WAR BY REVOLUTION

WAR BY
REVOLUTION

Germany and

Great Britain

in the

Middle East

in the Era of

World War I

Donald M. McKale

THE KENT STATE UNIVERSITY PRESS

Kent, Ohio, and London, England

© 1998 by The Kent State University Press, Kent, Ohio 44242
All rights reserved
Library of Congress Catalog Card Number 98-13285
ISBN 0-87338-602-7
Manufactured in the United States of America

06 05 04 03 02 01 00 99 98   5 4 3 2 1

LIBRARY OF CONGRESS CATALOGING-IN PUBLICATION DATA

McKale, Donald M., 1943–
    War by revolution : Germany and Great Britain in the Middle East in the era of
World War I / Donald M. McKale.
        p.   cm.
    Includes bibliographical references and index.
    ISBN 0-87338-602-7 (cloth : alk. paper) ∞
    1. World War, 1914–1918—Diplomatic history.   2. Middle East—Foreign
relations—Germany.   3. Middle East—Foreign relations—Great Britain.
4. Germany—Foreign relations—Middle East.   5. Great Britain—Foreign
relations—Middle East.   6. Great Britain—Foreign relations—Germany.
7. Germany—Foreign relations—Great Britain. I. Title.
D621.M628M38 1998   98-13285
940.3'2—dc21   CIP

British Library Cataloging-in-Publication data are available.

to the Clemson College Class of 1941
for its heroic and courageous service
in World War II and its leadership
in the postwar world

CONTENTS

Preface   ix

Acknowledgments   xv

Maps   xvii

Abbreviations   xix

1. Introduction: Britain, Germany, and the Middle East, 1871–1904   1

2. The Specter of Muslim Unrest and German Support, 1905–1914   17

3. Germany as Wartime "Revolutionary," Fall 1914   46

4. The Thickening Plot and Holy War, Fall 1914   69

5. Failed Expectations on Both Sides, 1915   97

6. The German Threat on the Periphery, 1915   120

7. A Sense of Crisis on Both Sides, Fall 1915   152

8. Britain as Wartime "Revolutionary": The Arab Revolt, 1916   170

9. Toward an Allied Victory, 1917   200

10. Epilogue: The War's End, 1918   220

Notes   231

Bibliography   293

Index   315

PREFACE

This book examines issues from World War I (1914–1918) in the Middle East that are still relevant today.[1] Even at present, problems in the region stem from the war and the postwar peace settlements—contradictory agreements and broken promises made by Britain and France with Arab leaders, most notably—which today remain unresolved sources of frustration and bloodshed.

Historiography on the war in the Middle East has emphasized overwhelmingly Britain's role in encouraging the Arab revolt in 1916 against Turkey and in establishing the Allies' controversial peace settlements. The latter dismantled what remained of the Ottoman Empire and placed almost all of its former Arab territories under British and French rule. Most writers have focused on a key question: what influenced the British to implement these policies? They represented at the time a radical break with Britain's traditional foreign policy of preserving the Ottoman Empire, and they were to have major, long-range consequences for the Middle East and the world.

T. E. Lawrence, the principal British figure in the Arab revolt, asserted in the 1920s that Britain had acted to assist the Arabs in achieving independence from a rotten and dying Turkey.[2] Subsequently, however, historians George Antonius, Elie Kedourie, Brinton Cooper Busch, C. Ernest Dawn, Roger Adelson, Suleiman Mousa, and Albert Hourani, and most recently the journalist David Fromkin, have discredited that view. Their research demonstrates that Britain based its World War I policies in the Middle East on military expedience, on the fear of Russian and French expansion in the region, and on London's intention to dominate the Arabs and Jews and use them to replace the Turkish empire as a safeguard for Britain's postwar imperial interests in India, Persia, and Egypt.[3] Much of this extensive literature provides the foundation of the British portions of the present study.

Nonetheless, such interpretations, while not incorrect, fail to explain fully the reasons for Britain's wartime policy in the Middle East. What has escaped the notice of scholars is the significant influence of Imperial Germany in shaping Britain's decisions, both before and during the war. Before the war, as the studies by Gregor Schöllgen and Ulrich Trumpener illustrate and the first chapters of this book affirm, Germany replaced France and Russia as Britain's leading rival in the region.[4]

Also, both the British and Germans seemed obsessed with pan-Islamism, an Ottoman doctrine that proclaimed the sultan-caliph's religious authority over Muslims all over the world. The doctrine further called on Muslims to defend the Ottoman Empire and caliphate, as the "true" faith, against others, particularly the Western infidel. For different reasons, London and Berlin significantly overestimated the power and unity of pan-Islamism, considering it before World War I to be the greatest threat to the West posed by the Muslim world.[5]

Some German leaders, including the emperor, Wilhelm II, worked to expand the Reich's influence in the Ottoman Empire in the belief that, in the event of a future war among the European powers, Germany could organize and exploit a fanatical and unified Islam for Berlin's wartime aims. These aims, once the world war began, were grandiose in the extreme and generally directed at rallying the German populace behind the war effort. They included strengthening Germany's power in Europe by diverting elsewhere the resources of its Great Power rivals, Britain, France, and Russia, and weakening or destroying their overseas (or other) empires. The British Empire especially contained vast numbers of Muslim subjects, who in the view of Wilhelm II and other German officials might be used against Britain. In 1898 the kaiser, in a visit to the Ottoman Empire, proclaimed himself the protector-friend of the earth's three hundred million followers of Islam.[6]

Similarly, Britain's prewar leaders tended to believe that the world of Islam was monolithic, that it took its cues uniformly from the sultan-caliph. These British officials, because of their longtime preoccupation with the defense of India, held deeply engrained attitudes that linked events geopolitically throughout the Middle East.[7] As tensions mounted among the European powers after 1905, and particularly between Britain and a Germany expanding its presence in Turkey, so did anxiety among some British leaders about pan-Islamism, specifically about a fanatical Muslim "holy war" (jihad) directed against Britain's rule in India and in the other large Muslim parts of the British Empire.[8]

The rise after 1908 of the Young Turk regime in Constantinople (which, ironically, initially downplayed pan-Islamism in favor of pan-Turanism) did little to allay British unease. Key officials in both London and Cairo urged that Britain counter the possibility of an anti-British jihad by exploiting the nascent Arab nationalism in Syria and elsewhere, and concluding an Anglo-Arab alliance against Turkey. Only in 1913–1914 did strategic and other interests result in an Anglo-German rapprochement in Turkey—which the outbreak of World War I destroyed.[9]

During the war, fear of pan-Islamism and association of it with German power, coupled with Allied military defeats at Gallipoli and in Mesopotamia, caused British leaders to panic. They nearly always believed, erroneously, that Germany controlled its Ottoman ally. To forestall what the British perceived was a serious threat to the future existence of their empire in India and Egypt, they allied themselves with the Arabs and at the war's end purposely destroyed the Turkish empire and divided its former lands among Britain, France, and the Arabs. Immense frustration resulted among Arabs, who responded with violence to the Allies' failure to provide them the independence and land they believed the British had promised them during the world war. Britain's wartime pledge to establish a "National Home" for Jews in Palestine was a further catalyst to violence in the Middle East. By 1922 the Allies had fashioned there "a peace to end all peace."[10]

What, specifically, did Germany do to prompt such an extreme response by Britain to the "Middle Eastern question"? The Reich, in addition to assisting the Ottomans militarily in the war, sought, like Britain, to incite revolution among the native peoples of its enemies' empires.[11] Once the Ottomans had joined Germany in the war in 1914, the Germans persuaded the sultan-caliph to declare a jihad of all Muslims against Britain, Russia, and France. This Turkish-German wartime appeal to pan-Islamism, an idea that had developed among German and Ottoman leaders before the war, aimed at stoking the fire of native revolts against the British in their chief imperial hold-ings, India and Egypt. It also focused on enflaming anti-British pas-sions in the surrounding Arab and other lands—in North Africa, Abyssinia, Somaliland, the Sudan, Turkey (including Syria, Palestine, Arabia, and Mesopotamia), Persia, and Afghanistan.[12]

This study deals with all of these geographical areas, including German policy toward the Arabs in Arabia and their leaders, whom the British and Lawrence succeeded in persuading to revolt in 1916. Despite the German alliance with the Ottomans, Berlin learned in the war that without Arab support neither Germany nor Turkey could undertake anything of military or political value in the strategic re-gion of Arabia, the Red Sea, and eastern Africa. Yet, as the present study will show, Germany failed for numerous reasons—including its leaders' confusion and indecision—to develop an effective and use-ful Arab policy or to influence its Turkish ally on the subject. Also, the Germans seemed wholly unconcerned about the contradiction in a Christian state's—Germany's—involvement in efforts by the sul-tan-caliph to wage a jihad against other Christian nations.

Several questions, therefore, dominate this book. Why, for ex-ample, did Britain and Germany engage in the Middle East in this waging of "war by revolution," or in using dissident groups within the enemies' states or empires to revolt and thereby weaken them?[13] For the Germans, their revolutionary policy represented less a confi-dent *Weltpolitik* ("global policy") and "bid for world power"[14] than an attempt to secure a victory for itself in Europe by diverting else-where the resources of Britain and its allies. Britain acted from a long-held fear of pan-Islamism and German power in the Middle East, which in combination appeared to London to threaten Britain's rule in India and Egypt.

Why, in the short term, did the Germans and Turks fail in their revolutionary policy, while the British succeeded? Contrary to what British leaders believed during the war, neither Berlin nor Constan-tinople based its important decisions on religious-revolutionary con-siderations; rather, they based them on strategic, and often conflict-ing, interests. Also, non-Turkish Muslims in the Ottoman Empire, including the Arabs, acted less for religious than national, tribal, or dynastic reasons. For their part, the Young Turks resented the involvement of Germany—a foreign and Christian state—in pan-Islamic and intra-Turkish affairs; it appeared to Constantinople to threaten both Ottoman sovereignty and foreign political interests. Yet despite these many problems and failures, in the long term the German war, both military and revolutionary, in the Middle East between 1914 and 1918 helped weaken Britain's global empire. How?

Still other issues, of a more contemporary nature, are worth pondering. For instance, the behind-the-scenes, "low-intensity" political war—complete with sabotage, terrorism, and propaganda—introduced by each side to the Middle East to destabilize the enemy's position and protect its own, may have had more lasting effects for the region today than is generally recognized.[15]

Finally, what might the experience of the European powers in World War I with what they perceived as a fanatical, monolithic, and aggressive pan-Islamism tell us about today's popular Western and American view of Islamic "fundamentalism"? What I call the "wars by revolution" waged by both Britain and Germany in World War I in the Middle East were the most extensive efforts by the West in the twentieth century to manipulate and oppose what it considered the most radicalized form of Islam: pan-Islamism. Much as the British and Germans held pan-Islamism, some Western observers today ascribe to Islamic fundamentalism—a phenomenon with a variety of meanings—a unity and authority over Islam that it does not, in fact, possess.[16] In the pages that follow, I demonstrate the religious, political, and national diversity of Islam and the difficulty the West had in this earlier age, attempting to manipulate or control it.

ACKNOWLEDGMENTS

This book could not have been researched and written without a great deal of help. The Class of 1941 Memorial Endowment at Clemson University, along with other monies and a sabbatical leave from the university, made much of the research travel possible and have been helpful in innumerable other ways. Also, a grant from the National Endowment for the Humanities that I received for a previous project assisted the research for this study.

Archivists at the National Archives and Records Administration in Washington, D.C., as well as the Yale University Library at New Haven (Connecticut), the Military History Institute of the U.S. Army War College at Carlisle Barracks (Pennsylvania), the Public Record Office at Kew (near London), the India Office Library and Records in London, and the Political Archive of the German Foreign Ministry (Politisches Archiv des Auswärtigen Amts) in Bonn were all courteous and helpful, either by finding for me documents in their archival collections or by answering my inquiries, in person or in writing, about their holdings. I am also indebted to the interlibrary loan department at the R. M. Cooper Library of Clemson University.

The Hoover Institution on War, Revolution, and Peace at Stanford University holds a major collection of the diaries and papers of a key source for this study—a German consular and intelligence agent, Curt Prüfer. I am particularly grateful to his son, Olaf H. Prufer of Kent, Ohio, who generously made these materials available to me before giving them to the Hoover Institution. Also, several scholars have read all or portions of the completed manuscript and have made suggestions for revision; I would especially like to thank George O. Kent, William Ochsenwald, James A. Miller, and Sylvia Haim.

I owe the greatest debt of gratitude, however, to my wife, Janna, and my children, Emily, David, and Susan. I have been blessed with their presence as well as with their inspiration and support, not only in this project but in the living of life itself.

All mistakes of judgment, interpretation, or fact in the book are my responsibility.

MAPS

The Middle East in World War I   5

Arabia in World War I   18

Africa and the Middle East in World War I   60

Asia in World War I   121

ABBREVIATIONS

AA   Auswärtiges Amt
The German foreign ministry, with headquarters in Berlin. Today the ministry is located in Bonn.

Bd.   (pl. **Bde.**): *Band*
Volume or folder, used in the endnotes to cite documents from the Politisches Archiv (Bonn).

CGS   Chief of the [British] General Staff

CIGS Chief of the [British] Imperial General Staff

CUP   Committee of Union and Progress
The principal party of the Young Turk movement, which except for a brief period ruled the Ottoman Empire from 1908 until 1918.

DMI   Director of [British] Military Intelligence

DMO Director of [British] Military Operations

EEF   Egyptian Expeditionary Force
The British army that advanced in 1916 across the Sinai Peninsula and, in conjunction with the Arab revolt against the Turks, invaded and defeated the Ottomans in Palestine and Syria during 1917–1918.

FO   FOREIGN OFFICE
The British foreign ministry, with headquarters in London. Also used in the endnotes to designate collections of documents from the ministry, now deposited in the PRO.

GOC   GENERAL OFFICER COMMANDING [British]

GP   DIE GROSSE POLITIK DER EUROPÄISCHEN KABINETTE 1871–1914. SAMMLUNG DER DIPLOMATISCHEN AKTEN DES AUSWÄRTIGEN AMTES
A major German collection of documents published in the 1920s to counter what Germany claimed was the Allied accusation that the Reich had started World War I.

HIWRP   HOOVER INSTITUTION ON WAR, REVOLUTION, AND PEACE [Stanford University, Palo Alto, California]

IEF D   INDIAN EXPEDITIONARY FORCE D
An element of the British India Army, operating in southern Mesopotamia. In April 1915, the unit was reorganized as a regular army corps and reinforced with more Anglo-Indian troops.

IO   INDIA OFFICE
The ministry in London responsible, along with the Foreign Office and Government of India, for British policy in India.

IOLR   INDIA OFFICE LIBRARY AND RECORDS [London]

IWM   IMPERIAL WAR MUSEUM [London]
The publisher of a volume, *Operations in Persia, 1914–1919*, of the British government's official history of World War I.

MEF   MEDITERRANEAN EXPEDITIONARY FORCE
The British army that carried out the Gallipoli campaign

against the Turks, from February 1915 to January 1916. From mid-1916 to 1918 the designation signified a different army, the Mesopotamia Expeditionary Force.

MI   [British] MILITARY INTELLIGENCE

MIL   MILITARY

MIS   MISCELLANEOUS

n.   FOOTNOTE OR ENDNOTE

n.d.   NO DATE

NARA   NATIONAL ARCHIVES AND RECORDS ADMINISTRATION [Washington, D.C.]
The main United States government archive, it holds and reproduces extensive microfilms of collections of captured German records from 1871 to 1945. Microfilms are cited in the endnotes by microcopy, reel, and frame numbers.

NfdO   NACHRICHTENSTELLE FÜR DEN ORIENT
Information Service for the East, an agency established by the AA at the beginning of World War I to assist in organizing and directing Germany's policy of inciting revolution in the Middle East and North Africa. The agency mainly published and distributed pro-German and pan-Islamic propaganda in the Muslim world and engaged in political surveillance of Orientals living in Switzerland.

PA   POLITISCHES ARCHIV DES AUSWÄRTIGEN AMTS
The archive of the German foreign ministry in Bonn. Documents are cited in the endnotes by reference name and volume.

P&S   POLITICAL AND SECRET DEPARTMENT
A section of the India Office; its historical records are deposited at the India Office Library and Records (London).

PRO   PUBLIC RECORD OFFICE [London]
The main British government archive. All documents from it cited herein are located in the new building in Kew.

R   File designation in the India Office Library and Records (London) for the Persian Gulf.

Sektion IIIb Politik
The policy office in the reserve section of the German General Staff that organized the army's political operations in foreign countries. Also, Sektion Politik acted in such matters as a liaison for the General Staff with the foreign ministry.

WK   *WELTKRIEG*
A reference *(Aktenzeichen)* in the Politisches Archiv (Bonn) for files and records from World War I documenting German revolutionary activities in the Middle East, North Africa, and India. Many of the files are microfilmed and available through the National Archives and Records Administration (Washington, D.C.).

WO   WAR OFFICE
British government ministry in London. In the endnotes, used to designate collections of documents from the ministry, now deposited in the Public Record Office (London).

Yilderim   "THUNDERBOLT," "LIGHTNING" [Turkish]
Nickname for German Army Group F, created in 1917 for use against the British in Mesopotamia but used mainly during 1917–1918 in Palestine and Syria.

YUL   YALE UNIVERSITY LIBRARY
Manuscripts and Archives, Sterling Memorial Library (New Haven, Connecticut).

Introduction
Britain, Germany, and the Middle East, 1871–1904

"To defeat the enemy," a key British official concluded during 1915, in the midst of World War I, "the destruction of the Ottoman Empire would be a decisive step."[1] How could Britain best achieve this radical break, discussed even before the world war, with its longtime foreign policy that had aimed at preserving the Turkish state? What would replace Turkey as the bulwark safeguarding Britain's shortest route to India, the heart of Britain's vast global empire?

According to the official, Britain should "back Arabic speaking peoples against the Turkish Government," destroy the Ottoman Empire, and create from its ruins an independent confederation of pro-British Arab states.[2] A few months later in 1916, with Britain's encouragement and military assistance, the Sharif of Mecca, Husayn ibn Ali, the guardian of the holy places of Islam, led a revolt of Arabs in the Hijaz, a region of western Arabia, against their Ottoman ruler, the sultan-caliph.

The British-sponsored Arab revolt, assisting as it did the triumph of Britain and its allies in the war in the Middle Eastern theater, had a vital impact on the future of that region and of the Islamic world. As this study illustrates, important roots of the revolt in 1916, like those of other wartime policies pursued by Britain in the Middle East, were deeply embedded in Britain's prewar antagonism toward, and rivalry with, Imperial Germany. The policy of waging "war by revolution" in the Middle East, pursued by both Germany and Britain between 1914 and 1918, had its origins long before the world war, in the arrival there of the first imperial powers—Britain and France, and later Germany.

The British Empire, the Sultan-Caliph, and Pan-Islamism

By 1907 the largest European empire, that of Britain's, included India, southern Persia, the principal shaykhdoms of the Persian Gulf, Aden, Egypt, and a portion of the sultanate of Zanzibar along the East African coast. The empire numbered ninety-six million Muslim subjects, almost one-third of the world's Muslim population. In contrast, the number of Muslims under French rule in Africa and Asia totaled nineteen million, roughly as many as lived under Russian rule in Central Asia.[3]

London exercised much of its vast influence in the Middle East and southern Asia through its colonial, but powerful and often independent, Government of India. Not only did the Raj win or force promises from local Arab shaykhdoms (which included Kuwait and Muhammarah) in the neighboring Persian Gulf to keep foreigners out, but it handled Britain's relations with Aden, Afghanistan, and the Ottoman provinces of southern Mesopotamia.[4]

Britain also attempted, as part of its Middle East policy, to preserve the most powerful, but continuously declining, Muslim state, the Ottoman Empire, which lay on the route from Europe to India. Since, particularly, 1830 Britain had engaged in what Englishmen called "the Great Game," protecting India from Russian attack; it was for that purpose that the British extended their influence into Turkey, and into other Islamic states, including Persia and Afghanistan, as well.[5]

The Ottoman Empire, despite the effective loss of its rule in Egypt to Britain in 1882, of Tunis to France in 1881, of Libya to Italy in 1911–1912, and of the Muslim khanates of Turkestan to Russia, remained the only significant focus of Muslim power in the world. The despotic sultan-caliph, Abd ul-Hamid, in part to offset the loss of Ottoman territories to the West and Russia, attempted not only to centralize his power in the remainder of the empire but also, in the process, to establish the doctrine of pan-Islamism. According to that ideology the Turks proclaimed the sultan the true and rightful caliph who, having inherited his office from the last Arab caliph in 1517, held a religious authority, distinct from political authority, over all the world's Muslims. Furthermore, pan-Islamism called on all Muslims to defend the Turkish empire and caliphate against the infidel, even by waging holy war.[6]

The extent to which Muslims accepted these doctrines is problematic; some found it convenient to embrace them, while others rejected them as false arguments. By the end of the nineteenth century a handful of Arab writers who urged a reform and reawakening of Islam viewed the Turks as degenerate Muslims who, unlike the Arabs, had not received the original revelation and whose rule should be replaced by an Arab caliphate. Nevertheless, most Arabs and other Muslims looked to the Ottoman sultan as the most powerful independent Muslim ruler, a pillar of support in a world increasingly hostile to Islam—a world in which the great majority of Muslims lived under alien rule.[7]

In the view of Englishmen and other Europeans, pan-Islamism posed a serious menace. They believed only too easily the idea, medieval and Social Darwinian in origin, that Muslims were essentially inferior and fanatical savages, prone to violence in response to religious appeals. Furthermore, Europeans viewed the sultan as the murderer of Christians, particularly because of the Ottoman massacres during the 1890s of Armenians in the eastern Anatolian provinces of the empire.[8] Accordingly, the Europeans feared that if they pressed the sultan too hard they might be confronted with pan-Islamic agitation, and even revolt, in their Muslim colonies. This especially haunted Britain after the Great Rebellion of 1857 in India, although that revolt had nothing to do with pan-Islamism. Twenty years later, however, during the Russo-Turkish War, the Muslims of India for the first time demonstrated their sympathy for the Turks on a significant scale.[9]

German Interest in the Muslim World

During the 1880s and 1890s a new factor appeared in the Middle East, one that the British believed threatened their supreme position in the region: the growing prestige at Constantinople of Imperial Germany. Among the European powers the German Empire arrived late as a global imperialist competitor. Because this was particularly true in the Middle East and Africa, Germany appeared free from the taint—as the Turks viewed it—of snatching land from the Ottomans. Berlin, in sharp contrast to Britain, ruled only a few overseas lands, which contained a small number of Muslim subjects—in 1914, roughly 2,600,000, scattered through East and South-West Africa and the Kamerun.[10]

Only during his last years had the "iron chancellor," Otto Prince von Bismarck, involved Germany in the affairs of the Middle East. Concerned mainly with the security of the new German Empire in central Europe, he had encouraged the diversion to Europe's periphery—the Middle East and Africa—of the attention of Europe's other Great Powers, including Britain.[11] But by the end of the 1880s, Bismarck's entry into the race for overseas colonies led him to side with France against Britain, encouraging the latter to make concessions to Germany in South-West Africa, the Kamerun, and Togoland, and in such islands as Zanzibar, New Guinea, and Samoa.[12]

Bismarck's policy also included preservation of what remained of the Ottoman Empire, despite its serious internal problems and losses of land to Britain, France, and Russia. German interest in Turkey long predated the Bismarckian era;[13] nonetheless under his leadership Germany saw the Turkish state as a bulwark against Russian expansion into the Middle East and Balkans. Consequently, Bismarck consented in 1882 to Turkish requests for a military mission to Constantinople to assist in reforming the sultan's army. The dispatch of the officers soon began a steady German *pénétration pacifique* of the Ottoman Empire. This included shipments of armaments to Turkey and concessions for construction of the Anatolian railroad.[14] Despite his support for the Ottoman Empire, Bismarck exerted himself for none of the non-Turkish peoples, including the Arabs, who lived under Ottoman rule. Moreover, he remained silent about the severe mistreatment by the Sublime Porte (the Turkish government, so named for the gate of the sultan's palace) of the Christian peoples in its provinces of the Balkans and eastern Anatolia. German officials were as little concerned for such peoples, or the Arabs, as they were for their own national minorities at home.[15] Nevertheless, the German leaders viewed them and that part of the world as having increasing importance for Germany, as illustrated by the founding in 1887 in Berlin of the Seminar for Oriental Languages.[16]

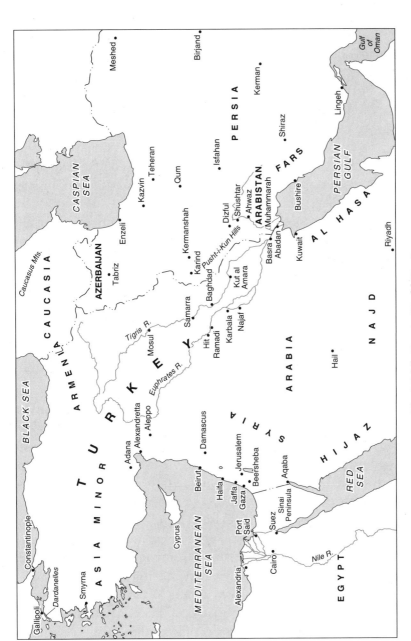

The Middle East in World War I.

In the Bismarckian view, the only possible value of foreign peoples, particularly minorities, was in producing problems for a military or political enemy of Germany. For instance, as early as 1866, during the Austro-Prussian War, the Prussian government established contacts with nationality groups in Austria, including the Hungarians and Slavs, with the idea of persuading them to revolt against the government in Vienna. After the formation of the German Empire, its army high command envisioned striking Russia, as one officer said, by fomenting revolution or insurgency among the non-Russian minorities along Russia's "vulnerable borders."[17]

The idea of inciting revolt among the minorities of a foreign enemy of Germany did not end with Bismarck's dismissal in 1890. Thereafter the German emperor, the young and belligerent Wilhelm II, and others in his government, expanded the concept. While intensifying Germany's role in Turkey, they discussed pan-Islamism and its potential for promoting insurgency in the vast colonial holdings around the world of competing imperialist nations.[18]

In part this idea reflected the kaiser's "new course" in German foreign policy, officially proclaimed during 1896 and 1897 by Wilhelm and his foreign secretary, Bernhard von Bülow: pursuing expanded German influence overseas—in fact, global power.[19] The resulting Weltpolitik, based on the construction of a powerful new battle fleet and on Berlin's eagerness to push its advantage at every international crisis point, produced sharp disagreements with other nations, particularly Britain, France, and the United States, over colonial territories in the Far East, Latin America, and Africa.[20]

Moreover, both Britain and Russia felt endangered by the steadily expanding German economic and military influence in the Ottoman Empire. Although London, as well as some historians much later, eventually believed that Germany intended to turn Turkey into a satellite or colony of the Reich, German policy toward Constantinople seemed much less defined and consistent at the time. Actually, Berlin's approach to the Ottoman Empire was dictated to a considerable extent by the kaiser's personal and quixotic views on the potential usefulness of Turkey and Islam against Britain, identified by Wilhelm II and many other Germans as their nation's archenemy.[21]

Britain's unhappiness with Germany in Turkey first emerged in the mid-1890s. The British disliked Berlin's refusal to oppose the Porte's massacre of the Armenians, as well as German support of the Ottomans in the Turkish-Greek war over Crete in 1897. While Turkey and Greece fought, Muslims in India conspicuously displayed their sympathy for the Turks.[22]

Furthermore, throughout the 1890s the *amir* (a Muslim ruler) of Afghanistan spread anti-British propaganda among the predominantly Muslim tribes along the northwest frontier of India. He opposed any extension of British influence across the border into his country and incited the tribes on both sides of the frontier to rise in revolt. Also from 1898 to 1902 the amir employed a German cannon maker of the Krupp company at an armaments factory in Kabul. The problems with Afghanistan awakened in Britain and the Government of India renewed anxiety about pan-Islamism (although in fact such actions had less to do with fanatical pan-Islamism than with nationalism and a wish for independence on the part of some Indian Muslims).[23] Still other British fears resulted from the long effort in the Sudan by Anglo-Egyptian forces, which finally succeeded in 1898 in defeating the *khalifa*, the successor to the *mahdi* (messenger of God), who had ruled the country since 1883 by playing on the Muslim fanaticism of the tribes.[24]

Other factors added to Britain's concern about India, pan-Islamism, and the growing German presence in the Middle East. These included Britain's clashes with Russia in central Asia and the fact that the British navy, which was badly overtaxed by defending Britain's far-flung empire, could no longer protect the Black Sea straits from a Russian attack. By the end of the 1890s Britain's conservative government under Lord Salisbury even began lessening its role in Constantinople in favor of building up British strength in Egypt.[25]

The Kaiser and the "Red Sultan"

Especially disturbing, however, to Britain—as well as to France and Russia—was the involvement of Germany in the politics of pan-Islamism. During October and November 1898 Wilhelm II journeyed

for the second time in nine years to Turkey, where he embraced publicly the world of Islam and its people. The kaiser, according to Bülow,
who accompanied the emperor to Turkey, held an "excessive enthusiasm and exaggerated zeal for everything Turkish and Mohammedan."[26]

The reasons for his fascination with the Orient (a word used by
nineteenth-century Europeans to describe the "Eastern" or Middle
Eastern world) and Islam were various. On the one hand, Wilhelm's
views reflected the attitudes and prejudices of most Germans at the
time. Partly because Germany had arrived later in the Middle East
than had the British and French and possessed far less firsthand experience with it, the Orient for Germans seemed almost exclusively
an academic, even romantic, phenomenon. Also, the kaiser, like most
Germans and Europeans, spoke of Muslims in monolithic terms and
as subjects of the sultan-caliph. Wilhelm viewed Islam as a unifying
force that beckoned to true believers with the appeal of a set of ide-
als, the attraction of which he compared to the spell of the virtues of
old Prussia. The kaiser admired the despotic rule of the sultan, believing it emanated from God, whom the sultan served as earthly regent.[27]

On the other hand, practical reasons also fueled the kaiser's interest in the Orient. For him Turkey served as a vehicle by which the
Reich could oppose rival Great Powers and also enhance its foreign
trade (which had steadily improved with the Ottomans since the end
of the 1880s). Wilhelm intended his first visit to Constantinople in
June 1889 to cultivate the sultan as an ally, at a time when he believed
Russia was Germany's principal enemy.[28] He had been encouraged to
visit Turkey by reports in the fall of 1898 from Adolf Freiherr Marschall
von Bieberstein, the ambassador in Constantinople, that the sultan
wished to extend the Anatolian railroad toward Aleppo and Baghdad,
possibly using German financing and builders. At the embassy a feeling existed that Germany should quickly seek the new railroad concession, mainly because of potential competition from other Great
Powers, like Britain and France.[29]

But the Turks also had a special interest in Germany building the
new section of the railroad. Apart from the rail line's economic value,
the sultan, Abd ul-Hamid, intended it for political and military use,

to strengthen his rule over distant and rebellious Arab tribes not only in Mesopotamia and the Persian Gulf but also in southern Syria and the Hijaz in western Arabia. In this respect the proposed rail line—and also the later (1901) Hijaz railroad, which Abd ul-Hamid was determined should run from Damascus to Mecca—resulted from the pan-Islamic and political-strategic interests of the Turks.

Consequently, in awarding the concession for the newly proposed railroad to Baghdad the sultan believed it essential to choose a Great Power that would sympathize with pan-Islamism. He settled on Germany because, unlike Britain, France, and Russia, it had practically no Muslim subjects and therefore little reason to fear Muslim discontent.[30] The sultan eagerly welcomed Wilhelm II and his lavish entourage, at a time when no other European sovereign would even meet the despotic Abd ul-Hamid. The latter's notoriety as the "Red [bloody] Sultan" resulted from his regime's brutality, and particularly the murder of the Armenians. Further, the sultan used the visit to impress on his guest the doctrine of pan-Islamism and his own claim to the caliphate.[31]

While in Damascus the kaiser wrote his cousin, Nicholas II, the czar of Russia, that "our reception here is simply astounding[.] Never has a Christian . . . Monarch been so fêted and received with such unbounded enthusiasm. It is because I am a friend of their Sultan and Kaliph and because I always pursued an open and loyal Policy toward him."[32] In return for his festive welcome, Wilhelm obliged the sultan by associating himself closely with all Muslims. In a speech in Damascus he made the famous announcement that particularly unsettled Britain and France: "Let me assure His Majesty the Sultan and the three hundred millions of Moslems who, in whatever corner of the globe they may live, revere in him their Khalif, that the German Emperor will ever be their friend."[33]

Stories abounded that Wilhelm II would soon convert to Islam. Although they had no basis in fact, no German official, including the kaiser, denied them.[34] The government did its best to counter strong criticism of the visit in the foreign press and to minimize nationalist comments in German newspapers. The foreign ministry spread the view that Wilhelm II had made the voyage solely for religious purposes, to enable the kaiser to make a pilgrimage to the Holy Land.

But Wilhelm's own actions, if not in Damascus then in Jerusalem, clearly belied the claim. He entered the holy city as a conquering hero, riding on a white stallion and his spiked helmet glistening in the sun, accompanied by dozens of Prussian and Ottoman cavalrymen.[35]

Furthermore, Wilhelm seemed to connect the warm welcome he received in Turkey with what he perceived as Ottoman dislike of the British and French.[36] Even as Berlin attempted to downplay the emperor's visit to Turkey in the German and European press, privately he and his officials studied the potential value of pan-Islamism for producing revolts among the Muslim subjects of the British Empire. Much of the impetus for the idea apparently stemmed from the kaiser himself. As early as 1896, during Germany's crisis with Britain over the Transvaal, he had alleged to a Russian diplomat that a German agent in Baghdad had uncovered an Islamic prophet from whom one word would unleash a huge anti-British Muslim uprising in India. In August 1897, Wilhelm told Nicholas II, in connection with Britain, "never to forget that the Mahometans were a tremendous card in our game in case you or I were suddenly confronted by a war with the certain meddlesome Power."[37]

Finally, and despite the superficial nature of Wilhelm's interest in the Orient and of his relationship to Abd ul-Hamid, his visit to Turkey inspired a myth among some Muslims, particularly in North Africa, that there existed a "traditional" or "natural" German-Muslim friendship. The myth asserted that the association between Germans and Muslims extended back even to the time of the Prophet, Muhammad, and that Wilhelm might be a son of Abd ul-Hamid, come to liberate the world of Islam from its French and British oppressors![38]

Oppenheim and Other Pan-Islamists

Some controversy exists about how much the kaiser's views on the Middle East and pan-Islamism resulted from the notorious German archaeologist-spy and Jewish convert to Christianity, Max Freiherr von Oppenheim. Oppenheim, born in 1860 to a family of Cologne bankers, joined the active movement of German archaeologists and scholars studying the Orient. As Germany's relations with Turkey expanded, this group followed other European Orientalists to the Ottoman provinces in North Africa and the Middle East. In 1875, for example, the Egyptians had appointed a German, Wilhelm Spitta, director of the national library in Cairo, a position held by German scholars until 1911.[39] The Berlin government, which limited its contacts in the Middle East mainly to the Turks, who in turn jealously guarded their rule over the other peoples of the Ottoman Empire, often used these German scholars to collect intelligence in the Arab hinterland.

Oppenheim's travels and archaeological research, financed by his family and facilitated by his fluency in Arabic, took him to Greece and Constantinople (1883), the Maghreb (1886, 1892), and Libya (1892). During the fall of 1892, he visited Cairo for the first time, meeting leading Egyptians, traveling the Nile River, studying the Arabic language, morality, and customs, and learning about Islam. Inasmuch as the German foreign ministry had to approve his travels, Oppenheim used his friend and mentor, the noted African explorer Gerhard Rohlfs, to establish close relations with several ministry officials and diplomats. These included Paul Graf von Hatzfeldt, the ambassador in London, and Paul Kayser, the influential director of the foreign ministry's colonial department. Consequently, during Oppenheim's visit in 1893 to Syria, Mesopotamia, the Persian Gulf, Muscat, Aden, Zanzibar, and German East Africa, he filed extensive reports on political and military matters. He especially recommended, regarding the relationship of the Ottomans to the Arabs, that the Turks display considerable armed power and build strong garrisons.

Returning to Germany, he visited London and numerous British Africanists. In October 1895 he journeyed again to Constantinople; the sultan, acknowledging his growing reputation as both an Orientalist and someone with ties to his home government, received him in an hour-long audience. Back in Germany he received from the foreign ministry a commission to lead an expedition to the Lake Chad area to secure it for Germany, a trust that further evidenced his blossoming relationship with the ministry.

In March, with the assistance of Hatzfeldt, Oppenheim gained entry into the consular service, overcoming considerable anti-Semitic opposition in the foreign ministry. Through the appointment he hoped, albeit without success, to win admission to the prestigious diplomatic corps and thereby the German upper class.[40] The ministry canceled the Lake Chad mission and decided to send him to Egypt;[41] it assigned him to the consulate general in Cairo, with the rank of attaché. Except for a trip to Syria in 1899, during which he discovered the ancient Hittite ruins at Tell Halaf, and a visit during 1903–1904 to the United States, he remained in Cairo until 1910.[42]

Once in Egypt, Oppenheim, an extreme Anglophobe, immersed himself in anti-British politics. The origins of his intense dislike of Britain remain unclear. His passion for Islamic and Arab culture, coupled with Britain's control and influence over Egypt, several zones on the Persian Gulf, and other Islamic states, may have contributed to it. So also could have his ambition to move from the German consular service to the diplomatic corps, a distinction obstructed by his Jewish background; he may have felt that anti-British views (while they were not as widespread in the foreign ministry as elsewhere in the Berlin government, for instance in the navy) would facilitate such a promotion.

Oppenheim financed much of his work in the consular service from his private resources and seemed to possess a free hand in establishing intimate ties to Egyptian leaders opposed to the British occupation of their country.[43] Soon after arriving in Cairo he met the young Austrian-educated khedive, Abbas Hilmi II, the Turkish viceroy in Egypt. The khedive, who had ascended the Egyptian throne in 1892 and resented openly the British occupation of the country, received the German attaché in a private audience. Thereafter, much to the anger of the British consul general (often referred to by Britain as its Agent or Resident) in Egypt, Evelyn Baring Lord Cromer, Oppenheim befriended Abbas Hilmi.[44]

Moreover, the German met often with anti-British Egyptian nationalists. These included the editor of the Cairo newspaper *al-Muayyad,* Shaykh Ali Yusuf, and the later founder of the nationalist party, Mustafa Kamil; both men supported the claims of the khedive, the Ottomans, Islam, and secular nationalism. Oppenheim also mixed with teachers and students at the al-Azhar University in Cairo, where he met Muhammad Abduh, a noted Egyptian and Islamic reformer, in 1892.[45]

For his superiors in Cairo and Berlin Oppenheim wrote countless reports about Muslim affairs from Morocco to China and the Caucasus to Yemen. He gave special attention to the politics of pan-Islamism, which he considered of major importance.[46] His opinions in this regard resulted from the response of some Muslims to the Turkish-Greek war and from his acquaintance with Muhammad Abduh, whose ideas he erroneously interpreted as wholly anti-British.[47] According to Oppenheim, Islam was undergoing "a regeneration of power and vitality" that was producing an increase in pan-Islamic sentiment in Egypt, Russian central Asia, and northwest India. He recommended that the foreign ministry establish a central office in Cairo for "special observation" of the Muslim world.[48]

Scholars dispute how much influence Oppenheim had in shaping Germany's Middle Eastern policies and statements, like those of Wilhelm II during his visit to Turkey in 1898, promoting pan-Islamism.[49] Other German officials before World War I also believed in the usefulness of pan-Islamism for the kaiser's new Weltpolitik, and they helped disseminate the idea in the government. These included Marschall von Bieberstein, the ambassador in Constantinople (1897–1912); Alfred von Kiderlen-Wächter, the foreign secretary (1910–1912); and Arthur Zimmermann, a counselor in the foreign ministry's political department (1905–1910), later the ministry's director (1910–1911), and eventually its under-secretary and secretary.

In the army, too, support existed for mobilizing the Muslim world against Britain, particularly among officers who did not consider the Ottoman armed forces sufficiently trained and equipped to make much of a contribution in a major European war. Field Marshal Colmar Freiherr von der Goltz, a member of the German military mission to Constantinople from 1883 to 1895, envisioned Turkey as a principal means of threatening India. By the beginning of World War I, General Helmuth von Moltke the Younger, the chief of the army high command (1906–1914), thought similarly.[50]

However, the politics of pan-Islamism did not appeal to everyone in the Berlin government. Some in the foreign ministry, such as the anglophile minister Friedrich von Rosen, the minister to Portugal, and the later ambassador in Constantinople, Baron Hans von Wangenheim, warned against using pan-Islamism and inciting religious passions to further German objectives against the Reich's European rivals. Paul Graf Wolff-Metternich zur Gracht, although he had accompanied the kaiser to Turkey in 1898 and carefully provided Wilhelm with Oppenheim's reports and discussed them with the emperor, emphasized how much Germany benefited from good trade relations with the British Empire. So did the commercial department in the foreign ministry.[51]

Germany, Turkey, and the Anglo-French Entente

Important consequences flowed from the kaiser's visit to Turkey. In December 1899 the Porte granted a preliminary concession for railroad construction to the group of German industrial and financial institutions, led by the Deutsche Bank, that had built the Anatolian railroad. The agreement provided for the extension of the railroad into Mesopotamia and toward Baghdad, terminating in the Ottoman province of Kuwait on the Persian Gulf. On 5 March 1903, after unsuccessful attempts by Germany to acquire financial assistance from France and Britain for construction of the railroad, the Ottomans and Germans signed the Baghdad railroad convention. Along with acquiring the railroad concession Germany increased its armaments trade with Turkey and founded the Deutsche-Palästina Bank, with branches in Jerusalem and Jaffa, and in 1906 the Deutsche Orientbank.[52] Moreover, as the British observed, the Reich suddenly expanded its activity in the Persian Gulf. Although only six German citizens lived in the Gulf region, Berlin established a vice consulate at Bushire, on the Persian side, in November 1897; a private shipping and pearl-trading company owned by Robert Woenckhaus began doing business at Lingeh on the Gulf coast.[53]

The potential value of the railroad, the most visible and controversial aspect of Germany's *pénétration pacifique* of Turkey, was lost on neither the Germans nor the British. When completed the railroad would link Constantinople, and Europe in general, with Baghdad and the Persian Gulf, thereby allowing Germany to enter

Mesopotamia, Persia, and the Gulf region economically, and possibly threaten India.[54] British fears for the security of India had traditionally centered on Russian expansion into nearby Afghanistan and Persia, but in 1903 the Baghdad railroad alarmed George Curzon, the British viceroy of India.[55] Consequently, to gain control over the final, southernmost section of the railroad, in January 1899 the Government of India concluded a secret agreement with the Shaykh of Kuwait, Mubarak as-Sabah, whose province lay under Ottoman rule.[56]

Thus, as the new century dawned, Anglo-German tensions had emerged clearly in the Middle East. But far more serious problems divided the two powers. These included an intense economic rivalry and Germany's continued construction of a large battle fleet. However, building the fleet was to bring disaster for Germany; it involved the nation in a massive and costly arms race with Britain, and it would complete the isolation of the Reich that had started with the Franco-Russian alliance of 1894. Although Anglo-French conflicts remained acute in Africa and southeast Asia, as did Anglo-Russian differences in Persia, the Dardanelles, and China, in time such issues no longer dominated international relations. Instead, the flowering of the "Anglo-German antagonism" prevailed increasingly on the European and world stages.[57] When Wilhelm II and his advisers rejected during 1899 and 1900 Britain's feelers for an alliance with Germany, London, its imperial position weakened by the Boer War, settled its colonial differences with France and Russia. It concluded an *entente cordiale* with France in April 1904 and a formal agreement with Russia in 1907, thus completing the Triple Entente that enveloped the Reich before World War I. This alliance dramatically heightened Germany's paranoia, its conviction that its rivals were imposing on it a hostile encirclement, an iron ring.[58]

Most notably, the entente cordiale of 1904 represented a severe blow for German diplomacy in the Middle East, particularly in Egypt. France, by virtually abandoning the administration of Egypt to Britain, made obsolete Germany's old device of exploiting Anglo-French tension over Egypt to acquire colonial concessions from Britain and otherwise advance German policy in the Orient. Also, with the Anglo-French entente Britain's occupation of Egypt gained de facto international acceptance. Not surprisingly, German assent to the changes in Egypt came only in July 1904, after long and bitter negotiations that left much ill feeling on both the German and British sides.[59] After 1904 divisions and fears among the Reich and its European rivals, particularly Britain, intensified—not only in Egypt but elsewhere in the Middle East.

2   The Specter of Muslim Unrest and German Support, 1905–1914

In a New Year's Eve letter in 1905 to his chancellor, shortly before the crisis in Morocco, in which Germany failed to break up the Anglo-French entente cordiale, Wilhelm II mentioned the possibility of a future European-wide war. Germany, he wrote to Bülow, should not enter the conflict until it had concluded an alliance with the Ottomans and with "all Arabian and Moorish rulers." The Reich, the kaiser continued, could not begin a war until such a pact with Islam could be sealed.[1] During the decade before World War I concern, much of it exaggerated, intensified among the British over the combined threat to the British Empire of the increasing German influence in the Middle East and the Ottoman doctrine of pan-Islamism.

Ironically, both the British and Germans emphasized pan-Islamism—each for a different reason—as much or more than did the Turks and most other Muslims. The Europeans, including their rulers, held a popular misperception of the Muslim world: that it formed a monolithic pan-Islamic entity, guided by the caliph—the successor of the Prophet, Muhammad—in Constantinople. As this chapter emphasizes, both Britain and Germany believed erroneously that whoever controlled the caliph dominated Islam.[2]

"Of Course Our German Cousins Are Behind It All"

After its failure in Morocco, Germany engaged in anti-British activities in Egypt and the Persian Gulf region, and it continued its rivalry with Britain for influence in the Ottoman Empire. In Egypt, during 1906 the British suspected German involvement in the Anglo-Turkish dispute known as the "Aqaba incident." This particularly

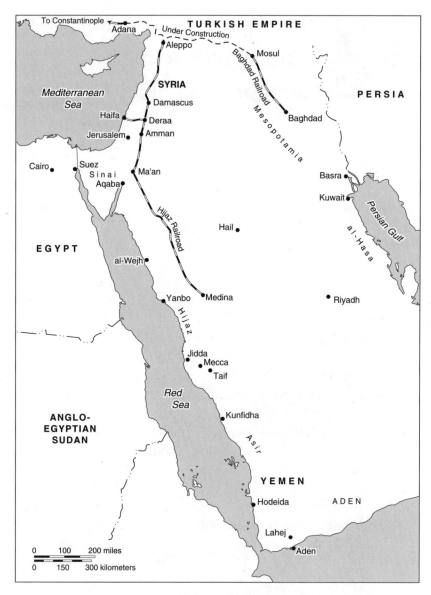

Arabia in World War I.

awakened British fears of a threat from the east to Brit
of the country.[3]

The dispute involved the Turkish-Egyptian boundary c
Peninsula. During the conflict Britain forced the sulta
Hamid, not to occupy land around Aqaba, a town 150 mi...s east of
the Suez Canal. The British found especially worrisome the sultan's
construction of the nearby Hijaz railroad, begun in 1901 and intended
by the Turks to run from Damascus to Mecca. Britain worried about
the railroad for a variety of reasons. The line eased the movement of
Turkish troops toward Egypt and the Red Sea. Furthermore, it represented a physical embodiment of Ottoman pan-Islamism: it was being built with monies solicited by Abd ul-Hamid from Muslims outside the Ottoman Empire, particularly in India and Egypt; it would
help the world's Muslim pilgrims travel to the Islamic holy places in
Medina and Mecca; and it would aid the sultan in shipping troops to
southern Syria and Arabia to assert his rule there over the often anti-
Ottoman and rebellious Arabs.[4]

The fact that German engineers directed the construction of the
Hijaz railroad added to Britain's uneasiness during and after the
Aqaba incident.[5] The aging and authoritarian British resident (consul general) in Cairo, Lord Cromer, accused Germany of inspiring
the Turks to occupy Aqaba and the surrounding land. He worried
that backed by Berlin, Abd ul-Hamid aimed at pushing forward the
limits of Ottoman rule to a point in the Sinai Peninsula that endangered the navigation of the Suez Canal. His Oriental secretary and
confidant, Harry Boyle, declared, "Of course our German cousins are
behind it all."[6]

In April Cromer warned the British Foreign Office that the attaché
at the German consulate-general in Cairo, Max von Oppenheim, "has
been in constant communication with Moukhtar Pasha," the Ottoman high commissioner in Egypt. Moreover, Cromer advised British officials in Syria, where Oppenheim was visiting at the time, to
"keep an eye on his movements and proceedings."[7] As long as
Oppenheim remained in Syria and Mesopotamia, the British resident in Baghdad watched him closely. Cromer urged London to press
the German government to recall Oppenheim; on at least two occasions the British ambassador in Berlin, Sir Frank Lascelles, attempted

it unsuccessfully with the state secretary in the German foreign ministry, Heinrich von Tschirschky.[8]

Indeed, there existed little proof of Germany's connection with the Aqaba troubles; in fact the German ambassador in Constantinople, Marschall von Bieberstein, used his influence with the Turks to achieve a settlement of the dispute. Nevertheless, London accepted in large measure Cromer's interpretation of the question. While the British General Staff downplayed the threat to Egypt of a major Turkish presence in the Sinai Peninsula, the foreign secretary, Sir Edward Grey, agreed with Cromer and declared that possession of the Sinai was essential to the security of Egypt, the canal, and Red Sea.[9]

In the Aqaba crisis Britain forced the sultan to accept a Turkish-Egyptian border he had previously opposed, but even afterward the Hijaz railroad continued to concern the Foreign Office and General Staff. As early as July 1906 the Committee of Imperial Defence concluded that the Turks, if supported by the Germans, could move enough troops across the Egyptian border to threaten the Suez Canal. The army continued to work on plans, which it sent to the prime minister, for the defense of the canal and for a British counterattack against the rear of a Turkish force, by way of a landing in Syria. A General Staff memorandum argued in July 1907 that the presence of a large British force in Syria would prompt local uprisings of anti-Ottoman Arabs against the Turkish rear and force the Ottomans to recall their army invading Egypt.[10]

Cromer, however, now seemed more worried about the political situation inside Egypt. He disliked the hostile and highly agitated tone of the Egyptian nationalist press, which denounced Britain's role in both the Aqaba crisis and Dinshawai incident. In the latter the resident had ordered twenty Egyptian peasants executed or imprisoned for shooting a British soldier. Cromer especially disparaged Egyptian nationalists who, like Mustafa Kamil, identified themselves with the Turks and pan-Islamic doctrine and agitated in newspapers and schools for the removal of the British occupation. The resident blamed the opposition to Britain on what he called "hatred of the Moslem for the Christian."[11]

In London, Grey agreed. The foreign secretary commented in Parliament upon the occupation by Britain and France of lands belonging to the Ottoman sultan. "The fact had begun to have its effect in Egypt," he declared, alluding to the crises of the previous months, "and when you have conflict of that kind with the Turkish Government . . . you may be quite sure it is bound to have a certain effect on the Mahomedan races who are under British rule or in countries under British occupation."[12]

Despite the British maligning of them as merely religious zealots, the nationalists demanded some measure of self-government for Egypt, greater participation in the country's parliamentary bodies, and a reform of the "capitulations" (legal privileges granted by the regime of the khedive to Europeans in Egypt). Cromer agreed only with the last demand. The German consulate-general in Cairo, however, opposed change in the capitulations, viewing the laws as necessary for protecting the limited German trade in Egypt.[13] German opposition to altering the capitulations took various forms. Although Johann Heinrich Count von Bernstorff, the consul general in Cairo, carefully avoided discussion of the matter in meetings with Cromer, he warned the foreign ministry and Reich chancellor, Bernhard von Bülow, of the suspected British action. Anti-British articles on the issue appeared in the German press. Such accusations irritated London, and Lascelles, its ambassador in Berlin, complained to the Reich government. Ultimately, however, the British did not change the capitulations.[14]

A German activity that received most attention from Cromer and his successors centered on the consulate-general's ties to the Egyptian nationalists and the khedive, Abbas Hilmi II. The latter's influence had been steadily eroded by the British since his assumption of the throne and subsequent rebellion against them in 1892 and 1893. Since then the khedive, a master of political intrigue, had contracted with German firms, such as Krupp, to expand construction of railroads owned by Abbas. His negotiations with the recently established German Orientbank in Cairo to sell part of his extensive properties in order to protect them from confiscation directed by Cromer especially provoked the British resident's ire.[15]

Relations became so tense between Cromer, the khedive, and the German consulate-general that shortly before Cromer's resignation the German foreign ministry directed Bernstorff to persuade Abbas

Hilmi not to push the British too far. The ministry feared British reprisals, including the establishment of a protectorate over Egypt, that could jeopardize German political and economic activities there.[16]

Yet neither Bernstorff nor the foreign ministry attempted to halt the anti-British activities of subordinate officials in the consulate-general. These included the notorious Oppenheim, known to the British as "the Kaiser's spy," and Curt Prüfer, an ambitious young dragoman (interpreter) and specialist in Arab culture and language.[17] Using the pretext of excavating ancient ruins and archaeological sites in the desert and disguised in Arab garb, the two Germans visited Bedouin tribes in Egypt and Syria, presenting the shaykhs with gifts and denouncing the British.[18] Their contacts with the Bedouins also resulted from Oppenheim's long-held view that Germany should encourage pan-Islamism as a means of subverting the Muslim subjects of the Reich's potential European enemies.

In this regard, Oppenheim argued repeatedly to the foreign ministry that Egyptians would rise against British rule if troops of the leader of Islam, the Ottoman sultan-caliph, appeared at the Suez Canal, or if a war began in Europe that involved Britain. In the margin of one such report to the ministry, Wilhelm II, who read Oppenheim's memoranda, noted happily, "Good, correct!"[19] Pan-Islamism was on the rise in Egypt and elsewhere in the Muslim world, Oppenheim asserted, including among the Afghans, who wished to fight for Islam against the British in neighboring India.[20]

During his repeated visits to Constantinople Oppenheim also met Husayn ibn Ali, whom the Turks had appointed at the end of 1908 the new sharif of Mecca. In their discussions the German, on the pretext of his interest in archaeology, questioned Husayn about political relations in the Hijaz. Husayn impressed Oppenheim, who later described the Arab as "a clever man."[21] Both Britain and France accused Oppenheim of dabbling in pan-Islamic propaganda; Paris even blamed him for inciting rebellion in 1908 among the French Foreign Legion and Arab population in Algiers.[22]

Oppenheim especially cultivated ties to the Egyptian nationalists and the khedive, Abbas Hilmi, but he had little success in encouraging them to form an anti-British alliance.[23] Following Cromer's resignation in 1907, his successor in Cairo, Sir Eldon Gorst, attempted to blunt the nationalist reaction against Cromer's coercive tactics by pursuing a policy of reconciliation with the khedive and by liberalizing British control of Egypt. Gorst, much to the chagrin of the Germans, discouraged Abbas Hilmi's friendship with the nationalists, who were plagued by internal divisions, and exploited their differences over the form of Egyptian government they wanted to replace British rule.[24]

The extreme nationalist party, which the khedive had previously supported, was led after 1908 by Mustafa Kamil's successor, the fiery pan-Islamist Shaykh Abd al-Aziz al-Jawish, and Muhammad Farid. Both Jawish and Farid, inspired by European ideas of liberty, argued for the immediate forcible removal of British rule from Egypt and reestablishment of Turkish sovereignty, based on the spiritual-religious hegemony of the sultan. But a new and more moderate nationalist party, which included Ahmad Lutfi al-Sayyid, had no sympathy for the khedive or the Ottomans, calling instead for the gradual creation of a liberal European-style constitution and parliamentary regime.[25]

The programs of each nationalist group threatened the khedive's position and family as much or more than they did the British occupation. The cocky, arrogant, and autocratic Abbas Hilmi not only opposed British rule and an Egyptian parliamentary government but rejected efforts by the Turks to reassert the sultan's rights of ownership over Egypt. As part of his anti-Turkish policy he had since 1895 supported the idea of replacing the Ottoman caliphate with an Arab one, making himself caliph. Less for nationalist than for personal and dynastic reasons, Abbas Hilmi promoted his and Egypt's claims to leadership of the Arab world and also Cairo's suitability to be the seat of the new caliphate.[26]

But it is unlikely that Oppenheim's tie to the nationalists and the khedive were the main reason the British called him "the Kaiser's spy." Instead, it was because of his contacts with other groups and individuals. These included, first, a circle of Arabs, Syrians, and Turks who had been enemies of Abd ul-Hamid and fled from Turkey to Cairo; and second, representatives in the Egyptian capital of the Libyan religious order, the Sanussis.[27]

But not everyone at the German consulate-general in Cairo approved of Oppenheim's activities. Bernstorff, the consul general, disliked how Oppenheim repeatedly corresponded with the German chancellor without consulting him. Bernstorff also sharply disagreed with his subordinate's enthusiastic estimates of the pan-Islamic movement and of what Egypt would do in a European war. However, Oppenheim impressed Wilhelm II, who called him the "feared spy" and who continued to believe in pan-Islamism and its potential for fomenting revolts among Muslims in the British colonies.[28] Furthermore, Oppenheim attempted to influence the new rulers in Constantinople, the "Young Turks." He responded favorably to their revolution in Constantinople in 1908–1909, because he believed that it had strengthened pan-Islamism. Working particularly through Abbas Hilmi's new representative to the Porte, Yussuf Bey Saddik, a longtime friend, Oppenheim tried to encourage the pro-German sympathies of the Young Turk regime.[29]

But at the beginning of 1910 Oppenheim resigned from the consulate-general, ostensibly to pursue his archaeological excavations of an ancient Hittite city he had discovered in Syria, Tell Halaf. As emphasized later in this chapter, however, his work in Syria and Mesopotamia centered significantly on promoting the Baghdad railroad among local Arabs.

The Young Turk Revolution and Britain's View

During July 1908 a revolution placed the Young Turks and their principal party, the Committee of Union and Progress (CUP), in power in Constantinople. Their objectives centered on saving the Ottoman Empire from destruction by Europe and on changing it into a modern centralized state. Within the empire the threat of secession by the non-Turkish peoples, including the Macedonians, Albanians, Armenians, and Arabs, had grown, bringing with it the menace of foreign intervention. Initially the new regime restored the 1876 constitution, established a parliament, and introduced liberal reforms that seemed to herald the beginning of a new era of freedom and of cooperation between the Ottomans and other peoples of the empire.[30]

But beginning in the fall the Bosnian crisis, in which Austria-Hungary completed its takeover of the former Ottoman province, emboldened the enemies of the new government to attack it. Despite this threat, the CUP strengthened its position in the parliament. Amid bitter factionalism both in and outside of the committee an attempted counter-revolution in April 1909 resulted in enhanced influence for the army and in the virtual elimination of the powers of Abd ul-Hamid. The parliament removed the sultan from the throne in favor of one more amenable to its will, his brother Mehmed V.[31]

By the end of 1910 the British ambassador to the Porte, Gerard Lowther, who disliked the Young Turks, was accusing them of abandoning liberal Ottoman rule in favor of pan-Islamic and Turkish nationalist policies.[32] Lowther even thought, erroneously, that pan-Islamism constituted the distinguishing feature of the Young Turk movement and was a force that might affect lands as far away as Algeria and Persia. He also worried about the possibility that the new regime would enter a formal alliance with Germany.[33] His reports to London influenced both the foreign secretary, Grey, and after 1910 the permanent under-secretary of state in the Foreign Office, Sir Arthur Nicolson. The latter especially feared the specter of pan-Islamism and its potential association with Germany:

> I think that this Pan-Islamic movement is one of our greatest dangers in the future, and is indeed far more of a menace than the "Yellow Peril." . . . Germany is fortunate in being able to view with comparative indifference the growth of the great Mussulman military power, she having no Mussulman subjects herself, and a union between her and Turkey would be one of the gravest dangers to the equilibrium of Europe and Asia.[34]

Within the British government, the India Office shared Nicolson's apprehension about pan-Islamism, seeing it as a potential menace to India. Lowther, however, and although he continued to supply the Foreign Office with evidence of pan-Islamic activity, advised Nicolson and Grey at the beginning of 1911 that it was less dangerous than they believed.[35] He reminded his superiors that the Shiites, a sect of Islam dominant in eastern Mesopotamia, Persia, and Yemen, abhorred the Sunni Muslims, the mainstream of Islam, and that they would probably not collaborate with the Turks. Further, Lowther claimed, the Arab had no respect for the Turk as a Muslim and felt that the caliphate should be in Arab hands. Nor did Lowther regard pan-Islamism as dangerous in India: Indian Sunnis viewed the Young Turks as "sacrilegious revolutionaries" who had deposed God's elect, Abd ul-Hamid, from the caliphate and replaced him with a puppet.[36]

During 1911 and 1912 the Young Turks strengthened their authority and that of the army over the parliament and domestic opposition groups. Much of this resulted from the further Ottoman military losses to European forces. In the Turkish-Italian war of 1911–1912, Turkey lost Libya to Italy, and in the first Balkan War of 1912 the Porte lost nearly all of its remaining European territories.[37] The failure of Constantinople to defend Libya weakened its position in the eyes of the restive non-Ottoman peoples of the Turkish empire, particularly Arabs, and destroyed much of the confidence they had in a Young Turk revival of the country. Soon after the outbreak of the war with Italy a Turkish official warned Lowther that the surrender of Libya to a Christian power would mean a mass rising of the Arabs against the Turks. Nevertheless, during the war the Turks discouraged German efforts (taken to promote pan-Islamism) to recruit Egyptians to fight for the Ottoman and Arab forces in Libya.[38]

Emerging Arab Unrest

A major reason why the Porte intensified nationalist policies yet also appealed to pan-Islamism (as noted by the British) was to reconcile the Arabs of the Ottoman Empire to Turkish rule. By 1910–1911 a steadily unfolding "Arab question" existed in the empire. Serious Arab discontent with the Turks had appeared in Mesopotamia and Yemen, including violent assaults by Arabs on local Turkish garrisons and trade. The Turks had fought since 1869 a prolonged colonial war to subjugate Yemen, but beginning in 1905 the Yemeni rebellion intensified and caused serious problems for the Ottomans.[39]

Small groups of Arabs had thought of either political reform of the Turkish government that would grant Arabs greater autonomy from the Ottomans, or complete independence for Arabs from Turkish rule. Such ideas had circulated among a few Egyptian intellectuals at the end of the nineteenth century. Moreover, during the 1890s the Egyptian khedive, the young and ambitious Abbas Hilmi, had intrigued against his overlord, the Ottoman sultan, by spreading propaganda favoring the replacement of the sultan as caliph by an Arab caliphate, with himself, Abbas Hilmi, as the new caliph.[40]

The Young Turks, however, following their revolution in Constantinople in 1908–1909, pursued a vigorous defense of the Ottoman Empire and caliphate. The new rulers, by expanding the number of administrative institutions and schools in the empire, seemed more than previously to force Turkish political and cultural policies on the Arabs and other peoples. In response, the Arab nationalist ideology called "Arabism" slowly spread, proclaiming the Arabs to be a special people who possessed peculiar virtues and rights and who deserved some form of autonomy within the empire.[41]

Several Arab groups in the empire, mainly in Syria, Cairo, and the Persian Gulf port of Basra, demanded reforms that would ensure rights for Arabs. Some Arabs who participated in the movement also had in mind independence from the Ottomans, and they secretly worked for such a nationalist and revolutionary goal. At the beginning of 1911, thirty-five Arab deputies in the Ottoman parliament sent the guardian of the holy places in the Hijaz, the Sharif of Mecca, Husayn ibn Ali, a written appeal to lead an Arab rising against the Young Turks. Although even many Arab nationalists viewed Husayn as loyal to the Ottoman Empire, or at least pro-Turkish, the sharif ruled almost independently in the Hijaz.[42]

Moreover, Arabs were encouraged to seek autonomy from, or reform within, the Ottoman state by the series of wars that the Young Turks fought during 1911 and 1912, resulting in Turkey's loss of territory in Libya and the Balkans. In this sense, Arab nationalism was a reaction against the failure of the Ottoman Empire to resist the advance of Europe and its expansion into the Middle East.[43] Despite the rise of the Arab nationalist movement, however, most Arabs remained loyal to Turkey until World War I.[44]

The rise of the Arab movement had caught the attention of both Germany and Britain. Two principal factors dictated Berlin's response to it. The first was the intimate tie of Germany to the Ottoman government. Second was the German attempt, particularly after 1911 and 1912, to achieve a rapprochement with Britain, which meant doing nothing to encourage the opposition of Arabs to British influence in the Middle East.[45]

As early as 1907 and 1908 German consular officials in Syria, Mesopotamia, and Egypt had reported a multitude of anti-Turkish actions by Arabs. The officials stressed the serious nature of the revolt in Yemen against the Ottomans; the plundering by Arab tribes of Turkish and British commerce in Mesopotamia; the hatred for the Turks of Shiites in Karbala, Najaf, and Samarra; and the seizure by Bedouins in Medina of a train carrying Muslim pilgrims on the Hijaz railroad.[46]

In September 1910 the German consul in Beirut, Wilhelm Padel, reported to the foreign ministry the local Arab unhappiness with German press claims that the Ottomans must dominate the peoples of the Middle East. Padel discussed what he called "an Arab question" and emphasized that the Arabs formed a majority in the Ottoman Empire.[47] Yet he discounted any serious threat from the Arabs to Ottoman hegemony, arguing that Arabs were "considerably inferior" to the Ottomans "morally as well as intellectually," and that Arab attacks against the Ottomans were only of a local character and without any religious significance.[48]

The German consul in Baghdad, Dr. W. G. Hesse, viewed with greater concern the anti-Ottoman unrest of Arab tribes in Mesopotamia, including attacks on local Turkish garrisons and trade. "The situation could become dangerous," he warned, apparently referring to the Shiite-Sunni conflict in the region, "as soon as a religious event unites the previously divided tribes."[49] On another occasion Hesse declared, "Whether there will be large revolts will depend significantly on whether a leader is found who, by the force of his personality, can carry the Bedouins away with him and understands the exploitation of religious motives to hold together the tribes hostile to one another."[50] Hesse, moreover, observed the expanding influence in Basra of the Sayyid Talib al-Naqib, the local Arab representative to the Ottoman parliament and a member of the most powerful noble family and Islamic religious authority in the city.[51]

As reports about the Arab unrest and anti-Turkish activity mounted, German officials, searching for the causes, seemed to discount Arab grievances toward Ottoman policies; instead they blamed Germany's European archrival, Britain. For example, the German military attaché at the Constantinople embassy, Major von Strempel, accused the British of inciting the revolt in Yemen against the Turks, a revolt that the Turks ended only in 1911 with the assistance of the Sharif of Mecca and other Arab leaders.[52]

Moreover, the Germans erroneously accused the Egyptian khedive, Abbas Hilmi, of being a British tool. They had observed since 1909 that the khedive once again entertained the idea of an anti-Ottoman alliance of all Arabs, with himself preferably its leader and new caliph.[53] Moreover, the theme of British-supported Arab unrest appeared in the German press, as it did in reports to Berlin from the consulate-general in Cairo. As early as June 1909 Oppenheim argued that the British, working particularly through their Persian Gulf ally, the Shaykh of Kuwait, were supplying weapons to keep alive the conflict in northern and central Arabia between the two main rival chieftains, Ibn Rashid and Ibn Saud.[54]

During 1910 and 1911 Hesse, the consul in Baghdad, alleged that the British were smuggling weapons to Arab tribes in central Arabia. Also, Britain, he asserted, was encouraging an anti-Turkish alliance among several chieftains that included Ibn Saud, the shaykhs of Kuwait and Muhammarah, and Sadhun Pasha, the Muntafiq leader in Mesopotamia. In August 1911, the son of a shaykh from the province of al-Hasa in eastern Arabia visited Hesse; the Arab denounced the Ottomans and British, requested German protection for local Arabs, and prophesied that Arab attacks plundering shipping and caravans in Iraq and Mesopotamia would continue. Hesse lamented the turmoil, and especially the apparent unwillingness of the Young Turks to control the situation.[55]

For instance, in July 1912 he even criticized the pro-German Turkish governor (vali) of Baghdad, Jemal Pasha, who later in 1913 seized power in Constantinople as part of a Young Turk triumvirate. Jemal, according to Hesse, had done nothing to quiet local Arab unrest and had allowed anti-European sentiment to develop in the province. The consul, furthermore, refused German involvement with the Arabs and discouraged any action by them against either the Young Turks or British.[56]

During the fall of 1911, the Austrian priest and Orientalist Alois Musil traveled along the Hijaz railroad and to the Red Sea coast. In reports to his government in Vienna he too asserted that the British were involved in the region. According to Musil, the British expected to occupy the coast soon. He also relayed information that Britain had concluded treaties with a number of coastal shaykhs.[57]

Although the Germans privately criticized the supposed British involvement with the Arabs, Berlin seemed intent on doing nothing in Mesopotamia, the Persian Gulf, or elsewhere in the Middle East to provoke Britain to take a radical political or military step to strengthen its already strong position in the area. To avoid problems with Britain, the Germans even downplayed pan-Islamism. For example, in January 1911, the British consul in Baghdad, J. G. Lorimer, complained that a Young Turk officer had acted on behalf of the *imam* (the spiritual leader) in the Shiite holy city of Najaf by attempting to spread pan-Islamic literature in Baghdad. The German consul, Hesse, supported the restraining of the officer by the local Ottoman governor-general, Nazim Pasha.[58]

By September 1911 German suspicions, most of them based on local reports but unsubstantiated, of British involvement with the Arabs had reached the highest level of government in Berlin. The kaiser, apparently on the authority of Oppenheim, maintained that the new British resident in Cairo, Horatio Herbert Lord Kitchener, intended to take advantage of the Turkish-Italian war over Libya to establish an Arab caliphate under Egyptian and British protection.[59] Such claims of a British-controlled Arab caliphate had been the subject of rumors among some Arab nationalists since at least the 1880s, but the German emperor was only partly correct.

Extensive research has illustrated that British leaders before World War I, while they accumulated, like the Germans, substantial evidence of the existence of Arab unrest as well as of a small nationalist movement, disagreed over what these factors meant and what Britain's response to them should be. By 1910 British consuls in Syria, particularly H. A. Cumberbatch in Beirut, were observing the growing dissatisfaction of some Arabs with the Young Turk regime, although

neither the British nor the Turks realized until much later that leading Syrian and Mesopotamian Arabs had started to form clandestine
secret societies and develop explicitly nationalistic ideas. Through
the anti-Turkish Syrians exiled in Egypt, the British Residency in Cairo
was somewhat better informed, yet its officials too had little idea of
the depth of Arab feelings or of the extent of the secret Arab organizations.[60]

In February 1911, Gorst, the British resident, reported to Grey that
Egyptian nationalists suspected one of the best-known advocates of
the Arab cause and of pan-Islamism in Cairo, Shaykh Muhammad
Rashid Rida, and also local Syrian exiles of busily intriguing in the
Hijaz and Yemen against the Turks. Their efforts, Gorst added, "are
inspired or aided by the Anglo-Egyptian Government."[61] Apparently
the khedive, Abbas Hilmi, cooperated with Rida as part of the
khedive's aspiration to establish an Arab caliphate—politically, an
empire that would include Egypt, Syria, and Arabia. That Rida had
founded after 1910 one of the Arab secret societies, whose membership included Abdullah, the Sharif of Mecca's son, remained unknown
to the British.[62]

Britain's response to the Arab question was also colored by
London's fear of the activities of its main European rival in the Middle
East, Germany. Since 1906 the British General Staff had studied extensively the possibility of a Turkish-German invasion of Egypt. Grey's
remarks in Parliament on the importance to Britain of Arabia sparked
a British press attack on Turkish economic concessions to Germany,
concessions that, warned one paper, could "bring German interests
as a militant possibility into Arabia—on the flank of Egypt and the
British route to the East."[63]

In Egypt such opinions were commonplace by the end of 1911 and
1912 among the officials of the British Residency. They were shared
by their new chief, Lord Kitchener, the conqueror of the Sudan in
1898 and the greatest living hero of the British Empire. Influenced
by the Young Turk defeats at the hands of Italy and the Balkan
states, such officials argued that the Ottoman Empire could no
longer maintain itself. Only with powerful German support of the
empire, Kitchener believed, could Turkey preserve the status quo. In
his view, Britain should not assist the Turks to preserve themselves;

he prophesied that the Arabs of the Ottoman Empire would soon seek independence.[64] Moreover, Kitchener considered the Arab lands in the Middle East vital to Britain's position in Egypt and India, and thus he was attracted to the idea of providing support to the Arab movement. Specifically, he recommended that Britain seize a part of southern Syria from the Turks and encourage the Arab provinces of the empire to form themselves into one or more autonomous and pro-British states.[65]

From 1911 to 1914 the influence Kitchener exerted from Cairo increasingly replaced that of the Constantinople embassy in shaping Britain's relations with Turkey and the Arabs. In September 1913 he sent to southern Palestine a small military mission, disguised as an expedition of the Palestine Exploration Fund (whose members included the archaeologists Leonard Woolley and T. E. Lawrence), to survey the region. Six months later Kitchener helped persuade the Young Turks to free from prison Major Aziz Bey al-Masri, a former Egyptian officer in the Ottoman army whom the Ottomans had arrested for treason and had become a hero of Arab nationalists for his participation in Ottoman negotiations in Yemen and in the Libyan war against the Italians. Furthermore, since his appointment at Cairo Kitchener had taken a keen interest in the Hijaz and in its Arab prince, the guardian of Islam's holy places, the Sharif of Mecca.[66]

Much of Kitchener's concern for Arab nationalism resulted from the continued anti-British activity of the Germans in Egypt. Despite Oppenheim's departure from Cairo at the beginning of 1910, his work there continued through his protégé, Prüfer, and the new German consul general, Hermann Count von Hatzfeldt. Prüfer, with Hatzfeldt's assistance, published articles in the German press hostile to British policy in Egypt, and he increased ties to the most radical anti-British Egyptian nationalists, Farid and al-Jawish.[67]

The German intrigue with the Egyptian nationalists concerned the Foreign Office in London especially because of anti-British outbursts of the nationalists in 1910 and 1911. Kitchener, almost from the moment of his appointment as resident, had reinstated the harsh policies of Cromer toward the khedive, decreasing the latter's authority over even ceremonial matters and threatening to depose him. Kitchener also tried to weaken the nationalist movement by playing on its divisions. He cooperated with its moderate party but refused to tolerate the extremists Farid and al-Jawish, whom he exiled.[68]

Kitchener's crusade also touched upon the Germans. Continually apprehensive about Berlin's meddlesome policy toward Egypt, he kept the size of Britain's peacetime military garrison in the country at roughly six thousand troops. Moreover, in September 1911 he unleashed a bitter, if minor, controversy with the Germans by rejecting their suggestion that the Egyptian national library appoint Prüfer as its new director and that the Cairo museum name a German as its second in command.[69]

The Germans also presented yet another problem for the British in Egypt. During the Turkish-Italian war of 1911–1912, in which Turkey lost Libya to Italy, the German consulate-general in Cairo pursued a pro-Turkish and pan-Islamic policy. Part of the consulate-general's assistance to the Turks in the war was to collect money from Egyptians and, by emphasizing pan-Islamism, to recruit Bedouins as soldiers to help their fellow tribesmen and Turkish forces in Libya fight the Italians.[70] The project foundered, however, partly because the Young Turks did not support it, resenting the involvement of Germany, a foreign and Christian state, in pan-Islamic activity. The war ended with Turkey's defeat and loss of Libya; the Ottoman failures in Libya and in the Balkan wars of 1912 and 1913 persuaded the Germans to study more extensively British military and security measures in Egypt. Fritz Klein, a German officer assigned to the consulate-general, reported in April 1912 on Britain's increased fortifications along the Turkish-Egyptian border and on the Sinai Peninsula meant to prevent Turkish troops from penetrating to the canal. Klein in addition investigated possible Ottoman invasion routes through the peninsula.[71]

The Young Turks and Arab Policy

The loss of Libya and the remnants of Turkey's European empire prompted, on 23 January 1913, a coup in Constantinople that finally placed the CUP fully in power. A triumvirate that combined committee and army influence dominated the new regime: Enver Pasha, a former military attaché in Berlin and an admirer of Germany; Jemal Pasha, an army colonel and military governor of Constantinople; and

Talaat Pasha, a parliamentary deputy and the government's minister of the interior.[72]

The events in the Balkans, including the wars of 1912–1913, particularly persuaded the CUP of the necessity of strengthening both Turkish nationalism—especially of the pan-Turanian brand, which demanded the extension of Turkish rule over the Turkish portions of Russian central Asia—and pan-Islamism. The new leaders at the Porte needed major changes if the only non-Turkish element of any significance—the Arabs—were to remain within the Ottoman Empire.[73] Consequently, although the government continued with the modernization of the army (with the aid, significantly, of the German and British military missions in Constantinople), the education system, and the economy, they attempted several measures to placate Arab opinion. These included decentralizing the administration of the Arab provinces, permitting the Arabic language in schools and certain government departments, and in June 1913 appointing an Arab, Said Halim Pasha, as prime minister *(grand vizier)*.

An ardent pan-Islamist, Said Halim helped fashion a CUP Arab policy that made concessions to the Sharif of Mecca, Husayn ibn Ali, and that was to prevent the latter's break with the committee until after World War I had begun. The Porte offered Husayn, in return for his support of the Hijaz railroad to Mecca, the lifetime *amirate* (the office of commander, governor, or minor ruler of a province) of the holy city, and to make it hereditary in his family.[74] Despite these concessions to the Arabs, complaints of discrimination against them continued and some anti-Turkish feeling spread, particularly in Syria and Mesopotamia.

The Young Turks, in addition, moved in October 1913 to modernize and improve the Ottoman army. That month the Porte announced the appointment of a new and larger German military mission to Constantinople, led by General Liman von Sanders. The Arab response to the mission is unknown, but the ensuing international crisis, in which the Russians bitterly protested the mission and demanded Anglo-French support in opposing it, quickly raised the fears of both London and St. Petersburg.[75]

In December the British foreign secretary, Grey, began a concerted effort to strengthen Anglo-Turkish relations, replacing the anti-

Young Turk Lowther with a new representative to the Porte, Sir Louis Mallet. But Mallet had little success, mainly because Russian hostility toward Turkey continued and the Porte resisted British attempts to persuade it to introduce reforms in the Ottoman Empire that would satisfy the grievances of oppressed minorities, like the Armenians.[76]

The Anglo-German and Anglo-Turkish Agreements of 1913–1914

Despite these political problems, Britain successfully safeguarded its strategic and economic interests in the Ottoman Empire. This held especially true in Mesopotamia and the Persian Gulf, where British concern revolved significantly around the issue of the Baghdad railroad. The latter presented a potential and wide-ranging threat to Britain's interests in both Turkey and the Gulf, as well as in India.

The railway ran through the heart of Mesopotamia, a region where Anglo-Indian trade had long been paramount and unrivalled; it also passed the towns of Karbala and Najaf, where stood religious shrines of the Shiite sect, visited annually by thousands of Anglo-Indian subjects. Further, London viewed the mineral rights granted to Germany along the railroad as a danger to British aspirations for acquiring oil in the Mosul and Baghdad provinces. Finally, navigation privileges afforded to Germany on the Tigris River and its port rights at Baghdad and Basra challenged the concession held for years on the main local waterways by the British-owned Euphrates and Tigris Steam Navigation Company.[77]

Anglo-German and Anglo-Turkish negotiations regarding the railroad dragged on interminably. They were shaped in part by the general winding down of tension after 1910 between London and Berlin on numerous broader colonial and naval issues and in part by the ever-present apprehension of several key British leaders about pan-Islamism. Although some officials demanded a harsh policy in dealing with the Young Turks, including partitioning the Ottoman Empire with Britain acquiring a part of Mesopotamia, a feeling also existed, and was shared by Grey and Nicolson, that Britain should adopt a moderate line in the negotiations. For example, at the end of 1910 both the India Office and the British resident in the Persian Gulf clamored for the use of military force to secure Britain's position in the region; Nicolson and the new viceroy of India, Sir Charles Hardinge, cautioned against it. Both feared anti-British pan-Islamic outbreaks in India, Persia, and Egypt.[78]

Hardinge particularly exaggerated the threat of pan-Islamism and Muslim unrest in India; of the several hundred million people in the country, Muslims numbered seventy million, with most of them living in Bengal and the North-West Frontier Province. Although some Muslims in India expressed pan-Islamic sentiments and even solidarity with the Ottoman caliph, Muslims were almost wholly absent from the growing reign of terror in India waged by the Hindu-dominated, anti-British nationalist movement.[79] Other British officials, including Lord Crewe, the secretary of state for India, and Sir Arthur Hirtzel, the India Office's political secretary, downplayed Muslim threats to British rule in India.[80]

Other factors provided Britain with incentives to conclude an agreement with the Ottomans on the Baghdad railroad and related issues. There was concern in some circles that by threatening the Turks Britain might drive them completely into the arms of the Triple Alliance. The British, furthermore, wished to retain control of much of the Gulf area, more in fact than it wished to expand their influence in Mesopotamia. This led the British to negotiate with the Turks for an agreement on Kuwait, the Gulf terminus for the Baghdad railroad, and on the other issues regarding the Gulf and Mesopotamia.[81]

Also, from 1911 to 1914 at least two agents of the Government of India—Captain William Shakespear, the political agent in Kuwait, and Lieutenant-Colonel Gerard Leachman—frequently visited Abd al-Aziz ibn Saud, a rising Arab chieftain in north-central and eastern Arabia, a region known as the Najd. Headquartered in Riyadh and allied to the puritanical Islamic movement, the Wahhabis, Ibn Saud in 1913 extended his sway to the Gulf by seizing from the Turks the province of al-Hasa. As a result, the Porte had thought it necessary to appoint Ibn Saud as vali of the Najd; he in return promised not to give concessions to, or enter into direct relations or treaties with, foreign powers. Ibn Saud continued his bitter struggle for domination of the area against another Arab rival, Abd al-Aziz ibn Rashid, of Hail.

Both Shakespear and Leachman, despite opposition from the Foreign Office, which feared incurring the wrath of the Young Turks, hoped to aggravate the religious and political differences between Ibn Saud and the Turks and to establish friendly relations with the chief.[82] On the Persian side of the Gulf, Britain had by 1910 an arrangement with the Shaykh of Muhammarah, Khazal, that resembled the one with Kuwait. Sources of oil on Khazal's land, and the lease of Abadan by the Anglo-Persian Oil Company for a large oil refinery to produce fuel for the British navy's new dreadnoughts, made for an agreement doubly important for Britain.[83]

So did the increased activity of the Germans in the Gulf and southern Persia. By 1906 the German shipping and pearl trading firm of Woenckhaus possessed branches throughout the Gulf. In addition, the Hamburg-Amerika Line had established a regular commercial service from Europe to the Gulf that charged lower rates than British companies. Also, during 1906–1907 a mini-crisis erupted when Woenckhaus obtained a concession to mine iron oxide on the small Gulf island of Abu Musa. The conflict reached the highest levels in British and German diplomacy, and a British ship forcibly removed from Abu Musa Arab miners employed by the Germans; the affair remained unresolved until World War I.[84]

In southern Persia, the German vice consulate at Bushire, particularly under the leadership during 1909–1910 and 1913–1914 of the German agent Wilhelm Wassmuss, engaged increasingly in anti-British activities, including illegal gun-running, among the surrounding Arab and Persian tribes. Tribesmen and pirates of the Gulf, supplied with German, Belgian, and French weapons through Turkey and Oman, smuggled the arms to Baluchistan and then to rebels hostile to Britain in Afghanistan and the North-West Frontier Province of India. Wassmuss's animosity toward the British and their resident in the Gulf, Sir Percy Cox, led the German minister in Teheran in 1910 to remove Wassmuss for a time from Bushire.[85]

On another level as well the expansion by Germany of its activities in Persia, where Britain controlled the south and Russia the north, alarmed the British. Germany had increased its trade with Persia, establishing a bank in Teheran in 1906, and soon began urging that

Persia include Berlin in important railroad and shipping concessions previously enjoyed by Britain and Russia.[86]

Meanwhile, the British embassy in Constantinople observed carefully the activities of Oppenheim and other Germans, mostly archaeologists and engineers, in Syria and Mesopotamia. Oppenheim not only worked at his archaeological site at Tell Halaf but visited among the Arabs living along the construction route of the Baghdad railroad. During 1911, he and the former German head of the Egyptian national library in Cairo, Bernhard Moritz, won support for the railroad from Arab and Kurdish tribal chiefs in the Khabur valley region. Encamped beside the upper Euphrates River, Oppenheim and Moritz pitted the Arab tribes against one another; they intrigued with the Anaza and Muntafiq, hoping thereby to undermine neighboring tribes like the Shammar, who opposed the railroad running through their land.[87]

Moreover, in Mesopotamia, along the Tigris and Euphrates rivers, other German archaeologists, led by Dr. Friedrich Sarre of the Kaiser Friedrich Museum in Berlin, established close relations with local tribes while excavating the sensational palace ruins at Samarra of the ninth-century Abbasid caliph, al-Mutasim.[88] Another Orientalist, Alois Musil, a Catholic priest and professor at the University of Vienna whose work the Germans knew well, traveled among the Bedouins in the Sinai Peninsula, northern Arabia, and southern Mesopotamia. In northern Arabia especially, Musil established friendly ties to the Anaza tribe and its leading chieftain, the shaykh of the Rualla, Nuri ibn Shaalan.[89]

Thus, the British possessed plenty of reasons to negotiate a settlement with the Young Turks—as well as with the Germans—regarding the Baghdad railroad and related issues. In August 1913 Britain concluded with the Porte a convention on the railway. In return for a significant financial payment from Britain, the Young Turks agreed to termination of the line at Basra, to request Britain's permission for any track built beyond Basra to the Gulf, and to equality of treatment for British and Indian trade on all railways in Turkey. Grey and the British also concluded with the Turks, on 29 July 1913 and later, agreements that secured Britain's navigation rights on the Tigris and

Euphrates Rivers, its interests in Mesopotamian oil, and its domination over Kuwait.[90]

As for Germany, its leaders too had incentives by 1912–1913 to settle the railroad problem, as well as other issues in Turkey, with Britain. The recent crises over Morocco and in the Balkans had intensified the perception in Berlin that France, Britain, and Russia had "encircled" Germany—even though much of the "encirclement" had been self-imposed—and that a two-front war with Russia and France seemed ever more likely. Anxiety also existed in some government circles—particularly the kaiser and the chancellor, Theobald von Bethmann Hollweg—that Turkey had been so weakened by its recent wars that it might not survive. Others however, like the German ambassador in Constantinople, Wangenheim, and the foreign secretary, Alfred von Kiderlen-Wächter, believed that Turkey could continue to exist, even without its European territory.

Bethmann Hollweg, who hoped to achieve a rapprochement with Britain, thereby dividing it from its allies and securing London's neutrality in the event of a continental war, sought to turn a partition of Turkey to Germany's advantage by using the issue in negotiations with Britain. In order not to arouse anti-British protests from the German public and pressure groups, particularly the Pan-German League, Berlin delayed for as long as possible publication of the Anglo-Ottoman railway convention of August 1913.[91]

Not only the pan-Germans but also some German industrialists, government officials, and publicists demanded that their government transform Turkey into a satellite, which Germany could exploit economically in unlimited fashion. These groups urged completion of the Baghdad railroad to the Persian Gulf. Beginning in 1913, Germany's new foreign secretary, Gottlieb von Jagow, together with leading industrialists, envisioned the Reich dividing the Middle East and gaining control of its economy. Also, various nationalist writers and Orientalists, such as Ernst Jäckh (who had joined the foreign ministry in 1912) and Paul Rohrbach, urged the government to settle German colonists in Turkey. This, they argued, would strengthen Young Turk rule over the hostile and supposedly degenerate non-Turkish peoples of the Ottoman Empire.[92]

The Anglo-German negotiations on the Baghdad railroad continued during 1913 and the first months of 1914. In March 1914 Britain
and Germany reached an agreement on oil in Mesopotamia, by which
the Germans received a share of 25 percent and Britain the remainder. Only at the end of July did Berlin, apparently as part of a last
attempt to acquire British neutrality in the coming world war, agree
to sign a Baghdad railway agreement.[93]

By the beginning of 1914, therefore, Britain had protected and even
consolidated its position in the Ottoman Empire. To be sure, London had not lessened the political and economic inroads which Germany had made. Nevertheless, the Porte was nowhere near being converted into a satellite of the Reich, or even into its reliable ally.
Germany's trade with Turkey had increased significantly, yet it still
ranked behind that of Britain, France, and Austria-Hungary.[94] Much
of this had become apparent to the Germans, particularly regarding
the issue of oil rights. By April 1914 the German ambassador in London, Karl von Lichnowsky, was informing Berlin of British estimates
of the major oil sources on the Mekran coast of the Gulf. Two months
later the German consul in Baghdad, Hesse, emphasized to his government the importance of the Abadan oil refinery.[95]

Rejections by Britain and Germany of Arab Approaches

Britain's success in Turkey pleased the Foreign Office and Grey. The
latter continually sought to reassure Berlin and Constantinople of
Britain's wish not to partition the Ottoman Empire, but to reform it
and consolidate Ottoman authority. Grey had no intention of allowing this subject to undermine Britain's negotiations for agreements
with the Turks regarding the Baghdad railway and other issues.

In the foreign secretary's view the Turkish empire was enfeebled
by its internal weaknesses and corrupt administration. But this attitude notwithstanding, he believed that Turkey continued to offer
Britain a balance of power in the Middle East and the best protection
for its interests there, particularly from the threat of Russian expansion into the region. Furthermore, partition of Turkey inevitably
implied German predominance in Asia Minor and French supremacy
in Syria, thus making more acute Britain's weakness in Mesopotamia

and the Gulf. Finally, the Government of India opposed dividing Turkey, because it might alienate India's Muslim subjects.[96]

But not everyone in his government agreed with Grey. Some urged the dissolution of a declining Turkey among the Great Powers. These included his ambassadors in Constantinople, first Lowther and then Mallet. They received numerous reports from their consuls in Mesopotamia that demonstrated mounting dissatisfaction of local Arabs with Turkish rule. Also, persons of lesser stature believed in partitioning Turkey, like David G. Hogarth and T. E. Lawrence, Oxford archaeologists concerned with protecting Britain's interests in explorations of ancient ruins in northern Syria along the route of the Baghdad railroad. Perhaps more important, Grey's chief officials in Cairo, including after 1911 Lord Kitchener, urged that Britain protect itself from the growing German influence in the Ottoman Empire, alleged to be a danger to Egypt from the east, by allying with the anti-Turkish Arab movement in Syria and Iraq.[97]

But Grey and the Foreign Office held sway on the issue. Consequently Britain officially rejected opportunities before World War I to encourage the Arabs to revolt against the Ottomans. Only Kitchener tried to keep a line open to the Arabs by responding to a feeler extended to him on 5 February 1914 from Abdullah, the son of the Sharif of Mecca, during a visit to the khedive in Cairo. During the meeting Abdullah inquired whether if the Arabs resisted Ottoman attempts to remove the sharif from power, Britain would help prevent it. Kitchener disclaimed any interest in interfering in the affair.[98]

The Germans, too, received and rejected approaches from anti-Ottoman Arabs, but such contacts illustrated the Arabs' anxiety at the prospect of British and French rule replacing the Turkish one in the region. For example, during 1912 and 1913 the Cairo consulate-general reported to Berlin on Syrian Arab exiles in Egypt led by the local pan-Islamist and Arab nationalist Rashid Rida. Rida met with a German emissary and discussed his dream of the creation of an independent Arab caliphate, of which the new caliph, the Egyptian khedive, would rule Syria and Arabia. Although according to Rida the British and French were encouraging "the Arab revolutionary movement," they were not to be trusted. Rida thus asked Germany for diplomatic support and assistance in acquiring armaments to be used against the Anglo-French—a request that Hans von Miquel, the new consul general in Cairo, quickly refused.[99]

Moreover, at the end of 1912 a representative of the youthful tribal chieftain at Hail in north-central Arabia, Abd al-Aziz ibn Rashid, contacted the German embassy in Constantinople, asking Germany for protection for himself and his followers. According to the emissary, Rashid Pasha, Ibn Rashid was convinced that the Ottoman Empire would soon collapse, thereby allowing Anglo-French influence to expand into the region. Rashid Pasha had several meetings in June and July 1913 with the ambassador, Wangenheim, as well as with officials of the Baghdad consulate; the Germans refused to provide Ibn Rashid with weapons, but they ultimately persuaded the Young Turks to do so.[100]

Other Arab leaders who mistrusted the British and contacted the Germans for assistance had organized reform committees in Basra and Beirut favoring greater Arab autonomy. The Basra Reform Committee, founded in February 1913 and led by the Sayyid Talib al-Naqib, opposed centralized Turkish rule over, in the sayyid's words, "the oppressed Arab nation," but the committee's greater fear was British expansion in Mesopotamia. Members of the Sayyid Talib's family approached the German consulate in Baghdad requesting protection from the Reich for them and their leader; the Germans refused and even took the unprecedented step of informing Britain of the decision.[101] In Beirut the German consulate watched closely the local Arab reform committee; the office instructed Berlin in May 1913 that committee members had ties to the Arab congress then meeting in Paris.[102]

By the beginning of 1914 the Arab question clearly worried German officials; above all, they suspected that Britain played a role in it. In addition, they realized the issue's potential for undermining Berlin's attempts at an agreement with London on the Baghdad railroad and on much larger matters in Europe. In January the German embassy in Constantinople showed greater alarm than did the Young Turks when Kitchener dispatched the British mission, disguised as an archaeological expedition, to southern Palestine to survey the area and the Egyptian border. A few weeks later the foreign ministry asked its embassies in London and Constantinople if they had heard about a secret meeting of Arab chieftains in Arabia. The alleged meeting, said the ministry, had aimed at separating the Arab leaders from the Ottoman Empire and establishing an Arab caliphate. On 9 March Wangenheim replied from Constantinople that the embassy had no knowledge of such a meeting.[103]

Almost simultaneously, Miquel in Cairo learned of the recent visit of Abdullah, the Sharif of Mecca's son, to the Egyptian capital. While the consul general apparently knew nothing of Abdullah's meeting with Kitchener, Miquel nevertheless received information unwelcome to the Germans: Abdullah had met the khedive and complained to him about Young Turk attempts to centralize control over his father's domain, the Hijaz, which contained the Islamic holy places. Furthermore, Miquel learned, Abdullah did not believe assurances given him by the Ottoman commissariat in Cairo that the government in Constantinople "was well disposed toward the sharif."[104]

On 28 March Wangenheim dispatched a report to Berlin describing in bleak terms Young Turk relations to the Arabs. A part of Yemen had been lost to the Ottomans, said the ambassador; also, all the principal Arab chieftains in Arabia, except for Ibn Rashid, despised the Turks. The Sharif of Mecca, for example, had demanded greater autonomy from Constantinople. Wangenheim discounted foreign—meaning British—influence in the matter but concluded that the Young Turks considered the situation serious enough to have developed plans for armed attacks, first on the sharif and then on Yemen.[105]

Two months later the ambassador informed Berlin that the "Arab movement" was on the rise and that he feared the emergence of a popular leader who might unite the Arabs against the Turks. Such a person, he suggested, could be Aziz Bey al-Masri, the former Egyptian officer in the Ottoman army whom the Turks had arrested in February for treason but had recently released (in part because of the intercession of Kitchener and Britain). Wangenheim's warning resulted partly from news that an Arab nationalist group had emerged for the first time in northern Syria at Aleppo.[106]

A similar alarm came from Hesse, the consul in Baghdad. On 16 July, amid the crisis in Europe that would soon explode into World War I, he expressed to the foreign ministry pessimism about the decline of Ottoman control over Arabia and Basra. In his view the turmoil among the Arabs in the region, including the armed attacks of the Muntafiq and their chief, Ajaimi, on the forces of the Basra nationalist, the Sayyid Talib, endangered German interests, especially the further construction of the Baghdad railroad. The consul urged that Germany increase its influence in the area, suggesting that it establish a consulate in Basra and send a German battle cruiser there.[107]

Berlin never considered such proposals seriously, because they would hardly have assisted the efforts of Germany during the July crisis in Europe to persuade London to remain neutral in a war on the continent.[108] Indeed, only in a final desperate attempt to gain British neutrality in the coming world war did the German government agree at the end of July to conclude the settlement with Britain, which had been under negotiation for nearly two years, regarding the Baghdad railroad.[109]

By then, however, it was far too late for such an agreement to affect the deteriorating situation in Europe. Furthermore, German policy in 1914 toward Britain, plus the knowledge of German officials in Turkey about the Arab unrest there, may explain why Wangenheim showed little interest in the pan-Islamic activities suggested to him in March by the extremist Egyptian nationalist exiled in Constantinople, Shaykh al-Jawish. The latter, recommended to Wangenheim by Enver Pasha, urged that in the event of a war between Germany and Britain, anti-British insurrections among Muslims be ignited in Egypt and elsewhere.[110]

Also, Germany's policy in Turkey seemed to have reached a point of crisis. During the previous months the Young Turk government, unable to raise a large enough loan from a Germany severely hampered financially by the Reich's grand political schemes in the Middle East and elsewhere, had procured the money in Paris, in the process making major railroad and harbor concessions to France in Asia Minor and Syria. Even the kaiser, a longtime rabid supporter of the Porte, complained that Germany's shortage of money meant that it could not count on the backing of the Ottomans in the future. Wilhelm accused the Young Turks of disloyalty to Germany and of making dishonest and corrupt advances to the Entente.[111]

Nevertheless, while the Germans wished to do nothing to alienate Britain, Berlin also could not afford to anger the Turks. During the summer of 1914 the Deutsche Bank, aided by the foreign ministry and its under-secretary, Arthur Zimmermann, placed a new loan on the Berlin market—a loan urgently needed for extending the Baghdad railway and demonstrating to Turkey and the Entente powers Germany's economic strength.[112] By July 1914, therefore, the Balkan crisis that soon produced the world war was threatening to lose for Germany not only its bridge to the Middle East but also the object of its political and economic expansion in the region, the Ottoman Empire itself.

3

Germany as Wartime "Revolutionary," Fall 1914

The onset of the "Great War" in Europe in August 1914 shattered any opportunity in the Middle East for implementing the agreements concluded there during the previous year among Turkey, Britain, and Germany. Following Austria-Hungary's attack on Serbia, Germany declared war on Russia and France and invaded France and Belgium, forcing Britain's entry into the conflict against the Central Powers of Germany and Austria-Hungary.

During the conflict's first months the German goals included weakening the Allies by diverting their resources away from Europe and particularly to their empires in the Middle East, North Africa, and southern Russia. German officials envisioned waging war against the far-flung British Empire, which the kaiser and his subordinates envied and despised, by inciting anti-British, pan-Islamic rebellions—and eventually a "holy war" (jihad)—among its many Muslim subjects. But although the idea of promoting uprisings as a means of warfare had existed among German leaders for at least two decades, they quickly found themselves nearly wholly unprepared for organizing the revolts.[1]

The Turkish-German Alliance and First Preparations for Inciting Muslim Rebellions

Almost until 4 August, when Britain declared war on the Central Powers, key German leaders, especially the chancellor, Bethmann Hollweg, and foreign secretary, Gottlieb von Jagow, held to the illusion that Germany could convince Britain to remain neutral. Thus when the world war began, Germany possessed no military strategy by which to confront Britain. The Reich's massive prewar naval buildup had failed either to offset or out-produce the British Royal Navy. However, few leaders in Berlin, except for Admiral Alfred von Tirpitz, who had built the German fleet, realized the latter was nowhere near ready for war with Britain.[2] This would make ever more problematic—not to mention unrealistic—the German plans to instigate, with the help of Turkey, anti-British rebellions of Muslims in faraway Egypt, India, and elsewhere.

Another difficulty with the German program to stir up anti-British revolts in the Middle East in 1914 resulted from the Reich's prewar policies in the region. Except in Turkey, they had done little to enhance Berlin's influence there. In Egypt, Persia, and Afghanistan a German presence barely existed. Even in the Ottoman Empire, despite the major advances the Germans had made since the 1880s, the other European powers effectively counterbalanced Germany's economic and financial power. Britain's military position in the empire and rest of the Middle East appeared as strong as ever.[3]

Therefore, the Young Turks caught Berlin by surprise when during the July crisis of 1914, a small faction among them proposed to the Germans that the Central Powers and Turkey conclude an alliance directed against Russia. A majority of the Turkish government knew nothing of the alliance until its conclusion. The group that arranged it, composed of the grand vizier, Said Halim, the interior minister, Talaat Pasha, and the war minister, Enver Pasha, were worried about the Turkish weakness made obvious in the wars of 1911 and 1912.

This minority faction also believed that, in the event of a European war, Turkey had much more to fear from Russia than Germany. The pro-German Enver, who presented the proposal to Germany on 22 July, in particular judged the Central Powers as the strongest alliance in the European crisis and the side that could win a war. The German ambassador at Constantinople, Wangenheim, quickly rejected the feeler. While Wangenheim may have acted on policy orders from Berlin, he also doubted, as did the chief of the German General Staff, General Helmuth von Moltke, the usefulness of the Turkish armed forces for Germany.

Two days later, however, on 24 July, Wilhelm II intervened. Frustrated over the recent failures of German policy in Turkey, he overruled Wangenheim and ordered him to open negotiations with the Porte.[4] During the ensuing discussions with the Young Turk faction, the kaiser became, in the words of the German historian Fritz Fischer, the "emperor as revolutionary."[5] Wilhelm II returned to his prewar fixation on using pan-Islamism as a tool of war, mainly because he seemed concerned with Britain as much as with Russia and France. He believed that both the continued authority of his monarchy at home and Germany's rise to world power depended on the destruction of the British Empire.[6]

On 30 July he expressed even more clearly his plan for revolution against Britain and for expanding the revolt beyond simply a means of warfare. Now he envisioned it as a means of dismantling the British Empire. He scribbled on a diplomatic dispatch from Russia: "Our consuls in Turkey and India, agents, etc., must inflame the whole Mohammedan world to wild revolt against this hateful, lying, conscienceless people of hagglers; for if we are to be bled to death, at least England shall lose India."[7] In part, therefore, Germany negotiated with the Turks with the intention of using them to produce a pan-Islamic movement that would begin with a holy war proclaimed by the Porte against Britain and its allies.

On 2 August the German-Turkish discussions resulted in a secret treaty between the two states. In the pact the Turks agreed to intervene on Germany's side if the latter and Russia went to war over the Austro-Hungarian and Serbian conflict (an eventuality that in fact had already happened); in return Germany obligated itself to protect the territorial integrity of the Ottoman Empire. With the Turkish treaty concluded and with Britain's entry into the war imminent, several of the highest officials in the German government immediately began implementing the kaiser's ambitious policy of waging war against Britain by inciting insurrections among its Muslim subjects in Egypt and India.

Moltke, the chief of staff, approved fully of the plan in letters to the German foreign ministry on 2 and 5 August, the second one—full of bitterness prompted by Britain's declaration of war—urging the ministry to incite the fanaticism of Islam. In the ministry, Jagow and his under-secretary, Zimmermann, whose stern demeanor and strong support of the Reich's Oriental and pro-Turkish policy made him popular with the kaiser, assented immediately. Jagow directed the embassy in Constantinople to spread propaganda among Muslims in British colonies, especially in India, and to ensure that the British naval mission did nothing to utilize the small Turkish fleet for Britain's purposes.[8]

Following the conclusion of the treaty, the Porte mobilized its armed forces. However, some Young Turks in the government had neither wanted nor even known about the alliance with Germany. Furthermore, the Allied powers soon proved stronger than expected in the European battles. The Porte, as a result, adopted a policy of armed neutrality and pursued it for several months.

The German and British embassies in Constantinople competed feverishly with one another to influence Turkish policy. Wangenheim, his military and naval attachés, and Liman von Sanders tried to force the Porte to enter the war against the Entente; Sir Louis Mallet, on the other hand, worked to keep the Turks neutral for as long as possible. Enver Pasha and his subordinates slowly prepared Turkey for war and made several concessions to the Central Powers. These included allowing two ships of Germany's Mediterranean fleet, the *Goeben* and *Breslau*, to enter and remain in the Turkish straits, and also assisting (as discussed below) German preparations for an attack on Egypt to trigger a pan-Islamic rising. However, neither Wangenheim nor Liman could persuade the Porte to abandon its neutrality.[9] Until Turkey entered the war, the Germans had little hope of conducting a military operation anywhere in the Middle East.

Nevertheless, with the conclusion of the treaty on 2 August discussions began immediately in Constantinople between the German embassy and Turkish war ministry about a Turkish-German military expedition against Egypt. On 10 August and 4 September Moltke telegraphed Liman about the importance of the Egyptian operation. While Liman, for strategic reasons, viewed this campaign as useless, Wangenheim and his military and naval attachés urged on the Turks the German General Staff's idea of an attack, specifically on the Suez Canal.[10]

Even before the war, the German General Staff had rated British colonial troops average at best and predicted that war in Europe would provoke native Muslim rebellions in both India and Egypt.

The Germans did not expect a large uprising, but they did envision that the excitement caused by the unrest would force Britain to send troops to the endangered regions, thus removing such forces from the main war theaters in Europe.[11] The high command saw an assault on the Suez Canal as a blow upon the British Empire at its most sensitive point. A Turkish triumph over Britain in Egypt seemed the most effective method for promoting a holy war of the Islamic world against Britain and its allies.

During the first week of August, the Young Turk war ministry ordered the Ottoman Fourth Army in Damascus to prepare for an expedition against the canal. Simultaneously, on 5 August Enver Pasha established formally in the government his previously private secret service, the *Taskilat-i Mahsusa;* headed by its cofounder, Sulayman Askeri, it was now to function as a wartime intelligence and guerrilla organization. Enver also created in the war ministry a Central Office for the Islamic Movement, appointing as its leader an anti-French Tunisian, Ali Bas Hamba, to coordinate pan-Islamic revolutionary activities with the Germans.[12]

In Berlin the foreign ministry and the army's reserve section of the General Staff *(stellvertretende Generalstab)* began dispatching individuals and political missions to Constantinople and Tripoli, in order to promote from there Muslim rebellions. The Reserve General Staff's *Sektion IIIb Politik,* directed by Captain Rudolf Nadolny, organized the army's political operations in foreign countries. The foreign ministry's political department created an Islamic section to guide its work in the Middle East, North Africa, and southern Russia.

To head this new department the ministry recalled Oppenheim to service in August, with the rank of minister in residence. It chose the Jewish archaeologist-spy because he was the only person in Germany who possessed both extensive knowledge of the Middle East and Africa and also experience in a consular office. Oppenheim's colleague in the ministry, and the most important propagandist of Germany's Oriental policy, was Ernst Jäckh. Another key official in the political department, also recalled to service at the war's beginning, was Otto Günther von Wesendonk; he served as the ministry's coordinator of revolutionary activities in the Middle East, India, and Russia and as its liaison with the General Staff.[13]

Wesendonk and Nadolny dispatched the first of the Reich's groups to North Africa, with the task of provoking Islamic uprisings against the French in North Africa. As early as 1 August Nadolny sent to Tripoli a reserve officer, the industrialist Dr. Otto Mannesmann, along with an interpreter and Hans Steinwachs, the director of the Morocco Mine Syndicate and Remscheid-based mining company of his brother, Reinhard Mannesmann. Before the war, the Mannesmann brothers had received mining concessions in Morocco and had cultivated political relations with several Arab and Berber tribal chieftains.

Otto Mannesmann, who spoke little Arabic, arrived in Tripoli on 8 August and presented himself as a deputy of the local German consul, Dr. Alfred Tilger. Mannesmann had orders to subvert French rule in Morocco, Algeria, and Tunis.[14] German plans for Algeria also received a boost from an entirely different quarter. The Algerian shaykh exiled in Syria, the Amir Said, a grandson of the nineteenth-century anti-French Algerian rebel Abd al-Qadir, telegraphed the foreign ministry offering to lead five hundred riders against France.[15]

In Berlin, the political department of the foreign ministry discussed Mannesmann's mission to North Africa and agreed on plans to incite anti-British revolts in India and Egypt. Also, Oppenheim recommended to Bethmann Hollweg the formation in the ministry of a central propaganda agency aimed at Muslim peoples and at countering the "shameless lying proclamations" allegedly issued by the British embassy in Constantinople. Sounding during the war's first days as heady and arrogant as the kaiser, Oppenheim emphasized the vulnerability of Britain to Muslim revolution in India.[16] At this point Ernst Freiherr Langwerth von Simmern, the assistant director of the ministry's political department and an expert on Morocco, informed the General Staff of the ministry's planned operations, highlighting the idea of spreading propaganda and agitation to India through Arabia. "One hopes," said Langwerth, "that a movement beginning in Egypt will reverberate through Mecca to the rest of the Islamic world and that its waves strike India."[17]

Oppenheim soon informed Bethmann Hollweg that raising a holy war among Muslims in India had been discussed with Enver Pasha and asserted that such an insurrection, promoted by emissaries from Turkey and "unleashing Afghanistan on the Indian borders," would

convince Britain to make peace.[18] He alleged—without official information—that the Afghan army had fifty thousand troops ready to
invade India. Germany and Turkey, he urged, should send an expedition of military advisers to the army of the Amir of Afghanistan,
Habibullah Khan.[19] During the ensuing weeks (as discussed later in
this study), the foreign ministry and General Staff organized two expeditions to the amir.

Preparing the Assault on Egypt

While ideas circulated in Berlin about attacking Britain in India and
the Germans began mobilizing for that purpose expeditions to Persia and Afghanistan, both Berlin and Constantinople focused much
of their activities on Egypt. Not only did they push forward Young
Turk preparations for an eventual military invasion of Egypt, but they
spent a great deal of time and energy attempting to block the Suez
Canal and raising an anti-British rebellion inside the country. As early
as 14 August, the British deprived German ships in the canal of their
wireless sets, to prevent them from communicating local British naval movements to two German warships in the Mediterranean Sea.[20]

By 20 August the German navy had added its voice to those of the
foreign ministry and General Staff in calling for a Turkish offensive
against the canal. But even in the first days of the war the Germans
encountered serious problems in implementing their ambitious plans.
Without an Ottoman entry into the war on Germany's side and without adequate German naval power to challenge Britain on the high
seas, the Reich had no means of launching a military strike against
Egypt.

Despite such issues, intelligence agents of the German navy in Egypt
tried (unsuccessfully) to obstruct the canal, by sinking a large German freighter, the *Barenfels,* loaded with coal for India. The plot,
which involved the German chargé d'affaires in Cairo and one of the
last German consular officials to leave Egypt, von Pannwitz, misfired
when seamen on the *Barenfels* betrayed it to the British, who seized
the vessel a half hour before it was to set sail.[21]

By the end of August the German navy was being pressured by
Bethmann Hollweg to block the canal; the chancellor realized that

the German armies in France had not achieved their planned lightning victory and that Britain apparently intended to remain in the
war. Although the navy's chief, Tirpitz, called the operation difficult
and promised nothing, the navy nevertheless collaborated with the
foreign ministry in planning another attempt to disrupt the canal,
recruiting for the task Robert Mors, a German policeman in Egypt.[22]

Meanwhile, Berlin eagerly welcomed an offer of assistance in the
attack on Egypt from the country's anti-British khedive, Abbas Hilmi.
The outbreak of the war had found him visiting Constantinople,
where he was forced to remain. The cavalier manner in which the
Young Turks investigated an attempted assassination of him there
in July 1914 angered Abbas Hilmi. He believed that his cousin and
Ottoman grand vizier, Said Halim, with whom Abbas Hilmi had poor
relations and who had ambitions of his own to rule Egypt, had either
perpetrated or planned the attempt.[23]

The khedive found himself, thanks to his prewar anti-British, pro-
Arab, pro-German, and pro-Islamic policies, in a precarious situation. Both the Ottomans and British mistrusted and disliked him.[24]
Abbas Hilmi, with his retinue of servants, secretaries, and his French
mistress, was a virtual prisoner of the Young Turks. Immediately he
turned for assistance to the Central Powers, first to his longtime friend
Germany, and later to Austria-Hungary. On 22 August he approached
Wangenheim, declaring his readiness to cooperate with Germany to
destroy British rule in Egypt.[25]

Abbas Hilmi's ideas fit well with the German plans to exploit pan-
Islamism. For a time, during the first months of the war, the khedive
played a primary role in such thinking; he hoped thereby to use his
Young Turk adversaries and German allies to help him return to an
Egypt freed of both British and Turkish control, but under his rule. At
the khedive's urging, Wangenheim arranged for a meeting of Abbas
Hilmi with Enver Pasha, who disliked the khedive; when they met on 4
September, the two argued loudly but finally promised to reconcile.[26]

In addition, the extreme Egyptian nationalists and students living in exile in Switzerland, led by Muhammad Farid, offered their
assistance to the Egyptian campaign. Farid, an anti-British fanatic
and pan-Islamist, had founded in Geneva an organization called
the Society for the Progress of Islam (Société Progrés de l'Islam),

which recruited exiled Egyptian nationalists. The German consulate-general in Geneva provided Farid with funds to travel to Constantinople to assist in the attack on Britain in Egypt. In Bern, the German minister, Baron Gisbert von Romberg, attracted to Germany's cause another Egyptian, Dr. Mansur Rifat, the publisher of an anti-British newspaper in Geneva, *La Patrie Egyptienne*. But Rifat feuded with other Egyptian nationalists and the khedive; in November 1914 the Swiss authorities, who had uncovered a plot involving Rifat to assassinate British officials in Egypt, expelled him from the country.[27]

By the beginning of September the Germans had received conflicting information from various quarters regarding the political and military situation in Egypt. On the one hand, the Reich's legation in Athens first claimed that "serious unrest" against British rule existed in Egypt and then retracted its assertion, reporting instead the arrival there of some forty thousand Indian troops to guard the country. On the other hand, Germans forced to leave Egypt gave information to the foreign ministry that suggested initial Egyptian sympathy for the Central Powers and Turks. Moreover, Enver Pasha claimed to Wangenheim that the Porte had agents in India, Persia, Morocco, southern Tunisia, and Algeria promoting native rebellions against the British and French. The war minister also told Wangenheim that four important tribal chieftains from Arabia—Ibn Saud and Ibn Rashid of Najd, the Imam Yahya of Yemen, and Sayyid al-Idrisi of Asir—had personally delivered gifts to the Porte and volunteered to assist the Turks in a war against Britain.[28]

The optimism of the Turkish war minister, the initial reports of Britain's buildup of its troops in Egypt, and the advance of German armies in France combined to encourage Bethmann Hollweg to push even more the plans against Egypt and India. By 4 September the chancellor had received unmistakable indications of British resolve to remain in the war. "One of our chief tasks, therefore," he stressed to the foreign ministry, "is to soften up Britain gradually by harassment in India and Egypt, which can only be possible from there." He ordered the ministry to do its utmost to make it happen.[29]

Three days later he approved the Turkish-German military expedition against Egypt, directing the embassy to win Enver Pasha's agreement for a raid on the Suez Canal of about twenty or thirty thousand men and promising Berlin's support with money and weapons.[30] It is unclear how much, if at all, the planned operations against Britain in Egypt and India encouraged the chancellor to issue his vast war aims' program, which he intended as eventual conditions of peace. Historians have noted that his so-called "September Program" resulted in large measure from long-held German imperialist views and from the expectation, popular in the government and public, of a quick German military victory in France.

The chancellor's war aims program symbolized the wave of annexationist feeling that swept over Germany during the initial military successes of August and September, expressed in the most extreme form by the demands of the Pan-German League. Bethmann Hollweg represented the ideas of many German industrial and military leaders when he called for using the war and the subsequent peace settlement to establish Germany's economic domination throughout central Europe, the Balkans, and Turkey, and to expand the country's colonies in East and Southwest Africa into a vast central African empire.[31]

The initial attempts to stop traffic in the Suez Canal, urged upon the foreign ministry and navy by the highest levels of the German government, proved to be failures. On 3 September Curt Prüfer, the former dragoman in Cairo, arrived in Constantinople with instructions to prepare an anti-British rebellion in Egypt, first by spreading reports that the leader of Islam, the sultan-caliph of the Ottoman Empire, intended soon to join Germany in the war. The extravagant plan, ordered by Zimmermann, also included liquidating the British officer corps in the Egyptian army, obstructing the Suez Canal, and blowing up railroads and important port installations.[32]

Prüfer observed during a meeting the next day at the German embassy with Wangenheim and the naval attaché, Captain Hans Humann, the personal rivalries between the ambassador and Liman von Sanders; the discussion also revealed to him the divisions in the Porte over whether to join Germany in the war. Nevertheless, Wangenheim introduced Prüfer to Robert Mors, the principal agent for sabotaging the British in Egypt until a Turkish expedition could attack the Suez Canal. Mors, of German descent, was a lieutenant in the Egyptian police on leave in Constantinople.[33]

The two conspirators then met with Omar Fauzi Bey, an official in the Porte's war ministry, who promised to cooperate with the Germans. They devised a plan to send secret agents to Egypt to organize terrorist bands *(comitaji)*, each numbering ten to fifteen Egyptian marauders recruited from criminals; the bands were to attack railroads and British property, and force the British to scatter their troops throughout the country. Fauzi intended moreover to form groups of Bedouins to raid British posts along the canal and fire on ships passing through it.[34]

Prüfer, however, learned soon that implementing the plans for a rebellion in Egypt would not be nearly as easy as either he or his superiors in Berlin had assumed. He faced problems in recruiting agents to carry out such operations, problems made worse by Turkish reluctance to allow the Germans to operate freely in Ottoman lands, and by the traditional mistrust and rivalry between the Turks and Arabs in the Ottoman Empire. The Turks refused to work with two Egyptian leaders whom Prüfer knew well, the khedive Abbas Hilmi and the nationalist and pan-Islamist Shaykh al-Jawish. The Porte even mistrusted Ibn Rashid, the pro-Turkish prince in Najd, and discouraged Prüfer from approaching him for help.[35] Despite such difficulties, and following a meeting of Prüfer with Enver Pasha on 7 September, the war minister confirmed the plans worked out by Turkish officials and the German agent for triggering a rebellion in Egypt.[36]

That same day Bethmann Hollweg approved the even more radical project of the combined Turkish-German military expedition against the Suez Canal;[37] the Reich's military mission in Constantinople began immediate preparations. Nonetheless, bitter conflicts regarding this and other issues raged between Wangenheim and Liman. Wangenheim pressed for a cautious German policy, fearing that the Reich's preparations for a military attack on Egypt might alienate Italy, Germany's partner in the Triple Alliance, which had chosen to remain neutral in the war. The Italians opposed any political or military action by the Turks or Central Powers in North Africa. They feared it could undermine Italy's already unstable position in Libya, caused by the hostility of the key Bedouin tribal and religious group, the Sanussis.[38]

Germany's problems with Italy became apparent as early as 29 August, when the Rome government protested to the German ambassador, Johannes von Flotow, the activity of Otto Mannesmann's mission in Tripoli and secured the return home of everyone in the group except its leader. Mannesmann, who operated under the codename of "Dr. Mann," soon sent eastward into the Libyan desert a Turkish envoy with gifts and a message to the Sayyid Ahmad al-Sharif, the shaykh of the Sanussis, an Islamic religious order to which the main Bedouin tribes of Cyrenaica (eastern Libya) belonged. Although Mannesmann had never met the Shaykh al-Sanussi, he showed no reluctance, and in fact the greatest of confidence, in urging the chief to attack the British harbor at Sollum on the Egyptian border and march into Egypt.[39]

Wangenheim, in addition to worrying about German policy alienating Italy, also interfered with Prüfer's activities; the ambassador particularly opposed the agent's independence from the embassy and his reception of orders from Oppenheim. The ambassador also disliked Prüfer's involvement with Shaykh al-Jawish, with whom Prüfer had been friends since the latter's days in Cairo, but whom Wangenheim and some Turkish officials distrusted. Despite Prüfer's conflicts with the ambassador, the agent dispatched Mors with dynamite, detonators, propaganda leaflets, and several Egyptian cohorts on a ship to Egypt. Mors had orders to carry out the planned comitaji operations there and, if possible, blow up the Suez Canal.[40]

Moreover, during the first half of September, Prüfer received his first information on the strength of British forces in Egypt. One of his spies reported that four thousand troops had left for the Sudan and that of the forty to fifty thousand remaining, London had shipped thirty thousand to France. The report, while inaccurate as to the figures, reflected Britain's actual transfer of Egyptian soldiers to the Sudan and its shipment of units from India to Egypt and France.[41]

Amid the German activities under way in Constantinople, Wilhelm II approved the combined German-Turkish expedition planned against Egypt. The kaiser's agreement prompted both Bethmann Hollweg and General Erich von Falkenhayn, Moltke's successor as German chief of staff, to emphasize the Egyptian project even more strongly to the foreign ministry and to German officials in Constantinople.[42] The ministry and the General Staff increased their pressure on Wangenheim and Liman, respectively, to persuade the Young Turks to enter the war. At Bethmann Hollweg's order, Jagow informed Zimmermann that Germany would send money to equip the Turkish attack on Egypt only after Turkey had joined the war against Russia.[43]

Simultaneously, Jagow discussed with Zimmermann the problem raised previously by Wangenheim about Italy. Both Zimmermann and Jagow seemed unconcerned about Italy joining the Entente. According to Jagow, who spent much of his time at General Staff headquarters, a Turkish assault on Egypt and the incitement of Muslim unrest there would really be an asset, rather than a liability, in keeping Italy from joining the enemy![44]

Although the intensified German pressure on the Porte failed to persuade it to enter the war, Enver Pasha inched closer to conflict with Russia and grew more confident of Turkey's defenses along the Dardanelles. On 20 September he assigned the task of organizing and carrying out the Ottoman military attack on Egypt to a unit in Damascus of the Fourth Army, the VIII Corps. Dispatched as advisers to the corps were five German officers, including the unit's chief of staff, the Bavarian major Friedrich Freiherr Kress von Kressenstein, and the intelligence agent and interpreter Prüfer.

Kress, who immediately visited the Turkish-Egyptian border at the eastern end of the Sinai Peninsula, discovered serious obstacles to the attack on Egypt. The VIII Corps badly needed equipment and supplies, but the transport available was poor, and problems loomed in provisioning the corps with water in the Sinai desert. Further, Kress and Prüfer learned of conflicts in Syria and the Sinai region between Arabs and Turks, an issue about which Kress claimed after the war he had known nothing.

Kress and his staff in Damascus also discovered that the Turkish troops often bitterly resented directives issued by the German officers, in part because the orders were often abrupt and categorical. The fact that few of the Germans knew Turkish or Arabic, and that they viewed the Orientals with racial and cultural contempt added to the problems.[45] Finally, the Germans had little geographic knowledge of Palestine, Syria, and Egypt; they had to rely, ironically, on British maps of the region.[46]

Prüfer, too, found difficult organizing an anti-British rebellion and terrorist campaign in Egypt while at the same time helping recruit Bedouins for the Turkish military expedition. Enver had ordered the creation of a special Arab auxiliary unit within the VIII Corps. In Damascus, Beirut, and elsewhere, Prüfer, usually in Arab dress, cultivated friendly relations with influential shaykhs, other Arab notables, and Turkish officials, bribing them with gifts and decorations. He assisted in enrolling fifteen hundred volunteers, but the number fell far short of the several thousand which the Germans hoped for, and many, Prüfer observed, were unreliable.[47]

In addition, and with the blessing of Kress, he continued to seek spies to enter Egypt, including some to join the planned comitaji units and to mine and dynamite the Suez Canal. His efforts generally failed, however. The dubious plan of recruiting Bedouin criminals from Lebanon displeased Turkish leaders, who delayed releasing some from prison, and money proved insufficient to transform the new recruits into trustworthy agents.[48]

Expedition Mania, the Arabs, and Propaganda

Meanwhile, in Berlin the foreign ministry and General Staff continued in furious fashion to push forward Germany's hastily conceived plans for the Middle East. Jagow approved Oppenheim's formation of a small translation office within the Prussian ministry of culture to produce pro-German propaganda pamphlets in Arabic and modern Indian languages.[49]

But the most noticeable activity in this regard involved a flurry of German expeditions and individuals sent by the foreign ministry and General Staff to the Middle East and North Africa to incite Muslim rebellions. Most of the missions, which Berlin organized with only the nominal approval of the Turks and in complete disregard of Islamic—and particularly Arab—customs, were designed to assist the operations already unfolding against Egypt. The expeditions aimed

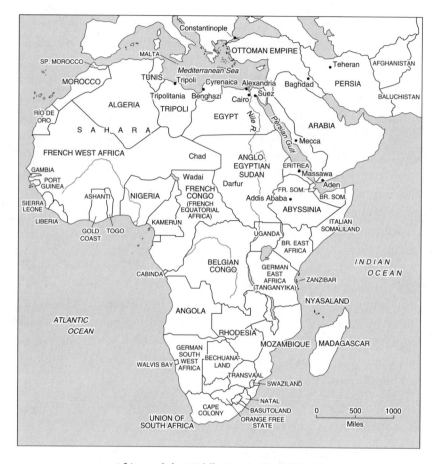

Africa and the Middle East in World War I.

at reaching Egypt either directly through Syria and the Mediterranean or indirectly through western Arabia, across the Red Sea, and into the neighboring Anglo-Egyptian Sudan and Abyssinia.[50]

As the campaign against Egypt developed, the number of Germans entering the Ottoman Empire, mainly as expedition members and military advisers, grew. Berlin seemed increasingly concerned, particularly as some moved south toward Arabia, the Sinai Peninsula, and the Red Sea, about how the Arabs of the empire responded to the German-Turkish calls for Muslim rebellions against the British. Arab support for the revolts was a necessity; however, as noted previously, plenty of evidence before the world war had indicated Arab unrest arising from dissatisfaction with Turkish control. Still other prewar information on the Arab question, compiled by the Reich's consuls and embassy in Turkey, suggested that many Arab nationalists feared British and French designs on their lands.[51]

During the fall of 1914 the staff of Germans serving in Damascus with the Turkish Fourth Army, preparing for the assault by its VIII Corps on the Suez Canal, experienced difficulties in recruiting Arabs in Syria and Palestine to form an auxiliary unit in the corps. Unrelated to this effort, the German embassy and consulates in Turkey, using mainly Arab agents, distributed anti-British propaganda leaflets to Muslim pilgrims in Mecca and Medina.[52]

Since before the war the kaiser and other German officials had suspected that Britain was making efforts to gain the support of the influential Sharif of Mecca, Husayn ibn Ali, by proclaiming him caliph to replace the Ottoman caliphate. In mid-September 1914 Oppenheim alleged this to be true and obviously dangerous for the German-Ottoman alliance. Consequently he flatly rejected a suggestion from the German minister in Athens, Albert Graf von Quadt, that Turkey could win Arab support for an attack on Egypt if the Porte appointed Husayn Shaykh al-Islam, the chief *mufti* (a learned exponent of Islamic law who issued decisions or opinions regarding the law) and leader of the religious hierarchy in Constantinople.[53]

By the end of October concern was mounting in Berlin regarding Arab support for the planned Turkish attack on Egypt. Information arrived at the foreign ministry from Prüfer in Syria and another agent, the Orientalist Bernhard Moritz, that the two principal tribal

chieftains of Najd, Ibn Saud and Ibn Rashid, had again declared war
on one another and thus could be of little use for the Turks against
Egypt. Both Moritz and Prüfer, moreover, believed that Ibn Saud
was in the pay of the British, and also the Sharif of Mecca. Regarding the sharif, however, Prüfer seemed convinced that the Turkish
governor of Mecca, Wahib Bey, controlled Husayn; Oppenheim
agreed.[54]

Throughout the fall of 1914, therefore, awareness of the Arab question steadily increased in Berlin, and so did the pressure to foment
the rebellions in Egypt. But emblematic of the poor quality of the
missions the Germans sent to Arabia and the Red Sea for such purposes was that of the German journalist Max Roloff. Sent to Egypt
and then to Mecca disguised as a Muslim pilgrim, Roloff was to recruit Muslims, in return for a handsome sum of money, to support
Germany in the war. However, neither Oppenheim nor anyone else
in the foreign ministry had checked carefully Roloff's background
or ability to make the trip, and he turned out to be a swindler. Roloff
never traveled further than Holland; he then returned to Germany
and published his supposed experiences in Mecca. The publications
threatened to damage German-Turkish relations, with their claim
that an unbeliever dressed as a Muslim pilgrim had entered Arabia
and the holy cities of Islam. The foreign ministry and General Staff
ordered Roloff arrested, but he avoided trial throughout the war,
because the government did not wish to give him publicity.[55]

In mid-September the embassy in Constantinople sent a Turkish
agent, Sami Bey, the former governor of the Ottoman province of
Fezzan in Libya, first to Egypt to gather intelligence information, and
then to the Sudan. His ultimate goal was Libya, where he hoped to
incite the Sanussis to attack the British in Egypt and the French colonies to the west. The Italians, however, arrested him as he tried to
reach Egypt through Italy and Tripoli carrying propaganda leaflets
in Arabic.[56]

The Orientalist Moritz left Damascus disguised in Arab dress for
Arabia, intending first to establish for Oppenheim an information
center in Medina, and second to reach the Sudan from an Arab port
on the Red Sea. Moritz also had orders from Kress von Kressenstein,
the German chief of staff of the Ottoman VIII Corps, to collect intel-

ligence information about British and Egyptian troop strength in the Sudan and to incite unrest there. Before he departed at the end of October, however, Moritz filed with the foreign ministry a discouraging report in which he declared that the planned campaign to raise the Egyptians in rebellion had poor prospects for success because of the "unwarlike" Egyptians and the lack of support from the Arabs, especially the pro-British Sharif of Mecca.[57]

Still another expedition began forming during November 1914, headed by Leo Frobenius, a veteran prewar German explorer of West Africa. In Constantinople the German embassy and Turkish war ministry negotiated to send Frobenius with a seventeen-member mission of Germans, Turks, and Arabs first to Abyssinia, to reach the German legation there, and then to the Sudan. Once the world war began, Berlin had lost all contact with the legation and, thus, with the government in Addis Ababa. The Entente powers controlled the lands that encircled Abyssinia; the French also owned the postal and telegraph offices in the Abyssinian capital and had suspended local communication with Germany and Austria-Hungary.[58]

Simultaneously with the political expeditions, the Germans ordered five military missions to the Sinai region and Red Sea. A most bizarre one arrived there in mid-October. A German naval officer, Lieutenant Hilgendorf, attempted to cross the border of Turkey and Egypt with a small party of German colonists from Palestine disguised as an Arab comedy troupe. Apparently with Kress's blessing, Hilgendorf developed a scheme to block the Suez Canal: he intended to cross the Sinai desert to the canal, shoot the pilot of a passing ship, and thus run the vessel aground.[59]

An entirely different expedition, assembled by Liman von Sanders, the head of the German military mission in Constantinople, sent two Austrian officers to Gemsah, a town south of the Gulf of Suez; there the officers had been ordered to dynamite local British fuel depots. At the end of December, Prüfer ordered two other missions to southern Egypt and the Sudan to destroy British oil and other installations. One was headed by a Hungarian officer, Franz Gondos. Still another December expedition, sent by the General Staff and headed by Major Schwabe, left for Syria to join the Turkish Fourth Army, with the Sudan its ultimate goal.[60]

For a variety of reasons, none of the military missions had much success. Vigilant police in the town of Hafir al-Auja on the Turkish side of the border with Egypt detained Hilgendorf's group of Germans, apparently at Enver Pasha's order, following a protest by Mallet, the British ambassador, who had learned of Hilgendorf's intentions. Gondos failed twice to traverse the Red Sea into Upper Egypt, the first time because a British sea patrol spotted his boat and forced it back to a small port on the northern Arabian coast.[61] The highly secret Schwabe expedition only reached the Sinai Peninsula; it fell into disfavor with the foreign ministry when its commander overstepped his orders. Schwabe, apparently desperate to find a way to reach the Sudan, sent his interpreter, Karl Neufeld, who had been a German adventurer in the Sudan before the war, to Medina. But the action violated a custom in the Hijaz, enforced by the Sharif of Mecca, that no non-Muslim foreigner may enter the Islamic holy land without his permission.[62]

The sharif also played a role in undermining Moritz's mission. On 10 November Moritz arrived at Jidda, the Arabian Red Sea port. He distributed propaganda materials in the area and hired Sudanese agents to smuggle anti-British propaganda into the Sudan. But what Moritz's emissaries achieved remained unknown, because British ships patrolling the Red Sea prevented their return to Jidda. Furthermore, when Moritz left Jidda to return to Syria he fell captive in Rabigh, a port a few miles north, to Husayn. The sharif's son, Faysal, recognizing the German, imprisoned him for a few days, and threatened his life for not receiving permission from the sharif to travel in the Hijaz. On Moritz's arrival finally in Damascus in January 1915 he had only minimal success to report to Kressenstein and the foreign ministry. He warned his superiors in Berlin about British propaganda filtering into western Arabia from Egypt and the Sudan and about the bitter struggle for power in Mecca between the sharif and Turkish governor, Wahib Bey, a struggle in which Husayn held the upper hand.[63]

Problems also plagued Frobenius's expedition. It lost much valuable time in leaving for Africa because of quarrels in Constantinople between its leader and the Young Turk government. Oppenheim and the foreign ministry ordered him to establish a base of operations in Medina and then cross the Red Sea to Abyssinia. Frobenius carried with him orders to the German minister in Addis Ababa, von Syburg, to use every means to induce the Abyssinians to intervene against Britain in the Sudan. The ministry authorized Syburg to promise the Abyssinian government, in the event it entered the war on the Reich's side, Germany's support for its territorial acquisitions in the Sudan region of the Blue Nile.

Frobenius took along as well a message from the Porte to the Abyssinian government, pledging that if Abyssinia attacked southward against British East Africa and Uganda, the Abyssinians would receive a harbor on the Red Sea. Neither the Germans nor the Turks seemed concerned that the harbor could only be carved from Eritrea, a colony held by Italy that blocked Abyssinian access to the sea.[64] This contradicted, however, the official German policy at the time of keeping Rome from joining the Allied side in the war. Finally, at the beginning of January 1915, after nearly five weeks of conflict with the Turks over mainly frivolous matters, Frobenius left Damascus.[65]

The Germans, with Austrian assistance, also attempted to unite behind the Turks in the attack on Egypt two leading tribal chieftains in Arabia, Ibn Saud and Ibn Rashid. This task fell to the Austrian professor and Orientalist Alois Musil, whose extensive prewar travels in northern Arabia had enabled him to establish a close relationship with the paramount chief of the Anaza tribe, the Rualla shaykh Nuri ibn Shaalan. On 13 October Musil informed the German ambassador in Vienna, Tschirschky, that the Austro-Hungarian government had approved his going to Arabia.[66] Musil asked for German backing of his mission, particularly with money, weapons, and munitions for the Arab tribes and with helping to assure his "freedom" of movement in Arabia.[67] Oppenheim, when questioned by the German foreign ministry about Musil's trip, immediately gave his approval. He judged Ibn Saud pro-British, Ibn Rashid pro-Ottoman, and the "very energetic and clever Grand Sharif of Mecca" pro-Turkish. Musil's mission, Oppenheim concluded, could be of great political significance for the future.[68]

Musil left Constantinople on 8 November, arriving in Damascus nine days later. Preparing for his entry into the desert, he soon learned of the difficulties of his task. He complained to the Austro-Hungarian foreign ministry about a lack of cooperation from the Young Turks, particularly Enver Pasha, and about their poor treatment and knowledge of the Arabs.[69] Although Musil ranked as one of Europe's premiere experts on Arabia, Enver disliked his mission, arguing that the Arabs probably knew that the Austrian was a Catholic priest and thus would not tolerate him. It seemed impossible that the caliph and Turkish government would employ such a person to negotiate with the Arabs. Nevertheless, the Ottoman interior ministry permitted Musil's mission. Three weeks after leaving Damascus and traveling south, the Austrian met Nuri ibn Shaalan and his son, Nawwaf. Both chieftains denounced Ibn Rashid for using weapons and monies given him by the Turks to attack Nuri and other tribes loyal to the Porte rather than using such resources against Turkey's enemies. Also, Nuri viewed Ibn Saud as increasingly powerful. Finally, after much discussion with Musil, Nuri agreed to engage in negotiations with Ibn Rashid for peace between the two.[70]

As Musil continued to prepare for his sojourn in central Arabia, the flood of expeditions sent by Germany to the Middle East in the fall of 1914 apparently even confused the Germans themselves. Evidence of this is a lengthy memorandum given by Oppenheim at the end of October to Zimmermann at General Staff headquarters for transmission to the kaiser. In it Oppenheim described the numerous uncoordinated plans developed by the foreign ministry, General Staff, and the embassy and military mission in Turkey. He focused on the importance of striking a blow against Britain by raising revolts in Egypt and India. Crucial to the success of Germany's revolutionary activities, he declared, would be Turkish entry into the world war and the Porte's proclamation of a jihad against Britain and its allies. Much of the memo analyzed the potential for rousing the different Muslim peoples to oppose the Allies, listing the missions already begun to incite rebellions in Egypt, India (including neighboring Afghanistan and Persia), North Africa, and central Russia.

To promote a jihad aimed principally against Britain he urged that Germany establish a propaganda center in the Hijaz, making the Sharif of Mecca responsible for such activities. To gather intelligence in the region and to ship weapons and propaganda to the Sudan and ultimately from there into Egypt, Oppenheim proposed that the Reich establish a consulate at Jidda, a port on the Red Sea coast of Arabia.

His memo reflected a concern for the Arabs, about rumors that Britain sought to create an Arab caliphate to replace the Ottoman one, and over the rising power in central and eastern Arabia of the pro-British chieftain, Ibn Saud. For the Reich to have any chance of success in its revolutionary program, he concluded, the government must provide the foreign ministry and military at least one hundred million marks—an amount that eventually had to be doubled and tripled.[71]

Oppenheim's memo and the weak beginning of Germany's wartime activities in the Orient produced an administrative change in Berlin. During the rest of 1914 the foreign ministry transformed, under Zimmermann's guidance, Oppenheim's translation office in Berlin into a much larger information bureau to translate, publish and distribute in the Muslim world pro-German and pan-Islamic propaganda in Oriental languages.[72]

Oppenheim and two collaborators, the Oriental scholar Eugen Mittwoch, and a dragoman in the foreign ministry, Karl Emil Schabinger Freiherr von Schowingen, established the new bureau, called the Information Service for the East (Nachrichtenstelle für den Orient). Oppenheim headed the agency, but he possessed little talent for organizational and administrative affairs. From the outset, deficient leadership and a lack of careful monitoring by the foreign ministry limited the success of the Information Service.

The new agency published and distributed in the Middle East prisoner-of-war newspapers, German and non-German publications, and war reports; it also assumed a role in German foreign intelligence and revolutionary operations, particularly in Switzerland and North Africa. Among the nearly forty full-time and occasional workers in the Information Service, many of them university scholars and other specialists trained in Oriental languages, arose petty jealousies, envy, and rivalries that undermined both discipline and productivity.

Equally damaging for the Information Service's work, the agency experienced difficulties in sending propaganda materials, most of them printed in Berlin or at the Constantinople embassy, to Oriental countries. In this regard, it encountered resistance not only from the enemy—the British, French, and eventually the Italians—but also from the Turks, who did not welcome German or any other foreign propaganda in their midst.

Despite the multitude of problems that plagued it, the Information Service received tens of thousands of marks from the foreign ministry to finance its work. The agency sent its first published materials in October and November 1914 to Turkey for delivery to Egypt and Arabia. Throughout the war it produced 1,012 different publications—newspapers, books, journals, pamphlets, and leaflets—in nine European and twelve Oriental languages, and it distributed more than three million copies of them.[73]

One of the first projects of the Information Service was the distribution of propaganda by the agency and Oppenheim among French Algerian and Tunisian troops seized by Germany as prisoners of war. The Germans held most of the Muslim prisoners in a camp at Zossen, near Potsdam, with others at Altengrabow and Senne outside Paderborn. Oppenheim accepted without question that the prisoners hated the French and could be persuaded, in part by building a small mosque at the Zossen camp and providing it with a Muslim cleric, to desert France and join the pan-Islamic movement being organized by Germany and Turkey. The Germans planned to send some of the deserters to Constantinople and either use them for the Ottoman expedition against Egypt or return them to their homelands as anti-Allied propagandists.[74]

Nearly everyone in Berlin arrogantly persuaded themselves that Germany, with Turkey's assistance, could rally the Muslims of the Middle East to support the Central Powers in the war. Oppenheim and other officials believed, in simplistic and doubtless nationalistic fashion, that the world of Islam loved Germany and hated Britain and that consequently the Reich only had to convince the Turkish sultan-caliph to declare a holy war to rouse the anti-British passions of Muslims to action. This view blinded officials in Berlin not only to the mistrust and dislike felt by many Muslims toward the Turks, but also to the fact that while Muslims may have opposed British rule, they were unwilling to exchange it for what they perceived would be Ottoman or German control.

4 The Thickening Plot and Holy War, Fall 1914

Despite the fact that the Turks had not entered the world war when it began, and knowing nothing of the German-Ottoman alliance of 2 August 1914, British officials in both Constantinople and Cairo observed carefully Turkey's preparations for war and its cooperation with Germany's pan-Islamic and revolutionary policies in the Orient. When the German warships *Goeben* and *Breslau* entered the Dardanelles on 10 August, the Foreign Office in London doubted, sometimes against the opinion of Mallet, its ambassador in Constantinople, that Britain could prevent the Porte's entry into the war on Germany's side.[1]

Britain, Egypt, and the Arabs

British officials in Constantinople and Cairo believed that a severe threat existed to Egypt from Germany and Turkey. At the war's beginning, intelligence reports indicated that Egyptian public opinion favored the cause of the Central Powers and Turks. The Egyptians estimated German military power highly. Also, most Muslim Egyptians gave allegiance to the Ottoman Empire and its sultan-caliph; prayers in Egyptian mosques for the caliph continued throughout the war.[2]

Yet while the Germans and Turks hoped to exploit Egyptian opinion by attacking the Suez Canal, which would incite anti-British rebellions in Egypt, both Berlin and Constantinople failed to consider in their calculations another factor at work. Considerable ambivalence existed among Egyptians about the possible results of a Turkish defeat of Britain in Egypt and whether it would mean the replacement of one arbitrary and alien regime, the British occupation, by a Turkish one.

Britain's major concern centered on protecting the canal from a Turkish and German attack—"less for its military effect," recalled Sir Ronald Storrs, the Oriental secretary at the Cairo residency, after the war, "than for the repercussion upon a Moslem Egypt."[3] Already, on 19 August, the British had foiled a German attempt to block the canal. Because Egypt was not at war, and because of the anomaly that the diplomatic agents of the states with which Britain was at war were accredited to the Porte, the Austro-Hungarian consul and German chargé d'affaires remained in the country as late as the end of August, intriguing against the British.[4]

Sir Milne Cheetham, the British resident in Cairo following Lord Kitchener's appointment as war minister, informed Grey and the Foreign Office of numerous signs, including Turkish officers passing through Egypt to the Red Sea, that an attack on Egypt formed part of Turkish plans in the event of war. Cheetham also reported that emissaries were being sent to Egypt, India, Yemen, and the Sanussis to stir up trouble, and that the British military command in Egypt hoped for the arrival soon of Indian troops.[5]

Throughout September and October, Cheetham and Mallet reported to the Foreign Office further Turkish preparations against Egypt, noting especially the steady Ottoman troop movements southward to Syria and Palestine and toward the Sinai border. By 10 October Mallet had learned of the arrival at the Turkish Fourth Army in Damascus of German officers, the party that included Kress von Kressenstein and Prüfer. A few days later Mallet warned London that Muslims in northern Syria had been "reported to have been so inveigled and incited by German and Turkish deliberate official misrepresentations and falsehoods of every kind that masses seem to believe [the] German Emperor has embraced [the] Islamic faith, and that Germans are fighting for Islam against Russia."[6]

In Cairo, Sir John Maxwell, the recently appointed commander of Britain's troops in Egypt, pointed out to the War Office in London that German officers were regularly visiting the frontier posts along the Sinai border. Military intelligence showed that as many as a hundred thousand Ottoman troops might be amassing in Syria and Palestine for action against the canal. Furthermore, Cheetham had learned that the khedive, Abbas Hilmi, and the Egyptian nationalist Muhammad Farid had involved themselves with the Germans in fomenting trouble in Egypt and preparing the way for a Turkish invasion.[7]

On 16 October Maxwell informed Kitchener that while he had found little evidence of German agents in the country, he had recently captured "an undoubted spy of Enver's," caught with a secret code, maps of the Suez Canal, and two boxes of detonators.[8] The capture of the German agent Mors and his trial in Cairo at the end of October provided the British with extensive information about the German and Turkish attempts to infiltrate Egypt with Muslim terrorists and to block the canal. Mors described how the German agent Prüfer and Shaykh al-Jawish had sat together in a hotel in Constantinople "copying in Arabic a recipe for making bombs." The Germans had recruited Mors, the latter told British interrogators, to smuggle detonators into Egypt, along with instructions in Arabic on how to build and use bombs against British officials.[9]

London immediately announced a reward for the capture of Prüfer, Kress, and the other German officers associated with the Ottoman Fourth Army preparing the assault against Egypt. Shortly after Mors's trial, the Foreign Office ordered Mallet to warn the Turks that a military violation of the frontier of Egypt would place them in a state of war with the three Allied powers; he mentioned Prüfer in his complaint.[10]

By then the British had implemented a series of measures in Egypt that effectively closed the country to penetration by German and Turkish agents. Britain had identified and arrested a number of Turks and Egyptians suspected of spying for the Ottomans and Germans. In addition, Maxwell had registered nearly eight hundred German and Austro-Hungarian citizens still in Egypt; they soon lost their shops, other businesses, and government positions, and the British interned many of them on Malta. The Cairo government expelled the last of the German and Austro-Hungarian consular officials on 9 October.[11] With Egypt not at war, the fifteen German ships remaining in the Suez Canal were ordered to sea, where a British cruiser seized them as prizes.[12]

The British also made extensive military preparations to protect the country, and particularly the canal. They evacuated the Egyptian camel corps from the Sinai Peninsula and placed it in positions on the western bank of the canal; the British left the Sinai desert to its twenty-five thousand Bedouins and converted the canal into a defense-barrier for Egypt.[13] In addition, however, Britain needed sufficient troops to protect the country. With the garrison of regular British troops in Egypt destined for the fighting in France, the government in London began dispatching forces to Egypt from the British Indian Army. The first of these landed at Suez on 8 September, but Kitchener and the War Office in London soon ordered most of them sent on to France. During October, as news worsened about enemy activity along the Sinai border with Turkey, the War Office promised for Egypt's defense six more Indian brigades, a camel corps, and eight battalions.[14]

To protect Egypt and the other British interests from the growing Turkish menace, Britain moved toward using the Arabs of the Ottoman Empire against the Turks. Before the war, the British, like the Germans, had possessed ample evidence of Arab unhappiness with Turkish rule; this had given birth to the idea among some British officials that if war occurred between Britain and Turkey, with the latter supported by Germany, London could strike a blow by encouraging the Arabs to revolt against the Turks.[15]

On 9 August 1914 Aziz Bey al-Masri, the former Egyptian officer in the Ottoman army whom Enver Pasha had arrested at the beginning of the year for treason but then released, approached Gilbert Clayton, the official representative in Egypt of the British-controlled Sudan government. Al-Masri claimed that Enver had called him to Constantinople "to raise the Arabs against England"; instead, he now offered "to lead the Arabs (Syria and Irak [sic]) against the Turks in order to form an Arab empire under British suzerainty." The Foreign Office ordered Cheetham to tell al-Masri to remain quiet and leave the Arabs alone.[16] Nevertheless, several weeks later Clayton, with the help of Storrs, the Cairo residency's Oriental secretary, sent a secret memorandum to Kitchener, urging him to enter into conversations with the Sharif of Mecca, Husayn.[17]

Clayton raised with the war minister the issue of whether the Ottoman sultan could be replaced as caliph of Islam by an Arab leader friendly to Britain. If so, Husayn, the guardian of the Islamic holy places, seemed the obvious candidate. But to support his argument Clayton made claims based on erroneous intelligence information. For example, he asserted to Kitchener that the rival leaders of the Arabian Peninsula—the rulers of Asir (Sayyid al-Idrisi) and Yemen (the Imam Yahya), as well as Ibn Saud and perhaps Ibn Rashid of Najd—had moved closer to Husayn, in part encouraged by agents of the khedive in Constantinople, to work for "an Arabia for the Arabs."[18] Such a rumor had existed before the war among German officials in Turkey, but the story contained little truth, as the continued bitter conflict between Ibn Saud and Ibn Rashid, described in the previous chapter, illustrates.

But faulty intelligence also buttressed Clayton's most important justification to Kitchener for approaching the Sharif of Mecca. Clayton warned that reports received lately indicated that the Turks had successfully elicited the neutrality or active assistance of the leading chieftains of Arabia.[19] He concluded "that the Sherif of Mecca has now definitely thrown in his lot with Turkey. This action appears to have formed part of a general Pan-Islamic movement, engrained from Constantinople."[20] But while both Constantinople and Berlin promoted pan-Islamism, the sharif had hardly joined the Young Turks. In fact, many Germans and Ottomans viewed the sharif and other key Arabian chieftains, except for Ibn Rashid, as pro-British.[21]

Kitchener and Clayton, however, were not the only ones in British officialdom to suggest the possibility of waging war against the Turks by allying with the Arabs. Grey proposed to Mallet warning the Porte about it, whereupon the ambassador replied that supporting an "Arab movement" would be one of the most effective weapons in a war against Turkey.[22] Also, Sir Andrew Ryan, the acting chief dragoman at the Constantinople embassy, wrote a spirited memorandum on the possibility of engineering an Arab revolt that would establish a stable authority "strong enough to administer, but weak enough to be dependent on us."[23]

The India Office advised caution, informing the government that its use of the Arabs, along with the latter's wish for autonomy from the Turks, could be a two-edged policy. The Government of India viewed Muslims as an important section of India's population, which

Delhi wished not to risk offending by pitting Arabs against the sultan-caliph in Constantinople. India did not want either an Arab caliphate or a united Arabia but rather a weak and disunited one, divided into small principalities that were as far as possible under India's suzerainty. Sir Arthur Hirtzel, secretary to the India Office's political department, wrote on the issue: "The strength of our position vis a vis the Arabs has lain in their own divisions and in their hostility to Turkey. . . . Moreover, Pan-Islam is a danger that must be steadily born[e] in mind, and it seems highly probable that eventually a consolidated Arabia would be a far greater danger, alike in Africa and Asia, than the Jewish free-masons who now control the Caliphate."[24]

While such fears of pan-Islamism also characterized Kitchener's attitude, the war minister nevertheless seemed unconcerned about the potential problems posed by the India Office regarding an Anglo-Arab alliance. He had believed since long before the war that the Turks and pan-Islamism formed a major threat to British interests in the Middle East, all the more so because they possessed German backing. This was apparent in his directive to Cheetham on 24 September to continue secret negotiations with Abdullah, the Sharif of Mecca's son, which Kitchener had already started before the war. The minister told Cheetham that he wished to determine the sharif's attitude toward Britain in case the "present armed German influence at Constantinople coerce Calif [sic] against his will and Sublime Porte to acts of aggression and war against Great Britain."[25]

Simultaneously, and unknown to Mallet or the embassy, the India Office and Government of India voiced alarm at British policy. They were especially worried about the effect on the Arabs in the Persian Gulf of Britain's inaction while the Turks made preparations for war and a possible future declaration of jihad.[26] Consequently, the Indian authorities, supported by Kitchener and Eyre Crowe, the Foreign Office specialist on Germany, suggested to the British cabinet that India send one of its army divisions to the head of the Persian Gulf. On 2 October the London government approved this proposal and also ordered Captain William Henry Shakespear, the India government's political officer in Kuwait, to visit Ibn Saud to persuade him not to side with the Turks should war break out between Turkey and Britain.[27]

By then the initiative in the Arab question had passed from Mallet's hands to the Cairo residency. On Cheetham's advice, the Foreign Office decided to approach soon the Imam Yahya of Yemen and Sayyid al-Idrisi of Asir—before, as London feared, the Young Turks won them over. In mid-October Gerald Fitzmaurice, the influential former dragoman at the Constantinople embassy, recommended to the Foreign Office that in the event of war with Turkey, Britain exploit Arab opposition to Turkish rule in Mesopotamia and also, provided France could be reconciled to it, in Syria. In his view, the probability existed that an Arab caliph would replace the Ottoman one and thus remove the "sting" from pan-Islamism, whose roots lay in the union of the spiritual and temporal powers at the Porte.[28]

These ideas formed the guidelines of the subsequent revolutionary policy pursued by Britain toward the Arabs. With France, London was to have almost instant disagreement on the issue of which of them, England or France, should approach the Arabs. French military leaders, eager to enhance France's future claims to Syria, and apparently independently of the British, had already suggested to their government organizing an Arab or Arab-Syrian rebellion against Turkey, led by the Sharif of Mecca, that might prevent anti-French Turkish activity among Muslims in France's North African colonies.[29]

Also, apparently with Cheetham's collaboration, adherents of the Pan Arab movement in Cairo had sent emissaries to Arabia, Syria, and Palestine to communicate Britain's message to the Arab chieftains and urge them not to join the Porte. If war came, the messengers told the Arab leaders, the latter could expect armaments and ammunition from Britain. By the end of October Cairo received a reply from the Sharif of Mecca, through his son Abdullah, to the question put to him a month before by Kitchener. His father, said Abdullah, would not willingly support the Turks.[30] Kitchener replied quickly, again through Egypt; on 31 October, he sent a message that Abdullah received two weeks later, promising that if the "Arab nation" allied with Britain in the war, Britain would ensure Arabia's safety and freedom from the Ottomans. Kitchener, moreover, mentioned the possibility of establishing a new caliphate at Mecca or Medina—but as solely a spiritual, rather than political, office.[31] The principal impetus for an Anglo-Arab alliance would come only after

Turkey joined the Central Powers in the war and Britain began both its military assault on the Dardanelles and its plans to dismember the Turkish empire.

Organizing against Britain in India

At the end of September 1914, the Foreign Office learned, apparently from the British consul in Basra, that thirty-two secret emissaries from Turkey, including German officers, were "on their way to preach a 'jehad' in India, Afghanistan, and Baluchistan."[32] A few weeks later the British legation in Switzerland reported to London the cooperation of local Indian revolutionaries with Germany "with a view to making trouble in India."[33]

Of all the foreign schemes for the Middle East developed by Germany during World War I, its plans for India were probably the most far-fetched and illusory. On the one hand, Germany had on the eve of the war almost no presence in India, except for consulates in Calcutta, Bombay, and Madras, which looked after German trade.[34] Its only other major link with India involved German scholars; several, including Helmuth von Glasenapp, hired during the war by the foreign ministry and the Information Service for the East, studied Indian philosophy and other aspects of the subject of Indology. On the other hand, even if Germany had had enough troops at its disposal in 1914, which it did not, and if they had been transported to India somehow, it still seems highly dubious that the Reich could have aroused the Indians to rebel against their colonial masters.[35]

The Indians did not rebel during the war, and in fact they supported Britain with both money and troops, of which thousands fought and died in Europe and the Middle East. This resulted not merely from conciliatory policies toward India adopted before the war by the viceroy, Hardinge. What particularly helped dampen Islamic fervor was the loyalty of the Muslim princes in India, including the Aga Khan, who owed much of their authority to Britain. Furthermore, from the war's beginning the Government of India successfully implemented political measures that rendered virtually impossible German, Turkish, and even nationalist Indian infiltration. In addition to police vigilance toward revolutionaries, especially in the

Punjab, the government made ruthless use of the Press Act and the Defence of India Act; the latter superseded the provisions of criminal law, set up special courts that could hold summary proceedings, and allowed the government to intern suspected persons without trial. An Arms Act denied Indians the freedom to carry arms, and another law regulated the arrival in India of emigrants suspected of revolutionary activities.[36] The only direct taste of war for India resulted when the German light cruiser *Emden* raided British shipping in the North Pacific and Indian Ocean.[37]

In Berlin, partly because of the tight security in India, Oppenheim and his cohorts possessed little accurate knowledge of the situation there. They accepted without question unsubstantiated reports, most of them from German diplomats in Persia and China, claiming India was ripe for rebellion.[38] The German leaders believed that if weapons and propaganda were supplied to Indian revolutionaries for an armed rising and Turkey called upon Indian Muslims to rise against colonial rule, large numbers of British troops would be tied down and unavailable for use in Europe. Oppenheim overestimated the strength of pan-Islamism in India immediately before the world war.[39] To be sure, many Indian Muslims expressed themselves in pan-Islamic terms, and during the Turkish-Italian and Balkan wars of 1911 and 1912 nearly the entire Muslim press in India had supported the Turks. But pan-Islamist organizations in India hardly flourished.[40] Berlin, however, hoped to use pan-Islamic and also Bengali revolutionaries (who desired immediate independence for India by overthrowing British rule, violently if need be), to Germany's advantage.

At the end of August 1914, Oppenheim gathered together in Berlin an Indian Independence Committee. It included Indian revolutionaries willing to collaborate with Germany in the potentially dangerous work of instigating anti-British insurgency in India. The Germans recruited two groups of Indians: students living in Berlin and other university towns who sympathized with Germany in the war; and extremists from Bengal and the *Ghadr* (Mutiny) party, a largely Sikh movement with widespread support among the emigrant Indian communities of western North America and East Asia.[41]

Before 1914 the Bengal nationalists had bitterly opposed British rule in India, with violence and terrorism; a number of nationalist groups were active in the Bengal province, while police pressure had forced others abroad. The Ghadr party's origins in 1913 lay in the discrimination suffered by Sikh peasants from the Punjab who had emigrated to the west coast of the United States and Canada. Although the party's initial leaders were revolutionary exiles, the Oxford-educated anarchist Lala Har Dayal and a pan-Islamist professor Maulvi Barkatullah, its strength lay in the devoted allegiance of the Sikh peasant emigrants and the support Ghadr leaders could potentially arouse in the villages and military regiments of the Punjab.[42]

Oppenheim recruited into the Berlin committee members from Switzerland (the Bengali activist Virendranath Chattopadhyaya and an exile from southern India, Chempakaraman Pillai), Germany (the Marxist historian Bhupendranath Datta and Heidelberg student Marthe Prabhakar), the United States (the Ghadr leaders Barkatullah and Taraknath Das), and Syria (two brothers living in Beirut, Abd al-Jabbar Kheiry and Abd al-Sattar Kheiry).[43]

The Germans, however, had less success in recruiting Har Dayal, the most notorious Ghadr leader. Following arrest in the United States in March 1914 for an inflammatory speech at an anarchist meeting in San Francisco, he jumped bail and fled to Switzerland. During the fall Har Dayal traveled for the Germans to Constantinople to assist in sending Indian revolutionaries to India. But he soon left in anger, apparently mistrusted by the Young Turks, and settled in Geneva. Moreover, as a fanatical Hindu he denounced the emphasis by Oppenheim and other Germans on pan-Islamism and Indian Muslims in the plans for India.[44] So within the first two months of the war the Germans discovered firsthand a problem among the Indian revolutionaries that would continue to undermine the latters' work, as well as that of Germany, toward the goal of destroying British rule in India.

Through the Indian Independence Committee in Berlin the foreign ministry contacted Indian revolutionaries in the United States. For this purpose, and with the full collaboration of the ambassador, Count Johann Heinrich Bernstorff, the ministry turned the German embassy in Washington into a communication center for messages between the revolutionaries, the ministry, the General Staff, and Indian agents in the Middle and Far East. The embassy also provided money and forged papers that enabled the Indians to travel between the United States, Europe, and Asia, and it provided large amounts of money to the Indians for publishing propaganda.

Perhaps even more significantly, the military attaché at the embassy in Washington, Captain Franz von Papen, organized revolutionary action groups and, beginning in October 1914, arms shipments for India. With the cooperation of the Krupp representative in the United States, Hans Tauscher, Papen purchased at least $140,000 worth of rifles, pistols, and ammunition and stored them in various places.[45]

Berlin's Decision to Contact Afghanistan

Germany also made preparations to dispatch from the Reich via Turkey a military mission to Afghanistan to persuade its ruler, Habibullah, to attack India. The foreign ministry and General Staff accepted Enver Pasha's claim (contrary to the facts) to Wangenheim that the war minister had frequent contact with Habibullah, and that he was ready for any hostile operation against England and Russia.[46]

By 19 August 1914 Enver had already proposed sending a mission of Turkish officers to the amir, accompanied by a German military contingent to enhance the group's prestige with the Afghans. But, and as yet unbeknownst to the Germans, the war minister had previously ordered a small Turkish mission to Kabul, led by a deputy in the Ottoman parliament from Smyrna, Obeidullah Effendi. However, Obeidullah had not yet left Constantinople.[47] Enver's principal goal in suggesting a joint Turkish-German mission to Afghanistan reflected the Porte's desire to maintain close supervision of the Germans as the latter moved through Persia and Afghanistan. The Young Turks, with their fanatical pan-Turanian aspirations, which envisioned uniting under Ottoman rule the Turkish peoples of southern and central Russia and Persian Azerbaijan, considered both countries within their sphere of influence.[48]

During the weeks that followed a special commission in Berlin organized the German expedition to Persia and Afghanistan. The commission included Oppenheim, Jäckh, Arndt von Holtzendorff (the director of the Hamburg-Amerika shipping line), Reinhard

Mannesmann (the industrialist and official in the Reich colonial office), and a captain from the Reich naval office. The presence of Holtzendorff and Mannesmann on the commission illustrated the widespread feeling among the German leadership that the war would be short and victorious, and that it would produce possibilities for future economic expansion in Persia and Afghanistan.

To lead the Germans the commission chose Oskar von Niedermayer, a twenty-nine-year-old Bavarian geologist and artillery officer who had traveled extensively in Persia and India. The mission also included Wilhelm Wassmuss, the former consul at Bushire who had returned to Berlin; Max Otto Schuenemann, a former administrator of the German consulate at Tabriz and director of the Persian Carpet Company; and Professor Erich Zugmayer, a zoologist and specialist on Tibet and Persia.[49] As the expedition took form, reports from the chargé d'affaires at the German legation in Teheran, Radolf von Kardorff, as well as from Wassmuss urged that Germany also employ the mission for political and military purposes in Persia. Kardorff, a thirty-three-year-old diplomat who possessed little experience in Persian affairs, repeatedly telegraphed Berlin that Germany needed only to supply Persia's tribes with weapons, munitions, and money to set an anti-British and anti-Russian rebellion in motion. Previously, Persia, which had declared its neutrality in the war and which suffered at the hands of Russian occupiers in the north and British in the south, had played no role in Germany's Middle Eastern policy.

Oppenheim and the foreign ministry persuaded the chancellor, Bethmann Hollweg, to alter the policy. Oppenheim insisted that an opportunity existed to convince the Persian government to join the Central Powers in the war, particularly if Turkey entered the struggle. Persia's entry in the war against the British and Russians, Oppenheim declared, would make an enormous impression on India.[50]

From the time the Berlin government decided on the Afghan and Persian expedition, eight months passed before its first members left Mesopotamia to begin their work. Delays resulted not only because Turkey did not in fact join the Central Powers in the war until November 1914, but also because of problems in shipping German weapons, supplies, and money through neutral Bulgaria, and particularly Romania, to Turkey.[51] The expedition also suffered from the fact that most of its members had little or no knowledge of Oriental languages and cultures. Consequently, Zimmermann, Langwerth von Simmern, Niedermayer, and Zugmayer recruited mainly Oriental experts for work in western Persia and Mesopotamia. They included a team of German archaeologists who had returned at the breakout of war from digging among ancient ruins in Mesopotamia and had cultivated close relations with local Arab tribes (including the Anaza and Shammar): Conrad Preusser, Hans Lührs, Paul Maresch, and Walter Bachmann.[52]

Wassmuss and his group waited in Aleppo throughout October and November, where Zugmayer and Schuenemann soon joined them; Niedermayer and other expedition members remained in Constantinople, awaiting supplies, until 5 December. During that time quarrels over leadership further plagued the expedition; in Aleppo, commission members complained about Wassmuss's authority over them. The grumblers were dismissed and replaced by persons more experienced in Oriental affairs, such as the dragoman Eduard Seiler, Günther Voigt, and Wilhelm Wagner.[53]

Indecision, moreover, developed at the highest level in the German government—over whether the kaiser should send along with the group special gifts, decorations, and a handwritten letter to the amir of Afghanistan. Zimmermann drafted a letter that emphasized Wilhelm's desire "to help the Mohammedan peoples in their struggle for independence" from British and Russian rule. But Muslim autonomy mattered little to the Germans; the General Staff rejected sending either the letter or decorations, fearing they might fall into enemy hands.[54]

Still another reason for the delay of the German mission involved the attempt by the Turks, who held the ultimate authority over the expedition, to keep it from entering Persia. Rauf Bey, the Turkish official given ultimate control by the Porte over the German and Turkish expedition, refused to contact Wassmuss and the other Germans waiting in Aleppo and Constantinople.[55]

In fact, as Niedermayer informed Wesendonk on 18 October from Constantinople, the Turks had sufficient cause for delaying entering either the world war or Persia. Not only did the British possess a significant number of ships and troops in the Persian Gulf, but they also had paid subsidies for years to the tribes of southern Persia to secure their loyalty. Finally, Niedermayer warned, although many of the tribes of western and central Persia—the Kurds, Arabs, Bakhtiaris, and Qashgais—supported the Turks and Germans, the latter faced serious obstacles in provisioning the tribes with weapons, munitions, and money. "From where do they come," he asked, "if Rumania prevents transit?"[56]

Also, the Germans awakened mistrust among both the Young Turks and Persians by proposing to send through Turkey, to incite the tribal revolution in Persia, a wholly disreputable and untrustworthy Persian prince, Salar ud-Daula (in 1914 living in exile in Switzerland). The choice of the prince, made primarily by Oppenheim and the Information Service for the East, was an improvised and uninformed one. Before the war, the prince, a member of the ruling dynasty in Persia, had involved himself in the struggles for power there and intrigued unsuccessfully against the shah. The Germans paid for Salar ud-Daula's travel to Constantinople, where he met with Young Turk leaders, who mistrusted him. When the Persians declared their neutrality on 1 November, even Kardorff, the German chargé d'affaires in Teheran, urged that the prince not be sent to Persia; to do so, Kardorff feared, might anger the Teheran government and persuade it to join the Allies. The Turks eventually imprisoned Salar ud-Daula.[57]

A second German expedition to Persia, organized during September and October, also began slowly. On 22 September, a representative of the Hamburg-based Woenckhaus shipping and trading company, which had operated since 1897 in the Persian Gulf, proposed to the foreign ministry and General Staff that Germany destroy the oil tanks and refinery of the British-controlled Anglo-Persian Oil Company at Abadan, at the head of the Gulf along the Persian side of the Shatt al-Arab.[58] Pipelines connected the refinery to the oilfields along the Karun River, which ran northeast through the Persian towns of Ahwaz and Shushtar. Since the British fleet had recently changed its fuel from coal to petroleum, Persian oil had assumed considerable significance for the British admiralty.

As early as 22 August the German consul in Bushire, Helmuth Listemann, had reported to the foreign ministry, erroneously, that the British had moved two hundred troops of the Indian army to

Abadan and would soon increase the force to fifteen hundred.[59] Oppenheim discussed the matter with Robert Woenckhaus and Albert Ballin, the latter the owner of the Hamburg-Amerika shipping line, which like Woenckhaus had done business in the Gulf and still had ships at Basra. From the meetings, which involved neither the General Staff nor admiralty, Oppenheim produced a plan whereby if Turkey joined Germany in the war, a steamship at Basra owned by Ballin, the *Ekbatana,* and a Turkish gunboat would sail down the Shatt al-Arab, obstruct the river below Abadan, and set the oil tanks and refinery afire.

Woenckhaus and Ballin, however, after addressing the issue with Holtzendorff, the director of the Hamburg-Amerika line, disagreed with Oppenheim's proposal. Ballin urged the foreign ministry not to destroy the Abadan oil installation but rather to capture it, by sending (with Turkish cooperation) a German expedition there. According to Ballin, Germany could acquire "an oil source of unending wealth" that "would be of the greatest value for the Reich naval office."[60]

Meanwhile, the foreign ministry had notified Wangenheim and Enver Pasha of the plan to block the river and destroy the refinery. Enver favored the project, and by 17 October Niedermayer, the leader of the German expedition to Afghanistan, had readied himself to leave from Constantinople for Basra to supervise the operation.[61] But a meeting in the foreign ministry of Jagow, Holtzendorff, Ballin, Woenckhaus, Oppenheim, Langwerth von Simmern, and representatives from the General Staff and admiralty decided against the *Ekbatana* scheme and in favor of sending a large detachment of German troops, together with Turkish forces, to occupy Abadan and the entire oil-rich Karun region.

According to Jagow, the revised operation would not only benefit the German navy but deny the valuable oilfields to the British, force them to send several thousand troops to the Gulf to protect their interests, and embarrass them in India. Several days later the foreign ministry ordered Niedermayer not to leave Constantinople for the Gulf; on 4 November the General Staff and ministry named Captain Fritz Klein, a former military attaché in Teheran, to lead the expedition of troops to the Karun region.[62]

The decision, however, which had taken over two months to make, came too late. As Berlin was ordering the Klein mission to Turkey, the British Indian Army landed its Expeditionary Force D (known as "IEF D") at the head of the Persian Gulf. Simultaneously, the India Office was organizing the dissemination of pro-British propaganda among the local Arab tribes. Furthermore, the Indian government now ordered one of its key political officers in the Gulf, Shakespear, to travel to the Arab ruler of Najd, Ibn Saud, to persuade him to take sides with Britain when war came with Turkey.[63]

IEF D apparently knew nothing of the plans developed in Berlin to capture the Abadan oilfields for Germany. Once in the Gulf it awaited the outbreak of war with Turkey—which the Porte forced on 29 October by shelling bases in the Black Sea of Britain's ally, Russia. On 6 November the expeditionary force landed at Abadan and drove back the Turkish soldiers above the oil installations, whereupon the government in London sanctioned the capture of Basra, seventy-five miles north of the Gulf. IEF D seized the city on 22 November, and by the beginning of December it had advanced to the junction of the Tigris and Euphrates rivers.

Historians have debated energetically the goals of IEF D; the weight of the evidence, however, falls heavily on the argument that Britain intended primarily to demonstrate power to the Arabs, whose backing against the Ottomans London had now decided to enlist.[64] That decision resulted in part from the wish of the British to preserve their powerful position in the Persian Gulf and Mesopotamia. But what generated such thinking was the strong feeling among Britain's leaders in London and the Middle East that not only did the Young Turks intend to enter the war but that the combined strength of Germany and Turkey seriously threatened the heart of the British Empire, in Egypt and India. Fears of such a menace had emerged among important British circles even before the war.[65]

Britain's move to secure military control of the Gulf, as well as the difficulty of shipping weapons and troops through Romania to Turkey, forced the Germans to change the nature of the Klein expedition. On 10 November the General Staff and foreign ministry decided against sending a large number of German troops to the Gulf; instead they adopted a modified form of Oppenheim's original plan. They dispatched Klein and a small contingent of twelve officers, not to try to capture the British oilfields and refinery but to attack and destroy them, with the assistance of local pro-German Persian gendarmerie and well armed nomads like the Bakhtiaris, Qashgais, and Arabs.[66] Klein arrived in Constantinople five days later, to a cool reception from the Turks. In December he assembled his forces in Aleppo; from there, despite obstacles placed in their way by local Turkish commanders, they accompanied Niedermayer and his Afghanistan expedition to Baghdad.

The Germans and the Call to Holy War

On 17 and 21 October 1914, a loan from Germany, two trainloads of Turkish pounds in gold, arrived safely in Constantinople. The transfer of the money removed the final obstacle to Turkey's entry into the world war; Enver Pasha now used his position as war minister to draw the Turks into the fighting. He urged the commander of the German Mediterranean naval squadron to open hostilities against Russia. The *Goeben* and *Breslau* bombarded Russian Black Sea ports on 29 October; St. Petersburg declared war on Turkey on 2 November; three days later, London and Paris joined their Russian ally.

The Ottoman sultan, Mehmed V, too weak to challenge the war faction in the government and acting as caliph of all Muslims, declared a jihad against the Allies. Unconcerned by the fact—peculiar from an Islamic perspective—that Turkey had joined certain Christian powers in war against others, he called on Muslims to defend their faith against its "mortal enemies."[67] Government-sponsored demonstrations flooded the streets of Constantinople. The Young Turks unleashed in their heavily censored press a barrage of pan-Islamic propaganda, hoping thereby to overcome the difficulties that had prevented a spontaneous revolutionary movement of Muslims against Britain and its allies. In the Shiite cities of Najaf and Karbala in eastern Mesopotamia, the press and *ulamas* (persons learned in Islamic theology and law) emphasized the community of Shiites and Sunnis.[68]

Within a few weeks the Turks began an invasion of the Caucasus and Russia. Enver Pasha's pan-Turanism produced a particular, personal interest in this campaign and in pursuing it as long as necessary to seize the region from the Russians. The Caucasus campaign, however, took away troops and armaments from the planned attack on Egypt, preparations for which the Porte now increased: in mid-November the Young Turks appointed one of their own as the new commander of the Fourth Army in Damascus preparing the expedition. This was Jemal Pasha, a pronounced pan-Islamist who likewise held the positions of naval minister and governor of Syria.[69]

Berlin received the news of Turkey's entry into the war with delight and satisfaction. Zimmermann, the "strong man" in the foreign ministry who wished to prosecute the battle against Britain to the bitter end, particularly welcomed not only Turkey's military forces but also what he saw as its moral power to fanaticize the Islamic peoples of the world by proclaiming a holy war. Partly because of his concern to retain Ottoman assistance against Britain, Zimmermann (along with his chief, Jagow) played a major role at the end of 1914 in helping the German General Staff scuttle a proposal by chancellor Bethmann Hollweg that the Reich conclude a separate peace with Russia.[70] In Constantinople too, some German officials expected the holy war and ensuing Turkish assault on Egypt to destroy Britain's global empire. Only Wangenheim disagreed and expressed misgivings about the jihad, predicting that the holy war would likely "coax only a few Muslims from behind the warm stove."[71]

In Berlin part of the euphoria over the sultan-caliph's proclamation resulted from the attitude, popular among Zimmermann and the foreign ministry, that the holy war would benefit significantly the Reich's struggling efforts to raise Muslim rebellions against Britain in Egypt and elsewhere in the Middle East. The Germans now intensified pan-Islamic propaganda aimed at Egypt. During December their agents in Syria smuggled to various notables in Egypt a strongly worded manifesto appealing to their loyalty to the caliph and khedive, and urging the Egyptians, in the name of Islam, to revolt against the infidel and occupying power.[72]

However, at almost the same moment that news of the jihad reached Germany, Oppenheim complained to Zimmermann that the information on Egypt produced by the foreign ministry's agents in Turkey (Prüfer, Moritz, and the consul in Haifa, Julius Loytved Hardegg) and the embassy in Constantinople was incorrect or partially contradictory. To remedy the situation, Oppenheim proposed establishing an information service of German and trusted Oriental officials stationed at posts throughout Turkey, including areas off-limits to non-Muslims in Arabia (Maan, Jidda, and Hodeida). Also, the foreign ministry, even before Oppenheim had expressed his concern, had asked the embassies in Constantinople, Rome, and Athens for reports on Egypt.[73]

These resulting reports produced minimal results. Only during the latter part of December did the embassies provide relatively accurate news about Egypt. Their information indicated that between thirty-eight and seventy thousand Indian troops guarded the Suez Canal, that warships patrolled the waterway, and that more troops had recently landed from Australia and New Zealand. The reports also suggested that Arabs along the western Egyptian frontier with Libya worried British officials.[74]

Despite the approval by the Berlin government of nearly three million marks for the Turkish invasion of Egypt and for the other German missions to the Middle East, the basic problems limiting the effectiveness of the German policy remained.[75] For one thing, after Turkey's entry into the war, bitter factionalism existed at the highest levels of the Young Turk regime regarding foreign policy. The direction of policy lay in the hands of a sizable group of CUP officials, chief among them Enver, Talaat, and Jemal, but another faction included the capable but anti-interventionist and pro-French finance minister, Javid Bey, and the grand vizier, Said Halim. Javid resigned from the government at the end of 1914 but retained considerable influence in the Porte's negotiations with the Central Powers before his return to the government in February 1917. These divisions in the Turkish leadership complicated the attempts by Germany to influence the Porte's foreign policy.[76] Also, the very nature of Germany's revolutionary policy aimed at the Islamic world and pursued through Turkey presented difficulties. In a blunt memorandum of 6 December to Oppenheim, Dr. Theodor Weber, the chief dragoman at the Constantinople embassy, condemned the confusion at the embassy regarding the many different German expeditions and agents besieging Turkey. He doubted whether any of them would succeed, and he urged the establishment of a central office at the embassy to coordinate everything with Turkish officials and protect against "errors and also treason."[77]

The Mannesmann mission, sent in August to Tripoli by the General Staff, provided a classic example of the diplomatic blunders wrought by Germany's Middle Eastern policy during the war's first months. Mannesmann's contact with the influential Sanussi prince in Cyrenaica, the Sayyid Ahmad al-Sharif, and the arrival in the latter's camp at the end of October of Sulayman al-Barani (an emissary from Turkey and former Ottoman parliament member from Tripoli) and several Turkish officers had alienated the Italians. Fears intensified in Rome that German and Turkish plans for an attack on Egypt would spill over into Libya and incite the Sanussis even more in their guerrilla struggle against the Italians. Austria-Hungary, furthermore, urged the Germans and Turks not to push the Italians into the Allied camp by angering them over Libya.[78]

The foreign ministry, and particularly Jagow, continued to discount Italian concerns. They believed arrogantly that Italy had little choice but to remain friendly with Germany and Turkey to protect its position in Libya. Nonetheless, and although both Wangenheim and Enver Pasha tried to assure the Italians that the Porte did not wish for Muslim unrest to spread into Libya, the Italians refused to permit Germany to send to Libya a retired Prussian army officer, Baron von Bentheim.[79]

Berlin's relations with Italy slowly deteriorated. At the beginning of November Rome protested that it had discovered Arabs in Cyrenaica using German money, and it implied that the Reich's agents had intervened in Libya by bribing the Arabs. The Italian prime minister, Antonio Salandra, asked Johannes von Flotow, the German ambassador in Rome, about the affair; the ambassador replied that no German agents had spent money in Libya and "that real emissaries would scarcely have proceeded so clumsily."[80]

Simultaneously, Enver Pasha, who envisioned Turkey's eventual recapture of Libya from Italy, discussed with the German naval attaché, Humann, the war minister's plan to send his younger brother,

Major Nuri Pasha, along with other Turkish officers, to Libya.[81] But twice during November Rome refused to allow Nuri Pasha even to enter the country, arguing ostensibly that Britain would view such permission as a break of Italy's neutrality. Despite the Italian attitude, the Young Turks prepared to send Nuri's mission secretly by Greek or Italian freighter, departing from Trieste and moving along the coasts of Italy and Sicily to Libya.[82]

In mid-December tension between Berlin and Rome worsened dramatically over an incident involving Mannesmann and the German consulate in Tripoli. Local Italian authorities captured a letter from Mannesmann and the consulate to the Shaykh al-Sanusi, and along with it a bundle of manifestoes intended for Arabs near the Egyptian border, urging them to attack the British.[83] The foreign ministry and General Staff immediately attempted to control the damage by returning Dr. Alfred Tilger, the German consul, to Tripoli. Tilger received the nearly impossible order to end the undeclared war between the Italians and Sanussis and thereby create a friendlier attitude among the Italians in Tripoli toward Germany's revolutionary activities aimed at Britain. Wangenheim, however, argued that sending a German to the Sanussis would not have the same effect as using a Muslim or Turk, and he reminded the foreign ministry of Enver Pasha's intention to send his brother to Libya.[84]

Also, at the year's end the Germans experienced other frustrations in their Middle Eastern policy. For example, the Reich was unable to persuade the Porte to reconcile the Egyptian khedive, Abbas Hilmi II, with the Egyptian nationalists who, like Muhammad Farid, resided in Constantinople and hoped to participate in the upcoming Turkish attack on Egypt. The Ottomans ignored a request from the German embassy on 25 November to place the khedive back in power once Turkish troops invaded Egypt. Instead, according to Humann, the Turks planned to name as khedive either Said Halim, the grand vizier, or the Libyan Bedouin leader, the Shaykh al-Sanussi.[85]

The Germans also worried about Britain's rumored ties to Abbas Hilmi. In fact, however, the British had refused contacts with Abbas Hilmi since the war's beginning. The khedive had approached Britain through the Italian ambassador in Constantinople, expressing his wish to settle in Italy, but the Foreign Office in London had angrily rejected the feeler and urged Italy not to allow him residence there. On 18 December Britain announced that it had deposed Abbas Hilmi, established in Egypt a British protectorate for the Ottoman suzerainty, and in place of the khedivat had raised Abbas Hilmi's uncle, Husayn Kamil, to the throne, with the title of sultan.[86]

When news of his deposition by the British arrived in Constantinople, Abbas Hilmi no longer lived in the Ottoman capital; tensions had risen between him and the grand vizier, and he had left the city and settled in Vienna. There he hoped to utilize the Central Powers further to force the Turks to affirm him as khedive. The Germans and Austro-Hungarians, for their part, although disappointed at the failed reconciliation between the ex-khedive and Young Turks, seem to have been pleased to have an Islamic figure of Abbas Hilmi's stature much closer to them in Europe; they hoped throughout the war to ensure his loyalty in the event the Central Powers won the struggle and the prince returned to the Egyptian throne. The Young Turks, for their part, welcomed the removal of the ex-khedive, whom they viewed as both a troublemaker and rival, from their midst.[87]

By the year's end, Germany's disappointing experiences with the ex-khedive, with the Sanussis in Libya, and the confusion that characterized Berlin's revolutionary activities in the Middle East suggested that the Turkish proclamation of jihad had not immediately benefited the Reich's policy. Pessimistic reports about the holy war and the Arab question arrived in Berlin from German agents in Mesopotamia and Syria. From Baghdad, the dragoman Kalisch declared that the British Indian Army, which had reached as far north as Qurna in Mesopotamia, had made a great impression on the local Arabs. He prophesied that there would be no anti-British Arab revolt in those regions as long as Britain's power remained evident.[88] Prüfer, assigned in Syria to the Ottoman corps preparing to attack Egypt, predicted to Oppenheim that neither the Egyptians nor the Sudanese would rebel against the British. Also, he complained bitterly about the problems that confronted the corps: its inability either to find enough camels for transport to Egypt or to recruit reliable Bedouins for an Arab unit; and its failure to procure sufficient weapons. Of the Arabs, Prüfer concluded, "One need not be deceived about the fact that the enthusiasm for the holy war in Syria and Palestine, the recruiting districts for the Eighth Corps, is an artificial one." More specifically, he warned, the Sharif of Mecca was "in the pay of the English"; pilgrims returning from the Hijaz had told him that the sharif's attitude was "very lukewarm at the least." Also, said Prüfer, relations seemed strained between the sharif and Ottoman governor of Mecca, Wahib Bey, who had sought to break the local influence of the sharif.[89]

The Austrian Orientalist Musil also portrayed a bleak picture for Vienna and Berlin as he embarked on his mission into northern Arabia. There he hoped, with the blessing of the Central Powers and Porte, to reconcile the feuding Arab princes—Ibn Rashid, Ibn Saud, and Nuri ibn Shaalan—and persuade them to join the holy war. Musil complained to Vienna, however, that despite his meeting on 28 December 1914 with Ibn Shalaan, he now had serious difficulties. "The tribes flee the requisitions of the [Turkish] government," he reported. "I searched alone with my small caravan for Nuri. There is no enthusiasm for Islam. The tribes are little interested in the war between Britain and Turkey. British agents work hard to prepare the ground." Ibn Rashid, declared Musil, had recently plundered the tribes of Nuri and his son, Nawwaf, thus preventing them from sending at the least five thousand camel riders needed to assist the Turks in attacking Egypt. Despite such problems, Musil left Nuri's camp at the beginning of January 1915 for Ibn Rashid's residence in Hail, about 450 miles south in the desert. There he hoped to persuade Ibn Rashid to conclude peace with Nuri and Nawwaf as well as with Ibn Saud.[90]

Britain's Response

The problems experienced by the Germans and Turks in unleashing the holy war remained almost wholly unknown to the British and their allies. Among the Allied powers, Britain felt most acutely the danger of a holy war and its possible consequences. The British Empire possessed many more millions of Muslim subjects than did the imperial holdings of France, Russia, and the rest of Europe combined; moreover, both India and Egypt lay geographically near Turkey. In India, the viceroy immediately moved to keep the situation calm, by securing declarations of allegiance from the native princes and other notables.[91]

In Egypt, Maxwell, the British commander, called nearly five hundred shaykhs to Cairo, where according to a report of the Egyptian interior ministry, "they professed fervent expressions of loyalty" to the government. Maxwell forced the few shaykhs the British mistrusted to swear loyalty on the Koran and confined others to their residences.[92] In the region of the Suez Canal a special British inspector, assisted by a secret service of faithful Bedouins, kept watch over local Arab chiefs.

On 2 November, after news that the khedive, from Constantinople, had asked Egyptians to oppose the British armies, Maxwell proclaimed martial law. The government banned seditious literature, closed the Deutsche Orientbank, and deported to Malta nearly four hundred more German and Austro-Hungarian citizens, along with forty-nine Turks and sixteen Egyptians. Further, the government arrested several hundred known and suspected Turkish, khedivial, and nationalist agitators, and forced the leading princes of the family of the absent khedive—Muhammad Ali (Abbas Hilmi's brother) and Aziz Hassan—to leave the country.[93]

To reduce the shock of these events on public opinion, the British in Egypt waited nearly six weeks to make the most stunning changes in response to Turkey's declaration of war. Thus it was not until 18 December that, as noted above, they made Egypt a protectorate of Britain announcing the next day that they had deposed the khedive, Abbas Hilmi (for having "adhered to the King's enemies"), and raising his uncle, Husayn Kamil Pasha, a loyal supporter of Britain, to a new sultanate.[94] These moves officially ended Turkish suzerainty over Egypt, by which the caliph had appointed the Egyptian ruler; henceforth a Christian power governed Egypt and named its monarch.

Meanwhile, on 16 November, the Indian troops destined for the defense of Egypt reached Suez; two weeks later, Australian and New Zealand forces arrived. Two Indian divisions, as well as British artillery brigades and a battery of the Egyptian army, now guarded the canal. Warships in the canal, however, acting as floating batteries, provided the main artillery defense. To assist the British against discontent among the Muslim Indian forces, Cairo arranged for the pro-British Indian prince, Aga Khan, to visit Egypt, speak to the troops, and proclaim that the Ottoman jihad had fallen on stony ground.[95]

In the neighboring, British-ruled Sudan, Egyptian army units sent at the war's outbreak provided the government-general with security. Egyptian officers received the news of the political changes in Cairo with little surprise and took an oath of allegiance to the new sultan. Leading Sudanese shaykhs and ulamas, called to Khartoum by the British governor-general and commander of the Egyptian army, General Sir Francis Reginald Wingate, gave similar assurances of loyalty. Also, the governor-general ordered pilgrims returning from the holy places in the Hijaz to be transported to Khartoum, before going to their villages, for interviews with loyal religious authorities so as to be disabused of false notions regarding the holy war.[96]

British intelligence in both Khartoum and Cairo received less positive news from the neighboring territories. A British agent and coast guard officer at al-Sallum on the Libyan-Egyptian border, Major L. V. Royle, retained close contact with the Sanussi shaykh in Cyrenaica, the Sayyid Ahmad al-Sharif. As early as 6 September Royle had learned of the expected arrival at the Sanussi camp of Germans—undoubtedly Mannesmann's messengers—and the Turkish emissary, Sulayman al-Barani. In the ensuing weeks, the Italians, concerned for their position in Libya against the Sanussis and worrying about German and Turkish intervention, attempted unsuccessfully to involve the reluctant British against the Sanussis. The government in Rome claimed to the British ambassador, Sir Rennell Rodd, that the Sanussis intended to ally themselves with the Turks against Britain.

But in Cairo, British officials, already worried about the pan-Islamic threat to Egypt from Turkey, wished to do nothing on Egypt's western frontier to anger the Sanussis or their religious brethren on the Egyptian side of the border. On the other hand, Britain used the issue eventually to persuade the Italians to abandon their neutrality and join the Allies. In this regard, the Foreign Office directed Rodd to advise the Italians that the Sanussis had been approached by the Germans about joining them, and that an attack on Egypt would likely create a disturbance in other Muslim areas of North Africa and must affect Italy.[97] The Shaykh al-Sanussi, for his part, negotiated with all sides. He not only received the emissaries of the Germans and Turks but repeatedly told the British of Turkish and German pressure on him to attack Egypt, and of his refusal to do so.[98]

At the end of November Royle met twice with the shaykh at al-Sallum. The shaykh indicated his displeasure at Egypt's new frontier policy of closely checking persons and provisions passing from Egypt into Libya. Many Sanussis lived in western Egypt, traded extensively with their fellow tribesmen in Libya, and acknowledged the Sayyid Ahmad's religious leadership. Although the sayyid had no quarrel with the British and in the past had expressed himself favorably disposed toward them, Royle's visits with the shaykh left Cairo uneasy about the situation. Cheetham identified a certain restlessness on the part of the Egyptian Bedouins in the western desert, with whom German and Turkish agents, he declared, "have unquestionably been intriguing." On the Libyan side of the border, some two thousand armed men had gathered at the sayyid's camp near al-Sallum; this force, he assured the British, was directed solely against the Italians. Britain thought this explanation seemed reasonable enough but nevertheless reinforced its troops in western Egypt.[99]

Elsewhere in the Middle East, the British found even less reason for optimism. By November and December their intelligence sources described a distressing situation in Arabia. Pilgrims at the holy cities and the port of Jidda suffered from near starvation because the Ottomans refused to ship food to the Hijaz, apparently wishing to blame the pilgrims' condition on Britain's control of the Red Sea. Britain's naval vessels patrolled much of the long sea-route from Suez to Aden; they attacked Turkish shipping, blockaded Arabian ports, and seized Arabian *dhows* (small boats). Nevertheless, the British attempted to alleviate the food crisis in the Hijaz, shipping supplies to the pilgrims and local Arab tribes through Jidda. In addition, Britain declared to the Arabs that despite the war with Turkey, the Allies would respect the sanctity and safety of the holy cities.[100]

In contrast, however, the British learned that initial approaches by the Turks to tribal chiefs in Arabia had failed to enlist their backing for the Porte. The Sharif of Mecca, for example, had refused the Young Turk request that he supply Arab troops and camels for the Ottoman forces in nearby Asir. In southwestern Arabia, the Porte had attempted to convince the Imam Yahya in Yemen, whose assistance the Turks had tried to secure with special privileges and subsidies, that he should join the holy war against the Christian powers. British intelligence concluded, however, that his inclinations were anti-Ottoman.[101]

Amid this information, the British extended their influence in southwestern Arabia. As early as September the British agent in Aden and India's voice in the Red Sea, Lieutenant Colonel H. F. Jacob, had proposed to begin negotiations with the Sayyid al-Idrisi, the Arab ruler of Asir. Three months later, with the blessing of the Foreign Office and Cheetham, Jacob began discussions in Aden with an emissary of al-Idrisi on an alliance between Britain and the Arab chief.[102]

Thus, by the end of 1914 Britain's leaders in Egypt, the Sudan, India, and the Persian Gulf showed increasing concern for the holy war proclaimed in November by Turkey and supported by Germany. These officials, although they occasionally realized the contradictions in a jihad fought partly for one Christian power against others, exaggerated the strength of religion in the war in the Middle East—more specifically of pan-Islamism, in which the Turks, backed by German arms, would unite the Islamic world in a fanatical and violent revolt against Britain.

It is unclear how much influence, if any, this situation exerted on the furious debate that arose during the fall of 1914 in London over Britain's military strategy. Kitchener, the forceful war minister, had long worried about the danger to Britain's position in the Middle East posed by an Ottoman-sponsored pan-Islamism bolstered by German power. He and other so-called "Easterners" in London advanced the idea that in view of the deadly and costly stalemate on the front in France, the French armies should hold the Western Front while Britain devoted its newly raised armies to attacking the enemy in some more vulnerable spot, preferably in the Middle East. The plan seemed brilliant; it aimed at forcing Turkey out of the war, relieving the Serbians and Russians, exerting pressure on the Austro-Hungarian armies, and ending the deadlock in France.[103]

Already on 3 November 1914 the admiralty, without consulting the British cabinet, had ordered a brief naval bombardment of the Ottoman forts in the Dardanelles. But the attack proved a serious mistake.[104] It alerted the Turks, who immediately paid more attention to the advice of Liman von Sanders and the German military mission that Turkey must strengthen the minefields and inner defenses of the straits and the Gallipoli Peninsula. The action would lead in the new year to a military disaster for Britain. Instead of eliminating Turkey from the war, Gallipoli inflicted heavy casualties and defeat on the British and intensified their paranoia over pan-Islamism and its German ally.

5 Failed Expectations on Both Sides, 1915

The war in the Middle East during 1915 was more than a "sideshow," as some British army leaders in Europe described it, for the gigantic battles unfolding on the Western Front. It produced on each side a whole series of political and military ventures. Germany and Turkey continued to struggle to incite Muslims, from Libya to India, to revolt against the British, and Britain experienced one of its greatest military defeats in history at the Dardanelles. Also, the Anglo-Indian attack in southern Mesopotamia ground to a halt along the Tigris River forty miles south of Baghdad. These Allied setbacks, when combined with the steady advance of the German and Austro-Hungarian forces against the Russians on the eastern front, provided the Central Powers a measure of ascendancy in the world war.

The Suez Canal, Gallipoli, and British Concerns for Egypt

As the new year opened, German officials increasingly saw the Middle East as an area in which the Reich could most effectively strike and damage Britain. In this regard, they held views remarkably similar to the so-called "Easterners" in Britain.[1] The Germans seemed worried only about their inability to acquire intelligence information from Egypt, which the Turks planned soon to attack.

The Reich's estimates of the numbers of British troops defending Egypt, which in reality numbered seventy-thousand, varied widely. In mid-January information still remained scarce when the Turks brought the flag *(sanjak)* of the prophet Muhammad from Medina to Jerusalem to symbolize the beginning of the jihad. Simultaneously, when the bulk of the Turkish VIII Corps, about twenty thousand men, invaded Egypt—leaving Beersheba to cross the Sinai desert to attack the Suez Canal—the corps's officers possessed little correct information on the canal's defenses.[2]

Kress von Kressenstein later acknowledged the failure to construct an effective intelligence network. Indeed, the paucity of information, combined with the conviction of German leaders that Britain could be attacked most productively in the Middle East, contributed significantly to the decision by the Turks and Germans to launch the assault on the canal at all. They ignored the VIII Corps's severe deficiencies in troops, modern weapons, supplies (especially water), and transportation across the Sinai desert. Kress, Prüfer, and other German officers with the corps realized such problems and feared for the outcome of the operation, which the Germans counted on for setting the jihad truly aflame.[3]

Further uncertainties about the holy war resulted from the meeting of Prüfer and several other German officers with the Sharif of Mecca's son, Abdullah, on 11 January as the Germans left Palestine with the corps. They visited with the amir in a tent near Hebron, and Prüfer seems to have been uneasy about what he saw and heard. Regarding Abdullah, he recorded in his diary that the Arab chief "gossiped much and emphasized to excess his friendship for the Ottomans."[4]

The apprehension of some Germans about the Arabs, jihad, and the attack on Egypt was not misplaced. Oppenheim, while he visited the ex-khedive in Vienna, seemed horrified at the possible consequences of a failure of the Turkish attack on the canal.[5] The British would, he prophesied, use the new Egyptian sultan to march into Syria and on to Mecca and Medina.[6] The Turkish VIII Corps, commanded by Jemal Pasha and composed of both Ottoman and Arab divisions as well as an auxiliary unit of Bedouins, departed for the Sinai Peninsula to attack Egypt, having received no support from the principal tribal chiefs of Arabia.[7]

Britain too by the end of January had learned, through the Government of India, of the lack of Arab enthusiasm for the holy war proclaimed by the Turks. Delhi had sent an emissary, Captain Shakespear, to the central Arabian prince, Ibn Saud, to encourage his friendship for Britain and utilize him, along with the shaykhs of

Kuwait and Muhammarah, in helping Anglo-Indian forces in Mesopotamia fight the Turks. Shakespear reported that the Porte had made
repeated requests to the chiefs of Arabia to proclaim a jihad against
the British.[8] The Turks had assigned Ibn Saud to defend Basra and
Baghdad from a British advance in southern Mesopotamia; Ibn Rashid
was to join the Turkish assault on the Sinai Peninsula and Egypt;
and the Sharif of Mecca, the Imam Yahya of Yemen, and the Sayyid
al-Idrisi of Asir were to secure the holy cities in the Hijaz and also the
Red Sea coast and ports.

But the plan had miscarried, Shakespear informed Sir Percy Cox,
Delhi's political agent in the Persian Gulf,

> for the same reasons that the attempt to provoke a "Jihad" has failed—
> the Ottoman government failed to take into account the irritation its
> policy for the last five years has produced in Arabia, failed to foresee
> that combined action between the tribes would be impossible without
> some more or less lasting composition of their feuds, enmities and
> jealousies, and failed to realize that religious enthusiasm could not be
> invoked on the flimsy pretexts it advances.[9]

Consequently, Shakespear continued, the Arab chiefs had consulted
one another after the Young Turks approached them and concluded
that they would await events rather than join the Ottomans. Ibn Saud
had informed the Porte that because of his continuing feud with Ibn
Rashid he could not use his armies to protect Mesopotamia, leaving
Najd open to attack, unless Ibn Rashid's forces moved against Egypt.[10]

Two weeks later Shakespear told Cox that he had discussed with
Ibn Saud the replacement of the Ottoman caliphate by an Arab one,
with the probability that the new office would be held by the Sharif
of Mecca. Shakespear also assisted Ibn Saud in writing the sharif to
urge him to temporize should he receive further Turkish requests to
join the jihad. In the political officer's view, Ibn Saud was doing all in
his power, short of an open rupture with the Turks, to further British interests; the Arab prince, he believed, deserved a close and bind-
ing understanding—specifically a treaty—with Britain.[11] But on the
morning of 24 January, before he could complete the agreement with
the amir, Shakespear died, on a central Arabian plain called Jarrab

while witnessing a battle between the armies of Ibn Saud and Ibn Rashid.[12]

Thus, the Turkish VIII Corps, which took two weeks in January to cross the nearly one hundred miles of Sinai desert to attack the Suez Canal, received no support from the leading Arabian princes.[13] Along the way bitter differences over strategy and other, less important issues separated Kress and his staff from Jemal Pasha, the Turkish commander, who usually settled the disputes in his own favor. Whereas Turkish reconnaissance patrols used camels (with which they scouted almost to the Suez Canal), the British used airplanes, which kept Cairo well informed of the Turkish advance and enabled the British to increase the canal's defenses even more. In addition, British planes bombed the invading force repeatedly, frightening both the Turks and Germans.[14]

The Turkish assault on the canal began early on the morning of 3 February. The British had stationed no troops on the eastern bank of the canal but had heavily fortified the opposite side. Also, Royal Navy cruisers fired on the Turks, particularly shelling the latter's field hospital. When forty Turks reached the canal's west bank by pontoon, they were massacred. By nightfall the British forces had routed the invaders. Total Turkish losses numbered at least fifteen hundred; British casualties neared 150. Jemal Pasha quickly ordered his remaining forces to retreat into the Sinai, which the Turks accomplished without difficulty. While Jemal led most of the corps back to Palestine, where some of the German officers arrived in Jerusalem on 11 February, Kress remained in the desert with several battalions and a squadron of camel riders.[15]

The attack on the canal failed for several reasons. Although the Turks organized, led, and constituted most of the expedition, much of the blame for its outcome rested with the Germans. The latter had pushed their allies into a premature operation without providing them adequate weapons and supplies. Moreover, the German leaders had deceived themselves as much or more than had their Turkish counterparts like Jemal Pasha, by expecting the appearance of the Turks near the canal to set Egypt ablaze in holy war against Britain.[16]

The Turkish advance prompted neither a native uprising in Egypt nor any Sanussi activity in the country's western desert. For their part, Kress and Prüfer refused to blame the Germans for what had happened; instead, they placed much of the responsibility for the defeat on others whom they considered inferior. For example, Prüfer claimed later to Oppenheim that the Arab—mostly Syrian and Palestinian—units in the Ottoman VIII Corps "were of no use. The old hostility toward the Turks stirred itself again among the officers." Many of the Arabs had deserted during the fighting. "The holy war is a tragicomedy," he declared. "The Egyptians are even cowardly in desperation and lack any genuine love of fatherland."[17]

Although the assault on Egypt disappointed the German high command, it soon concluded that the attack had achieved one of its original objectives: it had alarmed Britain sufficiently to retain large numbers of troops in Egypt, which removed such forces from the western front in Europe. For the moment, the German and Turkish commands agreed not to resume large-scale operations against Egypt.

On the one hand, the German belief about the value of the attempt against the canal was correct. British anxieties for Egypt's security continued, in part because the Turkish troops had reached all the way to the canal; also, those who remained in the Sinai desert made subsequent minor raids on the canal and a larger one in August 1916. Moreover, as early as three weeks after the battle, on 3 February 1915, the British learned of the German and Turkish strategy of attempting to force Britain to keep large numbers of troops in Egypt and away from Europe.[18] On the other hand, the campaign against the canal probably diverted British troops less from Europe than from the costly and disastrous Gallipoli campaign.

On 19 February Britain began its military assault on the Dardanelles and the Gallipoli Peninsula. Henceforth Egypt served as the major base for Britain's Mediterranean Expeditionary Force (MEF). The commander of the MEF, General Sir Ian Hamilton, learned when he arrived in Egypt of the large number of troops stationed there to defend the country. Kitchener ordered a strengthening of the Egyptian garrison and told Maxwell, its commander, to supply for Gallipoli any troops from Egypt that could be spared.[19]

But with questions of the security of Egypt and the canal still uppermost in his mind, Maxwell naturally delayed relinquishing anything. Nevertheless, during March and April a substantial portion of the Australian, New Zealand, and Indian divisions that had defended Egypt during the Turkish attack departed for Gallipoli. Other divisions of the MEF soon landed in Egypt, both imperial and British troops, and they too left quickly for the new front.[20]

Although problems at Gallipoli emerged immediately for Britain, its leaders—including Grey and Kitchener—expected victory and envisioned adding territory from the defeated Turkey to the British Empire.[21] As the Gallipoli campaign proceeded, the London government, in part because of its fears of Russian and French claims on the Ottoman Empire, formed a special interdepartmental committee, headed by Sir Maurice De Bunsen. To it fell the task of examining how Britain could dissolve the Turkish state during the war and yet secure long-term British interests in the region.[22]

But in one of the most poorly mounted and ineptly controlled military operations in Britain's history, the landings on Gallipoli in April and August ended in failure and large numbers of British casualties.[23] As the disaster unfolded, the British commander in Egypt, Maxwell, worried about its impact on the Muslim world and about the steady loss by the Egyptian garrison of units to the MEF.[24] He warned Kitchener that the failure of Britain at Gallipoli "would bring about a critical situation all over the Moslem world, and I think we should take all legitimate risks to avoid this." Yet Maxwell also pleaded with the war minister not to weaken the defense of Egypt too greatly.[25]

Despite the steady departures of troops from Egypt to Gallipoli, as well as occasionally to the growing Anglo-Indian forces in southern Mesopotamia, the number of men in the Egyptian garrison remained essentially the same, between roughly seventy and a hundred thousand (except that the garrison grew weaker and less efficient because it lost its best formations).[26] Britain, moreover, strengthened security measures in Egypt, as illustrated by a far-ranging search and reward offered to capture three German spies allegedly operating in the country: Baron Otto von Gumppenberg, Baron von Bentheim, and Solomon Inger.[27]

Also because of Britain's apprehension over public opinion in Egypt, Sir Henry McMahon, the new British High Commissioner in Cairo, rejected Italian suggestions that Britain and Italy negotiate a policy for a joint political and military operation against the Sanussis.

To do so, McMahon informed Grey, "would probably have far reaching effects on Moslem feeling, not only in Egypt and the Sudan but in Arabia and possibly even in India."[28]

Still another sign of British unease regarding Egyptian public opinion involved Britain's initial interest in a settlement with the ex-khedive, Abbas Hilmi, who still resided in Vienna. By this agreement he would renounce the Egyptian throne in return for financial compensation from Britain. Apparently the initiatives for such an agreement originated with (separately) both the ex-khedive and the new sultan of Egypt, Husayn Kamil.[29] The latter, influenced by a recent attempt to assassinate him and by fears that Britain might name Abbas Hilmi's youngest son, Abd al-Moneim, as his successor, pushed the British to establish the order of succession through Husayn's son, brother, and cousin. But while McMahon assured the sultan of Britain's loyalty to his family's succession, the High Commissioner only sequestered Abbas Hilmi's properties in Egypt and did nothing at the time to exclude officially the ex-khedive from the Egyptian throne.[30]

McMahon also made a concerted effort to centralize and coordinate Britain's Arab policy in Cairo. While Egypt handled the negotiations with the Sharif of Mecca, which resumed in July without the knowledge of the Government of India, the latter controlled Britain's relations with Ibn Saud, the Persian Gulf shaykhs, and the Sayyid al-Idrisi of Asir. The India Office viewed with alarm hints made previously of putting Arabs fully in control of the Islamic holy places in the Hijaz, and of the assumption of the caliphate by Husayn, the Sharif of Mecca.[31]

McMahon, who had been appointed High Commissioner in Egypt after service in the Government of India's foreign department, knew about the policy disputes between Cairo and Delhi. Once in Egypt he determined to continue the negotiations that Cairo had begun with the sharif's son, Abdullah. In this regard he resented India's contacts through Aden with al-Idrisi, contacts which on 30 April 1915 produced a treaty that bound the sayyid and Britain to cooperate against Turkey. McMahon feared that the treaty might undermine his dealings with Husayn, who disliked al-Idrisi. But other differences also separated Cairo and Delhi. They disagreed over policy in the Red Sea, over McMahon's suggestion that Cairo make an overture to Ibn Rashid (the northern Arabian prince and enemy of Ibn Saud), and over Cairo's dispatch of pan-Arab agents to the Persian Gulf to incite Arab rebellion in Mesopotamia.[32]

German Efforts to Strengthen the Holy War

Information had also arrived in Cairo and Delhi in the first months of 1915 not only about increased German activity in Turkey (particularly among the Arabs and Jews and Armenians of the Ottoman Empire) but also about attempts by the Reich to reach eastern and central Africa. The German foreign and colonial ministries as well as General Staff hatched repeated schemes to send emissaries across the Red Sea to Abyssinia, the Sudan, and further into Africa to distribute arms to Muslims and incite holy war against the British. Some of the plans reflected the wish of Berlin to retaliate against the intense pressure already applied by the British and French to Germany's colonial holdings in Africa. Anglo-French troops had seized Togoland and the Kamerun, and British and imperial forces had invaded German South-West Africa and East Africa.[33]

The Germans intended to reach Africa through Turkey; throughout the war, however, such plans bore little relation to the realities of the Reich's military and political position in the Middle East and Africa. British control of the high seas as well as of Egypt, the Red Sea, and much of East Africa precluded nearly any chance of a successful German penetration of the huge continent.[34] Nevertheless, during January 1915 the foreign and colonial ministries discussed a plan devised by Duke Adolf Friedrich zu Mecklenburg, the former governor of Togoland, to create a military expedition comprising Sudanese and Egyptian troops for attacks on the Belgian Congo and British East Africa. A few weeks later, despite the Turkish defeat at the canal, an official in the colonial ministry and former officer in German East Africa, the retired Lieutenant Fritz Bronsart von Schellendorff, submitted a plan to the German chancellor, Bethmann Hollweg, which called for "white" Christian Germany to conquer central Africa.[35]

Also, Wilhelm Solf, the colonial secretary, discussed sending a special reconnaissance unit to Turkey and the Sinai Peninsula to investigate the possibility of utilizing Arabia and Egypt as bases for a military campaign against British colonial possessions in central Africa. Solf agreed with numerous other German leaders that one of their nation's primary aims in the war should be to increase its colonial possessions and create a central African empire.[36]

However, only one German agent dispatched to Africa even reached its coast. Leo Frobenius's long-delayed expedition to Abyssinia and the Sudan left Damascus at the beginning of January 1915, with orders to foment among Sudanese tribes a jihad against their British rulers. With Ottoman assistance he traveled down the Red Sea coast, passing through Yanbo and Jidda to Kunfidha. From there the mission crossed the sea in a dhow southwest to Massawa, on the coast of Italian-controlled Eritrea. But when Frobenius arrived in Eritrea the Italian authorities, hoping not to alienate the British, who worried about his presence in Abyssinia, refused to allow him passage.

Nevertheless, the pro-Islamic and pro-German heir to the throne in Abyssinia, Lij Iyasu, gave Frobenius permission to enter his country.[37] Moreover, Frobenius recruited agents and sent them to the Sudan. He attempted as well to contact Ali Dinar, the anti-British sultan in the Darfur region of western Sudan. But despite Frobenius's lengthy negotiations with the Italians, during which the Germans informed Rome that the mission had "no military character," the Italians and British collaborated in removing him from Eritrea. At the beginning of April they returned him to Europe and sent the other expedition members back to Syria.[38]

Frobenius's mission occurred at an inopportune time for German diplomacy. At that moment Berlin still hoped to keep Italy from entering the war on the side of the Allies; yet with regard to Eritrea and Libya Germany pursued a confused and fumbling policy that could only have encouraged the Italians to accept the secret offers they received from Britain and France for a wartime alliance. Rome feared, with some justification, German and Turkish incitement of Abyssinia to attack Eritrea. Moreover, German and Turkish attempts in Libya to persuade the Sanussis to invade Egypt seemed likely to cause the

Sanussis to intensify their guerrilla war against the Italian colonies along the Libyan coast. On 23 May Italy joined the Allied side in the war, an event that angered Bethmann Hollweg and prompted him to make public his government's extensive list of war aims in both Europe and Africa.[39]

Still other events signified not only the near impossibility of Germany reaching Africa through Arabia and the Red Sea but also the ineffectiveness of the holy war. During April most of the surviving crewmen of the German cruiser *Emden* (sunk by the Australians in the Indian Ocean), making their way north along the Arabian Red Sea coast toward Europe, only narrowly escaped Bedouin attackers.[40] Perhaps the most significant aspect of the harrowing experience of the sailors was that it illustrated again the unfriendliness of the Sharif of Mecca, the dominant ruling force among the Hijazi Bedouin and along the Arabian Red Sea coast, toward both the Turks and Germans.

The importance of the sharif and of his tie to the British particularly caught the attention of the acting German consul in Damascus, Wilhelm Padel. On 20 February he denounced the Turks to the Constantinople embassy for failing to do more to recruit the support of the sharif and other Arab leaders. Padel especially urged that Germany intensify its efforts to unite behind the Ottomans the two powerful feuding chieftains in northern and central Arabia, the pro-Turkish Ibn Rashid and pro-British Ibn Saud. That the sharif and Ibn Saud were friends, said Padel, had emerged from letters that had been seized by Ibn Rashid, whose emissary had visited Damascus and had shown the documents to the consul. The Porte, he warned, erred in not taking the sharif more seriously and in having removed the hard-line, anti-sharif Turkish governor of the Hijaz, Wahib Bey, from his post.[41]

Padel's alert, coupled with previous concerns about the sharif raised by other German agents in Turkey and with the failure of the Arabs to join the assault on the Suez Canal, alarmed both the embassy and Berlin. Several weeks later Zimmermann, the under-secretary in the foreign ministry—who had no intention of alienating the Turks by seeking to befriend the Arabs—reacted to Padel and apparently also to the urging of Nadolny, the head of the Reserve General Staff's political section.[42] Zimmermann directed the Constantinople embassy to devise measures, in association with Enver Pasha and Alois Musil, "for the energetic combatting of English influence in Arabia."[43]

Berlin placed high hopes on Musil, the Austrian Orientalist, who had been in northern Arabia since January, dressed like an Arab and accompanied by an assistant and several servants. His orders were to produce peace among Ibn Rashid and Ibn Saud and persuade them to join the jihad. At first, German wishes seemed to be realized. At the beginning of April Enver Pasha, who had originally disapproved of Musil's mission but who now wished to assert full Turkish supremacy in Arab affairs, informed the Germans that the holy war was succeeding in Arabia. As proof the war minister told Humann that Ibn Rashid and Ibn Saud had concluded peace and that the latter had declared his willingness to place himself under a court of mediation of the sultan.[44]

But Musil, who had met with Ibn Rashid in the desert and arrived in Baghdad on 20 April, portrayed the opposite to Hesse, the German consul. The Austrian traveler reported to the embassy that he had learned in Arabia of "the complete indifference of the tribes toward the holy war and pan-Islamic ideas."[45] Musil stunned both the Turks and Germans by placing much of the blame for the feuding and civil war in north-central Arabia not on the pro-British Ibn Saud but on the allegedly pro-Turkish Ibn Rashid and the latter's chief minister, Saud ibn Subhan.[46]

Upon returning to Constantinople in June 1915, he met with Enver Pasha and the Young Turk interior minister, Talaat Pasha. His denunciation of Ibn Rashid as a traitor to the Turks angered Enver, whose traditional backing of Ibn Rashid was well known.[47] Also, his report bewildered the Germans; the embassy in Constantinople and the newly appointed consul in Damascus, Julius Loytved Hardegg, doubted the reliability of Musil's judgment of Ibn Rashid, but Wesendonk in Berlin believed that the Orientalist portrayed correctly the often-confusing Arab relationships.[48]

The Oppenheim Mission

Meanwhile, the near-complete lack of response to the jihad among the Arabs of the Ottoman Empire worried Berlin. On 2 March 1915 the Information Service for the East and its leader, Oppenheim, pro-posed to the foreign ministry that he travel soon to Syria. He intended to improve the content and distribution of pan-Islamic and German war propaganda in Syria, Arabia, and Mesopotamia, and to counter the enemy's. The trip, he said, should last three to four months and enhance the work of the Information Service.[49]

In Constantinople Wangenheim gave his approval for the journey only reluctantly, and only after Langwerth von Simmern, the coun-selor in the foreign ministry's political department, had interceded with him. Oppenheim arrived in the Turkish capital at the end of March.[50] He met Enver Pasha, who later complained to Humann about Oppenheim's plans to issue caliphate propaganda in the Ottoman Empire; the war minister opposed a Christian or infidel discussing among Muslims a topic with such religious implications.[51]

Wangenheim especially emphasized to the foreign ministry Enver's disapproval of much of the Reich's activity in Turkey. Enver disliked the mass of German propaganda aimed at Arab shaykhs (e.g., the German consul in Aleppo had distributed 163 newspaper articles writ-ten by himself), efforts by Germans—Christians—to incite a holy war, and German agents sent to Turkey who lacked the knowledge and sensitivity to influence native Muslims. Above all, said Wangenheim, Enver had declared that the CUP feared the Germans in Turkey viewed the latter as a kind of German "protectorate."[52]

Zimmermann stubbornly rejected the criticisms of Enver and Wangenheim, showing a characteristically unsympathetic and arro-gant attitude toward both Turkey and Islam.[53] Likewise, differences appeared between the foreign ministry and embassy, when the former proposed that Germany seek the Porte's approval for establishing a German consulate in Jidda and posting there Dr. Edgar Pröbster, an Arab specialist in the ministry. On one side of the issue, Wangenheim and the Porte argued that such an appointment would anger the Sharif of Mecca, Husayn; they also agreed to a future meeting of Oppenheim with Faysal, one of the sharif's sons, aimed at persuad-ing Husayn to distribute propaganda in the Arab world and supply the Germans and Turks with intelligence information on the en-emy. On the other side, Zimmermann disagreed with the ambassa-dor and Turkish leadership. He mistrusted the sharif, recalling for

Wangenheim previous reports from several German agents in Turkey alleging ties between the sharif and Britain. According to the under-secretary, the sharif should welcome "as a special honor the sending of an Imperial consular representative to Jidda." In Jidda, said Zimmermann, Pröbster should "not only construct an intelligence service, but supervise the Grand Sharif, [and] counter English agitation in Arabia."[54]

Although Turkish opposition prevented realization of the foreign ministry's scheme for the consulate, Wangenheim apparently soothed slightly Enver Pasha's unhappiness with the German activities in the Ottoman Empire. He asked the war minister to assume personal leadership of the many German expeditions operating in Turkey.[55] Enver then agreed to permit Oppenheim to meet with Faysal.

Despite the growing evidence from German sources, even stretching back before the war, that underscored the pro-British sympathies of the sharif, Oppenheim believed that the mistrust of the Germans and Young Turks of Husayn was unjustified. In part he based his view on the pro-Husayn opinions of the ex-khedive and Shaykh Salih al-Sharif al-Tunisi (a former Young Tunisian, dedicated propagandist of pan-Islamism, and favorite of Enver Pasha), whom Oppenheim met in Constantinople. Further, an investigation by Oppenheim convinced him that the intrigue at the Porte against Husayn, as well as efforts there to remove him as sharif, were unwarranted.[56]

To a significant degree Oppenheim evaluated accurately the situation involving Husayn. To be sure, the sharif had continued his negotiations with the British. In addition, the secret Arab nationalist societies in Syria, comprising officers in the Turkish army, had approached Husayn in January 1915 about assuming leadership of an Arab revolt against the Turks. But the sharif still leaned toward seeking autonomy for himself and his family within the Ottoman Empire. Perpetuating the sharifate in his descendants was a significant part of what he sought.

But in January an agent of the sharif had discovered in Medina documents of the local Turkish governor, Wahib Bey, that outlined a plot to depose Husayn and his family and end the special status of the Hijaz. The outbreak of the war had prevented the Turks from acting on their plan. The sharif sent Faysal to Constantinople to present the evidence to the Porte and ask for redress. Simultaneously, at his father's directive, Faysal made contacts with the nationalists in Syria to assess their strength.

Faysal arrived in Damascus on 26 March and spent nearly four weeks with the nationalist leaders. He then moved on to Constantinople, where the Porte gave him only limited satisfaction for his family's grievance, mainly Wahib Bey's dismissal as governor of the Hijaz. The Turkish leaders held out the possibility of redressing the situation for the sharif if he joined the jihad. Faysal, on the one hand, assured the Turks of his family's loyalty and promised to lead a force of Hijazi Arabs in the planned second Turkish attack on the Suez Canal. On the other hand, he concluded, partly because of his misplaced faith in the then-expanding British attack on the Dardanelles, that conditions favored an Arab revolution to free and separate Arabia from Turkey.[57]

Oppenheim met Faysal at the beginning of May. How much the Arab had learned by then from the Porte regarding his family's situation is unclear; Oppenheim later summarized their conversation in a memorandum. During the meeting, in which an agent of the ex-khedive and acquaintance of Faysal, Ahmad Sheffik Pasha, participated, Faysal assured Oppenheim that even if the Porte did not give his father a vote of confidence, the sharif "would, as always, remain loyal to the government."[58]

The only reason the sharif would negotiate with the English, Faysal claimed, was "if he was convinced that the Turks had decided to remove him." Oppenheim, in turn, emphasized to Faysal that Germany sought in the war only to strengthen the Turkish government and sultan-caliph. Faysal agreed on behalf of his father that the latter would assume responsibility for German and Turkish "propaganda in the entire Islamic world as well as for providing regular reports from Mecca" for the Turks.[59]

The Arab also explained to the German that his father had sent him to Constantinople to ascertain whether the sharif's enemies at the Porte intended to replace him and to defend him against the intrigue. But Faysal naturally said nothing about meeting in Damascus with members of the secret Arab societies; in this regard, Oppenheim apparently had no idea of Faysal's activity. It is unclear whether the

Arab leader sought to use the meeting with Oppenheim to pressure the Arab nationalists even more to urge the sharif to lead a revolt against the Turks. Faysal's account of the meeting—a rather amusing one given in 1917 to T. E. Lawrence—mentioned nothing of the agreement made by Faysal for his father, emphasizing instead Oppenheim's intense pressure on him "to make rebellions of Moslems against Christians."[60]

Despite the Faysal-Oppenheim meeting, Enver Pasha, for his part, still thoroughly mistrusted the sharif and, seeking to divide the latter from the British, insisted that Husayn provide a contingent from his armies to assist another planned Turkish invasion of Egypt. Wangenheim hailed the German agreement with the sharif on propaganda and political reporting as a great success for the Reich, claiming, erroneously, that it avoided an attempt by the Porte in the near future to replace Husayn. It is unlikely that the agreement delayed such a prospect, but rather that Turkey's involvement in the war did. Removal of the sharif, the ambassador asserted, would be exploited by Germany's enemies for their own interests.[61]

Faysal, following his month-long visit in the Turkish capital, returned to Damascus, where he continued negotiating secretly with the Arab nationalists. He also paid a courtesy visit in Jerusalem to Jemal Pasha, to whom he agreed to send a voluntary force of fifteen hundred camelry for another Ottoman attack on Egypt. When he returned to Mecca, on 20 June, his family decided to lead a general rising of the Arabs against the Turks and resume negotiations with Britain, despite the poor showing of the latter at Gallipoli.[62]

Oppenheim, after meeting Faysal, also left for Damascus, to organize an intelligence and information center at the local German consulate that would establish more effective contact with Arabia and Egypt. Using Damascus as his headquarters, he spent the next four months traveling in Syria, Palestine, the Sinai Peninsula, and even northwestern Arabia. Dressed like a Bedouin, carrying a considerable supply of money, and accompanied by Prüfer, several Indian Muslims, and a wagonload of propaganda materials, he stopped in cities, villages, and oases.

In mosques he delivered inflammatory speeches that emphasized pan-Islamism and added an element of nationalism to the holy war by preaching hatred for Christians, especially the British. He revealed an amazing insensitivity to Turkish and Arab cultures, by emphasizing monogamy, abandonment of the fez (the national headdress of the Turks), and practice in using arms for the jihad against the Allies. Such exhortations did not impress those who heard them, nor did the fact that Oppenheim had once been Jewish and that he represented a Christian state. He also met with little success in establishing a network of information centers in the major cities; it was to be under the Constantinople embassy's branch office of the Information Service for the East, staffed by local Turks and Arabs, and provided with pan-Islamic and German war propaganda.[63] While traveling, he focused on sending propaganda into Egypt and also, despite his recent agreement with the Sharif of Mecca, to Arabia.[64]

Germany's Relations with Ottoman Jews, Armenians, and the Porte

Similarly, an attempt by Oppenheim and Prüfer to send Jews from Palestine as spies to Egypt produced small results. Many of the eighty-five thousand Jews in Palestine by 1914 had come from Russia, fleeing persecution by the czarist government; some were Zionist, others orthodox and assimilationist. The war's impact on trade had impoverished the Jews in Palestine; the Porte classified the roughly fifty thousand Jews who held Russian citizenship as enemy aliens; and the virulently anti-Jewish and anti-Zionist Jemal Pasha, the Young Turk governor of Syria, persecuted them. The German government, whose officials were either apathetic about or prejudiced against Jews, nevertheless feared that the Turkish action would alienate public opinion abroad, especially American Jews, whose influence Berlin believed significant in world finance. Consequently, at the urging of Zionist leaders Germany cooperated in 1914 and 1915 with the United States and Italy in persuading the Turks to moderate their policy.[65]

As early as February 1915, Wangenheim had suggested to Bethmann Hollweg that the Reich seek to exploit the hatred of the Russian Jews in Palestine for the czar's regime. A month later Prüfer outlined an elaborate scheme for creating espionage networks of Palestine Jews in Egypt. During the ensuing months, and with Oppenheim's approval, Prüfer sent at least three Jews on missions to Egypt: two Jewish-

Americans from Palestine, Moritz Rothschild and Isaac Cohn; and a young Russian émigré, Minna Weizmann, the youngest sister of Chaim Weizmann and a leader of the Zionist World Congress. Hiring Jews for such work, however, proved risky. The British seized Weizmann in Cairo and returned her to Russia in May, while Cohn worked for British intelligence.[66]

It is unclear how much Oppenheim's activity in Turkey, particularly his pan-Islamic and hate-filled anti-Entente propaganda, helped to inflame the Turkish persecution of other non-Turkish peoples in the Ottoman Empire, including Christian groups like the Armenians. The Turkish massacre of a million or more Armenians in eastern Anatolia began in April 1915 and lasted into the following year. The Porte was still infected with an excessive nationalism, pan-Turanism, and xenophobia that collectively sought to transform the Turkish part of the empire from a multinational state into one of relative ethnic homogeneity. The Young Turks accused the Armenians of sympathizing with the neighboring Russians and of planning a massive revolt against Turkey.

Germany's laissez-faire attitude toward the massacres resulted from widespread indifference among German officials, both in Berlin and Turkey, who viewed the Armenians as an inferior and backward people unworthy of attention. The Germans were morally callous and did simply what they believed politically expedient, which meant keeping Turkey in the war rather than applying strong pressure on the Porte to halt the persecution.[67] Evidence recently produced from Turkish sources implicates the Germans even more significantly in the ghastly affair. It indicates widespread complicity on the part of Wilhelm II, of high-ranking German officers stationed in Turkey, of Orientalists like Ernst Jäckh and Paul Rohrbach, and of the ambassador, Wangenheim.[68]

The Germans rarely mustered the courage to criticize the Turkish policy, and after October 1915 they even forbade their own press to discuss Armenian affairs.[69] On 4 July and 11 August Wangenheim and his deputy at the Constantinople embassy, Ernst Fürst zu Hohenlohe-Langenburg, did express mild displeasure about the persecution to the Porte, but the ambassador studiously avoided interceding on behalf of the Armenians.[70] Wangenheim's successor, Paul

Graf Wolff-Metternich zur Gracht, disapproved much more strongly of the Turkish policy, which produced bitter conflicts with the Turks. Still other Germans, particularly Johannes Lepsius, the president of the German-Armenian Society, who possessed good connections with the foreign ministry and who visited Turkey during July and August, protested the Turkish policy to the ministry. But Zimmermann and other ministry officials downplayed the information, censored (as noted) the issue in the press, and blamed the persecution on the Armenians and the Allies.[71]

Some German eyewitnesses to the atrocities against the Armenians claimed that both Turks and Armenians either blamed the horrors on the Germans or believed the latter approved of them.[72] British intelligence sources in the Middle East in particular emphasized that numerous German officials in Turkey, including Oppenheim, approved of and incited the Ottoman attack on the Armenians. German pan-Islamic propaganda, the British maintained, inflamed anti-Christian feelings and attacks on the Armenians and asserted that the German emperor and his agents in Turkey had converted to Islam.[73]

The evidence indicates, however, that this incitement was in fact the despicable act of individual fanatics, not the result of official German policy. Such actions may explain, however, why numerous Turks in the provinces asserted that the persecutions originated with the Germans and also why the German government objected to the Turkish claims.[74] Most unfortunately, the Germans responded during 1915 and 1916 with a similar combination of disregard and enthusiasm for the persecution by Jemal Pasha, the Turkish governor and commander of the Fourth Army, of Arab nationalists in Syria.[75]

Among Muslims, Oppenheim's mission to the Ottoman Empire did little if anything to kindle their interest in the holy war. His presence in Turkey rather increased the tension that already existed between local Turkish and German officials. While the Germans believed Oppenheim's meeting with Faysal had achieved a coup in Turkish-Arab relations, Enver Pasha, possibly fearing that the Germans were becoming too friendly with both the Turks and Arabs, complained sharply about the German propaganda and other activities in Turkey. Furthermore, Enver rejected German proposals to bribe the Sharif of Mecca with large sums of money and warned the German embassy not to raise the matter again.[76]

German relations to Jemal Pasha also declined steadily. The failure of his forces to mount an effective attack on the Suez Canal had intensified the already caustic disagreements between himself and Kress von Kressenstein, his principal German military adviser. Jemal, furthermore, angered Berlin when he repeatedly frustrated efforts by the German consulate in Damascus to arrange for the Ottomans to provide the forces of Ibn Rashid with money and munitions for the latter's armed conflict in central Arabia with Ibn Saud. The foreign ministry also charged Jemal with having permitted Anglo-French diplomats to remain too long in Damascus after the beginning of the war. As documents seized in the French consulate revealed, the diplomats had engaged in anti-Turkish activities with local Arabs and others.[77]

On 5 June Wangenheim presented the list of German criticisms of Jemal to Enver Pasha. The latter replied that he followed Jemal's work carefully, that he believed the Syrian governor did not always act in Turkey's interest, and that Jemal had not been suitable to lead the expedition against Egypt. However, Enver told the ambassador, although the Porte would find the removal of Jemal difficult, particularly for domestic political reasons, such a move might be worth considering.[78]

But two months later both Oppenheim and Kress von Kressenstein, in opposition to other German political officials and officers in Turkey, including those at the German embassy, judged Jemal Pasha "reliable" and pro-German. They recommended that he continue as chief of the Fourth Army planning a second attack on the Suez Canal, and concluded that he had no ambitions to make himself the new khedive of Egypt.[79]

By then, however, Jemal had begun to suspect an anti-Turkish conspiracy among Arab nationalists in Syria. He changed his policy toward them from one of conciliation and appeasement to repression. However, instead of acting against treasonous Arab officers in the Ottoman army, he arrested and executed Arabs known indeed as nationalists but who were not involved in traitorous behavior. As for Arab military units in Syria, he removed them from the province and replaced them with Turkish forces.[80] How much, if any, the German criticism of his previous Arab policy influenced his new campaign of terror is unclear. It seems likely that neither the Germans nor Turks knew of Jemal's secret approaches to the Allies beginning in October.[81]

These and the other, more notorious, Ottoman-German conflicts may explain why in May 1915 Wangenheim urged the foreign ministry not to negotiate with Aziz Ali al-Masri, the Egyptian founder of an Arab nationalist society in Syria, when he contacted the Germans and offered to work for them in Arabia. Wangenheim recommended that Germany ignore al-Masri, because of "mistrust against Aziz among the leading personalities of the Turkish government."[82]

Whether or not al-Masri's approach to the Germans was serious and could have been exploited by Berlin is uncertain. Possibly the timing was right: although he had been in secret contact with the British in Cairo since August 1914, he was an opponent of British rule in Egypt, pro-German, and a supporter of the Turkish government, objecting mainly to its failure to appoint Arabs to high offices. Only a few months later he and other Arab nationalists, fearing Jemal Pasha's campaign of terrorism against them, presented the British with the nationalists' ultimatum. The latter told the British either to support an independent Arab state, as the Sharif of Mecca outlined to McMahon in Cairo, or face the prospect of the Arab movement backing Germany and Turkey.[83]

The Ex-Khedive in Europe

An Egyptian nationalist who received even more attention during 1915 from both the British and German sides was Abbas Hilmi, the ex-khedive. The Central Powers hoped to persuade him to reconcile with the Young Turks. However, from his residence in Vienna the ex-khedive continued to intrigue against the Porte, even seeking to sow suspicion between the Central Powers and Young Turks.[84]

He also pressured the Porte, through the governments in Berlin and Vienna, not only to permit him to lead the Egyptian expedition but also to affirm him publicly as khedive.[85] The Austro-Hungarian government treated Abbas Hilmi as a head of state, granting him an audience with the Emperor Franz Joseph, but the Germans refused his request to meet with Wilhelm II.[86] Oppenheim, who visited the ex-khedive in Vienna, informed Abbas Hilmi that meeting the kaiser might damage relations further between the Porte and the ex-khedive, and even those between the Porte and Germany.[87]

The Turkish failure at the Suez Canal dealt not only a serious disappointment to the personal ambitions of Abbas Hilmi and the Porte to seize Egypt from Britain, but also a crushing blow to the pan-Islamism and jihad of the Turks.[88] Despite the setback in Egypt, however, the Germans continued to believe in the value of the ex-khedive for the Reich's political policies both in the Middle East and Europe. Throughout the remainder of 1915 the German ambassador in Vienna, Heinrich von Tschirschky, worked unsuccessfully for the rapprochement of the ex-khedive and Egyptian nationalists with the Ottomans.[89] Ironically, Germany may have been responsible for the ex-khedive's lack of progress in coming to terms with the Porte. Despite Enver Pasha's continued unease about Abbas Hilmi's relationship to the Arabs, Oppenheim used the cabinet chief of the ex-khedive, Ahmad Sheffik Pasha, to arrange for and assist Oppenheim's negotiations with the sharif's son, Faysal.[90]

Also, the Germans attempted to use the ex-khedive for their propaganda activities in Europe. During March, in Zurich, Abbas Hilmi assisted Matthias Erzberger, a German parliament (Reichstag) deputy and the chief of his government's propaganda in neutral states, in paying for Germany a French defeatist and Abbas Hilmi's friend from Egypt, Bolo Pasha, ten million francs to acquire for the Reich the newspaper *Le Figaro*. The ex-khedive also received a large sum from the Germans to purchase newspapers in Italy. However, the schemes collapsed, because Abbas Hilmi and his agents spent the money unwisely, keeping large amounts of it for themselves;[91] he returned only 723,000 francs to the Germans.[92]

By summer's end the position of the ex-khedive had become increasingly uncertain toward both Turkey and Germany. He and his costly entourage of servants and agents soon moved to neutral Switzerland. There the possibility existed for him not only to contact numerous Orientals in exile and remain close to the Central Powers but also to contact Britain about a settlement regarding his Egyptian properties, which could provide him with substantially more income. Both Britain and Germany expanded their surveillance networks in the country, primarily to observe the ex-khedive and other Orientals there. Berlin, for example, appointed as its principal agent Heinrich Jacoby, the director of the Persian Carpet Company in Berlin and a member of Oppenheim's Information Service for the East.[93] Jacoby and his superiors in Berlin accepted completely the ex-khedive's claims of his influence in the Middle East and with Britain, in part because Berlin continuously received and unquestioningly accepted reports from Egypt of his popularity there.[94]

Nonetheless, the claims by Abbas Hilmi of Britain's interest in him were untrue; the British repeatedly rejected his approaches.[95] On 4 November Kitchener flatly rejected Abbas Hilmi as a potential leader of the Arabs and instead encouraged Britain's secret negotiations from its Cairo residency for an Arab revolt led by the Sharif of Mecca.[96]

News of Abbas Hilmi's activities in Switzerland particularly alarmed the Young Turks. They feared that his remaining in Switzerland would enable him to deal with Britain; also, they criticized the Germans for paying the ex-khedive such large sums of money, thereby allegedly lessening his dependence on the Porte.[97] British sources in Switzerland learned not only of such differences in the enemy camp but also that the ex-khedive had fallen into disagreement with the Germans.[98] McMahon recommended that Britain should exploit the situation to conclude a settlement with the ex-Khedive regarding the Egyptian properties Abbas owned.

At a meeting on 13 December, Grant Duff, Britain's minister in Bern, met with Abbas Hilmi and a pro-British intermediary, Habib Lutfullah. Abbas claimed knowledge of "a scheme afoot," approved by the British, "by which active support was to be given to a general rising against Turkish rule in Syria and Arabia." Duff informed the Foreign Office that the ex-khedive "expected to replace the Sultan of Turkey as sovereign of these regions" in return for Abbas Hilmi's agreement to accept the present regime in Egypt.[99] The Foreign Office mistrusted the ex-khedive completely and discouraged Duff from further contact with him. Moreover, both Kitchener and Grey agreed that "so long as the negotiations with the Sheriff [of Mecca] are proceeding it would be a pity to undertake other negotiations on opposite lines with the Khedive and Lotfullah, neither of whom inspires confidence."[100] Nevertheless, McMahon urged an eventual settlement with Abbas Hilmi, to lessen problems in Egypt.[101] But only after the Arab revolt had started in June 1916 did the British re-enter negotiations with Abbas Hilmi.

Although news about the ex-khedive's contacts with the British reached the Germans, Baron Gisbert von Romberg, the German minister in Bern, on the basis of an investigation by the agent Jacoby termed the information empty talk and malicious intrigue. Jacoby and his small network of spies also kept watch on local Turks who opposed the regime in Constantinople, on exiled Indians, and on leading Egyptian nationalists in Geneva.[102] Jacoby also reported to his superiors the recent arrival in Switzerland of William Somerset Maugham, "a writer of books" who "came to watch me, straight from England." Jacoby's suspicions were correct; Maugham had arrived in Geneva in the fall, to help bolster a collapsing British spy network whose incompetence had compromised some of its agents, including British diplomats, with the Swiss authorities.[103]

6 The German Threat on the Periphery, 1915

Britain's growing feeling of vulnerability about its position in the Middle East also resulted from its enemies' policies toward India and areas that bordered on the subcontinent.[1] This chapter surveys the German and Turkish activities during 1915 in India, Persia, Afghanistan, and Libya. There too, as in Arabia and Egypt, Germany encountered significant problems and even failure. The British and their allies knew of some of these troubles, and the German and Ottoman operations east of Turkey did not seriously threaten Britain's rule in India; nevertheless, they added to the perception among the British that the Central Powers posed such a danger.

The Activities Aimed at India

Much of the German campaign to incite an anti-British revolt in India focused on Indians in the United States. During the first months of 1915, Indian revolutionary exiles, mostly from America, arrived in Berlin, Switzerland, and Constantinople. The German foreign ministry, Information Service for the East, and diplomatic missions in America and elsewhere assisted them in their travels, with money and false passports.

Maulvi Barkatullah, the Ghadr leader from the United States, arrived in Berlin on 9 January 1915 after visiting with Har Dayal and Chattopadhyaya in Geneva. Barkatullah and other members of the Indian Independence Committee headquartered in Berlin discussed with their German patrons schemes for smuggling revolutionaries, weapons, and explosives into India and persuading British Indian troops in the Middle East to desert or mutiny.[2]

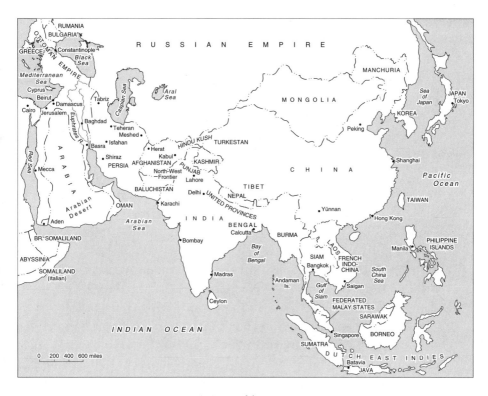

Asia in World War I.

But from its inception, the Indian committee in Berlin suffered from a lack of prestigious members of the Indian revolutionary movement. The committee counted as its only members of any stature the Ghadr leaders, Barkatullah and Har Dayal, and the Bengali activist, Chattopadhyaya. It was from these persons that Oppenheim and Wesendonk, whom the foreign ministry assigned as its liaison with the Indians, acquired their knowledge of Indian politics. Both Barkatullah and Har Dayal had been refugees living outside India for at least seven years.[3]

Nevertheless, the two Indians set much of the agenda for Germany's India policy. Har Dayal, who arrived in Berlin on 26 January, ordered the principal Indian revolutionary leaders in the United States, Ram Chandra (the editor of Ghadr publications and agent for Indian affairs at the German consulate in San Francisco) and Heramba Lal Gupta, to send Indian exiles in America through British East Africa to India. The Germans, who believed that widespread anti-British unrest existed in India, felt certain the exiles would reach their destination.[4]

Some of the German confidence resulted from a mutiny in the British Indian garrison in Singapore on 15 February and an abortive uprising of Indian revolutionaries in the Punjab four days later. The outbreak in Singapore was not directly connected with the insurrection in India, although Ghadr agents had previously made contact with the disaffected soldiers. But the British soon crushed both rebellions and learned from the conspiracy trials of the Punjabi defendants about the German role in Indian revolutionary activities.[5]

Despite the mutiny in Singapore, Indians in large numbers continued to volunteer to assist Britain in the war by serving in Indian army units fighting in France, Egypt, Mesopotamia, at Gallipoli, and elsewhere. Britain's dependence in the war on such troops weakened its hold over India and prompted British wartime promises that would lead later to dominion status for India.[6]

Furthermore, efforts by the revolutionaries to smuggle their followers into India, both from the United States and Far East, generally failed. The lack of success resulted from a combination of factors, including the incompetence, naiveté, and different cultural backgrounds of the Indians and German officials. Conflicts often developed among the Indians, particularly over leadership positions. Equally damaging to the Indian revolutionary schemes was Britain's vigilance, based on its worldwide network of diplomats and agents, in tracking and stemming such activities.[7]

The Government of India and British intelligence quickly established the links between the Germans, the Ghadr movement in America, and Sikh exiles returning to India. During the spring Delhi informed London that it possessed evidence associating Ghadr propaganda and the Germans with Sikh terror in the Punjab against police, army, and government officials. The Government of India responded to the Punjab uprising by arresting its ringleaders and executing eighteen of them.[8] Also, the authorities in India suppressed most of the locally produced Ghadr propaganda. When that happened, Ram Chandra and the German consulate in San Francisco smuggled it to India through business firms in the Netherlands and agents in the Dutch East Indies, Siam, and Shanghai. In addition, the British intercepted Indian revolutionary materials sent from America and Germany.[9]

The Germans and Indian committee had similar difficulties smuggling weapons into India. Since the war's beginning Berlin had noted correctly that a major revolutionary outbreak in India would need the assistance of a large-scale arms shipment. Barkatullah persuaded the Germans to ship weapons to India from the Far East rather than from the United States, where as early as the previous fall the German military attaché in Washington, Papen, had purchased and stored arms cargoes for India.[10] One of Barkatullah's fellow revolutionaries, Bhagvan Singh, a Sikh priest from the United States, had met while in Japan Sun Yat-sen and Chinese revolutionaries, who had proposed buying and sending weapons from there to India rather than from America. Another Indian revolutionary, Narajenawai Marathay in Shanghai, had suggested a similar plan. So had the anti-Dutch Javanese revolutionary Douwes Dekker.[11]

To coordinate these activities the German foreign ministry, working mainly through the German legation in Peking and Bernstorff, the ambassador in Washington, established in Shanghai a Central Office for the Indian Revolution.[12] During the spring the embassy, its consulate in Chicago, Papen, and several Indian revolutionaries, among them Jodh Singh and Heramba Lal Gupta, organized an operation sending revolutionary agents from the United States to India. Singh himself went to Siam, but not before he had stopped for instructions in Berlin. The other agents included Albert H. Wehde (who headed this far-flung project and posed as a collector of art objects and jewelry merchant), Max Schulze, and Georg Paul Boehm, a former German sergeant. According to Bernstorff's reports, Wehde planned to go to Calcutta to support the Indian revolution, while Schulze would go to Bangkok, and Boehm to the Punjab. The group intended to ship arms to a base of Ghadrite revolutionaries in the jungles of northern Siam; from there the Ghadrites would infiltrate the Burmese military police, which included some fifteen thousand Sikhs and Punjabi Muslims, and use them to invade India.

Wehde and his cohorts left the United States by the end of April. In Shanghai, the Central Office for the Indian Revolution expected them to arrive first in Manila, where the Central Office had purchased weapons and loaded them on a small ship, the *Henry S.* However, Bernstorff reported, the suspicious American authorities in the Philippines, whose neutrality did not extend to encouraging Asian nationalism, refused to permit the vessel to leave. Therefore the Wehde group left the weapons in Manila, mainly to conceal the purpose of the expedition, and boarded the *Henry S.* when it headed south on 15 July. It took on a mysterious cargo off the coast of Borneo, but shortly thereafter it developed engine problems that quickly terminated its journey. Wehde somehow reached Shanghai, where the Central Office for the Indian Revolution hired him for other similar activities; Boehm and Schulze traveled to Jakarta and contacted local German circles that included the Helfferich brothers, Emil and Theodor.[13]

The Ghadrite base in Siam fared equally badly. The local German consul, Dr. Voretzsch, and his chargé d'affaires, Dr. Erwin Remy, established with the assistance of the Peking legation a headquarters in the jungle near the Burmese border. However, although a hundred Ghadrites arrived there for training from Canada and China, the plot to infiltrate the revolutionaries into Burma misfired. The operation suffered from poor information about the political situation in India, from the failure of the Ghadrites to contact for training in revolution-ary activities a German expedition in Yunnan in southern China, and from the inability of the Germans to ship weapons to Siam.

The Siamese government's dependence on British India for infor-mation soon enabled Britain to uncover the plot. During July and August, at the urging of Britain's minister in Bangkok, Herbert Dering, the Siamese government arrested fifty-six Ghadrites, includ-ing the German-speaking Jodh Singh.[14] Because of intense British pressure, Siam and the Dutch East Indies also banned the importa-tion of seditious Indian literature into each country, although the prohibition in the Indies did not include German propaganda. In November the British arrested the Javanese revolutionary Dekker as he traveled from Europe to Siam for the Berlin Indian committee. He intended once there to publish German war news and Indian revo-lutionary materials for smuggling via Burma into India.[15]

Still another costly and unrealistic German adventure, begun in the United States, also ended in disaster. During the spring, the Ger-man consulate in San Francisco, with authorization and funds from the German navy, purchased a steamship, the *Maverick,* to transport to Asia the arms acquired by Papen in the fall of 1914. The Germans accepted the claims of Ram Chandra, who had purposely misled Papen and other Reich officials to believe that hundreds of thousands of revolutionaries waited in the Punjab and at Karachi to receive the arms. A German plan called for loading the weapons onto a schoo-ner, the *Annie Larsen,* owned by a German-American shipping agent, which would rendezvous with and transfer the arms to the *Maverick* off the coast of Mexico. From there the *Maverick* would carry the cargo to Bangkok under the American flag.

The scheme misfired, however, when both British and American authorities learned of it and stopped and searched the *Maverick* be-fore it could reach Mexican waters. The *Annie Larsen* finally docked near Seattle, Washington, where American customs officers promptly confiscated the ship and its cargo, which had been falsely declared for Mexico. The incident caused an unpleasant exchange between the U.S. State Department and Bernstorff, and it contributed to strained relations between Germany and America.[16]

Papen and Bernstorff failed to learn from either fiasco; Papen had been especially remiss in not anticipating the alertness of British intelligence and its cooperation with the Americans. Consequently, the Germans organized still more arms purchases, which produced the same results. In June British intelligence foiled an attempt to ship 7,300 Springfield rifles and 1,920 pistols on the Holland-America steamship *Djember* to the East Indies. German contacts in the East Indies with emissaries of a Bengali revolutionary in Calcutta, Jatin Mukherjee, produced a similar plan whereby the arms impounded in Seattle would go to Bengal. On 28 June, however, the British consul general in Batavia received an anonymous letter about the cargo; the British and Indian police not only destroyed the revolutionary organization in Calcutta but killed Mukherjee.[17] Still another German plan, based on freeing prisoners from the Government of India's penal settlement on the Andaman islands and using them to attack the Indian coast, collapsed when a German agent, Vincent Kraft, sold details of the operation to the British. Kraft also provided the British with extensive information on the Indian committee in Berlin and its activities in Washington, D.C., Siam, the Dutch East Indies, and Persia.[18] Later in the war he reappeared in Mexico, pretending to work for Germany but in fact spying for Britain.

Britain not only discovered and stopped most of the German activities aimed at India, but London used them to urge the United States government to prosecute Indian revolutionaries and German agents in America. By the end of 1915 Britain had accumulated a formidable documentary case for American action against the Indians and Germans. In December Britain provided the United States with a transcript of a trial in Lahore of local Indians. The defendants, who had conspired to overthrow British rule, had received much of their inspiration from Ghadr and other revolutionary sources in the United States. Nonetheless, and although Washington expelled Papen from the United States in December, America remained generally unresponsive to Britain in the matter.[19]

Only one other German and Indian intrigue in Berlin moved beyond the planning stage.[20] During the spring and summer of 1915 the Berlin Indian committee sent several of its members on missions to

Baghdad and Syria to infiltrate Anglo-Indian troops in southern Mesopotamia and Egypt, and to assassinate British officers. Both missions, however, because they included mainly Hindus (like Har Dayal who had returned to Constantinople), soon quarreled bitterly with local Indian revolutionaries already in Turkey, many of whom were Muslims. Oppenheim and Chattopadhyaya arrived in the Turkish capital during the spring, but neither succeeded in mediating between the factions.[21] Although the mission to Mesopotamia succeeded in distributing propaganda among Anglo-Indian troops and even in bombing an officers' casino, its Hindu members fell afoul of local Turkish authorities, who arrested one of the group.[22]

Despite such conflicts and the overwhelming lack of success of the Berlin Indian committee's revolutionary activities, the committee remained both fanatical and optimistic. It bombarded the Germans with demands for money and other support for the Indian revolution, including a German navy attack on Bombay and Karachi.[23]

In December Chattopadhyaya, writing for the committee, claimed that Punjab princes intended in March 1916 to incite a revolt in Peshawar and Quetta. The committee asked Jagow for assurances that Germany would assist the revolt with arms and money and would "have no other than commercial and cultural interests in furthering the cause of Indian National Independence."[24] The foreign secretary, obviously enthused by the committee's news, replied immediately, assuring the Indians "that Germany, the true friend of all oppressed nations, has no other than commercial and cultural interests in furthering the cause of the national independence of India."[25]

Afghanistan and Persia

Much of the Indian committee's claim that princes in the Punjab would revolt rested on information the committee had received from Harish Chandra. A Punjabi revolutionary living in Switzerland, he specialized in spreading defeatism among Indian soldiers in France and Britain. Chandra had returned to Switzerland in August 1915 after spending several months in India; while there, he had delivered to numerous princes messages from Mahendra Pratap Singh, who had joined the Germans. Chandra, Pratap's private secretary, had convinced himself that a public statement of German support for the Indian princes would ignite their rebellion.

The Germans placed great confidence in Pratap, a prince from Mursan and Hathras in India's United Provinces and a friend of Chattopadhyaya and Barkatullah; he had contacted Berlin in January 1915 from Switzerland.[26] The foreign ministry and General Staff accepted Pratap's proposal that he travel to Kabul, together with his friend Barkatullah, to persuade the amir of Afghanistan, Habibullah, to attack India and support the rebellion of the princes. Pratap, with the help of Chattopadhyaya and Barkatullah, received an audience with the kaiser, with whom he agreed to deliver letters from the German government to the amir and leading Indian princes, including the Maharajah of Nepal.

The foreign ministry and Nadolny assigned Werner Otto von Hentig, a former consular official in Washington, D.C., and an acquaintance of Barkatullah and other Indian revolutionaries, to escort Pratap to Afghanistan. Originally the ministry intended for the group to join the Niedermayer expedition headed for Afghanistan, which had already reached Baghdad and was to proceed together with a similar Turkish mission. Instead, during the preparations for the Pratap-Hentig expedition, the ministry ordered Hentig, once he arrived in Kabul, to open official relations with Afghanistan and establish a German diplomatic presence there.[27]

Pratap and Hentig arrived in Constantinople on 17 April and met with Enver Pasha and the sultan. Before they left Constantinople for the east they received letters from Wilhelm II and Bethmann Hollweg to deliver to Habibullah as well as to twenty-six princes in India and the Maharajah of Nepal. When their small band traveled further to Aleppo and Baghdad, however, it suffered delays and other difficulties like those experienced by the Niedermayer mission, caused mainly by conflicts with the Young Turks. The latter, principally because of the fanatical pan-Turanian ambitions of the faction around Enver Pasha and Talaat Pasha, viewed Persia, Afghanistan, and central Asia as the Ottoman sphere of influence; they opposed German activity east of Turkey. The Germans, however, saw Persia as a key link to Afghanistan and India, and hoped to persuade it to abandon its neutrality and join the Central Powers in the war.[28]

The success of the German armies in Russia in 1915 heightened Germany's interest in Persia. In this the Reich's inexperienced chargé d'affaires in Teheran, Kardorff, played a key role. He dispatched reports to Berlin that emphasized the eagerness of the Persians and the shah's government in Teheran to support the Germans and Turks in the war. The Persians, claimed Kardorff, hoped to free themselves from the Russian troops occupying much of northern Persia, and from British troops in the south. Kardorff, acting independently of the foreign ministry and using large sums of money for bribes, had won over to the German side the Swedish officers of the seven-thousand-man Persian armed force, the gendarmerie.[29]

On the one hand, this increased the interest in Persia of Nadolny and the General Staff. Nadolny argued that the possibility existed for Germany to unleash a massive anti-English and anti-Russian rebellion among the native peoples "from the Caucasus to Calcutta." On the other hand, Kardorff's activities hardened further the opposition of the Turks to German activities in Persia. The Ottoman military commanders in Mesopotamia, Rauf Bey and Sulayman Askeri, on orders from Enver Pasha, prohibited the Niedermayer expedition from entering Persia.[30]

The Turks also limited the work of another German mission that had arrived in Baghdad, one led by Fritz Klein and equipped with armaments from the General Staff. Enver, too, in the aftermath of the failed Turkish military attack against the Russians in the Caucasus, urged delaying the advance of the joint German (Niedermayer)–Ottoman expedition into Persia and Afghanistan until Turkish troops, which had invaded Azerbaijan, had pushed the Russians out of the area.[31]

A struggle on this question soon emerged in Berlin between the foreign ministry and General Staff. A multitude of issues, which undermined German hopes of persuading Persia to join the Central Powers, provoked it: Turkish obstinacy toward Germans in Mesopotamia and Persia, the mistreatment of Persians by Ottoman forces in Azerbaijan, and Persian fears that Turkey intended to seize Persian territory. The disagreement centered around control over Berlin's policy toward Persia and Afghanistan. Although the foreign ministry and Wangenheim urged cooperation in this matter with the Turks, several factors had increased the influence of the General Staff, which demanded a more aggressive German role. These included Turkey's recent entry into the war, the steady advance of German armies on the eastern front, a growing awareness in Berlin of Persia's potential importance in the war, the General Staff's equipping of Klein's expedition, and Niedermayer's request that his mission be subordinated to German military authorities instead of German and Turkish political ones.

A meeting of the principal Turkish and German leaders in Constantinople on 11 February reconfirmed Enver Pasha's military plans, but the German General Staff opposed what had been decided. Nadolny refused to accept the Young Turk leader's policy of invading Azerbaijan, on the ground that it would embitter the Persians toward the Turks and Germans, and delay the entry of the German expeditions into Persia. He argued that the presence in Persia of British troops in the south and of Russian forces in the north had long violated Persian neutrality, which Germany could not tolerate. He therefore issued orders designed to claim control from the foreign ministry over both the Niedermayer and Klein expeditions, whose objectives were to raise a large rebellion of the native peoples in Persia and Afghanistan against the British and Russians. He directed Niedermayer to separate his mission from the Turkish one and move immediately into Persia, without the Ottomans.[32] Nadolny also dispatched to Baghdad and the Turkish-Persian border Dr. Friedrich Sarre, a noted German archaeologist and scholar of Islam, to act as the staff's liaison officer in the region.[33]

During the ensuing weeks several small elements of Niedermayer's expedition entered Persia to establish supply bases for the support of not only his mission to Afghanistan but also that of Pratap and Hentig. Schuenemann traveled to Kermanshah, Peter Paschen to Kurdistan, Seiler to Isfahan, and Zugmayer and Walter Griesinger to Kerman. Wassmuss had left the expedition in January to advance independently into southern Persia, aiming at creating a base in Shiraz.[34]

In and around each city the German agents claimed special privileges as consuls and agitated among the local Persian population—Shiite religious leaders (ulamas), businessmen, government officials, the gendarmerie, and tribal leaders. To win the support of these groups and to pressure the government in Teheran to join the Central Powers in the war, the agents distributed propaganda and generous sums of money. They played on the animosity of the people toward British and Russian control of the country and called on Persians to join the jihad against the Allies. Reports from the Germans in Persia, however, soon arrived at the embassy in Constantinople, decrying how the armed Turkish incursions into western Persia had severely damaged attempts to mobilize Shiite support for the jihad.[35]

In southern Persia the British nearly captured Wassmuss twice, once in Shushtar in February and a month later at Behbehan; in the latter incident Wassmuss barely escaped, leaving behind much of his baggage, including a German code book. It fell into British hands and in 1917 assisted Britain in deciphering the infamous Zimmermann telegram.[36]

The British had better luck in seizing other Germans in the area. They captured Dr. Theodor Lenders, a German physician who belonged to Wassmuss's party, and upon occupying the German consulate in Bushire they caught the consul, Helmuth Listemann, as well. Furthermore, documents found at the consulate provided the British with information on Germany's numerous operations in Persia, including its agents' exhortations to the predominantly Shiite tribes to join the holy war against Britain and Russia, as well as on its plans for Afghanistan. Britain immediately protested to the Teheran government what it termed Germany's violation of Persian neutrality.[37] Wassmuss particularly concerned the British; the Government of India accused him "of trying to stir up the people of Arabistan to join in a Holy War against the British."[38]

The small Klein expedition included several German archaeologists—Preusser, Bachmann, and Lührs—with extensive knowledge of Mesopotamia. It formed both an example of and a major exception to Germany's policy toward Persia, which had become increasingly independent of the Turks. On one hand, Klein's attempt during his journey to Baghdad during January 1915 to persuade Shiite religious leaders in the holy cities of Karbala and Najaf to join with their rivals in the faith, the Sunnis, in the jihad against the Allies, produced little genuine Shiite-Sunni unity. Instead it served mainly to anger the Turks, who resented German interference in religious issues.[39] On the other hand, once in Baghdad Klein and his group joined the logistical unit of the local Ottoman army forces, commanded by Sulayman Askeri, fighting the Anglo-Indian army, the IEF D, advancing into southern Mesopotamia from the Persian Gulf. Askeri refused to allow Klein to carry out his principal assignment from the German General Staff: to enter southern Persia and, with the help of local, allegedly anti-British tribes, capture the lightly guarded British oilfields in the Karun River region and the refinery at Abadan.[40]

In place of Klein's group, two Turkish regiments, along with such pro-Turkish Arab tribes from southern Mesopotamia as the Bani Lam, crossed the border into Persian Arabistan, where they urged, with some success, local Arabs to join the jihad and attack the British from the east. On 5 February tribes incited by the Turks cut the British pipelines in several places. The oilfields, however, were never in serious danger, because the pro-British Persian tribe, the Bakhtiari, as well as Britain's ally, the Shaykh of Muhammarah, and a small Anglo-Indian force protected them. But following further Turkish and Arab agitation near Ahwaz and east of the Karun River, the British quickly sent reinforcements to the region. Simultaneously, Askeri's troops began an offensive against the British IEF D in southern Mesopotamia.[41]

In Berlin, Nadolny demanded that Germany participate in gaining control of the Karun oilfields by sending Klein's expedition there to assist the Ottoman attack.[42] Consequently, several members of the expedition, led by Lieutenant Hans Lührs, reached the Karun River and on 22 March and again in April dynamited the pipeline near Ahwaz. Groups of pro-Turkish Arabs, whom Lührs had contacted, also destroyed the line at several points.[43]

In the fighting along the Turkish-Persian border, however, British machine guns and artillery proved too much for the Arabs as well as for Askeri's Turkish forces. On 13 April Askeri committed suicide after the Anglo-Indian defeat of his troops near Basra.[44] Support for the jihad among local Arabs waned quickly, not only because of British predominance in firepower but also because of the extreme heat, lack of water, and British bribery of Arab shaykhs. The attacks on the Karun pipeline kept it from operating until June, when Britain concluded repairs.[45] The slow, but steady, advance of the IEF D, which had been reorganized into an army corps and reinforced with more troops, north along the Tigris River precluded further Ottoman and German operations on the Persian oilfields.[46]

Turkish-German Conflict over Persia

Despite the cooperation of the Klein expedition with the Ottomans, during the spring and summer of 1915 antagonism deepened between the Turks and Germans over policy in Persia. During the attack by troops of Rauf Bey into western Persia the invaders had plundered Persian and Kurdish villages and made known their intentions of annexing the region to Turkey. This produced bitter Persian protests and calls from Sarre, Kardorff, and Niedermayer for Rauf's removal.[47] When, however, Wangenheim and Zimmermann emphasized to Enver Pasha the harmful effects of Rauf's troops, the war minister rejected the criticism, refused to replace Rauf, and complained about the German advance into Persia.[48]

At the same time, however, the Germans pursued aggressively their policy in Persia, autonomous of the Porte, to persuade the government in Teheran to join the Central Powers. A Persian Committee, organized in Berlin by the foreign ministry, sent its members to Baghdad, Teheran, and Shiraz with propaganda demanding the liberation of Persia from British and Russian control.[49] In Kermanshah, in western Persia, the German agent, Max Otto Schuenemann, assisted by the gendarmerie's Swedish officers, incited local tribal leaders and townsmen against the British and Russians. The presence of Rauf Bey's troops nearby, moreover, forced the consuls of the Allied powers to flee the town.[50]

During April the German minister to Teheran, Prince Heinrich XXXI of Reuss, returned to the Persian capital along with the Austro-Hungarian minister, Count Logothetti. Reuss, accompanied also by Niedermayer and the remainder of his expedition, realized that Germany faced far more serious problems in persuading Persia to join the Reich in the war than Constantinople and Berlin had believed. He soon discovered that the British and Russians, thanks to Britain's capture of documents at the German consulate in Bushire, knew of the German strategy of persuading the Persian government to join the Central Powers.[51] In fact, at the end of April Britain and Russia moved quickly to blunt the threat. They posted new and more capable ministers to Teheran, and when the Persian prime minister and his government resigned, they pressured the young shah, Ahmad, an eighteen-year-old who had ascended the throne only in 1914, to name a new cabinet acceptable to the Entente.[52]

Reuss's return to Teheran did little to improve Germany's position in Persia. He failed to centralize leadership of Persian policy in his hands, and thus it remained distributed among a confusing array of German agents in the country, including Niedermayer, each pursuing his own, often contradictory, goals. Moreover, telegrams took from ten to fourteen days to travel between Teheran and Berlin. The transfer of money from Germany to Persia (done through banks in Amsterdam, Bombay, and Calcutta) often took even longer. This resulted in a lack of funds the agents required to pay for the support of Persian political and religious leaders and gendarmerie.

Furthermore, holy war propaganda had mobilized only a handful of Arabs and Kurds along the Turkish-Persian border, along with some south Persian tribes. Elsewhere the call for jihad had produced little response, falling victim to Persian fears of the Turks and to the Shiite-Sunni schism. Consequently, Kardorff had established contacts long before Reuss's arrival with the Persian nationalist party, the Democrats. This group in the Persian parliament in Teheran bitterly opposed Anglo-Russian domination of the country. The Democrats, however, remained cool to the holy war, fearing it might result in Turkish rule in Persia replacing that of the British and Russians. Kardorff, nevertheless, succeeded in establishing cooperation between Democratic officials and religious leaders.

As for the Persian tribes, they made a confusing picture. In the west, the Turkish invasion sabotaged pro-German sympathies; further south, where Wassmuss agitated among the traditionally anti-British Tangistanis, chances seemed greater that the tribes would join the Turkish-German side. But recruitment of the Persian tribes and gendarmerie for a military assault on the British and Russians in Persia suffered significantly from Germany's inability to ship weapons and money to its potential Persian allies. The Balkan supply route to Turkey remained closed to the Reich throughout much of 1915.[53]

At the beginning of May Reuss and his new military attaché, Count Georg von Kanitz, who had just arrived in Teheran, reported to Berlin that contrary to previous claims by Kardorff, Persia was not ripe for an anti-Allied revolt. Teheran, they declared, must remain neutral until the Persian gendarmerie could be increased in size to at least thirty thousand men and equipped with arms and munitions.[54] For these reasons, Wangenheim urged that the Germans in Persia move cautiously in raising a rebellion and that Berlin push the Porte to slow or halt Rauf Bey's advance into Persia so as to lessen Persian antagonism toward the Ottomans and their German allies. Nadolny agreed reluctantly, informing Kanitz that he should unleash the revolt only if the situation threatened to undermine its prospects for success.[55]

During June and July the position of the Germans in both Persia and Mesopotamia became even more problematical. Italy's entry into the war on the side of the Allies impressed the Teheran government. Rauf Bey's forces, as they plundered western Persia, advancing as far as Karind, threatened to sabotage nearly every German activity in Persia.[56]

Turkish behavior toward Persia also inflamed the hatred for the Ottomans among the Shiite religious leaders in the Mesopotamian holy cities of Karbala and Najaf. Violent anti-Turkish outbursts occurred in both places. Furthermore, setbacks suffered by Turkish troops in southern Mesopotamia, when an enlarged Anglo-Indian army (which included the former IEF D, now reorganized into an army corps) occupied Amara on 3 June and Nasirya on 24 July, damaged efforts by Klein and other Germans to recruit Arab support in the region against Britain.

Klein complained to Constantinople that because of a lack of money to pay Mesopotamian Arabs, only one shaykh, Ajaimi, supported the Turks and Germans. The Young Turks, he said, opposed using Germans to negotiate with the Arabs, fearing that Germany wished to seize Mesopotamia for its own economic purposes.[57] Finally on 4 July, Enver Pasha, who had stubbornly refused demands from Wangenheim and the German foreign ministry that the Porte remove Rauf Bey, informed Humann that he had prohibited Rauf to make further attacks.[58]

The Turkish incursions into Persia also threatened to undermine negotiations between Reuss and the Persian government for a loan from Germany to form and equip an army. During the summer a crisis had arisen in the Teheran government: a strong movement emerged under the leadership of the Democratic party opposing the Anglo-Russian domination of Persia and looking to the possibility of an alliance with the Central Powers. These elements seemed impressed with the success of the German and Austro-Hungarian armies in pushing the Russians eastward into Polish Russia and progressively out of Galicia. On 15 June the German foreign ministry, which hoped Persia would end its neutrality by joining the Central Powers, approved the loan and urged Reuss to continue the negotiations. Shortly thereafter the Persian government pushed for a formal alliance with Germany. But the continuing inability of the Reich to ship large amounts of money to Persia, as well as the Turkish attacks in western Persia, led the ministry to conclude that an alliance was premature.[59]

Meanwhile the German expeditions to Afghanistan—led by Niedermayer and Hentig-Pratap—advanced slowly across Persia. The Hentig-Pratap mission had crossed into Persia and on 15 June joined Niedermayer in Teheran. Niedermayer, who had arrived in the Persian capital with Reuss, remained there, spreading pro-German propaganda and attempting to organize a rebellion of Persians against British and Russian domination. Reuss quarreled with Niedermayer over which of them controlled Niedermayer's expedition members who had gone to various Persian cities to establish supply bases and win pro-German sympathy among the local populations.[60] Hentig and Niedermayer also argued about which of them should lead the combined expeditions into Afghanistan.

Despite this myriad of conflicts, which delayed the expeditions even further, Niedermayer and Hentig left Teheran at the end of June.[61] Both had agreed on one aspect of their journey: that the presence of Russian troops in northern Persia and British forces in the south dictated that the German advance should go through the central part of the country. They moved separately with their small caravans through Isfahan, where the bulk of Niedermayer's expedition remained behind. Then they advanced eastward across the Dasht-i-Kavir, the vast, roadless, and waterless salt desert of central Persia. Each caravan endured torturous travel through what Niedermayer called "Iran's hell," plagued by severe heat, thirst, dysentery, and malaria; the missions joined together in Tabas and on 1 August reached Birjand, roughly a hundred miles from the Afghan border.

The British and Russians had received reports of the approaching expeditions, and because the Government of India could spare few troops for intercepting them, the Russians established a cordon of soldiers along the east Persian border. But the expeditions executed several maneuvers to deceive the Allied forces, and both crossed the frontier on 19 August.[62] Five days later they arrived in Herat, from where they moved on to Kabul, the Afghan capital, reaching it on 1 October.[63]

Revolution or Negotiation?

While the expeditions moved across Persia into Afghanistan, German agents in several Persian cities continued to incite local populations against the British and Russians. Reuss objected to their activities, fearing they would undermine his negotiations with the Persian government, aimed at persuading the latter to abandon its neutrality and join the Central Powers.[64] The minister's disapproval went unheeded. In Kermanshah, the main German supply base in western Persia, Schuenemann prevented the return of the Anglo-Russian consuls to the city: as the consuls and their escorts neared the town limits, he led pro-German tribes in an armed attack that forced them to retreat.

Reuss opposed the assault on the consuls, fearing it would provide the Russians with a pretext for pushing their troops southward to Kermanshah, thereby threatening the German supply lines into Persia. His opposition proved justified. The British and Russians, capitalizing on local Persian animosity toward the Turks, quickly increased their activities in western Persia. Britain delivered more weapons and money to local tribal leaders and established closer relations to the Persian governor of the western region called Pusht-i-Kuh. The Russians elicited the support of the large landowners of the area.[65]

In Isfahan, the key base of operations for the Afghan expeditions of Niedermayer and Hentig, Seiler had won over to the German side local religious leaders, gendarmerie, the Democratic party, and surrounding tribes, including the anti-British Qashgais and even some of the traditionally pro-British Bakhtiaris. Using promises of German money and weapons, he urged the tribes, which feuded with one another, to unite and join a revolt of southern Persia against the British. Also, the construction of a German telegraph station outside Isfahan enabled Seiler to receive war news, propaganda, and diplomatic messages. In September he arranged an assassination attempt upon T. G. Grahame, the British consul in Isfahan, which prompted both the British and Russian colonies to flee the city.[66] On 1 October the German agent received orders from Niedermayer in Kabul to advance immediately into Afghanistan with the remainder of Niedermayer's expedition.

The Germans had less success in Kerman, a traditionally British stronghold nearly two hundred miles south of Isfahan. There the attempts of Zugmayer and Griesinger to incite anti-British feelings among the inhabitants and surrounding tribes generally failed.[67] In contrast, the German activities against the British in southwestern Persia, at Shiraz and Bushire, proved more successful. Wassmuss moved among the south Persian tribes like a native, playing particularly on the anti-British resentments of the large south-Persian tribe, the Tangistani.[68] During 11–12 July several tribes attacked the small British Indian garrison at Bushire, resulting in numerous casualties. However, the attackers lacked sufficient armaments, munitions, and money; Wassmuss, in numerous telegrams to Reuss, pleaded unsuccessfully for more of each. He intended for the assaults on Bushire to force Britain to send more troops to the region, thereby violating Persian neutrality even more conspicuously and, ideally, persuading the Teheran government to enter the war on Germany's side.[69] But Reuss criticized Wassmuss's activities, arguing that they would lead the Persian government to accuse the Germans of an equal violation of neutrality. As the conflict deepened between the two, the minister forced Wassmuss to relinquish his post as consul in Shiraz; in his place Reuss appointed Wassmuss's friend Kurt Wustrow.

Nevertheless, Wassmuss continued his campaign to arouse the tribes against Britain. In response the British occupied Bushire with five hundred more Anglo-Indian cavalrymen on 8 August and appointed a new and even more pro-British Persian governor.[70] Five days later British ships bombarded the headquarters of the hostile Tangistani tribal leader, Rais Ali, at Dilbar; on 3 and 9 September the Anglo-Indians repulsed with moderate casualties several Tangistani raids, during which Rais Ali was killed, after which they used pro-British tribes to scatter the enemy into the hinterland. At Shiraz Wustrow exploited the British occupation of Bushire to kindle a local movement hostile to the British. Also local tribal leaders murdered the British vice consul (a Persian) in Shiraz.[71]

During the fall Germany's fortunes in Teheran seemed to peak. In August and September German-Persian discussions reached an advanced stage; the Persian government asked for a treaty by which Germany would provide a large loan and guarantee Persian integrity and independence. Reports of the landing of Russian troops at Enzeli on the Caspian Sea and their movement south toward Kazvin, roughly a hundred miles from Teheran, led Reuss to push Berlin to accept the Persian conditions immediately.

But for reasons still unknown, Reuss's telegram outlining the Persian offer reached the German foreign ministry only on 9 October 1915, a month after the minister had sent it. The ministry, Bethmann Hollweg, and Wilhelm II quickly agreed to the Persian terms; they seemed persuaded that Persia would soon conclude the agreement. The optimism in Berlin resulted from the apparently impending defeat of British and imperial forces at Gallipoli as well as from increasing signs that Germany's route for money and armaments through the Balkans to Turkey and Persia would soon open. Indeed, during October Bulgaria entered the war on the side of the Central Powers, whose armies soon defeated Serbia.[72]

Berlin was further encouraged by the arrival of news that Niedermayer and Hentig had reached Afghanistan and that the Porte had made concessions to Germany regarding Persia. The possibility of a German-Persian treaty led the Ottomans to remove Rauf Bey from his military post and halt, at least momentarily, Turkish opposition in Persia to German activities there. Also, at the urging of the German

General Staff as well as of Nadolny and Otto von Lossow (the Reich's new military attaché in Constantinople), Enver Pasha appointed the legendary and aging German field marshal Colmar von der Goltz supreme commander of a newly formed Ottoman Sixth Army. It included both Turkish and German troops and operated in Mesopotamia and Persia. Von der Goltz viewed it as his principal objective to apply military pressure on India, thereby diverting ever more British troops from the main theater of war in Europe to faraway imperial territory.[73]

The Fall Crises in Teheran and Kabul

On October 27, when Reuss finally informed the Persian minister-president, Mustaufi ul-Mamalik, of Germany's agreement to the Persian demands, the Persian leader delayed concluding the pact, raising the amount of Persia's financial requests. He was also under pressure from the British and Russians to stop his negotiations with the Reich or face punitive action. To stiffen the Allied threat, the Russians on 7 November sent a military detachment from Kazvin toward Teheran and landed more troops at Enzeli.

Thus the Persian government suddenly found itself in a delicate situation. The Russians threatened Teheran militarily, no money or armaments had arrived for the Persians from Germany, and the British had advanced into Mesopotamia to within thirty miles of Baghdad, threatening to cut Persia off from future German supplies sent through Turkey. Moreover, matters worsened with von der Goltz's appointment as commander of the Sixth Army. He accepted the claims of the German military attaché, Kanitz, that much of Persia was ready for rebellion against the Anglo-Russians and ignored Reuss's warnings regarding such a revolt.

Consequently, von der Goltz failed during October and November to stop Kanitz. In mid-August the latter had reported to the German foreign ministry from Baghdad "that the hour of decision for Persia approaches."[74] But Kanitz, who feared the Russians would soon attack Kermanshah, the German stronghold in western Persia, moved prematurely. He had not only neglected to expand and pay the center-piece of German military plans, the Persian gendarmerie, thus failing to secure its loyalty, but placed too much hope in the tribes of western and southern Persia attacking the Anglo-Russian forces. When he could not fulfil his generous promises to the tribal leaders, namely that Germany would supply them with money and armaments, the expected rebellion fizzled.[75]

In fact, money filtered by the Anglo-Russians to the tribes and gendarmerie led some of the latter to attack the Germans and their supporters in Kermanshah. Repeated requests to Berlin for more money—from Kanitz, who had returned to Teheran, and from Sarre, Klein, and Lossow—produced little response.[76] Small shipments of money arrived in Baghdad in October. Also, the foreign ministry appropriated a million gold marks for Kanitz's bizarre, and subsequently unsuccessful, plan to free fifty thousand Austro-Hungarian prisoners of war in neighboring Russian Turkestan, intending to use them in the revolt.[77]

The shah, in view of the advance of Russian troops on Teheran, refused on 12 November to sign a treaty with Germany. Since Kanitz had planned to use the treaty to signal the tribes to revolt, he quickly concluded that the Persian government did not possess the courage to resist the Anglo-Russians. In opposition to Reuss, who advised that Germany preserve Persian neutrality at all costs, Kanitz attempted two nights later to ignite a revolution in the capital among the nationalists and local Persian Cossack units. These comprised Russian-led troops that served as a personal force of the shah. Only a few of the Cossacks rebelled, and Allied officials, with Russian troops near the city, quickly gained the upper hand. On 15 November Mustaufi ul-Mamalik's government, the nationalist and Democratic members of the Persian parliament, and diplomats of the Central Powers (including Reuss) fled Teheran south to Qum, having, they thought, convinced the young shah to join them. At the last moment, however, the Anglo-Russian ministers, mainly with the help of Farman Farma, the pro-British Persian interior minister, persuaded the shah to remain in the capital.[78]

These events quickly undermined Germany's position in Persia. During the ensuing days Kanitz, with a force composed of a Turkish battalion, some gendarmerie, and tribal levies of west Persian Kurds and Lurs, attacked the much-better-armed Russians near

Kermanshah. The tribesmen fought poorly, often deserting the cause, and the attack misfired; Kanitz never realized his hope of awakening nationalist feelings among the tribes and stirring them to common action and courageous fighting. In a moment of panic he called for help from Turkish troops, but they could not be spared from Mesopotamia. Also, although a shipment of German money had arrived, he still had received no armaments and munitions.[79] Apparently realizing the failure of his policy, Kanitz disappeared and committed suicide.

Von der Goltz and the Turkish Sixth Army, which had halted the Anglo-Indian forces at Ctesiphon and Kut al-Amara in southern Mesopotamia, could also spare no troops. German agents including Schuenemann, Sarre, and Klein soon left Kermanshah for the Turkish border. Reuss, for his part, never returned to Teheran, despite the foreign ministry's order that he do so. His efforts in Qum to form a Persian government-in-exile among the nationalists and democrats foundered, and Berlin soon placed him on sick leave and ordered him home. At the end of December the Anglo-Russians persuaded the shah to form in Teheran a new and openly pro-Allied government led by Farman Farma as prime minister, and to name a new commander of the gendarmerie.[80]

Elsewhere, too, the German campaign in Persia faltered. In Shiraz during 9–10 November 1915 the consul, Wustrow, on orders from the beleaguered Reuss in Teheran, used local gendarmerie to occupy the British consulate and seize its chief officer, Major W. F. T. O'Connor. But soon news reached Shiraz of the unsuccessful German efforts to persuade the shah to join Germany. This encouraged the acting Persian governor, Qawam-ul-Mulk, a powerful local tribal leader assisted by the British, to attempt to arrest Wustrow. Also, the German consul and Wassmuss disagreed on strategy. Wustrow left for western Persia, ostensibly to ask the German agents there for more money and weapons; he never returned, and German influence in Shiraz evaporated quickly.[81]

In Isfahan, another German stronghold, Seiler, responding to Niedermayer's order, left for Afghanistan on 24 November. He took with him the remainder of Niedermayer's expedition and took up the difficult task of breaking through the armed Anglo-Russian cordon that stretched along the Persian-Afghan border. But when Seiler's group pushed eastward through the desert, the Dasht-i-Lut, it fell victim to robbers and was forced to retreat to Kerman.[82]

The tide in Persia had clearly turned in favor of the British and Russians. Von der Goltz's appointment and his subsequent visit to Persia in January 1916 did nothing to halt the Russians' advance deep into western Persia, or their occupation of Kermanshah, Isfahan, and Qum. This, as well as the Anglo-Russian triumph in Teheran, had isolated the German agents in eastern and southern Persia from their western supply and communications bases.[83]

In Shiraz too the German position had crumbled. Local Persian governors, gendarmerie, and tribal leaders who had once supported the Germans now joined the British, whose consuls and other officials returned to their posts throughout the region. Much later, on 21 April 1916, when Seiler and the remnants of his ravaged caravan staggered into Shiraz, unaware that the British had gained control of the city, they were arrested and imprisoned. A few weeks later, the British captured Zugmayer and Griesinger, who had been in Persian Baluchistan organizing anti-British revolts among local tribes, as they retreated northwest toward Shiraz to join Seiler.[84]

Of the Germans who had operated in southern Persia, only Wassmuss (whom a postwar legend labeled the "German Lawrence") remained free. But with the Russian occupation of Isfahan, by which the Reich lost its main supply base and telegraph station, Wassmuss found himself completely cut off from further German assistance. He continued, nevertheless, to move and agitate among the Tangistani tribes, using them to close the road between Shiraz and Bushire to British military traffic, and avoiding capture by the Anglo-Indian police force created in January 1916. Only in 1918, following the armistice, did the British apprehend him.[85]

Despite their collapse in Persia the Germans persisted throughout the final months of 1915, placing their hopes for a massive revolution east of Turkey on the Niedermayer and Hentig missions. They had arrived in October in Kabul. During their first audience Habibullah, the amir of Afghanistan, seemed uneasy toward his guests and showed little enthusiasm either for joining the jihad proclaimed by Turkey and attacking India or for establishing diplomatic relations with

Germany.[86] The Government of India had informed the amir of their impending visit. Delhi also asked him to contradict the rumors, then spreading in his country, that the Germans formed the vanguard of a Turkish-German army advancing eastward.[87]

Such stories had caused considerable unrest in the North-West Frontier province of India; the local British commissioner viewed the German expeditions as so potentially dangerous that he doubled the financial subsidies to the local tribes, to encourage them not to be influenced by enemy propaganda. Also, on the Afghan side of the border, the British raised the allowances they paid tribes and made strenuous attempts to bribe influential religious leaders. Unbeknownst to the Germans, Habibullah had responded to the Government of India that he would disarm the Germans, imprison them until the end of the war, and remain neutral.[88] A further advantage for the British occurred when they intercepted messages to Teheran from Niedermayer and Hentig in Kabul, one that revealed the Germans' lack of success with Habibullah. The amir had showed his guests friendliness and allowed them freedom of movement, even discussed a German-Persian alliance with Hentig, but all this was mainly designed to encourage them to remain in the city until December.

Yet just as the Germans decided to abandon their mission and return home, the amir's brother, Nasrullah, arranged an agreement between the amir and his visitors. Niedermayer mistakenly believed that Nasrullah, who belonged to a militant anti-British faction at court, had more influence in the Kabul government than the amir did. On 24 January 1916 Habibullah and the Germans signed the draft of a treaty that stipulated Afghanistan's entry into the war against Britain. In return, the draft provided a guarantee from Germany of Afghan freedom and of deliveries from the Reich of substantial money, weapons, and munitions.[89]

But poor communications between Kabul and Berlin helped doom the agreement. Kabul had no telegraph line connecting it with Persia, and a messenger took nearly three months to reach Teheran, from where the draft treaty arrived in Constantinople in July. Meanwhile the German and Turkish position in Persia had largely collapsed. Habibullah, whatever agreements he may have made with Hentig and Niedermayer, now apparently had no intention of entering the war;

he did little more than allow Niedermayer to help increase the efficiency of the Afghan army's arsenal, various factories, and troop formations.

The amir cleverly used the Germans as a counterweight to the British, whose viceroy in India had since long before the war pressured Afghanistan to subordinate itself to India. Further, the Afghan ruler apparently wished to wait and see which side won the war, in the hope that Afghanistan would be represented at the peace conference and recognized as a sovereign state.[90] In May 1916 Niedermayer and Hentig, frustrated by their lack of progress with the amir, finally left Afghanistan. The former returned to Germany through Russian Turkestan and Persia, the latter through China and the United States.[91] As for the Indian revolutionaries accompanying the German mission, Pratap and Barkatullah, they remained behind in Kabul and intrigued unsuccessfully against the British in India.[92]

Although the German expeditions to Kabul achieved little tangible result, their presence nevertheless helped prompt the Anglo-Russians in Persia to take substantial military countermeasures to isolate the Germans in Afghanistan. In the spring of 1915 the two allies divided among themselves the central zone in Persia that had remained neutral after their convention of 1907. Moreover, the Russians, whose troops had advanced into western Persia, and the British Indian government increased the size of their respective military forces in the country, each by several thousand men.[93]

Libya: The Sanussis' Attack on British Positions

The British found themselves on the defensive during 1915 in North Africa, where a German and Turkish campaign incited Muslims against British rule in Egypt. In Libya, where the Italians were involved in a steady guerrilla war with Bedouins who opposed Italy's extension of its colonial rule, German and Turkish activities continued to damage relations between Berlin and Rome. Most Bedouins in Cyrenaica, the eastern part of the country along the Mediterranean coast, as well as tribesmen in the western desert of Egypt and in the Sudan were followers of a Muslim religious sect led by a nomadic chief, the Sayyid Ahmad al-Sharif (Shaykh al-Sanussi).

Since August 1914 the German agent, Otto Mannesmann, had attempted to contact the Shaykh al-Sanussi from Tripoli; by February 1915, numerous Turkish emissaries, among them Sulayman al-Barani, Enver Pasha's brother Nuri, and a Baghdadi Arab, Jaafir Bey al-Askari, had arrived at the shaykh's camp, then located on the coast of Cyrenaica. Both the Germans and Turks sought to persuade the Sayyid Ahmad to join the sultan-caliph's holy war against Britain by attacking western Egypt.[94] The Turks particularly coveted the shaykh's assistance; his prestige, and that of his religious order, extended beyond Cyrenaica to Sanussi communities in Egypt, the Sudan, Arabia, and other parts of the Islamic world. Moreover, his support for the Turks could offset the Sharif of Mecca's lukewarm, if not disaffected, attitude toward the Porte.

But initially the Shaykh al-Sanussi showed dislike for the arriving Turks, imprisoning al-Barani and treating Nuri Pasha poorly. At the beginning of 1915 the shaykh had encamped at Masaad, a few kilometers from al-Sallum, a British coastal outpost on the poorly defined Libyan-Egyptian border. There thousands of tribesmen of the Aulad Ali, a people of the western Egyptian desert who had not previously seen the Muslim leader, visited him and paid their respects; he also collected food and supplies from the Aulad Ali—but often, the British observed, by force. Italian military pressure from Tripolitania, the western portion of Libya, had pushed the shaykh and his Bedouins eastward, farther from the Italians and closer to the protection of the Egyptian frontier.

The idea persisted among the Italians, despite assurances from both Germany and Turkey, that the Turkish agents wished only to raise the Bedouins against Britain, and that the agitation would also incite the tribesmen further against Italy. Rome, consequently, demanded that Berlin recall Mannesmann from Tripoli. But only at the end of March 1915 did he return, briefly, to Germany, following expressions of outrage from the Italian government and press at the confiscation of a cargo of German arms hidden in beer barrels aboard a ship in Venice, a shipment arranged for by Mannesmann and destined for Tripoli.[95] On orders from Nadolny and Wesendonk, Mannesmann soon returned via Crete to Libya, disguised as a salesman. He carried a promise to the Shaykh al-Sanussi that Germany would support the expansion of the chief's rule southward into French-owned Chad and Wadai, and into the Sudan.[96]

Meanwhile, during the spring of 1915, Italy's anger at the German and Turkish activities mounted, as the Sanussis attacked and routed Italian troops in the Syrte Desert, an inhospitable area along the coast of the Gulf of Sidra. The defeat marked the end of any semblance of Italian control over the Libyan hinterland. It also provided German and Turkish vessels, including submarines operating from Austrian naval bases at Cattaro and Pola in the Adriatic Sea, a place to land arms and money for the Bedouins.[97] A few weeks later, Italy entered the world war on the Allied side.

The Italians joined the British despite Britain's steady refusal throughout most of 1915 to assist Rome against the Sanussis. McMahon, the British High Commissioner in Cairo, urged against joining with the Italians in the Sanussi question. Above all, he emphasized to Grey, "it must be remembered that hostilities undertaken against [Shaykh al-Sanussi] by Great Britain would probably have far reaching effects on Moslem feeling, not only in Egypt and the Sudan but in Arabia and possibly even in India."[98]

The Foreign Office directed McMahon to do everything possible to cooperate with the Italians, particularly if Italy joined the Allies, but Cairo mistrusted the Italians. Maxwell suggested to Kitchener that Italy sought to assist its cause by encouraging hostilities between the Sanussis and British.[99] Not even Italian reports of German and Turkish arms shipments arriving for the Sanussis by boat on the coast of Cyrenaica and western Egypt could persuade Britain to change its policy. On 3 June McMahon advised the Foreign Office not to press the Shaykh al-Sanussi to conclude peace with Italy "until an issue is reached at the Dardanelles."[100]

In part McMahon's policy rested on amicable negotiations between Cairo and the shaykh, conducted for the British by Major L. V. Royle and Lieutenant-Colonel C. L. Snow, both Egyptian coast guard officers at al-Sallum.[101] Their intimate acquaintance with the local Bedouins enabled them to prevent, in large measure, enemy-inspired intrigues in Egypt and simultaneously to preserve the respect of the Shaykh al-Sanussi for British authority in the region.

As for the Germans, Mannesmann and a fellow spy, Baron Otto von Gumppenberg, who had previously worked in Egypt, attempted to smuggle through Crete and nearby islands small shipments of arms to the coast of Cyrenaica.[102] The first cargoes of weapons and money arrived by German submarine.[103] But Gumppenberg, traveling on a forged American passport to al-Sallum, near the Shaykh al-Sanussi's headquarters, ran afoul of Enver Pasha's brother, Nuri.[104] Nuri's large payments of money to the shaykh assisted the chief in acquiring food and supplies for his hungry people, and they had increased the Turkish officer's prestige with him. Also the Sayyid Ahmad relied on Nuri and the other Turkish officers to assist him in training his motley Bedouin army. The Young Turks still viewed Libya as a Turkish land, and although they needed German naval and other military assistance to send supplies to the Sanussis, they resented German interference with Turkish policy there.[105] In a meeting with Humann on 4 July Enver Pasha denounced Gumppenberg, who had served in 1912 with Enver in the Libyan war, for undermining Nuri's importance with the Shaykh al-Sanussi and for allowing the latter to play off Gumppenberg and Nuri against one another by raising his demands to them.[106]

But the British captured Gumppenberg on 11 July, as he left the Libyan coast on an Oriental schooner that had landed more arms and Turkish officers at al-Sallum. The Germans, instead of acceding to Enver's wishes, transferred to Mannesmann their smuggling activities in Cyrenaica and their contacts with the Shaykh al-Sanussi. Mannesmann, who established his headquarters at Dfna, a small coastal town west of al-Sallum, also argued with Nuri Pasha and in dispatches to Berlin disparaged the Turkish influence on the Sayyid Ahmad al-Sanussi. The Young Turks, for their part, apparently tried to flatter the shaykh into attacking Egypt; they nominated him for governor of Tripolitania and its dependent regions. Still the shaykh hesitated to open hostilities and ordered his Bedouins not to shoot at British ships patrolling the coast.[107]

On 15 August Mannesmann attempted to force the shaykh's hand. The German agent and several Arabs lured the commander of a British submarine into boarding a small boat and approaching the shore near al-Sallum. They then shot at the commander, resulting in an exchange of gunfire with the submarine that killed a British sailor and several Arabs. Mannesmann termed the affair an "accident," but when the Sayyid Ahmad, who apologized to the British, refused to arrest the German and turn him over to Britain, Mannesmann and Nuri set forth to manufacture a new incident.[108] A few weeks later Mannesmann led a force of Bedouins in attacking an Italian warship that had attempted without success to land troops west of al-Sallum. Mannesmann's actions, reports of which arrived in Berlin weeks after they occurred, seemed to improve his relations with Nuri and the Turkish officers. They also pushed the Sayyid Ahmad increasingly toward a more anti-British stance. Mannesmann impressed the shaykh with stories of Germany's power and military successes in Europe; such accounts, as well as the shaykh's experiences in fighting the incompetent and dilatory Italian colonial army, may have misled him into believing that war with the British would be similarly easy.[109]

Furthermore, the Sayyid Ahmad was an old-fashioned and headstrong Muslim; he thus found it difficult to refuse the Ottoman sultan-caliph's instructions to attack in western Egypt. Militarily, from the Porte's view such an attack would ease Britain's pressure on the Turkish forces in Palestine and the Sinai region, which threatened the Suez Canal. The sayyid dispatched letters to Muslim leaders in India and Arabia urging them to join the jihad against the infidels and announcing that he was the caliph's representative in North Africa.[110]

Moreover, he called the Germans his "brothers," leading Mannesmann, who had moved by October to the shaykh's camp at Masaad, to conclude that he would attack Egypt immediately once Germany sent more arms and money. The sayyid even emphasized the request in three letters he dispatched via Constantinople to the German emperor. In addition, the shaykh declared that he had contacted Ali Dinar, the sultan of Darfur, a province in western Sudan still not effectively under Anglo-Egyptian rule; the sultan had supposedly agreed to attack the British simultaneously with the Sanussis' assault on Egypt.[111]

Meanwhile, the British and Italians had observed the increasingly threatening attitude of the Sanussis. Not only did the British confirm Mannesmann's presence at the Shaykh al-Sanussi's camp, but also British intelligence accidentally discovered the letters dispatched by the shaykh to Muslim officials in Arabia and India.[112]

Despite the situation, Britain continued to resist pressure from Italy to help force the shaykh to conclude peace with Italy. The Foreign Office informed the Italian government on 29 September that "the general situation in the Dardanelles is for the moment exercising an effect in Egypt and North Africa generally which renders it most hazardous" for Britain "to take any action which tends to drive [the] Senoussi into open hostility."[113] Instead, at the suggestion of the British agent Snow and with Italian approval, Cairo paid the Shaykh al-Sanussi money to remove the Turkish officers from his camp and to avoid an open rupture.[114]

During the first week of November, however, German submarines off the coast of Cyrenaica sank a British steamer and transport ship, whose crews were landed at Port Sulayman and were imprisoned by the Sanussis. The activity of the submarines apparently provided the final encouragement for the Sayyid Ahmad to attack the British. Between 17 and 19 November small numbers of his troops shelled British outposts near al-Sallum and Sidi al-Barani, manned by only 124 British and Egyptian troops; during the skirmishes, 135 natives of the Egyptian coast guard deserted to the Sanussis. Almost simultaneously, the shaykh demanded substantially more money from the British and agreed in return only to remove Mannesmann from his camp.[115]

Immediately the British withdrew their western Egyptian frontier posts to Mersa Matruh, roughly 120 miles further east, and reinforced them with two thousand motorized and relatively well-armed Australian, Indian, New Zealand, Egyptian, and British troops; the Sanussis gathered 2,500 warriors south and west of Matruh. The British counterattacked during 11–13 and 25 December; amid the fighting, the British suffered numerous casualties, which included the death of the agent Snow. Many more Bedouins were killed, however, forcing most of those who remained to flee their encampments.[116]

During the fighting a German submarine carrying Edgar Pröbster, a former consular official in Morocco who spoke fluent Arabic, landed at Port Sulayman a large supply of gold marks, military decorations, and arms for the Shaykh al-Sanussi.[117] The Germans intended Pröbster's visit to Cyrenaica to impress on the Sayyid Ahmad Germany's loyalty to him. After meeting with Nuri Pasha and the shaykh on 19 December, the German emissary proceeded back to Port Sulayman, where he remained until his return to Europe, again by submarine, in February 1916.

Pröbster also carried orders from Nadolny to Mannesmann, directing the latter to leave the Sanussi camp, move west across Libya, and join German agents in Tunisia, Algeria, and Morocco in attempting to raise local Berber and Arab tribes against the French.[118] But the main reason for the removal of Mannesmann was Enver Pasha's repeated accusations that the German's presence among the Sanussis undermined the influence of Nuri Pasha and the Turks. Both Falkenhayn, the chief of staff of the German high command, and Zimmermann tried unsuccessfully to allay Enver's mistrust of German political ambitions in Libya and Egypt, goals that, the war minister believed, conflicted with Turkey's goal of reacquiring control over both lands. Nor did Enver accept the German foreign ministry's claim that Germany's alleged popularity among the Arabs in Libya and elsewhere provided an advantage for the Porte by helping lessen Arab hostility toward the Turks.[119]

During the hostilities, the British remained in contact with the Shaykh al-Sanussi through Bedouin messengers, who reported to Cairo Mannesmann's departure westward for Tunisia.[120] By the end of December the British military operations around Mersa Matruh had left many of the Sayyid Ahmad's forces retreating westward in confusion and had caused severe damage to the prestige of their leader. For the British, it only remained to clinch their success; had their cavalry intercepted the main body of the enemy on 25 December, as was to happen a month later, the campaign might have ended there, with the Sanussis' defeat.

7

A Sense of Crisis on Both Sides, Fall 1915

During the fall of 1915 a feeling of urgency regarding the war in the Middle East gripped both British and German leaders. One aspect of the crisis facing Britain—at the Dardanelles, in Mesopotamia, and from the wide-ranging "war by revolution" waged by the Germans and Turks, whose pan-Islamism played on the deeply implanted British fears for the safety of India and Egypt—would have a most important bearing on the situation in the region. The belief of key British leaders that Britain stood at a critical point in the war in the Middle East strengthened an idea that had mushroomed with the start of the Dardanelles campaign. This was the view that Britain could undermine Germany's thrust through Turkey into the Middle East as well as make substantial strategic and territorial gains in the region by destroying and then partitioning the Turkish empire among the Allies and Arabs.

Britain Moves Closer to the Arabs

Even before the war this idea had existed among British leaders like Kitchener and Grey, who worried about the steadily expanding German influence in Turkey.[1] The course of the war had confirmed them in the thought that the Ottoman Empire must not survive in its present form. But in 1915 Britain had to take into account its European allies' interests in the Middle East as well as its own. In March, London and Paris had concluded the Constantinople Agreement with Russia; it promised the Black Sea straits and the Turkish capital to the Russians in the event of an Allied victory. The crucial step, however, toward breaking up the Ottoman Empire occurred on 24 October 1915. The British government, acting through McMahon, the High Commissioner in Egypt, agreed in a letter to Husayn ibn Ali, the Sharif of Mecca, to his demand that Britain support Arab independence from the Turks in Arabia, Mesopotamia, and much of Syria.

By this agreement and in subsequent exchanges of messages, Cairo and London encouraged Husayn to raise an Arab revolt against the Turks, a matter that Kitchener and the sharif's son, Abdullah, had discussed during the fall of 1914.[2] Husayn, with his unique position in the Islamic world as guardian of the holy places, and his relative independence, was not only the obvious person to lead an Arab rebellion but also the one who could best counter the effect of the sultan-caliph's call to jihad.

The details of what has come to be known as the Husayn-McMahon correspondence, which resulted in an Anglo-Arab alliance later marred by great controversy, need not be recounted here. Nonetheless, the immediate factors producing that October a sudden British interest in the alliance with the sharif are of relevance for this study. Despite the almost universal rejection by Muslims of the holy war proclaimed by the sultan-caliph, and despite British intelligence reports stretching back to the spring illustrating the refusal of Arabs in Arabia and Mesopotamia to support the Turks, British leaders still seemed haunted by the prospect of a jihad assisted by Germany.[3]

This helps to explain the response of the British to a visit on 11 October by Muhammad Sharif al-Faruqi, an Arab officer in the Turkish army who had deserted from the Turkish forces at Gallipoli, to Colonel Gilbert Clayton, the head of British intelligence in Cairo. Al-Faruqi claimed to represent a secret Arab military and nationalist society (al-Ahd) in Syria and Mesopotamia, a group that was allied to the Sharif of Mecca and wished to collaborate with the British in return for Arab independence. Clayton believed al-Faruqi, although in fact he was no spokesman for al-Ahd. The apparent emissary asserted (erroneously) that both the Turks and Germans intended to grant the Arabs their territorial demands but that if Britain supported Arab autonomy along the territorial lines laid out by the Sharif of Mecca, the anti-Turk revolt would begin at once. The interview with al-Faruqi set off a panic, extending from Cairo's leaders up to Kitchener in the War Office, that the Arabs might go over to the enemy, thereby jeopardizing Egypt. British leaders also convinced themselves that a massive anti-Turk Arab movement existed in the Turkish empire, centered in Syria but led by the Sharif of Mecca. No one in Cairo or London realized that the alliance between the Syrian nationalists and sharif was in fact poorly coordinated and militarily nonexistent.

Clayton persuaded the Foreign Office to meet the Arab demands, which McMahon did, with few exceptions, only twelve days later. Scholars have speculated extensively about why al-Faruqi succeeded in duping Clayton and most of his colleagues in Cairo. Some argue that Cairo, influenced by Sir Ian Hamilton, the British commander at Gallipoli, believed an Arab rebellion would enable Britain to save its beleaguered armies on the peninsula. Other writers believe that Cairo was worried that Bulgaria's joining the Central Powers' attack on Serbia on 11 October might endanger the Allied situation at Gallipoli.[4] Still others emphasize that Cairo viewed al-Faruqi and his fellow military officers as unwitting instruments, much less interested in an Arab nation than in a pan-Arab union presided over by an Arab caliph, which Britain could utilize to preserve and even increase its power and influence in the Middle East.[5] But the evidence also suggests that the panic of officials in both Cairo and London resulted in large part from their fear of the German and Turkish campaign to unite the world of Islam in a holy war against the Allies. Since June 1915, for the specific purpose of countering German jihad propaganda in the Arabian Peninsula, Cairo had distributed along the Hijaz coast a leaflet declaring that Britain would neither annex any land in Arabia nor allow any other power to do so.[6]

In October the concerns of the British also involved what they thought were their enemies' military plans against Egypt. Maxwell, the commander of British forces in Egypt, along with Kitchener and the prime minister, Herbert Henry Asquith, expected a second attack by the Germans and Turks on the Suez Canal. For Maxwell an alliance with the Arabs was a necessity, in part because, as he told the War Office on 12 October, he felt that "the Arab party will go over to the enemy." Three days later, he advised Kitchener that "a satisfactory settlement of the Arab question would go far to make a serious invasion of Egypt impossible."[7] The discussion focused on whether

Britain should establish in Egypt its major line of defense or adopt a tactic suggested previously by Kitchener of launching an offensive against the Turks in Syria at Alexandretta. Kitchener and Maxwell emphasized to Asquith "the German and Turkish menace in the East" and opposed withdrawing to a heavily fortified position at the Suez Canal. Such a strategy, Kitchener argued, when combined with the evacuation of Gallipoli, would "have far-reaching result by throwing the Arabs into German hands and thus uniting them against us; French as well as British possessions would be endangered."[8]

Although the Germans and Turks were in fact making plans to attack Egypt anew, they could not implement them until the summer of 1916.[9] Nevertheless, the discussions among British leaders produced important decisions. For one thing, the Alexandretta scheme fell by the wayside, because of the potential reaction of France, which coveted Syria as a future territorial acquisition, and because the British General Staff believed the operation would not weaken Germany.[10] However, during 1916 the British pushed their defenses into the Sinai Peninsula, preparing for a possible drive later, in conjunction with the planned Arab revolt, against the Turks in Palestine and Syria.

But an Arab alliance seemed all the more attractive to the British because during October and November political crises inspired by German and Turkish agents peaked on the borders of both Egypt and India. The attack by the Shaykh al-Sanussi on British outposts in western Egypt coincided with the arrival of German officials in Afghanistan and with the zenith of agitation in Persia. From Kabul reports reached Delhi and Cairo that Hentig and Niedermayer sought to convince the amir, Habibullah, to declare holy war on the British in neighboring India; in Teheran the Germans nearly persuaded the government to sign a treaty with Berlin, despite Persian hatred for the Turks; and in southern and western Persia they were inciting tribes to attack the British and Russians.[11]

Regarding what he viewed as the seriousness of German activities among Muslims, McMahon sent a warning to Grey on 24 October, the day he dispatched his crucial message to the Sharif of Mecca. "German officials and private individuals," he said, "have in many cases supported the preaching of the Jehad and actively promoted an anti-Christian spirit among Moslems."[12] Moreover, said the commissioner, German agents in Syria, Mesopotamia, and Libya had created the impression that the German emperor had converted to Islam.[13]

The Growing German Influence in Abyssinia

Meanwhile, reports of similar enemy activity in Abyssinia and the Sudan had reached the Cairo and Khartoum intelligence offices. When World War I began, Abyssinia was ruled by Lij Iyasu (a politically inexperienced, nineteen-year-old prince and heir-designate to the imperial throne of his recently deceased Christian grandfather, Menilek) and by a regency council composed of Iyasu's ministers.[14] Since 1911, when the council declared Iyasu old enough to act for himself with its guidance, the power of the central government in Addis Ababa had deteriorated, in favor of provincial tribal leaders.

With the outbreak of the world war Iyasu began a flirtation with Islam, in part because his father, Ras Mikail, was a former Muslim. Also, Iyasu strengthened his already close ties to the German legation in Addis Ababa and its minister, von Syburg. Throughout 1915 the German General Staff and foreign ministry attempted to reach Abyssinia by sending emissaries sent through Turkey, Arabia, the Red Sea, and Italian Somaliland. At first Berlin intended to use the country as a base from which to enter neighboring Sudan to incite its tribes against the British.

But in March the Italians foiled the Frobenius expedition.[15] The General Staff then dispatched another mission to the Red Sea and thence to Addis Ababa, this one led by Salomon Hall, a Syrian-German. Hall carried letters from Berlin to Syburg, directing him to convince Abyssinia to join the Central Powers in the war and attack the Italians in their neighboring colonies, Eritrea and Somalia. The Italians arrested Hall off the coast of Italian Somaliland when his small boat sank in the Red Sea, and his mission never reached its destination; the German foreign ministry finally contacted Syburg through its legation in Greece, sending him the same letters Hall had carried.[16]

Syburg, despite the problems his government had transmitting political orders to him, spread among the Abyssinians Berlin's popular, but false, claim of major German victories in Europe. He also promised Abyssinia that it would receive land from neighboring countries in the postwar peace settlement if it joined the Reich in the war. The German legation negotiated with Lij Iyasu for a German-Abyssinian alliance. Further, German and Turkish agents sought to stir Muslim tribal leaders in northern Abyssinia to attack across the frontier into the Sudan.[17]

By the last months of 1915 such activities had produced limited, yet noticeable, results. The anti-Italian policy especially appealed to Iyasu, who believed that the defeat of the Allies might allow Abyssinia to push Italy out of neighboring Eritrea and Italian Somaliland. Iyasu therefore sought an alliance with the Somali chieftain, the Sayyid Muhammad Abdullah—known as the "Mad Mullah"—who long had pursued an anti-colonialist war. Since, however, the sayyid followed in Somaliland an anti-Abyssinian line, many Abyssinians thought Iyasu's policy treasonous. Moreover, the country's leading officials viewed with extreme displeasure Iyasu's efforts to court a neighboring Muslim leader and to integrate Muslims into the administration.[18]

As early as March the veteran British minister in Addis Ababa, Wilfried G. Thesiger, had reported to the Foreign Office Iyasu's intrigue with the mullah and the local Turkish consul general, Mazhar Bey, as well as the budding criticism of Iyasu's pro-Muslim policies. Iyasu visited the minister, who found the prince confused by the different views he was hearing as to the likely outcomes of the war. On the one hand, the Germans had told him they would seize the Sudan and French Somaliland and leave Egypt to the Turks. Thesiger, on the other hand, stressed to Iyasu that a German triumph would mean the end of his country's independence, whereas Great Britain had no need for territorial expansion at the expense of Abyssinia.[19]

By the summer both Thesiger and British intelligence agents at Khartoum were warning of the growing influence of Turkish and German propaganda on Iyasu and of cultivation of Islam to serve his political ambitions.[20] The British became increasingly jittery about the situation; the Colonial Office in London even reported, erroneously, that Frobenius had entered Abyssinia. Thesiger's reports described continued weakening of Iyasu's authority, the prince's long absences from the capital, and the division of the regent's council of ministers into pro-German and pro-British factions.[21] At the end of the year, Iyasu shipped weapons to Somaliland and its chief, the "Mad Mullah." But British officials in Abyssinia, British Somaliland, and along the Sudanese frontier thwarted the conclusion of a treaty between Abyssinia and the Somali leader to attack the Italians.

Also, Thesiger's close relationship with the pro-British prime minister of Abyssinia, Habte Giorgis, forced the German legation in Addis Ababa to await the return of Iyasu to the capital to learn whether or not, as Syburg informed the foreign ministry through Yemen, the prince was inclined toward cooperation with Germany.[22] For the moment at least, and despite potential problems, both the British and Italian positions regarding Abyssinia appeared safe.

Oppenheim, Sykes, and Britain's Agreements with the Arabs and French

The most vivid symbol to the British of what they viewed as a widespread German menace in the Middle East was the continued presence in Turkey of the notorious Reich agent Freiherr von Oppenheim. His activities provided Cairo with further ammunition for its belief that Britain should conclude an alliance with the Arabs. The British had first received information about Oppenheim's mission to Turkey in May 1915, shortly after his arrival there.

Apparently the British had not yet learned of his meeting with Faysal, the Sharif of Mecca's son. Intelligence reports reached Cairo, however, that Oppenheim, along with other German officials in Haifa, Aleppo, and northern Syria, had encouraged the Turkish massacre of Armenians.[23] Simultaneously, Britain's ambassador in Rome, Sir Rennell Rodd, received information that Oppenheim had left Constantinople for Persia and Afghanistan on a pan-Islamic crusade, "well supplied with cash."[24] From then on the Cairo residency and several other British offices carefully monitored Oppenheim's movements. Information on him reached the Government of India, which notified its embattled armed forces in Mesopotamia that the German agent was a "private spy of the Emperor and is very dangerous. . . . If he managed to enter Afghanistan or Persia he is capable of doing infinite harm."[25]

He also caught the attention of Sir Mark Sykes, an official of Kitchener's in the War Office charged with responsibility for Middle East affairs. In June 1915 Sykes had left London on a fact-finding mission to the Middle East and India. However, because he possessed less than expert knowledge of much of the region, he absorbed a good deal of war hysteria, including accepting exaggerations about Oppenheim. For example, Sykes notified the War Office on 1 July that Oppenheim had left Constantinople for Syria with the "intention to raise pan-Islamic feeling against Great Britain." He continued: "India Office may expect his activities in Persia about the middle of July. His propaganda not well received among Constantinople religious communities owing to his Jewish origin. He has large funds at his disposal and intimate knowledge of the country."[26]

A month later Sykes reported again on Oppenheim, basing much of his assessment not on hard intelligence but on what he had heard from a Russian source. He made out Oppenheim to be larger than life, "a Jew of great wealth" and a "personal friend of the German Emperor's." Moreover, said Sykes, Oppenheim was "one of the original propagandists of the Baghdad Railway" and "a violent Anglophobe."[27] Of Oppenheim's "violent religious war against Great Britain," Sykes continued, "His preaching has naturally not had much effect among the Old School Turks, but it is exactly in tune with the ideas of the modern European educated Moslem, who likes a cloak of liberalism and progress to hide an even more relentless fanaticism than before." Sykes insisted that Oppenheim was heading for Persia and Afghanistan. He concluded that the German would incite massacres of Armenians in Turkey and arrange for the murders of Britons in Persia.[28]

At the time Sykes arrived in the Middle East, secret contacts had resumed between Britain and the Sharif of Mecca. Meanwhile, Cairo was receiving a steady flow of information, often from questionable sources, about Oppenheim; much of it portrayed him as a major enemy force in the Middle East.[29] By October, Cairo's fear of an anti-British pan-Islamic jihad stretching from Libya to Afghanistan—and thus, possibly even to India—had reached epic proportions.

Reports of Oppenheim's presence in the Sinai Peninsula and Hijaz accelerated the panic by raising fears that he might jeopardize Britain's relationship with the sharif. He had traveled to within a few miles of Medina and some of Islam's most holy places before Husayn forced him to leave. Information about what had happened came to the British through Abdullah, Husayn's son; Clayton, Cairo's intelligence chief, reported the incident on 12 November to London. He linked Abdullah's message about Oppenheim's expulsion from Medina to the readiness and intention of the Arabs to begin hostilities against the Turks.[30]

Also from Cairo, Sykes emphasized to the War Office that Oppenheim's activity formed part of a German and Turkish policy "worked by highly efficient agents on a well-coordinated plan." The "plan," explained Sykes, was nothing less than to destroy the British Empire by "fomenting" in India, Persia, Egypt, and Arabia anti-British "Moslem discontent and fanaticism." "To defeat the enemy," he concluded, "the destruction of the Ottoman Empire would be a decisive step." According to Sykes, Britain should "back Arabic speaking peoples against the Turkish Government," dismantling the Ottoman state and making the Arabs of the Middle East the principal safeguard of Britain's imperial interests in the region.[31]

Thus, by the end of 1915 Oppenheim's activity and the threat perceived by the British in pan-Islamism was giving officials in Cairo a further weapon to help them persuade the London government, over the objections particularly of the Government of India and even some Foreign and War Office officials, to commit itself to the Sharif of Mecca. On 21 November, the War Office concluded:

> The German dream is, and has been for a long time, to arouse all Mohammedans in every part of the world against their occupying powers. Von Oppenheim in Syria at the present moment, and creatures like him elsewhere, are sending Pan-Islamist propaganda with all the forst and guile of which they are capable. . . . [I]f we remain supine, and do not seize the advantage we have, we run grave risks, not only of losing the assistance of the Arabs against the Turks, but of finding them alienated entirely and fighting against us.[32]

Furthermore, Cairo's Arab policy, as Sir Reginald Wingate, the Governor-General of the Sudan, informed Clayton, was dictated by the European situation and by the success of the Central Powers against Russia, which had upset Allied plans in the Balkans and influenced the sharif. Wingate continued:

> There can be no doubt whatever that [Husayn and the Arabs] are more anxious than ever to throw off Turkish domination and to place the destinies of their as yet unborn State in our hands. . . . I am lost in wonderment at the attitude of the Home Authorities who would hold a pistol at the wretched Sherif's head unless he rises instantly in revolt—how can he rise when he is neither prepared as to money, arms, ammunition and other necessaries which go to make a revolt successful?[33]

Notwithstanding the impatience of Cairo and Khartoum with London, the Foreign Office had in fact authorized McMahon to continue his contacts with the sharif. Sykes, too, while in Cairo learned of the approach to Husayn, as did some Muslim leaders like the Indian prince, Aga Khan, who received the information from the Foreign Office.[34]

By the close of 1915 the correspondence between McMahon and the sharif had produced agreement on the territory that would form a future independent Arab state, except for certain vaguely defined lands in Syria where French interests were involved. Britain promised as well to deliver to Husayn supplies of arms at the beginning of 1916, with the understanding that the latter would launch an Arab revolt. So as not to damage the Anglo-French alliance, the sharif informed McMahon, he would postpone his demands in Syria until the war's end. These events prompted Sykes and officials in Cairo to form a special agency for Arab affairs, the Arab Bureau, in the local intelligence department.[35] The British government also completed a treaty with Ibn Saud, the leading Arab chieftain in eastern and central Arabia. The agreement gave Britain a large measure of control over Ibn Saud's foreign policy, but it acknowledged the independence and territorial integrity of the Najd and granted him an annual subsidy.[36]

Several factors seemed to confirm for British leaders the wisdom of their increasingly pro-Arab policy. A War Office intelligence report claimed that the Turks now realized they had a serious problem with the sharif and that they intended to conciliate him.[37] Rumors abounded too that Oppenheim would accompany the next armed Turkish and German attack on Egypt.[38] In London the Foreign Office received renewed reports through Russia that Jemal Pasha would turn against the Porte if the Allies met the demands he had first floated in October.[39] Finally, even some in the India Office, a traditional bastion of opposition to destroying the Ottoman Empire, after learning of widespread demands of German professors and writers that the Reich expand its influence into Turkey, expressed fear at the prospect of it remaining intact.[40]

Sykes returned to London, where by mid-December major decisions were being made regarding war policy. Already Britain had begun negotiations with France on the latter's claims not only to Syria but also to Palestine. Sykes now bore in mind the provisions that he was to implement in May 1916 in the controversial Sykes-Picot Agreement with France. In the agreement, unknown to the sharif until November 1917, Sykes concluded with the French a secret deal for the postwar creation of a Greater Arabia for the Arabs and Husayn, but with the interior of the Syrian part under French control, and the British receiving Mesopotamia. The agreement, moreover, made Palestine an international zone.[41]

Sykes arrived back in London a very important figure. Since the beginning of his journey in June he had traveled from the Balkans to India, witnessed warfare from the Dardanelles to the Persian Gulf, and had met every important British officer in the region. His return coincided with the British withdrawal from Gallipoli, the Allied reverses in the Balkans, and the Anglo-Indian setback at Ctesiphon in Mesopotamia. He met with prime minister Asquith's War Committee, the government's leading policy-making body, and argued that a military offensive from Egypt against the Turks would bring the Arabs over to the Allies. Sykes also urged on the committee the completion of the alliance with the Sharif of Mecca, the guardian of the holy places. He warned that the Turks might kill the sharif and replace him with their own nominee, which would result in a "real Jehad" threatening the British not only in Mesopotamia but also in Egypt, Persia, Afghanistan, India, and the Sudan. Sykes's testimony made a favorable impression on the committee members, most of whom, because of their longtime preoccupation with the defense of India, held deeply engrained attitudes that linked events geopolitically throughout the East and held pan-Islamism and a jihad to be fearsome prospects.[42]

But ironically, by December 1915, the very crisis that Sykes portrayed so passionately to London and which British officials in Cairo believed surrounded them, a crisis caused by the enemy's pan-Islamic activities and by military defeat in the Dardanelles, had already begun to ease. British forces in western Egypt turned back the Sanussi uprising, and in Persia the British and Russians regained substantial control over the political situation. Moreover, the amir of Afghanistan had rejected the efforts of the German expedition in Kabul to persuade him to declare war on the British in India.[43] How much these considerations influenced the major military changes made in London at the year's end, changes that resulted in the transfer of greater numbers of British troops from Egypt to France, is unclear. In any case, Asquith now appointed a new head of the Imperial General Staff, William Robertson. Robertson, a so-called "Westerner" who believed the army should concentrate on the main war theater in France, termed the military and political events in the Middle East "sideshows," unworthy of further important operations.

Robertson soon replaced the "Easterner" Kitchener as chief military adviser to the British Cabinet. Robertson, displeased at the large numbers of British troops retained in the Middle East, ordered Maxwell in Egypt "to get every possible man, horse and gun on the Western Front."[44] Of the fourteen British divisions then in Egypt, nine were sent to France before the opening of the Somme campaign on 1 July 1916. In both Egypt and Mesopotamia Robertson directed his commanders to follow a defensive policy.[45]

The German View of the Moment

Berlin, too, concluded during the final months of 1915 that matters in the Middle East had reached a crucial juncture. The Turks had denied military victory to Britain on the Gallipoli Peninsula and in Mesopotamia, and the Central Powers were still in the ascendancy at the moment on the Russian front. It was a measure of Berlin's confidence in its position that the Germans now planned to capitalize on their alliance with Turkey to seize the military initiative in the Middle East and East Africa before Britain could recover from its disaster at Gallipoli.

Several old problems, however, complicated this German effort. First, despite the Turkish success at Gallipoli, the British still retained control of the Suez Canal, the Red Sea, and the waters surrounding Africa.[46] A second issue burdening any new German enterprise, political or military, in the Middle East and East Africa centered around the intensification of conflict between Young Turk and German leaders. Dissension had characterized their relationship from the beginning of the war. The first major Turkish military success, the triumph at Gallipoli, emboldened the Young Turks to resist German demands on Turkey even more than previously.[47]

Also differences stemmed from the death at the end of October 1915 of Wangenheim, the German ambassador at Constantinople. He had acquired the confidence of his Young Turk hosts, particularly that of the powerful war minister, Enver Pasha, with whose opposition to German political enterprises and intervention in the Ottoman Empire the ambassador had agreed on numerous occasions. Relations between the embassy and the Porte cooled immediately with the arrival in Constantinople of the elderly Wolff-Metternich. The new ambassador not only defended the Armenians too vigorously against the Turkish persecution but treated the Turks with arrogance and chided them for their financial demands on Germany.[48]

Difficulties continued to fester as well between the Germans and Jemal Pasha, the Young Turk governor of Syria and commander of the Fourth Army. According to the German foreign ministry, Jemal held much of the responsibility for the strong British position among such leading chieftains in Arabia as Ibn Saud in the Najd and the Sharif of Mecca. Despite Jemal's execution of Arab notables in Syria whom he suspected of treason, the ministry criticized what it termed the governor's permissive policy toward Arab relations with British and French diplomats in Syria, questioning his loyalty to the Porte. Jemal, claimed the ministry, had allowed the Anglo-French officials to remain in Turkey for several months after the latter had entered the war.

Although some German agents in Syria, including Oppenheim and Prüfer, believed him trustworthy, Jemal disliked Oppenheim's presence in Syria and asked that he be returned to Germany. The German foreign ministry and General Staff, which were now making plans for a second attack on the Suez Canal by forces from Jemal's army, refused to recall Oppenheim; instead, Zimmermann directed him to remain in Turkey to keep Jemal under surveillance, "especially considering the information from there about [his] dubious reliability."[49]

The German-Turkish friction also bore upon another obstacle that existed to any new German venture in the Middle East and East Africa: the Arab question. As the Germans had learned previously, without Arab support they could undertake little of political or military value in the pivotal region of Mesopotamia, Arabia, and the Red Sea. But German leaders, who always found their options constrained on this issue by Germany's alliance with the Porte, disagreed in their assessments of the Arabs and on policy toward them. This resulted in much confusion and in Germany's failure to urge the Porte energetically to ensure the support of Arab leaders. During August 1915 news arrived in the Constantinople embassy from Baghdad that the British victories in southern Mesopotamia over the Turks had resulted from a mass defection of Arab tribes to the enemy.[50]

Also, during the final months of 1915 German leaders differed sharply over their appraisal of the Sharif of Mecca and what their policy should be toward him. Rather naively the Germans had expected the mission of Oppenheim to Turkey in May 1915 and his agreement with Husayn's son, Faysal, to improve the relationship of the sharif to the Porte and its allies.[51] The Austro-Hungarians, even before Oppenheim's meeting with Faysal, believed that the Sharif of Mecca had changed to a pro-Turkish attitude.[52] Prüfer, a German agent in Syria and close friend of Oppenheim's, seemed to discount the Arabs as a factor; he had traveled throughout Palestine and Syria, disguised in Arab dress, surveying local opinion for Jemal Pasha. Prüfer's report to the Turkish governor deprecated the influence of Arab nationalism and revolutionary fervor among the population.

An Arab uprising, he declared, had little chance of success because of the "cowardice and frivolousness of the population."[53]

Reports also arrived at the German embassy in Constantinople, however, warning of the sharif's pro-British sympathies; during the fall, Husayn had forced Oppenheim's removal from Medina.[54] In Berlin the foreign ministry doubted the sharif's loyalty to the Young Turks and viewed Ibn Saud, the ruler of Najd, as wholly in the British camp.[55] Similar differences and confusion regarding the Arabs characterized the Constantinople embassy and its relationship on the issue to Enver Pasha. The newly appointed Wolff-Metternich tried to persuade Enver to permit the Germans to attempt to lure Husayn away from English influence with large sums of money. But Enver, who already had numerous disagreements with Wolff-Metternich, rejected the proposal.[56]

The ambassador quickly dropped the idea of approaching the Arabs. The dragoman at the embassy, Dr. Fritz Schoenberg, on whose advice the ambassador and Konstantin von Neurath, the chargé d'affaires, relied heavily for their views on the subject, also discouraged trying to recruit the sharif. Schoenberg (who argued that Germany would soon knock Russia out of the war, enabling the Reich to seize and exploit much of Russia's European territory) saw a possibility of relieving the traditional Russian pressure on the Black Sea straits and the Balkans, and also of pitting the Russians against the British on the frontier of India. To achieve both he suggested that Russia be permitted a railroad connection to the Persian Gulf and Arabian Sea.[57]

Consequently, by the end of 1915 the embassy was pushing the Turks to offer nothing to the Arabs that might later undermine a German agreement with Russia. Wolff-Metternich, who had no firsthand experience in Middle Eastern affairs, had little but contempt for Arab nationalism. He dismissed Husayn as an insignificant leader of a band of robbers, too fanatical to work with the infidel British and easily removed by assassination if he became difficult.[58]

Despite the problems with the Arabs, Turks, and with the logistics of reaching the Middle East and Africa with naval and other armed support, German planners pushed confidently ahead with their schemes for the Orient. They wished not only to expand the Reich's

presence and influence in Turkey but also to seize the military initiative against the British in the Middle East and East Africa. This involved a second attack on the Suez Canal. Although they still knew
little about the situation inside Egypt, the General Staff and foreign
ministry continued to hope that the appearance of Turkish troops at
the canal would ignite a pan-Islamic revolt of Egyptians against the
British. Berlin also intended to capitalize on the steadily growing
Sanussi unrest on the western border of Egypt.[59]

Since July 1915, Falkenhayn, the chief of the German General Staff,
had urged the Porte to undertake a new Egyptian campaign. Consequently, Kress von Kressenstein, the chief of staff of the Turkish
Fourth Army's VIII Corps, now stationed along the Sinai border between Turkey and Egypt, devised an operational concept for the offensive. The plan, accepted by both Enver and Falkenhayn on 24
November, called for Germany to supply the VIII Corps with a special, heavily armed force, code named "Pasha I," of 150 officers and
1,500 men.[60]

Kress, however, much like his superiors in Berlin, mistrusted the
commander of the Fourth Army, Jemal Pasha. In November the General Staff and foreign ministry directed Oppenheim to remain in Syria
to observe Jemal's work on the planned Egyptian offensive;[61] only
much later, in May 1916, did the first Pasha I units arrive from Germany in Turkey. Two months thereafter Kress attempted the assault.

Germany's renewed interest in attacking Egypt resulted furthermore from the struggle in German East Africa of General Paul von
Lettow-Vorbeck's force of 300 Germans and 11,000 native soldiers
against overwhelming numbers of British, Indian, Boer, and native
troops. Both the German colonial ministry and General Staff intended
the attack on Egypt to relieve the intense pressure on Lettow-
Vorbeck.[62]

Most of all, the ministry and its secretary, Wilhelm Solf, envisioned
using Egypt as a springboard from which to launch an eventual German invasion of much greater areas of eastern and central Africa.
Solf pushed to win back the German colonies already lost to Britain
and to establish a German central African colonial empire by acquiring French, Belgian, Portuguese, and possibly British colonies. The
colonial secretary, with the foreign ministry's approval, had sent a

special reconnaissance unit, headed by Colonel Rochus Schmidt, to the Sinai Peninsula to investigate utilizing Arabia and Egypt as bases for the annexations.[63] Still other Germans, including some serving in Turkey, believed in attacking Egypt for similar reasons.[64]

Such imperialist fantasies had existed among numerous Germans before the war, and they had grown steadily as the fighting progressed and discussions about war aims intensified. By the end of 1915 demands reached a fever pitch among the colonial ministry as well as German publicists, pan-Germans, and economic leaders that the Reich use the war to establish a central African empire.[65]

Despite incidents that indicated the fruitlessness of shipping weapons and supplies across the Red Sea, which British ships patrolled, the colonial ministry continued to develop schemes to attack East Africa.[66] For instance, the Turkish government approved a plan by Duke Adolf Friedrich zu Mecklenburg to use the Somalis and their chief, the Sayyid Muhammad Abdullah, the "Mad Mullah," long an opponent of Italian and British colonialism, to invade British East Africa and Uganda.[67] At the end of December Solf pushed the General Staff to send a mission to southern Arabia with the aim of establishing a base for communications with, and smuggling armaments to, East Africa. He acknowledged to Falkenhayn that the "closing of the transportation routes" to Africa "has made it nearly impossible to support from the motherland the troops defending the remainder of the German colonies."[68]

According to the German admiralty staff, no chance existed for naval operations to assist the German forces in Africa. Solf therefore proposed relieving German East Africa by diverting British troops from there and Egypt to the Sudan. He urged that Germany incite anti-British revolts by smuggling weapons to the Sudanese through neighboring Abyssinian and Somali border tribes. Solf envisioned establishing a German headquarters in southern Arabia, from which Arab traders could be used to transport the armaments into eastern Africa.[69]

The idea hardly struck Falkenhayn and the General Staff as novel. Since the beginning of the war the General Staff and the foreign ministry had attempted repeatedly, and with a remarkable lack of success, to raise the Sudan and its neighboring countries in rebellion against Britain and to establish German consulates in Jidda and Kunfidha. Falkenhayn, in his reply to Solf, blamed such frustrations on "the resistance of the Turkish authorities, who believed they must take into account the sensitivities of the Grand Shaykh of Mecca."[70] Nevertheless, Falkenhayn agreed fully with Solf's plan. The chief of staff now believed "that the relationship between the Turkish government and the Grand Shaykh apparently has been settled," so that the Reich should again attempt reaching East Africa by establishing a foothold in Arabia and on the Red Sea. He immediately ordered the General Staff to carry out the project.[71]

In fact, however, the German action (assisted by the Porte), based as it was on erroneous information about the attitude of the Sharif of Mecca, helped to precipitate an armed revolt among the Arabs against the Turks. The Arab rebellion of 1916 resulted in part from Britain's war-waging policy of allying with and encouraging the Arabs to rise in revolution against the Turks. It produced a crisis that made a German and Turkish victory in the Middle East much more difficult.

8

Britain as Wartime "Revolutionary" *The Arab Revolt, 1916*

During the first weeks of 1916, deeply discouraging news arrived in London from the Middle East. Britain withdrew its last forces from Gallipoli on 8 January. In Mesopotamia, nearly eighty thousand Turks of the Sixth Army, commanded by the German field marshal von der Goltz, besieged at Kut al-Amara a much smaller number of Anglo-Indians.[1] Further, the British received word that Germany not only intended to expand its control in Turkey but to seize the military initiative in the Middle East and East Africa.

Britain and News of the German-Turkish Plan

This situation persuaded more British leaders than ever of the necessity for Britain to destroy the Ottoman Empire. When during the spring rumors circulated of a separate peace between the Allies and Turkey, even certain officials in the India Office abandoned their traditional support for keeping the empire intact after the war. Sir Arthur Hirtzel, the India Office's political secretary, warned in a lengthy memorandum:

> Behind the military threat in the neighborhood of Egypt and in Mesopotamia is the common danger of Panislamism. . . . Of the Moslem population of the world some 100 millions are British subjects, and this fact necessarily invests the Turco-German alliance with a new significance, and makes the survival of the Ottoman Empire, in any shape in which it can again become a German tool, a peculiar menace to us.[2]

Only a few disagreed that Britain could protect its position in India and the Middle East from pan-Islamism and a German-ruled Turkey by not only defeating the Ottoman Empire but dismembering it. One who downplayed the danger of the Turkish-German alliance was T. W. Holderness, the under-secretary in the India Office. He cautioned that "both from the past history of Mohammedanism and from the events of the present war, . . . pan-Islamism as a motive force can easily be overrated."[3] In a lengthy reply to Hirtzel, Holderness emphasized Islam's "want of cohesion and its sectarian divisions and animosities" and how it "is inspired by nationality rather than by creed."[4] Holderness, however, had no suggestions for British policy.

During January and February Britain continued to solidify its alliance with the Arabs. Cairo arranged for a group of ulamas from the local al-Azhar University to publish a proclamation to Arab soldiers in the Turkish army accusing the Turks of deceiving the Arabs and robbing them of the caliphate and the Koran. In contrast, the statement said, the British and French had befriended the Arabs, even encouraging the use of the Arabic language in their Middle Eastern and African empires.[5]

Meanwhile, the Sharif of Mecca, although privately uneasy about his negotiations with Britain and about news from Syria that the situation there did not favor an Arab revolt, assured the British of his loyalty.[6] Hussayn's allegiance seemed confirmed by a steady stream of information reaching Cairo's new Arab Bureau emphasizing the sharpening of differences between the Arab chieftains, the sharif and Ibn Saud, and the Turks.[7] Still other reports, particularly from an Arab spy (Mustafa Bey, a wealthy Damascene living in Egypt and code-named "Maurice") who was visiting Constantinople and Salonika, discussed the anti-Turkish attitudes of Arabs and the possibility of exploiting disaffection in the Ottoman Empire and army.[8] This and other information also indicated that German attempts, including those of Oppenheim, to attract Arab backing in Syria and Arabia had generally misfired.[9]

Then on 18 February the sharif informed Cairo of his satisfaction with the agreement he had reached with Britain. He also warned of impending German activity in Arabia and East Africa. The Turks, he told McMahon, "order us to expedite the journey of a group of Germans to the coasts of Africa (I think the shores of the Red Sea) and we replied consenting with all readiness." However, Husayn continued, "upon their arrival here we will inform you by some secret means, explaining what is necessary about their journey and its destination."[10]

Husayn had learned of the German mission from his son Faysal. The sharif had sent him to Syria to allay Turkish suspicions of Husayn and, if possible, organize a revolt there of Arab divisions of the Turkish army, which would attack from the rear should the army advance on Egypt. While in Damascus, Faysal heard from the German military officer in charge of the Reich's mission to the African coast "that, from the Yemen, arms and ammunition were to be shipped across to Abyssinia, and an anti-foreign war begun in that country." The officer "was going afterwards to German East Africa."[11]

The Stotzingen Mission

The German with whom Faysal spoke was Major Othmar von Stotzingen, a senior officer in the German XII Army Corps in Württemberg. Stotzingen had traveled widely before the war in Africa and received a recommendation for his mission to Arabia in 1916 from the wife of Alfred Count von Schlieffen, the former chief of the General Staff.[12] Ironically, because of Stotzingen's indiscretion to Faysal the Sharif of Mecca knew of the planned German mission to Arabia almost before the Germans received permission from the Turks to carry it out. Husayn worried much more, however, about the intentions of the large detachment of Turkish troops assigned by the Porte to accompany the Germans.

The Stotzingen mission arose from several factors, which this study has already discussed. These included the long history of failed wartime German expeditions to the Red Sea and the recent military defeats suffered by the British in the Middle East, which made Britain seem more vulnerable to enemy military action. In addition, the mission grew out of the questioning by both the Germans and Turks of the loyalty and significance of the Sharif of Mecca, and also out of Berlin's plans, conceived first at the close of 1915, to take advantage of Britain's presently shaky position in the Middle East. Finally, the

Germans held the grandiose idea that the mission would remove the pressure from Germany's beleaguered forces in East Africa by inciting anti-British revolts in the Sudan and Egypt.[13]

The Germans and Turks remained uncertain about the loyalty of the Arabs, particularly that of the sharif, and disagreed on policy toward them. In mid-January Humann, the naval attaché, the German official in Constantinople closest to Enver Pasha, informed Berlin of new evidence that pointed to Husayn's tie to the British. Accusations of the sharif's treason came from an Afghan notable, Muhammad Anim Bey ibn Hassan Khan, who had arrived in Damascus from a pilgrimage to Mecca and discussed his views with the German consul, Loytved Hardegg, and Prüfer. This and other reports from people arriving in Damascus from Mecca claimed that the sharif intended to use Bedouin troops, which he was recruiting in the Hijaz, not in the service of the Turks but against them.[14]

But both Humann and the ambassador, Wolff-Metternich, downplayed the potential danger of the sharif and his relations to Britain. The Porte, Humann assured Berlin on 16 January, "is precisely instructed on the political events in Arabia." The Turks, the attaché continued, believed that their governor in the Hijaz, Ali Gali Pasha, could control the sharif; if the governor could not do so, Husayn would place himself in open opposition to the government, and a small "punishment squad" of Turks would "immediately murder the Grand Sharif."[15] Furthermore, claimed Humann, the Porte had secured the loyalty of the ruler of Yemen, the Imam Yahya, whom the Turks could use against Husayn. Finally, the Porte alleged that the sharif's tie to Britain depended not on political issues but on the British provisioning the Hijaz with food and on the attempt by the sharif's Egyptian wife to secure the income from her properties in Egypt.[16] A letter from Wolff-Metternich to Berlin of 22 January reiterated these points.[17]

The small importance placed by the Turks on the Arab question may have made easier their acquiescence in the German plans for utilizing western Arabia, an area traditionally off limits to non-Muslims, and the Red Sea to penetrate eastern Africa.[18] Regarding the Stotzingen mission, at the beginning of January Berlin worked through the Turkish minister in Switzerland, Fuad Selim, to kindle the Porte's interest in persuading Abyssinia to enter the war. The Abyssinian heir-designate to the throne, Lij Iyasu, had cultivated Islam and befriended the German and Turkish diplomats in his country. Fuad Selim informed Romberg, the German minister in Bern, that the Porte had agreed in principle to the construction of a wireless station in Yemen for daily contact with Addis Ababa.[19]

Shortly thereafter Major General Otto von Lossow, a veteran of service in Turkey whom Berlin had appointed military attaché at the embassy in July 1915, returned to Constantinople. Lossow was to secure approval from the ruling faction in Constantinople, headed by Enver Pasha and Talaat Pasha and supported by the new foreign minister, Khalil Bey, for a small German mission to go to Yemen.[20] On 3 February Enver agreed that Stotzingen could travel along the coast of western Arabia to Yemen with an assistant, the former German resident of the Sudan, Karl Neufeld, to Arabia.[21]

Meanwhile, the German General Staff produced elaborate plans for Stotzingen to construct a propaganda and intelligence outpost in Yemen, an outpost with a wireless station to contact not only Abyssinia but also the Reich's besieged troops in German East Africa. The plans further called for the new outpost to send Neufeld and locally recruited Arab agents the short distance across the Red Sea to the Sudan. There they would distribute jihad propaganda, and bomb communications and rail lines.[22]

Enver Pasha agreed to the German proposal, but the war minister sought the approval for it also from Jemal Pasha, the powerful governor of Syria. Since preparations had begun at the end of 1915 for another Turkish attack against Egypt, Jemal had conducted extensive negotiations with the Sharif of Mecca, who had again dispatched his son, Faysal, to Syria. The governor had sent money and arms to Husayn in the expectation that he would assist the holy war, proclaimed by the sultan-caliph, by producing a large volunteer Bedouin force to assist the Turks against Egypt. The sharif's motives in negotiating were his wish to lessen Turkish suspicion about his loyalty and to keep his option open for a future alliance with the Young Turks should his discussion with the British fail.[23]

On 12 February Enver embarked on a lengthy visit to Syria, from where at the beginning of March he traveled further to Medina; he was accompanied by Jemal Pasha, several Turkish officers, and Faysal. While in Medina Faysal performed ceremonies chosen to demonstrate his father's loyalty to the Porte; the Germans applauded the visit.[24] Also in Medina Enver received lukewarm support for the Stotzingen expedition from Jemal and local Turkish authorities—lukewarm because they disliked the idea of Germans in Arabia, feared the reaction of the sharif to the German presence, and worried that the mission would interfere with the Turkish plans for assaulting Egypt.[25]

On returning to Constantinople Enver expressed concern for the survival of Stotzingen's Germans and demanded safeguards for their protection. He ordered them to speak only Turkish (in which neither Stotzingen nor Neufeld was fluent), travel accompanied by an Ottoman army unit, and to send Neufeld, who had once visited Medina against the wishes of both Turks and Arabs, not through the Hijaz but along the Red Sea shore.[26]

Still another factor encouraged the Turks to agree to the Stotzingen mission. A message had arrived through Yemen from the German minister in Abyssinia, Syburg, arguing that a successful German-Turkish attack against Egypt would accelerate the conclusion of a German-Abyssinian alliance and thereafter an attack by Abyssinia on the Sudan. Syburg added, "This could also provide a breather for our East African protective region that is threatened from British East Africa and the Belgian Congo."[27] Meanwhile, German concern over Abyssinia intensified when the Italian press reported, albeit erroneously, that Lij Iyasu's father, Ras Mikail, had arrived in Egypt to conclude an Anglo-Abyssinian agreement.[28]

The Final Encouragements to Revolt

By mid-March Husayn had completed negotiations with the British. The latter promised to deliver money and war supplies to the sharif, and Husayn planned to begin his revolt against the Turks on 16 June. McMahon in Cairo urged him to delay the rising until Britain could equip the Arab forces adequately;[29] otherwise, the British did their utmost during the spring to urge Husayn to revolt.

On 10 March, for example, Cairo eagerly reported a recent victory in Cyrenaica to the Sharif of Mecca, reassuring Husayn with a badly needed British success and thereby adding encouragement to revolt. The British had struggled to gain control of the situation in Libya, but in the first weeks of the year, using armored cars and airplanes, they inflicted a decisive military defeat on the Shaykh al-Sanussi, the Sayyid Ahmad, and his Bedouin forces. The shaykh, his men hopelessly defeated and confused, retired south with a small bodyguard to the western Egyptian oasis of Siwa and then further to al-Dakhla.[30] McMahon told the sharif that the Sanussis had "fallen victims to the wiles of the Turkish and German intriguers." However, he added, with the defeat of the Sanussis "the eyes of the Arabs are now becoming open to the deceit which has been practised upon them."[31]

Although McMahon emphasized the Arab nature of the events in Libya and the failed attempt by the Young Turks to use the Bedouins to undermine the British position in Egypt, the Libyan revolt had not in fact been Arab at all, but Islamic. In one of the war's ironies, while the British capitalized on Arab hatred of Turkish rule in the east, the Ottomans—with some German assistance—had persuaded their coreligionists in Libya to cooperate against the Christian occupiers of Egypt.[32]

The British also attempted to move the sharif to act by discrediting the Germans. In April British forces seized, in the German East African village of Moshi, a 1913 proclamation signed by Heinrich Schnee, the German governor of the colony. In it Schnee had announced a regulation prohibiting Islam.[33] At the end of May, Storrs (the Oriental secretary at the British residency in Cairo) delivered copies of the anti-Islamic Moshi document to Abdullah, the sharif's son.[34]

How much these British actions influenced the sharif is unclear. The immediate causes of his revolt involved the collapse of his negotiations with the Turks and the arrival in the Hijaz of the Stotzingen mission, accompanied by a large contingent of Turkish troops. These events suddenly pushed forward the date on which Husayn meant to act.

His discussion with the Turks soon ended, the final break arising ultimately from a message from Enver Pasha directing the sharif immediately to provide volunteers for the Sinai front. Husayn agreed to do so, but only on condition that the Porte grant an amnesty to Arab political prisoners, set up a decentralized Turkish regime in Syria and Iraq, recognize Husayn's rule in the Hijaz as hereditary, and confirm the sharifiate's traditional status and privileges.[35] During the first weeks of April, Jemal Pasha—in connection with an announcement to Husayn that a special Turkish army unit numbering 3,500 troops would travel with the Stotzingen party to Yemen—rejected the sharif's demands and even threatened the safety of Faysal, who was still in Damascus. At the end of the month the Turkish unit arrived in Medina, clearly posing a threat to the sharif and his authority; by 2 May Stotzingen and Neufeld had left Damascus for the Red Sea.[36]

Husayn's anger toward the Turks increased when Faysal reported from Syria Jemal Pasha's continued arrests and executions of local Arab nationalists, which were eliciting approval from at least some Germans. This meant that the planned Arab revolt could not depend on Syria, as originally thought, but must be based in the Hijaz. These events also convinced Husayn that his revolt should begin much sooner than he had intended. In mid-May Jemal permitted Faysal to return to the Hijaz, ostensibly to help organize the volunteer corps ordered to join the Turks in the Sinai Peninsula.[37]

Apparently, however, and despite his recent threat against Faysal's safety, Jemal trusted the Arab chief in the Hijaz more than the Germans. On 25 May Jemal denounced to Loytved Hardegg, the Reich's consul in Damascus, the continued distribution of German propaganda in Arabia. To demonstrate his anger he closed a reading center in Medina that had been established by Oppenheim.[38]

During the ensuing days tension mounted at the German consulate in Damascus, which served as Germany's main outpost and observatory on the fringe of Arabia. On 3 June Loytved Hardegg telegraphed the embassy in Constantinople news of unrest among Bedouins around Medina and along the Hijaz railroad.[39] Two days later he advised that the Arabs had reportedly captured Stotzingen, that fighting between the Turks and the sharif's forces had erupted south of Medina, and that the British had blocked the Arab coast of the Red Sea.[40] The same day, in yet another telegram to the embassy the consul relayed with irritation Jemal Pasha's claim to him that the governor had allowed Faysal to return to the Hijaz only to test the Arab's loyalty to the Turks. "I told him politely," the consul declared, "that the present time did not appear suitable to me to check on Amir Faysal and lose the Hijaz railroad."[41] Loytved Hardegg also seemed unimpressed with Jemal's argument that he had not believed the sharif would risk opposing the Ottoman government in public.[42] On 7 June the consulate reported the dispatch by the Turks of a special mission of three pro-Ottoman Arabs to Medina carrying fifty thousand Turkish pounds in gold for use in bribing local Arabs to support the government against the sharif.[43]

Meanwhile Stotzingen, Neufeld, and four others, one an Indian, had left Damascus for the Red Sea, carrying with them a large number of propaganda leaflets and the apparatus for a wireless station they had orders to construct at the Yemeni port of Hodeida. Stotzingen hoped to charter a dhow at al-Wejh, the next city on the coast, north of Yanbo, but because of the British patrol of the sea the mission continued on land. It soon learned that north of Jidda Bedouins had massacred another German group moving northward up the coast—a party of sailors who had escaped from Java and were making their way back to Europe.[44]

Stotzingen's mission nearly met the same fate. On 5 June, four days after it reached Yanbo, the sharif's armed revolt against the Turks exploded. Faysal and his brother Ali cut the Hijaz railroad line near Medina; while Husayn in Mecca proclaimed the revolt, his forces attacked the Turks in several cities of the Hijaz. Only Stotzingen and two of his men, including Neufeld, managed to escape back north along the Red Sea coast and return to Syria; the others died at the hands of the Bedouin attackers.[45] In the group's frantic scramble for safety baggage and numerous documents were left behind, some of which the sharif soon turned over; from them the British learned the German plans.[46]

The Germans and Turks had miscalculated the ties between the Turks and the sharif, which the latter had severely strained with his demand that the sharifiate be made autonomous and hereditary in his family. Constantinople and Berlin had also failed to appreciate the degree of Husayn's allegiance to the British. As the present study has illustrated, the German and Turkish policy toward the sharif suffered from faulty intelligence information, indecision, and poor preparation. In German policy only the alliance with the Turks ultimately mattered, because Berlin intended to use Turkey to facilitate its future economic and political ambitions in the region. This precluded any support by Germany of Husayn and Arab nationalism.[47]

The German Response and Second Turkish Attack on Egypt

The sharif's uprising stunned the Turks and Germans, despite the many signs warning them of Husayn's disaffection and of his friendship with Britain. On 9 June Loytved Hardegg informed the embassy of allegations that Bedouins led by Faysal had severed the telegraph line north of Medina. Even as the revolt began, however, the consul seemed uncertain about what had caused it. "I still do not know," he told the embassy, "whether the Turkish government provoked conflict with the Grand Sharif, in order to conquer beyond Syria once and for all, including the Hijaz, or whether the Grand Sharif has begun an open struggle against Turkey at Britain's instigation."[48]

For eleven days following the outbreak the foreign ministry and other agencies in Berlin received little information on what had happened, mainly because of poor communication between them, the Constantinople embassy, and the Damascus consulate. News of the revolt caused a stupor in the Turkish government, and it was screened from the public for several weeks. Only on 21 June did the German ambassador, Wolff-Metternich, relay even to the foreign ministry in Berlin the note of 5 June from the consulate relating the outbreak of fighting between Arabs and Turks south of Medina.[49] As late as the end of the month the Damascus consulate held out the hope that there was no Arab revolt. On 25 June Loytved Hardegg informed the embassy that Jemal Pasha believed the sharif would do nothing against the Turks.[50]

This badly misplaced combination of naiveté and optimism soon dissipated. Wolff-Metternich, in two messages to Berlin, reported having learned that as early as mid-1915 the Turkish governor of the Hijaz, Wahib Bey, had informed Enver Pasha of Husayn's treasonous activity and even threatened to murder the sharif. The ambassador had now also discovered that as late as the beginning of June 1916 the sharif had told Jemal Pasha that Husayn had organized an armed unit for the upcoming Turkish expedition against Egypt. Jemal had then permitted Faysal to leave for the Hijaz, accompanied by twenty Turkish officers and carrying a gift to Husayn of five thousand pounds in gold, to lead the unit to the Turks. But scarcely had Faysal and the Turkish officers reached Mecca when the sharif's followers seized the money and forced the officers to return to Syria.[51]

At last, Wolff-Metternich continued, "the Porte is convinced that it should no longer trust the assurances of loyalty from Husayn Pasha and his sons." Accordingly the Turks now deposed Husayn, the "old master of the art of Oriental deception," and replaced him with his uncle, Ali Haidar, who resided in Constantinople. "I ask myself," the ambassador concluded, launching into an angry attack on the Turks' failed Arab policy, "whether [the Porte] arrived at this insight too late."[52] No German official, either in Turkey or in Germany, took even the slightest blame for the Arab revolt, although repeated questions about the sharif's loyalty to the Porte had been raised by German agents since 1914.

On 1 July the Damascus consulate instructed the embassy that the sharif had declared his autonomy and that the Hijaz port city of Jidda had fallen to Arab and British forces.[53] A few weeks later Weber, the dragoman at the embassy, was agreeing with the pro-Young Turk Tunisian, Shaykh Salih, in ascribing the revolt to the Turkish persecution of Arabs in Syria. Salih begged him repeatedly, Weber observed in a memorandum, not to allow Germany to take the revolt lightly.[54] In Germany the press grudgingly mentioned the revolt but termed it insignificant, accusing Husayn of selling out to British gold and the British of planning to dismember and destroy Turkey.[55]

But privately the revolt caused immediate and widespread concern among German officials. One of the first responses came from the German agent in Syria, Prüfer: he joined a small airplane unit of the German "Pasha" corps preparing with the Turkish forces in the Sinai desert to attack Egypt. Of the Arab rebellion, Prüfer first scribbled in his diary on 9 June: "The revolt in the Hijaz grows. I was right to warn about the sharif." A month later he recorded, "The Arab revolt is very bad for the Turks. The amir of Mecca has declared his independence."[56]

German military leaders seemed equally disturbed. Liman von Sanders, the commander of the Turkish Fifth Army, which had suc-

cessfully defended Gallipoli, judged the revolt to be "much more serious than it has appeared for us Germans" and expressed the fear
that it "could even endanger the existence of the present [Turkish]
government."[57] In Constantinople members of the German military
mission worried about the revolt's effect on the planned Turkish attack on Egypt. In Germany Falkenhayn, the chief of the army's high
command, declared that the revolt threatened to undermine the value
of the Turkish alliance; he asked the Reich treasury office to provide
fifty thousand Turkish pounds in gold per month to combat the
uprising.[58]

The Turks, reflecting their view of the Arabs as inconsequential
and their dislike of German involvement in the Arab question,
downplayed the revolt. Enver Pasha emphasized to Humann that the
rebellion had not surprised the Turks. The attaché, visiting Berlin on
12 July, told his superiors at the Reich naval office that based on what
Enver and others at the Porte had told him, the Turks had not only
planned what occurred but had it under control![59] During the fall of
1916 Enver continued to provide the Germans with similar favorable
reports.[60]

Other German officials worried that the Turks would bungle their
attempt to suppress the revolt. Loytved Hardegg particularly held
this view, in part because of a stream of reports from Jemal Pasha
portraying the situation in the Hijaz as rosy.[61] In mid-September
Stotzingen, who had returned to Jerusalem from his ill-fated mission to Arabia, sent the General Staff and foreign ministry a report
that accused the Turks of purposely keeping events in the Hijaz secret to hide the unpleasant truth about them from the Germans. In
Syria, he added, serious deficiencies of food as well as other economic
problems embittered the people even against the Germans and threatened to deliver them to the sharif's cause.[62]

Though the anxiety of most German officials about the effect of
the revolt on the Muslim world was probably warranted, at least initially no German leader attempted to persuade the Porte to stop the
uprising by engaging in serious negotiations with the sharif. From
Mesopotamia the consulate in Baghdad informed the embassy on
22 August, "The defection of the sharif has increased the already restive attitude of the Arabs."[63] During the next weeks the consulate

discussed possible British treaties with Arab tribes along the Euphrates River and encouragement by British agents of Arab assaults on the Turks. In November another message from Baghdad described "the Arab question" as "still very critical." While the Anglo-Indian army in southern Mesopotamia prepared to resume its advance northward, Shiite Arabs launched a furious attack on Turkish troops along the Euphrates, near the village of Hilla.[64]

The German consulates in Palestine and Syria also carefully monitored the revolt's impact on local Arabs. Heinrich Brode, the consul in Jerusalem, emphasized the dislike of Syrians for the Turks and urged that the Germans not identify themselves too much with their allies.[65] In Damascus Loytved Hardegg worried that the sharif's sympathizers would exploit recent attacks by nearby bands of Hauran Arabs on villages and grain stations along the Hijaz railroad south to Deraa.[66] Reports arriving in Berlin from outside the Middle East added to the warnings about the Arab uprising. The German embassy in Madrid quoted an exiled Egyptian prince, Aziz Hassan, then living in Spain, as calling the revolt "very serious" and foreseeing a "widespread effect not only on the Muhammadan world in Africa, Persia and India, but above all in Turkey itself."[67]

The German troubles in this and other respects only increased when the long-planned second Turkish attack on the Suez Canal, led by Kress von Kressenstein, finally began on the morning of 4 August 1916. The assault did nothing to disrupt either the Arab revolt or the extension by the British of their defenses into the Sinai Peninsula. Beginning in the spring of 1916 the newly formed British Egyptian Expeditionary Force (EEF) had advanced across the Sinai Peninsula toward the Ottoman border. In March 1916 General Sir Archibald Murray, Britain's new commander-in-chief in Egypt, decided to secure the defense of the country by occupying al-Arish and Kossaimi on the southern border of Palestine. To the north and east of the Suez Canal the EEF began building a railroad and pushing cavalry into the desert beyond it.[68]

The Turkish expedition, which totaled eighteen thousand soldiers (including the German "Pasha" corps) and nearly as many camels, attacked the main British outpost at Romani, east of the canal. But the fighting ended within the day. British air reconnaissance had anticipated the main Turkish thrust, and the Turks suffered from the fatigue caused by stifling heat and scarce water. The defenders counterattacked with well-equipped cavalry forces and heavy artillery from warships in the nearby Mediterranean Sea; the Turks quickly retreated into the Sinai under the cover of darkness. The British had won a considerable victory. Total casualties among the Turks amounted to nearly nine thousand, among their enemy barely a thousand.

The battle at Romani signaled the end of the long Turkish-German campaign to take the canal and Egypt from Britain.[69] The British now seized the initiative; in the ensuing months their forces steadily and methodically drove the Turks eastward across the Sinai to the Egyptian frontier, between al-Arish and Gaza.

In Arabia, by the end of 1916 the revolt had lost much of its initial momentum, and the sharif's forces had failed to capture Medina. Nevertheless they had registered significant victories over the Turks. In that year the rebels captured Jidda, Mecca, Yanbo, Rabigh, al-Wejh, Kunfidha, and Taif. Also, they seized six thousand prisoners of war, plus weapons and military equipment; forced the Turks to add a substantial number of troops to their Medina garrison; isolated the Turkish divisions in Asir and Yemen from the principal force to the north; and prevented the Germans and Turks from spreading hostilities to Africa. Moreover, they had begun threatening the Hijaz railroad and other communications between Damascus and Medina.[70]

While the insurrection remained for some time a minor affair militarily, German leaders recognized straight away its potential for undermining the Turkish and German war effort in the Middle East. This realization, in part, resulted from Berlin's (and the Porte's) failed campaign since 1914 to wage a similar war by revolution—to incite the Arabs and other Muslims of the region to join the sultan-caliph's holy war against the British. Not coincidentally, in November 1916, the Germans began publishing in Berlin a weekly pan-Islamic journal, *Die Islamische Welt*, edited by the fiery Egyptian pan-Islamist Shaykh Jawish.[71]

As the revolution in the Hijaz began, most German leaders supported the Turkish military strategy of defending Medina and holding the Hijaz front. In the fall of 1916 the number of Turkish troops in Medina reached fourteen thousand. Their commander, Khairy Bey, ordered frequent sorties aimed at recapturing Rabigh on the Red Sea coast and clearing the way for a march on Mecca.[72] The Germans, however, not only exercised little direct military influence on Turkish operations in the Hijaz but disagreed among themselves on other aspects of policy toward the revolt.

At least one German official, Loytved Hardegg, put forth a radical set of proposals to halt the Arab uprising. He reported to Wolff-Metternich that many Syrian Arabs excused the revolt because of Jemal Pasha's recent persecutions of them.[73] Consequently, the Damascus consul urged, Germany should attempt to conciliate the Arabs by distributing pro-Arab propaganda in Syria and elsewhere, by establishing a consulate at Jidda (long desired by Germany), and by forming a pro-Arab party that Germany could use against the Turks in public meetings, the press, and parliament.[74] Wolff-Metternich objected that this would anger the Porte.[75] For the same reason Lossow, the military attaché in Constantinople, forbade the spread of propaganda among Arab troops in the Ottoman army. Nevertheless, the German embassy's branch office of the Information Service for the East, with the Damascus consulate's approval, did distribute thousands of Arab brochures and leaflets in Syria that emphasized the economic strength of Germany.[76]

In part the concern of Lossow and Wolff-Metternich not to upset the Turks over the Arab question resulted from bitter criticism leveled against the Germans in October by the grand vizier, Said Halim. He characterized as failures Germany's political and military operations in the Middle East and accused Berlin of charlatanism in organizing them.[77]

Despite the grand vizier's attack, other signs at the end of 1916 indicated a growing interest of both Turkey and Germany in attempting to halt the sharif's revolt by reconciling with the Arabs. On 29 December Lossow received a request from Enver Pasha for £T200,000 per month for payment to the sharif and other Bedouin chieftains in Syria, Arabia, and Mesopotamia.[78] Simultaneously, Oppenheim, who had returned to Berlin from his long mission in Turkey, sought to negotiate a peace with the sharif, apparently with the Porte's permission, by dispatching a letter to Husayn's foreign minister, Fuad al-Khatib.[79] Neither the Germans nor the Turks, however, received a reply—except for a continuation of the revolt.

"The Biggest Thing in the Near East since 1550"

For the British, the Arab revolt had an immediate effect. To begin with, it destroyed the Stotzingen mission, leaving in shambles the major German effort, begun at the end of 1915 and carefully orchestrated to gain Turkish approval, to seize from a vulnerable Britain the military and political initiative in the Middle East and East Africa. Although the revolt failed to generate a mass anti-Turkish movement among the Arabs, it nevertheless brought the Allies welcome relief. According to the official British history of the Middle East war:

> It is hard to overestimate the importance of the [Stotzingen] expedition, which might have taken Aden by surprise. With these reinforcements the [pro-British Arab chief in Yemen] Idrissi might have been crushed and the [pro-Turkish] Imam [Yahya] left triumphant in the south. Of not less importance would have been its influence across the Red Sea, had Stotzingen obtained touch with German agents.[80]

Further, the revolt, taken in conjunction with the advance begun in the spring of 1916 by the newly formed British EEF across the Sinai Peninsula, provided the Young Turks with a major embarrassment. The Turkish forces opposing Murray's EEF suddenly found themselves hampered by Arab dissidents threatening their communications and transportation lines from the rear.

The revolt and new British strategy in Egypt particularly helped to offset the humiliating defeat of the Anglo-Indian army in Mesopotamia. On 29 April, Anglo-Indian troops had surrendered at Kut al-Amara, after the Turkish Sixth Army, commanded by von der Goltz, rejected an extraordinary offer of two million pounds and forty guns for the Turks to allow the defeated force to retreat on parole. Nearly 70 percent of the Anglo-Indian prisoners taken at Kut later died in Ottoman captivity. The fighting and intense heat left both the Turks and British in Mesopotamia exhausted; the British resumed their attack only seven months later, in December 1916, after the appointment as commander of Major-General Sir F. S. Maude.[81]

Maude refused to advance until he possessed sufficient troops, transport, and supplies and until his men had recovered from the appalling conditions they had endured. Moreover, by then the British had reaffirmed their alliance with Ibn Saud, the powerful Arab chieftain of the Najd. At the end of November 1916 the British hosted him and other Persian Gulf protégés at a lavish reception in Kuwait. Ibn Saud made an unprecedented public declaration of support for the Sharif of Mecca, even though there were conflicts between the two Arab leaders over authority and territory.[82]

Notwithstanding the immediate advantages for Britain from the Arab revolt, one should not overestimate its importance in the general history and in the outcome of World War I. Although it contributed eventually to accelerating the military defeat of Turkey, the rebellion, like the other campaigns in the Middle East, remained secondary in comparison to the huge offensives of Germany and the Western Allies in France. Nor did the revolt ever produce anything resembling a mass movement, as British leaders had hoped it would. Few of his contemporaries agreed with T. E. Lawrence's observation in Cairo that "this revolt, if it succeeds will be the biggest thing in the Near East since 1550."[83]

To be sure, during its first months the uprising achieved noteworthy victories. But despite the rapid spread of the revolt in the Hijaz, it also produced much anxiety among British officials. The army headquarters in Cairo received news of the uprising with little enthusiasm; the commander, Murray, viewed it warily as a political matter and a new, worrisome military front. The British government published in its Muslim lands a carefully worded statement disavowing British involvement in the revolt and promising "to abstain from all interference in religious matters" and "to secure [the] Holy Places of Islam from all external aggression."[84]

Also, the revolt increased French activity in the Middle East, much to the unease of British officials determined to use the war to expand Britain's influence in the region even at its ally's expense. France supported the revolt for several reasons. Politically, the spread of French-backed rebellion among the population of Syria, Palestine, and Armenia could prepare the ground for French intervention and ambitions in the region, especially in Syria. Militarily, the French hoped the revolt would paralyze the Ottoman capacity for war. They also expected the affair to convince a majority of Muslims in France's African colonies to abandon their support for the Turks in favor of France as the liberator of the holy shrines of Islam. During September 1916 the French sent two missions, one to Jidda and the other to Mecca, to assist Husayn's military operations and his procurement of weapons.[85]

Britain and France supplied arms, most of them of old vintage, to the Arab forces through the Red Sea ports of Jidda and Rabigh; the Turks retained control over Medina and the Hijaz railroad. The Arabs, their initial successes notwithstanding, were undisciplined, poorly organized, untrained, and despite Allied aid, ill armed; there was widespread apprehension among the British that the Turks would recapture Mecca. Alarming reports from intelligence sources arrived in Cairo of the Turkish and German efforts to reconcile with the Arabs by increasing shipments of gold and promises of greater autonomy.[86]

The revolt quickly embroiled British leaders from London to Cairo and Delhi in a further round of bitter conflicts over policy. The differences centered on whether Britain should send troops, including Muslim units, to Arabia to aid the sharif. Both Faysal, who commanded the northernmost Arab forces, and his father asked for such assistance. Generally Cairo and Khartoum supported the requests; in London, Sir Mark Sykes, along with other "Easterners," opposed sending British troops to Arabia, although they pressed for every other type of aid for the Arab rebellion. At a meeting of the British government's War Committee, which included a mixture of senior cabinet minsters and strategic advisers and formed a key policy-making body, both Sykes and Clayton, who had just arrived in London from Cairo, persuaded Grey to pay a subsidy of fifty thousand pounds monthly to the sharif.

Sykes in particular presented to the committee and others in London his view of the importance of the Arab revolt in destroying Germany's position in the Middle East. "As regards the Central Powers," he wrote in a lengthy memorandum, "Asiatic Turkey is the last German colony. If the revolt failed, the Turks and Germans would surely triumph, with disastrous results for Britain."[87] McMahon too worried about what would happen if Britain did not assist the sharif adequately. After consulting with Colonel C. E. Wilson, the British representative in the Hijaz, he wrote the Foreign Office on 13 September that recapture of Mecca by the Turks, "apart from grave damage which will ensue to our prestige throughout [the] Moslem world will open the whole of Arabia to [the] Turks and give them free access to [the] Eastern shores of [the] Red Sea."[88]

Notwithstanding, in October the War Committee in London, the Government of India, and the Arab Bureau and key military leaders in Cairo disapproved a request from McMahon and Wingate for troops to be sent to Arabia. Opponents of the plan disliked it for a host of reasons, foremost among them the Muslim world's response to the presence of Christian forces in the Hijaz. Some officials worried that sending the troops to Arabia would violate the pledge given by Britain of non-interference in the Islamic holy places.[89]

Still the debate continued, involving even the French, who alarmed the British by considering themselves sending a force to Arabia. Meanwhile Husayn declared himself "king of the Arabs" and requested that both Britain and France recognize him as ruler of the independent "Arab nation." In December both London and Paris granted Husayn the title of "king of the Hijaz."[90]

In London the "Westerners" and their leader, Robertson, the new Chief of the Imperial General Staff, turned down all ideas of dispatching troops to Arabia, despite gains made by the Turks southwest of Medina, which strengthened the threat of a Turkish advance on Mecca. The situation changed little with the arrival of the new British government led by David Lloyd George and other imperialists eager to use the war to extend Britain's power in the Middle East. Furthermore, the fact that the sharif himself refused to request British troops in writing helped torpedo the project. Only a few British officers, chief among them T. E. Lawrence, a young archaeologist who had been working in the Arab Bureau and General Staff in Cairo, served in the Hijaz, as instructors and advisors with the sharif's forces.[91]

The initial mixed reception of the Arab revolt by Muslims in the Middle East appeared to justify the decision not to land a British force in Arabia. In Egypt the revolt found little popularity in the native press or among military and political authorities, including the sultan, Husayn Kamil.[92] In India both the government and the All-India Muslim League viewed the Arab rebellion with a mixture of surprise and hostility. "All classes," the viceroy declared to the India Office, "bitterly resent any idea of [the] desecration of Holy Places whether by Turk, Arab, or Christian, and condemn [the] Sherif for jeopardising them."[93]

In the last analysis, however, the Arab revolt did not interest the majority of Indian Muslims. For one thing, the rebellion was too far away; many believed that God had ordered such things for reasons known only to Him. For another, the Government of India carefully guided influential Muslims, including princes who owed much of their authority to Britain, to the proper interpretation of these events, emphasizing that to be pro-Turkish was to be anti-British.[94] Additionally, the careful British surveillance of Indian ports and frontiers, together with tightened censorship, screening of the arrival of emigrants suspected of sedition, the ban on Indians carrying arms, and the power to intern persons without trial, effectively foiled efforts by the Germans and Turks to infiltrate India with revolutionary propaganda and agents.[95]

The British continued to monitor carefully Indian and German revolutionary activities in Asia and the United States. Britain's Far Eastern fleet carefully patrolled the waters around Asia, seizing foreign ships involved in shipping arms, ammunition, and revolutionaries—both Indian and German—to India. During the spring and summer of 1916, the British uncovered further information about the German and Indian conspiracy. This came from the trials in Burma of the numerous Ghadrite revolutionaries captured the previous summer there and in Siam; the defendants, who included Jodh Singh, admitted to everything.[96]

London continued to pressure the United States to halt the work in that country of Indian revolutionaries, whom the Germans were assisting and who were producing anti-British propaganda and agents for smuggling into India. At the beginning of 1916 Berlin had sent

Dr. C. K. Chakravarty to the United States to replace Heramba Lal Gupta as head of the Indian revolutionary movement in America. Although Washington refused to act against the Indo-German agents, on 19 April American authorities raided an office in New York occupied by the German consul, Wolf Walter Franz von Igel. They seized incriminating papers that they would use a year later in a trial in San Francisco of numerous Germans and Indians for using the United States as a base for schemes to promote a rebellion against British rule in India.[97]

Libya, Darfur, and Abyssinia

The British also worried about the impact of the Arab revolt on their continuing efforts to pacify the Sanussis in Libya and check the crises, promoted by the pan-Islamic agitation of Turkish and German agents, in Abyssinia and the Sudanese province of Darfur. Much to Cairo's relief, events in Libya had proceeded favorably since the spring of 1916 for the British and Italians; they had contributed, together with the Arab rebellion, to undermining the position in Abyssinia of the pro-Turkish and pro-German heir to the imperial throne, Lij Iyasu.

In Libya, in the aftermath of the defeat of the Shaykh al-Sanussi, the Sayyid Ahmad, the British and Italians negotiated with his cousin, Muhammad Idris, for the latter to replace the sayyid as Shaykh al-Sanussi. The British eventually persuaded Idris to assume the Sanussi order's leadership, mainly by forcibly removing the remnants of Sayyid Ahmad's troops, who suffered from exhaustion and lack of food, from their Egyptian oases to Tripolitania.[98] This ended Britain's extensive military commitments in the western Egyptian desert, which had tied down for months nearly thirty-five thousand imperial troops and caused prodigious expenses.[99]

The British by allying with Muhammad Idris outmaneuvered the Germans, who had also tried to approach Idris. Following the defeat of Ahmad's forces in February 1916 the German and Turkish influence on the Sanussis waned significantly. The German foreign ministry and General Staff failed to persuade the hard-pressed German navy to dispatch to the shaykh a freighter with food and weapons, accompanied by a submarine.[100]

During April a German fact-finding mission headed by Freiherr Wolff von Todenwarth landed by submarine near the port of Jahudie on the coast of Cyrenaica; the boat also had on board a cache of munitions and supplies for the German agent Mannesmann. Todenwarth learned quickly that Bedouins of the new Sanussi shaykh, Muhammad Idris, had murdered Mannesmann to seize money he carried and that the situation in Cyrenaica had worsened substantially for the Germans and Turks. Returning to Germany in May, Todenwarth reported bitter resentment between the Sanussis and their Turkish advisers, including Nuri Pasha. Todenwarth proposed an attempt to ally with Idris, the apparent new leader of the Sanussis, and construct a wireless station in Libya.[101] In July, again in Libya, he observed just how tense relations were between Idris and Nuri Pasha.[102]

Todenwarth also learned of the animosity between Idris and Ahmad, of Idris's refusal to join Nuri in attacking Egypt, and of Idris's negotiations with the British and Italians. In mid-October he boarded another submarine, which carried him west to the Tripolitanian port of Misurata. There, at Nuri Pasha's urging he unloaded munitions and two artillery pieces, not for the Sanussis but for the forces of their bitter enemy, Ramadan al-Suwayhli, and for Sulayman al-Barani, the newly appointed Turkish "governor" of Tripoli.[103]

On his return to Berlin in November Todenwarth reemphasized to the General Staff and the foreign ministry the Sanussis' fervent dislike of the Turks, their desire only for independence from both the Turks and Italians, and their lack of interest in the holy war. He held Nuri Pasha responsible for the anarchy and anti-Turkish attitudes among the Sanussis.[104] The report drew criticism from the German embassy in Constantinople; in addition, it led Enver to discourage even more than previously the dispatch of German agents to Libya, claiming that he did not wish to risk another "Mannesmann affair."[105]

By the end of 1916 German policy in Libya had failed in its objective of keeping the principal Arab elements on the side of Germany and Turkey. Although German submarines continued to land weapons at Misurata for Ramadan al-Suwayhli and al-Barani, both of whom fought the Sanussis and Italians, the Reich was unable to retain contact with the new Sanussi leader or prevent him from uniting with the British and making peace with the Italians.[106]

For their part, the British worried throughout much of 1916 about the impact of the events in Libya—and after June, in Arabia—on the behavior of Ali Dinar, the anti-British sultan whose tribes dominated Darfur. The latter was a state in western Sudan not effectively controlled by Khartoum. During the fall Wingate refused to spare two companies of Sudanese troops to assist the revolt in Arabia because of "Darfur requirements."[107]

Problems in Darfur had arisen at the very outbreak of war between Britain and Turkey. Ali Dinar, influenced by propaganda sent him from Nuri Pasha's Turkish mission in Libya, had proclaimed a jihad against the British. At the end of 1915 Wingate had discovered that Ali Dinar was planning to invade other parts of the Sudan in connection with the Sanussis' attack on Egypt.

During February 1916 Wingate warned Cairo that a buildup by the sultan of Darfur of his forces created "a serious menace to border tribes [of the Sudan]." In response he reinforced the Sudanese camel corps on the frontier with infantry and artillery and requested further armed assistance from French troops in the neighboring colony of Wadai. French intelligence alarmed the British even further by reporting that Ali Dinar expected soon the arrival of a shipment of armaments and munitions from the Sanussis and Nuri Pasha.[108]

British anxiety regarding the sultan's tie to the Sanussis, Turks, and Germans was not entirely unjustified. Berlin had hoped for a long time for an attack by Ali Dinar against the British in Sudan, and for Sanussi assistance in shipping him armaments. In April 1916 the German foreign ministry believed that the sultan and Sayyid Ahmad, then the beleaguered Shaykh al-Sanussi, had concluded an agreement for such collaboration. Todenwarth, the German agent who visited Libya during the summer, dispatched by caravan to the Sudan a letter to Ali Dinar emphasizing German and Turkish military successes and calling on him to join the Sanussis in attacking Egypt.[109] In August Enver Pasha reported to the Germans that Ali Dinar had waged war against the British since March, that Nuri Pasha had sent a caravan from Libya with gifts to the sultan, and that the latter had insufficient weapons and munitions; he requested shipments of them from the Turks and Germans.[110]

By then, however, British and Sudanese soldiers had invaded Darfur in a campaign made difficult and risky by the waterless and roadless terrain. They occupied Ali Dinar's capital, al-Fasher, on 23 May 1916; the sultan fled south with his remaining troops, numbering about two thousand, whom the British bombed with planes sent from Egypt. In al-Fasher the British seized copies of letters sent by Ali Dinar to Enver Pasha and the Turkish sultan-caliph confirming that the Darfur chieftain had joined the jihad. As Britain's forces pursued the sultan, some of his followers revolted, and he attempted to gain time for his escape by pretending to negotiate with the enemy. But at the beginning of November the British reached Ali Dinar's camp at Giuba, a village two hundred miles southwest of al-Fasher, and attacked his few remaining diseased and hunger-ridden followers. The sultan died in the fighting.[111] This ended the most serious danger during World War I of an anti-British revolt in the Sudan.

Britain's successes in Darfur and Libya, and particularly the outbreak of the Arab revolt in June, in turn assisted significantly its efforts to halt the continuing crisis in Abyssinia. The British feared that the upheaval there would spill over into several neighboring British colonial possessions. Throughout the world war Turkish and German agents in Abyssinia had befriended the heir-designate to the throne, Lij Iyasu. They had encouraged his conversion to Islam and urged him to adopt anti-Allied policies—which his council of ministers and important tribal chieftains, most of whom belonged to the Abyssinian Christian church, opposed.[112]

During the first months of 1916 Britain's troubles in Abyssinia mounted. The Italians in Eritrea intercepted a letter showing that the Turks had sought to establish a Muslim pedigree for Iyasu by claiming that he was descended through his father from Fatima, a daughter of the Prophet Muhammad. Also, a special mission from the "Mad Mullah" in nearby Italian Somaliland arrived in Abyssinia to visit Iyasu. The latter had declared to the German minister, Syburg, his readiness to join Germany in the war, but he was reluctant to do so because his influential prime minister, Habte Giorgis, favored the Allies.[113]

Tensions increased for the British when Muslim tribesmen, Ogaden Somalis from southeastern Abyssinia, attacked Britain's outpost at

Serenli, on the northern frontier of British East Africa. The assault killed a district commissioner and sixty-five border guards.[114] As the crisis sharpened, the British and Italian ministers in Addis Ababa, Thesiger and Count Colli respectively, intrigued with the many disappointed and unhappy native politicians, most of them Christian, who despised Iyasu's pro-Islamic course and who were living out their frustration in the capital. On 16 May, when an armed gunman attacked the Italian legation and wounded Colli, Thesiger blamed the Germans, recalling their similar policy in Persia. Nonetheless the British rebuffed Italian demands that the Allies send troops into Abyssinia to restore order and partition the country among them.[115]

When the Italians seized more letters from Iyasu to the "Mad Mullah" and other Somali chieftains, British fears increased of possible raids by Ogaden Somalis across the border into British Somaliland. By 1 June Thesiger and his fellow Allied ministers had uncovered Iyasu's plan to establish an Islamic empire in East Africa, an empire that would include the "Mad Mullah" and Somalis then under Italian, British, and French rule. They also received evidence that the prince had shipped more arms to the mullah.

Thesiger warned the Foreign Office that matters were becoming intolerable and that the Allies should soon issue a joint public protest "to denounce Lij Yasu and to range ourselves on the side of the Abyssinian Church and of those chiefs, and they form a large majority, who hate this Moslem influence."[116] Thus it was hardly surprising that when the Arab revolt began, the British attempted to use it to undermine Iyasu. On 21 June Thesiger met with the prince and informed him of

> the fact that the Sherif had asked for and accepted military assistance from Great Britain, pointing out that once the principal descendant of the Prophet and the guardian of the holy city had asked for our assistance against the Turks, the latter could no longer pretend that they were engaged in a holy war or claim to speak in the name of the Moslem world.[117]

Iyasu, however, seemed little impressed with the Arab revolt; he continued his pro-Turkish and pro-German policies and his shipments of weapons to the "Mad Mullah." In response, the British brokered a peace treaty between the Somali tribesmen in British Somaliland (the Ishaak) and Abyssinia (the Ogaden) that ended the intertribal raiding and counter-raiding of the previous years. Reporting to London the agreement and the resulting tranquillity in Somaliland, the local British commissioner, G. F. Archer, assessed "that the news of events at Mecca has met with a most favourable reception here," as had British assertion of control in Libya and Darfur.[118]

When Iyasu left Addis Ababa and removed his most powerful chieftain and rival, Tafari Makonnen, as governor of Harerge, the heavily Muslim province of eastern Abyssinia, rumors circulated that Iyasu favored a victory by the Central Powers, that he intended to rid East Africa of colonialism, and that he was arming non-Christians against the Europeans. Thesiger, Colli, and their French counterpart encouraged the gossip and met repeatedly in the capital with Habte Giorgis and other members of the council of ministers opposed to Iyasu. On 12 September the Allied representatives assisted in the formation of an anti-Iyasu conspiracy, dispatching a note to the Abyssinian foreign ministry asking for an explanation for Iyasu's belligerence and announcing an arms embargo against the country. The prince's many enemies among his ministers and tribal chieftains feared that his continued leadership would plunge Abyssinia into a war with the Allies and also into civil strife.

The crisis in Addis Ababa greatly alarmed the British government in London. Grey associated the upheaval in Abyssinia with the failed German and Turkish mission led by Stotzingen. The latter, Grey reminded Cairo, had aimed at "provoking an outbreak in Abyssinia and the adjacent countries from a base in Arabia." Both Grey and the military leadership in London opposed armed intervention in Abyssinia; the foreign secretary suggested as an alternative using the Sharif of Mecca to influence Lij Iyasu. Britain, Grey proposed to McMahon, might persuade Husayn "to pronounce against Lij Iyasu's claim to descent from Fatima" and thereby undermine the prince's assertion that he belonged to the family of the Prophet.[119]

A revolution in Addis Ababa on 27 September made this plan moot. An assembly of the anti-Iyasu faction in the Abyssinian government deposed the prince and proclaimed a new ruler and monarch, Zawditu, Menilek's daughter. Iyasu's enemies charged him with apostasy and internal subversion; the leader of the Abyssinian Christian church excommunicated him as an unbeliever. Tafari played a key role in the revolution, which resulted in his immediate promotion to *ras* (chieftain) and his nomination as heir-apparent to the throne and regent to the Empress Zawditu. The next day, Thesiger informed the Foreign Office, "The Government is now in the hands of those who are friendly to our cause."[120]

The Allies, however, had not heard the last of either Iyasu or his German and Turkish supporters. The Porte informed the German embassy in Constantinople that Lij Iyasu's overthrow was hardly favorable news, but both the Germans and Turks prophesied that the deposed prince and his father, Ras Mikail, would attempt a counter revolution.[121] But on 26 October the forces of the new regime defeated Mikail's army and captured the chieftain. His son, Iyasu, fled for sanctuary to his native province, Welo, northeast of Addis Ababa.

The Rivalry in Switzerland

In Europe the Arab revolt, although noticed by the press, hardly made an impression.[122] Neutral Switzerland, however, was an exception. There resided numerous Egyptian and Turkish exiles opposed to or courted by one side or the other in the hope that the Orientals could be used to advantage. Anglo-French agents exploited the revolt to distribute anti-German propaganda among the exiles. In Geneva, Prince Sabaheddin, an exiled former Young Turk and leader of a party of liberal Turkish dissidents, claimed—quite falsely—that he had helped prepare the Arab rebellion.[123]

The revolt, however, changed few political attitudes among the expatriates in Switzerland. For example, the leader of the exiled Egyptian nationalists, Muhammad Farid, whose Young Egypt party demanded the freeing of Egypt from foreign rule, remained alienated from the Young Turks. The nationalists and Egyptian students in Switzerland suspected the Porte of intending to use the war to replace Britain as the ruler of Egypt. Similarly, bitter conflicts existed between the Young Egyptians and the Turkish exiles; most of the latter had worked for sultan Abd ul-Hamid's regime and now formed a party hostile to the Young Turk government.[124]

Inasmuch as it feared that Germany intended after the war to create a vassal state of Turkey, the party tried to tie itself to France and Britain. Throughout much of 1916 German diplomats and spies in Switzerland alleged to the foreign ministry repeated French attempts to use the party to establish a separate Franco-Turkish peace. Especially during May (when pro-peace feelings surfaced briefly in France and a prominent French politician contacted the German minister in Bern about a Franco-German peace) the Germans carefully monitored discussions between Fuad Selim, the Turkish minister in Switzerland, and an emissary of Sabaheddin.[125]

German intelligence operatives in Geneva also reported increased contact by the Allies, specifically former French and Russian dragomen, with the Turkish opposition party. In July emissaries from Talaat Pasha, the Porte's interior minister, arrived in Switzerland; their task allegedly included persuading the party to act as an intermediary for concluding a peace. However, the British government ordered its minister in Bern to discourage all such proposals, absent evidence that they originated from fully accredited representatives of the Porte.[126]

During August a key German spy and member of the consulate in Geneva, F. Marum, observed a substantial increase in the number of French agents in the city. Also, Zimmermann and the foreign ministry discussed reported Allied peace feelers through Sabaheddin to the Turkish finance minister, Javid Bey, who was then visiting Berlin. Meanwhile, other German reports claimed that the Turkish party in Switzerland, assisted by French money, sought to organize a revolt in the Turkish army.[127]

It is apparent from the German and British archives that the Entente had no serious intentions of using members of the opposition party to facilitate a separate peace. Instead the Allies cultivated party members to gather bits of information about the enemy or to create unease. The Turkish oppositionists, for their part, hoped by claiming to represent the Allies to inflate their importance, ingratiate themselves with both sides, and receive financial subsidies from each.[128]

Despite Swiss neutrality, German and Allied spies both worked extensively to keep the Orientals in Switzerland under surveillance and from falling completely into the camp of the respective enemy. During 1915 the Swiss authorities broke up the poorly operated British intelligence network, whereupon it was steadily rebuilt during the ensuing year around the novelist W. Somerset Maugham and officials in Geneva.[129] On the other side, in March 1916 the Swiss arrested briefly the head of German civilian intelligence in the country, Heinrich Jacoby, as he returned to Germany. By November both the French and Swiss had begun closing in on Jacoby and his spy ring, which included two Armenians and an Irish journalist.[130] Some of the duties of Jacoby's group involved spying on Turkish officials like Zia Bey, the consul general in Geneva, and on Fuad Selim, the minister; the Germans suspected both of ties to the Allies and the Turkish opposition party.[131]

No Oriental in Switzerland, however, attracted more attention from both the British and Germans than did the ex-khedive of Egypt, Abbas Hilmi. He had lived in Switzerland since the summer of 1915, and both sides continued to court him to keep him from joining the other. The British negotiated sporadically with the ex-khedive during the summer and fall of 1916, hoping to persuade him to renounce officially his claim to the Egyptian throne.[132] Although Germany received reports that Abbas Hilmi was unhappy with the Reich and intended to abdicate his throne, Zimmermann, as under-secretary of state in the foreign ministry, concluded that "it would not be clever to let him fall completely and push him into the arms of England."[133]

When the Arab revolt erupted in June, Abbas Hilmi angrily blamed the Young Turk leaders, Enver Pasha and Jemal Pasha, for the uprising and attempted unsuccessfully to send an envoy to the sharif through Austria.[134] The feelings of the ex-khedive reached Tschirschky, the German minister in Vienna, who reported them to Jagow. Said Tschirschky, "Hilmi foresees a very severe crisis for the entire Turkish empire. If the sultan is stripped of his honor as caliph, the Turkish empire will possess no connecting link."[135]

Although the Germans and Young Turks differed in their initial responses to the sharif's revolt, they both nevertheless applied pressure on Abbas Hilmi to return to Constantinople and declare his loyalty to the Porte. Some in the German foreign ministry, including Wesendonk, believed that the ex-khedive had assisted Husayn in unleashing the revolt. But Abbas Hilmi, full of fear and dislike of the Turks, refused to go to Turkey, which in turn fueled the mistrust of the Porte and Berlin toward him.[136]

During October, the ex-khedive's problems mounted. Swiss authorities, on information supplied by a British spy named "Bernard" whom Abbas Hilmi had unwittingly hired, arrested his financial agent and cousin, Muhammad Yeghen Pasha. The Swiss discovered at Yeghen's house documents implicating the ex-khedive in espionage and propaganda activities during 1915 for the Central Powers. For a few weeks, until Yeghen's release, the ex-khedive feared the possibility of his own arrest or deportation from Switzerland for violating its neutrality laws.[137]

Although he escaped this embarrassment, the affair undermined further his position with both the Germans and Turks on one hand, and Britain on the other. His chances for a settlement with Britain that would provide him badly needed money from his Egyptian properties, had diminished significantly by the end of 1916, because the military situation in the Middle East had turned in Britain's favor. The EEF was preparing for an offensive into Palestine, while in Mesopotamia a reinforced Anglo-Indian army advanced north along the Tigris River, with the goal of capturing Baghdad.[138]

Furthermore, Britain steadfastly refused Abbas Hilmi's demand that it name Abd al-Moneim, his youngest son, to succeed to the Egyptian throne. Sir Horace Rumbold, the new British minister in Bern, who conducted Britain's negotiations with Abbas Hilmi, learned that the ex-khedive was likewise negotiating with the local Turkish and German legations. Much of the information came to the British from one of their principal agents, the Arab "Maurice," whom the British had sent to Switzerland to help them keep Abbas Hilmi under surveillance. When Britain's discussions with the ex-khedive stalled at the end of December, the Foreign Office gave him until mid-July 1917 to renounce his throne and accept a financial settlement on his Egyptian properties.[139]

9 Toward an Allied Victory, 1917

During the first months of 1917 the Allied war against Turkey took on a new importance, similar to that of 1915. In response to the failure of the Allies during 1916 to achieve any gains in the battles in France, the imperialists in London who dominated the Lloyd George ministry focused increasingly on the interests of the British Empire overseas. The government accelerated Britain's previous plans to partition Turkey, plans that included placing both Palestine and Mesopotamia under British control. The EEF attacked in Palestine, but it advanced deeply into the province only during the fall of 1917, after being reinforced and overhauled by a new commander, General Edmund Allenby. The EEF captured Beersheba on 31 October and Jerusalem on 9 December. In Mesopotamia, Anglo-Indian forces captured Baghdad and advanced further north along the Tigris River.[1]

Turkey, Germany, and the Arabs

The Turkish armies had suffered heavy losses in fighting at Gallipoli and in the Caucasus; during 1917 desertions increased, manpower dried up, and the strain intensified on Ottoman resources. After the fall of Baghdad the Turks persuaded the Germans to increase their military commitment in the Middle East. During the spring and summer the Ottoman and German military leaderships agreed to undertake a major offensive to recapture Baghdad and southern Mesopotamia from the British. For this purpose the former German chief of staff, Erich von Falkenhayn, assumed command of a newly created German Army Group F, or as the Turks called it, *Yilderim* ("thunderbolt" or "lightning"). The new force initially numbered eleven thousand German soldiers and officers. Moreover, for service under Yilderim and Falkenhayn the Porte agreed to form a new Turkish army, the Seventh, and reequip the Sixth Army, which had fought in Mesopotamia.[2]

The decision to recapture Baghdad instead of fortifying Palestine and Syria against British and sharifian attack rested significantly on a change in leadership at the Porte. During February the Young Turk faction around Enver Pasha and Talaat Pasha increased its power when Talaat replaced Said Halim as grand vizier. Following the Arab revolt, Said Halim had criticized German operations in Turkey. Both Enver and Talaat held extreme pan-Turanian ideas; these emphasized uniting under Ottoman rule the many Turkish peoples of southern and central Russia and northwest Persia.

The loss of Baghdad, which lay on the main route to Persia, had delivered a serious blow to such aspirations. Now, however, with the progressive Russian collapse leaving Britain as Turkey's sole serious opponent in the Middle East, Young Turk dreams of creating a pan-Turanian empire intensified. The failed pan-Islamist campaign, which the Arab revolt symbolized, helped shift the CUP leaders' attention even more toward central Asia.[3] The Germans for their part agreed to the new offensive in Mesopotamia because of the Reich's long-held ambition to complete the Baghdad railroad and make Turkey a base for extending Germany's economic influence into Asia as well as into the Middle East and Africa.[4]

The impetus and planning for much of the economic campaign developed in the German foreign ministry, particularly with Oppenheim. At its direction the embassy in Constantinople arranged for an agency of German heavy industry to act as a front organization to distribute economic propaganda in Turkey. The agency, however, had little success; its propaganda aroused further Turkish suspicion toward German interests in Turkey and contributed to the Porte's increasing censorship.[5] Prüfer, the head of the embassy's intelligence bureau, proposed that Germany change its propaganda, which portrayed Germans as superior warriors and industrialists, to emphasize their peace-loving nature and concern with Ottoman culture.[6] His idea of moderating German nationalism received little attention in Berlin.[7]

This emphasis on the nationalist nature of the Reich's propaganda paralleled the expanding German military presence in Turkey. The advance of the British EEF and its Arab allies into Palestine persuaded the Porte to transfer there both the new German Army Group F and the Ottoman Seventh Army and to shift much of the power of command in Palestine from Jemal Pasha, the commander of the Ottoman Fourth Army there and in Syria, to Falkenhayn.[8]

Both Kress von Kressenstein and Jemal, the latter a much greater pan-Islamist than Enver or Talaat, warned the government in Constantinople not to attempt to defend simultaneously Palestine and the Hijaz; instead Kress proposed that the Turks abandon the Hijaz and Yemen to the Arabs and focus on defending Palestine. Only in this way, he argued, could the Turks hold firm, eventually win the war against the advancing British and Arabs, and retain Arabia and even the province of Syria in their empire. The Porte, however, refused Kress's suggestion, fearing the political consequences of relinquishing the lands.[9]

Within the Young Turk regime, sharp disagreements surfaced over this and other aspects of Ottoman war policy. A faction friendly to the Allies and led by Javid Bey, the newly reappointed finance minister, tried unsuccessfully to assert itself against Enver and Talaat by opposing the rupture of diplomatic relations with the United States.[10] Richard von Kühlmann, the new German ambassador to the Porte, emphasized to the foreign ministry the conflict in the CUP regime. Both Kühlmann and his superiors in Berlin, not wishing to antagonize the Porte and risk losing it to a separate peace with the Allies, deferred to it on a variety of issues, including the Arab question.[11] How much the Arab insurrection concerned the Ottomans is unclear; the German documents suggest that throughout 1917 Turkey did little to make peace with Husayn and the rebels. Instead, until the fall much of Enver Pasha's attention centered on furthering his pan-Turanian ambitions by recapturing Baghdad from the British. In their approaches to the sharif the Young Turks limited themselves to vague suggestions about granting the Arabs autonomy; moreover, it was Jemal Pasha, who had ordered the bloodbath against Arab leaders in Syria, who now extended some of the Porte's feelers to the sharif about ending hostilities, which hardly inspired Husayn's trust.[12]

Despite Germany's deference to the Ottomans on the events in the Hijaz, the Germans feared the revolt and gave it careful attention. On 5 January Loytved Hardegg, the consul in Damascus, added to a lengthy report to the foreign ministry a conclusion mixing hope and pessimism. Emphasizing the former, he alleged that Ibn Saud, the leading Arab prince in eastern and central Arabia having close ties to Britain, had recently sent a delegation to the Ottomans at Medina and might soon join Turkey in the war against the sharif. The downside, he predicted, was that soon Husayn's forces would open "a passionate offensive with the assistance of England."[13]

The forecast proved remarkably accurate. Three weeks later, Arab troops under Faysal and accompanied by T. E. Lawrence arrived at the Red Sea port of al-Wejh, a day after the town had been taken. The capture of al-Wejh opened a new phase in the Arab campaign. The Arabs used it as a base from which to launch guerrilla attacks along a substantial section of the southern Hijaz railroad and to make it harder for the Turks to attempt to recapture Mecca.[14]

Meanwhile, Kühlmann described to the foreign ministry the confusion in the Turkish government's policy toward the Arab question. On one hand, Constantinople sought to expand the war against the sharif. The Porte still encouraged efforts to reconcile Ibn Saud and Ibn Rashid and to persuade them to enter the war against Husayn. On the other hand, the Turks dispatched to Mecca a close friend of the sharif, Ibrahim Bey, the president of the Ottoman council of state, to present Husayn an offer expanding the authority of the Hijaz amirate and making it hereditary. The emissary also carried the promise of a large financial subsidy for Husayn. Nonetheless, according to Kühlmann, inner circles in the CUP considered Ibrahim Bey's mission a failure before it started.[15] Rumors also abounded in Constantinople that to implement the new Arab policy successfully the Ottomans would replace the anti-Arab Jemal Pasha as governor of Syria. Yet, Kühlmann cautioned, that could backfire if the sharif and his followers sensed Turkish weakness in Jemal's removal.[16]

The Germans themselves seemed confused and divided over what to do with the Arab question. Kühlmann and other German officials did little to encourage either an Ottoman rapprochement with the

Arabs or an intensification of the Porte's military measures against Husayn, but privately they worried about the uprising and criticized the Turks for having caused the revolt. Kühlmann, much like his predecessors at the embassy, blamed Jemal Pasha's persecutions of the Arabs in Syria.[17]

For a brief time during March and April the Germans expected the fall of Medina to the Arabs. Arab forces under the Sharif of Mecca's son, Zaid, had captured a convoy of Ibn Rashid's, the young Arab prince and leader of the Shammar in northern Arabia; it had been attempting to deliver to the Ottomans at Medina food, guns, and livestock. Ibn Rashid and his followers then joined the Turks northwest of the holy city. But Ibn Rashid had lost influence in his own lands, and the Turks viewed him as a burden rather than a source of supply or assistance. To prevent him from returning east and possibly joining the enemy, the Ottomans detained him as a hostage against the good behavior of his tribesmen. This seemed to produce in Berlin a feeling of panic, and even the bizarre idea that Germany should force Turkey to transfer the grave of the Prophet from Medina to Jerusalem in order to keep it under Ottoman control. Wesendonk opposed the scheme; moving the grave, he argued, "would be interpreted . . . as robbery and a crime committed [by Turkey] against Islam, with the assistance or even at the instigation of the Germans."[18]

From throughout Palestine, Syria, and Mesopotamia, German agents reported rising Arab feelings against the Turks. Gerhard von Mutius, the consul in Beirut, denounced the Ottoman silence on the fighting in the Hijaz and southern Palestine. This policy, he informed Berlin, was producing the "wildest rumors" among local Arabs of the imminent defeat of the Turks. "Already they are talking among themselves," he continued, "about what they as Arabs would still have to do with the Turks if Mecca, Medina, Baghdad, and also Jerusalem were no longer in Turkish hands."[19] Walter Rössler, the consul in Aleppo, notified Kühlmann in May: "The attitude of the Arabs in Mesopotamia is evermore threatening. All of them seem to be armed in order to unite with the southern Arabs, who have joined the pro-British sharif."[20]

Britain and the Arabs: The Sharif, Ex-Khedive, and "Maurice"

The British believed increasingly that the Turks and Germans pursued a well-coordinated policy toward the Arabs and the sharif, one that meant to entice him into concluding peace with Turkey and ending his alliance with Britain. This view, which had dominated British thinking during much of the war, resulted from faulty reports by intelligence agents and perhaps from the sharif himself.

Husayn, a skillful politician, had doubts about British postwar intentions in Arab lands and thus sought to keep open his options by secretly preserving his lines of communication to the enemy. At the beginning of January the Arab Bureau in Cairo circulated information that Oppenheim was "in Medina . . . attempting to make terms for the Turks with the Sherif." Two weeks later Husayn contributed to the rumor by telling the British he had "heard from reliable sources that 22 Germans are now in Medina. Oppenheim is almost certainly there."[21]

During the ensuing weeks the India Office, the Foreign Office, and the Arab Bureau emphasized Britain's interests in Arabia and the value of the sharif in assisting Britain's future control of the Middle East.[22] At the end of March Colonel C. E. Wilson, the British representative in Jidda, asked the Arab Bureau to increase Britain's subsidies to Husayn from £125,000 to £200,000 per month. "As is well known," said Wilson, "the Germans and Turks have spent huge sums in the Hedjaz and neighbouring country on bribes to Sheikhs and Tribes. The Sherif informs me that he has certain evidence that £T1,000,000 was sent in all to Medina about six months ago for the purpose of bribes."[23] Above all, he emphasized to Cairo, the sharif's alliance with Britain and revolt had lessened the threat to British interests of pan-Islamism.[24]

During April reports flooded the Arab Bureau and other British intelligence offices that the Turks and Germans had offered "a spiritual caliphate" to Husayn if the latter halted his revolt.[25] This information, coupled with an unsuccessful attempt by British forces to take the Palestinian town of Gaza, damaged morale in Cairo. In addition, the Arab world received the fall of Baghdad to the Mesopotamia Expeditionary Force (MEF) with mixed feelings. Simultaneously, the sharif complained to Wilson about numerous issues, including, as Wilson informed the Arab Bureau, the boundaries of the kingdom Husayn was to receive after the war.[26]

In addition, Husayn's foreign minister, Fuad al-Khatib, expressed to Wilson the sharif's unhappiness at not being sent airplanes, and at Britain's involvement with other Arab chieftains without his approval. The minister reminded Wilson of Husayn's loyalty to Britain and of how the sharif had not only abandoned the Turks but had helped destroy the German attempt to penetrate (in the Stotzingen mission) Arabia, the Red Sea, and Africa.[27]

These factors gave added urgency to meetings held during May in the Hijaz between Husayn and Sir Mark Sykes, Lloyd George's recent appointee to the secretariat of the prime minister's powerful government body, the War Cabinet, as its expert on Islamic affairs. By then it was obvious that the Arab revolt would survive. Britain, therefore, could no longer ignore the problem of reconciling its previous commitments on the postwar Middle East to the sharif and those made, through the secret Sykes-Picot agreement of 1916, to the French. Some circles in London and Cairo now even questioned the Sykes-Picot partition and pressed for a revision to give Britain a stronger position in Palestine and in Arabia. How much the sharif, who asked that both Sykes and François Georges Picot visit him, knew about the Anglo-French agreement is unclear, although Husayn generally tried to exploit the two powers' rivalry in the region. Despite the secrecy of the document, the Italian government had learned of it.[28]

Sykes conferred with Husayn privately at the beginning of May in Jidda, and two weeks later both Sykes and Picot met the Arab leader. Whether the visitors gave the sharif the details of the Sykes-Picot agreement still remains uncertain. Little doubt exists, however, that they reassured him of their support of Arab independence and of the principle of a postwar confederation of Arab states. In addition they discussed with the sharif France's future role in Syria; Husayn understood that France was to have a place there and that Britain recognized the legitimacy of it. While in Arabia, Sykes witnessed the conflicts that the French military mission to Husayn, led by Edouard Brémond, was causing between the Arabs and British. For the first time he saw the advantage of removing the French from the Hijaz.[29]

Husayn's meeting with Sykes and Picot did little to lessen British fears that the enemy might persuade the sharif to stop the Arab revolt. An important question is whether Britain's concern about alleged German and Turkish approaches to the Arabs influenced it to renew during the summer and fall the EEF's advance into Palestine, coordinated closely with the activities of the Arab rebels. By June Faysal and his forces, following an operational plan suggested by T. E. Lawrence and approved in both London and Cairo, had moved north from al-Wejh. They recruited new followers among the tribes and destroyed bridges, track, and communications along the Hijaz railroad. On 6 July the Arabs captured Aqaba, for use as a center from which to cut the railroad between Maan and Deraa. The ultimate goal was to raise tribal forces that would harass the railroad from Damascus to Aleppo, from bases further north in Syria.[30]

During August the British moved Faysal and his force to Aqaba and, with Husayn's permission, incorporated them into the EEF under its new commander, Allenby. However, the British officials in Cairo hoped eventually to use the Arab forces for much more than simply military purposes; postwar political goals dominated their thinking. They favored a postwar Middle East composed of various Arab states, chiefdoms, or principalities, bound loosely together under sharifian leadership, but under British control exercised locally and through Husayn. Cairo, for its part, intended the sharifian army to assist the EEF to conquer Syria and unify it on a national basis, thereby placing Britain in a strong position for domination of the region after the war. As part of this scheme Cairo sought to undercut France's claims to portions of Syria as defined in the Sykes-Picot agreement and in Picot's May meeting with Husayn.[31]

Sir Mark Sykes, having returned to London, seemed less worried about the French than about world opinion toward the agreement between himself and Picot for postwar Anglo-French domination of the Middle East. During 1917, war-weariness among the belligerents on both sides had produced several proposals for a peace without annexations. Sykes urged that Britain remain faithful to the Sykes-Picot arrangement, but he failed to convince others in London, including Lloyd George. During May and June the prime minister and Lord Robert Cecil, the assistant foreign secretary, announced publicly Britain's intention of dismembering the Ottoman Empire. They demanded the curbing or elimination of Turkey's control over Arabia, Palestine, Syria, Armenia, and Mesopotamia. Lloyd George and the other imperial expansionists in his government wished to place as many as possible of the Arab regions of the former Turkish empire under exclusive British influence.

Still other powerful forces in London, influenced by the possibility that Russian Jews might persuade their fellow Russians to continue in the war, and by the desire to secure Britain's interests in Palestine against France, had begun discussing plans that would result on 2 November in the Balfour Declaration. Named for the foreign secretary, A. J. Balfour, it expressed Britain's support for "a National Home for the Jewish People" in postwar Palestine.[32]

In the fall of 1917, the raids by the Arabs and Lawrence on the railroad grew in number, as Allenby and the EEF drove northward into Palestine and toward Jerusalem. To prepare for this campaign the EEF had previously spread into southern Palestine propaganda identifying the Allied cause with that of Arab autonomy. In addition, the British sent into the region emissaries who dispensed large amounts of gold to induce local Arab tribes to withhold their support from the Ottomans and Germans.[33]

Still another factor added to Britain's fear that its enemies were making a strong effort to recruit the Arabs. In October the Porte announced that the ex-khedive of Egypt, Abbas Hilmi, had returned to Constantinople from Europe, where he had lived since 1915. Throughout 1917, while still in Switzerland, the ex-khedive had in his usual fashion played a double-edged game. Seeking to extract more money from the German and Ottoman legations, he had led them to believe that he would soon complete a deal allying him with Britain.[34] But when Talaat Pasha replaced Said Halim, Abbas Hilmi's cousin and arch-enemy, as grand vizier, the ex-khedive entered negotiations with the Porte for his return to the Ottoman capital. The Germans urged him to do so, in part because the ex-khedive and his son, Abd al-Moneim, had been spinning a web of intrigue against the Central Powers by negotiating with Britain and France.[35]

Still other factors persuaded Abbas Hilmi to move back to Constantinople. The British had ended their negotiations with him on 14 July without the ex-khedive either accepting or rejecting their offer of a financial settlement on his Egyptian properties were he to renounce his Egyptian throne. Thereafter Britain moved secretly to liquidate his properties and officially remove him from the succession.[36]

The ex-khedive's decision to live again in Constantinople especially pleased Berlin. The Germans seemed more determined than ever during the final months of 1917 to safeguard their future candidates for the Egyptian throne. They hoped to reconcile the ex-khedive and Young Turks, and to prevent his son from befriending the British (although Britain cared little for him).[37]

When the ex-khedive arrived in October in Constantinople, he announced that the Turks had agreed to place him on the Egyptian throne once again and that he would persuade the Sharif of Mecca to give up his revolt. The British both believed and privately expressed concern about what they heard. Also contributing to Britain's uneasiness were the death of the Egyptian sultan, Husayn, on 9 October, his replacement by a younger brother, Ahmad Fuad, and the first signs during the war of anti-British feeling in Egypt.[38]

In fact the Porte had little intention of using Abbas Hilmi to approach the sharif or participate in any other way in Ottoman efforts to conciliate the Arabs. Instead, as the German embassy in Constantinople reported to Berlin, the Young Turks had coaxed Abbas Hilmi back because they mistrusted him, wished to keep him under close scrutiny, and sought to destroy whatever influence they imagined he possessed with the British, French, Arabs, or the party of exiled Ottomans in Switzerland.[39]

The British, however, persisted in viewing Abbas Hilmi as part of a major Turkish campaign, promoted by Germany, to grant autonomy to Arabia and other Turkish provinces. Berlin, said reports reaching the British in Switzerland, was "prepared to sacrifice the whole of the Arab element in Turkey."[40] The visit of Wilhelm II to Constantinople in mid-October fueled the rumors.[41]

During the fall the British dispatched the Arab agent "Maurice" to Switzerland and Germany to discover more of the enemy's supposed machinations. First the spy met the German minister in Bern, Baron von Romberg, and told him that he had once worked for the British and a Syrian party against the Ottomans but that now, because the British owed him money and had tried to force him to go to France, he wished to join Turkey and assist it in persuading the Arabs to return to the Ottoman fold.

Wesendonk, also in Switzerland at the time, and Prüfer at the embassy in Constantinople suspected "Maurice" of being a Lebanese or Syrian spy for Britain;[42] however, the new German ambassador in Constantinople, Bernstorff (who had replaced Kühlmann when the latter returned to Berlin as foreign minister) believed him to be well informed on Arab tribes in Mesopotamia and northern Arabia. In mid-September the Porte, agreeing with its minister in Switzerland, Fuad Selim, concluded that "Maurice" possessed important information on British contacts in and plans for Turkey, and directed the Germans to send him to Constantinople.[43]

On his way to Turkey the British spy stopped in Berlin, where officials in the General Staff, as well as Kühlmann, questioned him about British intentions in Syria and Mesopotamia and about the Arab revolt. He wished, the spy said, for the Germans to convince the Turks to grant autonomy to the Arabs.[44] When he arrived in Constantinople, "Maurice" met and discussed the Arab question with both Talaat Pasha and Enver Pasha. Why the Young Turks treated him so well is uncertain, unless they were genuinely interested in using him against the British and to influence Arabs in Syria to remain loyal to Turkey.[45] Upon reaching Damascus "Maurice" had an audience with Jemal Pasha, who emphasized that he had repeatedly written to both the sharif and Faysal urging their reconciliation with the Turks but that they had not replied. He did not return to Cairo and relate his story to the British until January 1918, but "Maurice" nevertheless provided British intelligence with occasional reports during his mission.[46]

Mesopotamia and Palestine:
Declining Fortunes of the Turks and Germans

Britain took as a sign of its enemies' competition for Arab support the intense German effort to recruit hungry and destitute tribes in Mesopotamia against the Anglo-Indian army. For much of the war German agents in Mesopotamia had assiduously courted Ajaimi, the powerful Muntafiq chief. At the beginning of 1916, for example, the German commander in Mesopotamia, von der Goltz, had met with Ajaimi to enlist his forces in a planned Ottoman and German advance on Basra. In August 1917 the Germans discussed making Ajaimi the amir of Mesopotamia and acquiring from him land on which to extend the Baghdad railroad to Basra.[47]

When the Yilderim army was formed during the summer and fall, its main contact with the Muntafiq and other Arabs along the Euphrates River lay with a special German intelligence group called the Muntafiq Mission (or Missmont). Organized in Aleppo and headed by Conrad Preusser the archaeologist, Missmont had arrived on 24 September at Hit, a town on the western bank of the Euphrates. Missmont collected intelligence information, much of it from Arab spies paid to journey into British-held areas. The group disseminated propaganda aimed at inciting local tribes against the Anglo-Indian army and persuading them to attack behind its lines. Missmont also issued hundreds of rifles to shaykhs and lavishly spent money on the latter.[48]

However, at the end of September a victory by the Anglo-Indian forces over Turkish and German troops at nearby Ramadi broke the power of both Ajaimi and the Germans. Henceforth Ajaimi now aimed primarily at extorting more money from Missmont. Preusser, who believed that the main Turkish and German military offensive would occur in Mesopotamia, found his work undermined further when Yilderim and the Turkish Seventh Army were sent from Mesopotamia to the Palestine front. Moreover, local Turkish officials deliberately made it difficult for the Germans to contact the Arabs directly. Eventually the Yilderim leadership, on orders from the Porte, demanded that Missmont sever all relations with the Arabs.[49]

The German policy in Mesopotamia failed also because of extensive British activities among the local Arabs. Since January Sir Percy Cox, the Government of India's representative in the Persian Gulf, had tried unsuccessfully to persuade Ajaimi and the Muntafiq to join the British side. The Anglo-Indian army had even provided one of its agents, Colonel Gerard Leachman, with motorized vehicles to capture the Muntafiq chief.[50] The feverish hunt for Ajaimi continued to the end of the year, but increasing numbers of other shaykhs, many of their followers suffering from hunger, offered to surrender in return for foodstuffs and subsidies.[51]

In Palestine and Syria the British and Arab military campaign forced the Turks and Germans to intensify their political efforts to keep the local Arabs loyal to Turkey. Upon the arrival of Yilderim in Palestine and Falkenhayn's assumption of command the Germans assumed—apparently with the approval of the Ottomans—a greater role in appealing to the Arabs. They established a special bureau in Damascus to spread anti-British propaganda and dispatch agents with gold to sow discontent among the sharif's followers.[52]

Oskar von Niedermayer, the leader of previous German expeditions to Persia and Afghanistan, also arrived in Syria. He tried unsuccessfully to bribe the sharif's son, Faysal, to conclude an agreement with the Germans and Ottomans.[53] Still another sign of German interest in the sharifians was Prüfer's deluded suggestion to the foreign ministry that Germany use the Sanussis in Libya—with whom in fact the Germans had lost all influence—to induce the sharif to halt his revolt.[54]

The pro-Arab policy of the Turks and Germans seemed even more evident when the anti-Arab Jemal Pasha lost much of his military command in Palestine to Falkenhayn. The British and Arab advance into Palestine placed extraordinary pressure on Jemal's Fourth Army, which defended the province; weakened by three years of war, desertion, and serious deficiencies of armaments, food, and other war materiel, the Fourth Army had only twenty-five thousand troops to face the eighty-four thousand in the EEF. Then too, the British offensive threatened the rear and flank of the German and Turkish military operations in Mesopotamia.

This situation persuaded Enver Pasha and Falkenhayn, the German commander in Mesopotamia, to shelve momentarily their plan for the reconquest of Baghdad and to transfer the newly established Yilderim and the Turkish Seventh Army from Mesopotamia to Palestine. In addition, Germany sent to Palestine a heavily armed Asia Korps, or "Pasha II," as the Turks called it. There were problems, however, transporting the German forces to Turkey, and also bitter conflicts between Enver, Falkenhayn, Jemal, and Kress over issues of authority and strategy. At the lower levels of command the arrogance of German officers, coupled with their poor or nonexistent knowledge of the Turkish language and culture, alienated Turks. The latter engaged in widespread passive resistance to the Germans and even occasionally attacked and murdered them.[55]

It is uncertain how much such problems hindered German military preparations and thereby assisted the advance of the EEF and sharifian rebels into Palestine. Also unclear is whether they influenced the subsequent behavior of Jemal. On the German side the longtime mistrust of him remained unchanged. Jemal's bitterness toward the Germans so intensified with his loss of command to Falkenhayn that in the fall the Germans invited him to the Reich, where they might soothe his feelings. Berlin also hoped to lessen his antagonism toward the Jews and Zionism.[56]

But neither the visit to Germany nor the military situation in Palestine changed such matters. In mid-November the British, having captured Beersheba, broke through the Ottoman lines northward into the Judean hills; simultaneously, Faysal's guerrillas raided and harassed the Turkish and German forces from the rear, east of the Jordan River. The German consulate in Damascus reported Jemal's dejection from the military failures. He feared, said the consulate, the fall of Medina and Jerusalem, and with it "the worst political results, especially [Arab] revolts."[57]

Jemal's actions seemed to reflect his state of mind. On 14 November, on orders from the Porte, which in turn had received pressure from Falkenhayn, he issued a public appeal offering a pardon to all Arabs who had taken up arms for the sharif in the Hijaz. In the meantime he sent letters to Faysal and Husayn urging their reconciliation with the Turks.[58] Although scholars have made much of Turkey's approaches to the sharif and also of his mistrust of the British and of wish to retain contact with the Turks, Husayn in fact kept Cairo fully apprised of Jemal's entreaties. The British High Commissioner, Wingate, even proposed using Faysal to approach Jemal to learn more about Turkish policy toward the Arabs.[59]

On 6 December Jemal spoke publicly in Beirut about the Sykes-Picot agreement of 1916, whose provisions the new Bolshevik regime in Russia had just published. The agreement provided for the Anglo-French division of much of the Ottoman Empire at the peace settlement. Jemal accused Husayn of subjection to the enemies of Islam, who intended, as the agreement revealed, to dismember the empire. He also denounced the Germans, calling them a "savage race," worse than the British, between whom and the Turks there could be nothing but hatred. Turkey, he declared, had entered the war to rid itself of interference by Europeans but instead had handed itself over to Germany.[60] Three days later Jerusalem fell to Allenby and the EEF. The loss of the second of the three holy cities of Islam destroyed much of what remained of the awe once felt by Ottoman Arabs for Turkey.

Libya, Abyssinia, and India

A source of Britain's concern during 1917 to preserve Arab loyalty was a pattern of continued German efforts in Libya, Abyssinia, and elsewhere to influence events in the Middle East and India. In Libya the threat to Allied interests had shifted westward to Tripolitania, where the Germans and Turks incited Arabs against the Italians. On 14 and 17 April both the British and Italians concluded peace and trade agreements with the new Sanussi leader, Sayyid Muhammad Idris.[61] Consequently, a new German expedition, headed by Todenwarth, delivered weapons and munitions by submarine to the Arab chief and Sanussi rival, Ramadan al-Suwayhli, and to the Turkish agent in Tripoli, al-Barani. Their attacks on the Italians in October, however, produced little.[62] Throughout the fall the British watched carefully the continued German activity in Tripoli.[63]

Events in Abyssinia also continued to receive Britain's attention. There the German legation aimed both at allying once more with the deposed prince, Lij Iyasu (who now lived with the remnants of his armed followers in the eastern province of Welo), and at providing access for Germans in Africa to the Red Sea and Arabia. For some time Germany had coveted such an outlet for its colonial forces in nearby German East Africa, which remained heavily outnumbered in and isolated by their war with British imperial troops.[64]

In May, Syburg, the Reich's minister to Abyssinia, dispatched a German from Addis Ababa, Arnold Holz, an Austrian accomplice, and native servants and guards to destroy the railroad line that ran from the Abyssinian capital to Jibuti, the main port of French

Somaliland. The Germans intended the destruction of the railroad to be a signal for anti-French tribes along the line, including the Danakils and the sultan of Tadjura, to seize the small French colony.[65]

Holz and his followers reached French Somaliland in June and for a time threw the local colonial authorities and neighboring British Somaliland into disarray. Along the way the conspirators attracted several hundred tribal followers. The British tightened naval patrols along the Somali coast to assist the French by preventing Holz from escaping across the Red Sea to Arabia.[66] But Holz lacked food and weapons, which lost him the backing of further supporters. At the beginning of September French forces north of Jibuti captured him, along with numerous documents implicating the German legation in the plot and showing that Holz ultimately intended to reach Yemen.[67]

Although by year's end Holz had already been convicted as a spy and received a death sentence, complications from his adventure persisted for the British. During the crisis, Thesiger, the British minister, pressed Empress Zawditu's regent and co-ruler, Ras Tafari, to expel the German and Turkish diplomats from Abyssinia. When the empress learned of the negotiations, tensions between her and Tafari over this and other issues led her, much to the chagrin of the British, to allow Syburg and the other Germans at the legation to remain in Abyssinia.[68]

During 1917 the Germans continued to incite the anti-British nationalist movement in India. In Germany imperialist pan-Germans like Ernst von Reventlow, as well as industrialists and the government's naval and colonial offices, demanded the destruction of British rule in India and the Reich's annexation of naval and other strategic bases in the Indian Ocean. This, they argued, would safeguard the postwar German economic dominance they planned for the Middle East, the Persian Gulf, and Asia.[69] German intrigue directed at India, however, suffered from its usual problems; for example, bitter conflicts existed between the Berlin Indian committee, whose members were mainly Muslims, and its branch in Constantinople, dominated by Hindus.[70] Consequently it failed, as previously, to threaten British rule.

Also, the Berlin committee had disagreements with the Germans over a variety of issues. German border officials often harassed committee members as they left Germany for Switzerland, Turkey, and elsewhere. Furthermore, the committee's unending demands for money plagued its relationship with the Germans. A key member of the committee, Chattopadhyaya, spent large amounts of German money to attend the international socialist conference in Stockholm. While there, he opened a branch office of the Berlin Indian committee. Chattopadhyaya hoped to convince the Russian revolutionaries who had organized the conference and the socialist press of the importance of the India question in postwar peace negotiations.[71]

The Berlin committee also remained active in the United States, but not for long. In January 1917 it received word from C. K. Chakravarty, the German-appointed leader of the Indian revolutionary movement in America, that Jodh Singh, an agent of the committee arrested in Siam, had turned informer at the Lahore trial and had helped condemn numerous revolutionaries to death or deportation. "Fortunately," Chakravarty declared, "the informer did not know any of us and our plans."[72] Chakravarty's luck, however, soon changed. In February, mainly in response to Germany's unrestricted submarine policy, the United States broke off relations with Germany, subsequently entering the war on the Allied side. Washington now agreed to cooperate fully with Britain against the Indian revolutionaries in the United States. At the beginning of March, New York police raided Chakravarty's office in the city. Confronted with papers seized by the police, he confessed his role. This discovery, along with the Wolf von Igel papers already held by the Americans, soon led to a wave of further arrests of both Indian and German agents in the United States.[73]

On 20 November a spectacular and lengthy trial began in San Francisco for thirty-five persons of various nationalities, including nine Germans and seventeen Indians. The American government charged them with violating the neutrality of the United States by using American territory as a base for German-assisted plots to promote a rebellion against British rule in India.[74] The trial delivered the death blow to the Indo-German movement in America.

In addition, little of value resulted from either the German or Indian campaign to spy on and recruit Indian nationalists living in Switzerland. For example, at the beginning of 1917 a prominent Indian prince who had lived in London, Thakur Shri Jessrasinghi, betrayed to the British secret papers given him by Germany's chief Swiss agent, Jacoby, and intended for other princes in India.[75] The Germans, moreover, competed with the British consulate in Geneva for influence among local Indian nationalists. The latter suspected Germany of wanting to replace British rule in India with its own. On orders from the German foreign ministry, Jacoby and another German spy, Gerald Gifford (an Irish writer who once worked in Egypt for *The Times* of London), tried to convince the Indians of the Reich's anti-imperialist intentions toward India.[76]

But by the year's end the Berlin Indian committee learned that German policy was in fact quite different. The committee requested a public statement from the Reich that it supported India's independence; B. N. Datta, the committee's secretary, alluded to the Allied calls for the freeing of Belgium, Rumania, and Serbia and for the autonomous development of the subject peoples of Turkey. "The time has arrived," he insisted, "for the German government, as a counterweight against the enemy's demands, to declare its wish that the nationality principle be applied to India and other nations under British domination."[77] Berlin refused to issue such a declaration, however, which revealed the German government's (and especially the army's) imperialist ambitions in Asia.[78] The rejection also disillusioned the Indian nationalists in Berlin and Stockholm. They soon turned increasingly for help to a new quarter—Bolshevik Russia.

Peace Overtures

By the summer and fall of 1917 several factors convinced Britain to consider a negotiated peace, first with Germany and then with Turkey. These included the war-weariness of France and Italy, the revolution in Russia and further weakening of that nation's war effort, and the intensification of Germany's submarine war. A flurry of peace resolutions and feelers appeared from both sides as well as from neutrals like the Vatican.[79]

Some British leaders in London, particularly Lloyd George, believed that Britain's success against Turkey would force it to sign a separate peace and leave its key territories—Mesopotamia, Palestine, and Arabia—subject to Britain's direct rule or dominant influence.[80] At the end of December, the Foreign Office dispatched orders to Sir Horace Rumbold in Bern to develop peace approaches with the Turks.[81]

Because of the Russian collapse, there was interest in peace at the Porte, but it centered around the relatively weak faction that included Talaat Pasha and the Entente-ophile Javid Pasha. As early as June 1917 Talaat suggested to the Central Powers that they offer a non-annexationist peace to all the Allied powers. But neither Berlin nor Vienna intended to renounce the extensive annexations they planned; moreover, each saw little danger that Turkey would abandon it by concluding a separate peace with the Allies, because of the Allies' publicly announced plans to dismember the Ottoman Empire.

During the ensuing months the Turks and British engaged in secret, but rarely serious, negotiations. In Geneva an agent of Lloyd George offered an emissary of Enver Pasha bribes for Turkey to leave the war on Britain's terms. Other feelers involved Talaat. The first was in June, in Geneva: a former Ottoman interior minister, Rashid Pasha, who claimed connections to the grand vizier, delivered to Dr. H. Parodi, an Anglo-Egyptian functionary supervising Egyptian students in Switzerland, the peace program of the local party of Turkish exiles. A month later, again in Switzerland, Nureddin Bey, a friend of Talaat, told a British official that the grand vizier wished to send emissaries to Bern to discuss peace. In Smyrna, furthermore, the local Turkish governor contacted a French resident about peace negotiations.[82]

The Turkish overtures appealed to some in the British Foreign and War offices who still believed that Britain's long-term imperial interests in the region remained safer in the hands of a strong Turkey rather than—as others in the government hoped for—a cluster of Arab successor states. However, the Turkish feelers, because of the continued weakness of the peace party in Constantinople, produced no success. They aimed less at concluding a separate peace with the Allies than at applying pressure on the Germans not to conclude a peace of their own that would violate Ottoman sovereignty, territorial or otherwise.[83]

For instance, the Porte claimed to Berlin that Britain had offered it peace proposals, wherein the British supposedly agreed to return to Turkey its territory presently occupied by the Allies. The Foreign Office, in fact, immediately and furiously renounced the claim. However, an investigation of the matter by the foreign secretary, Balfour, revealed that possibly a British agent had made the unauthorized proposal to the Turks. Lloyd George, the prime minister, together with Britain's military intelligence, had sent an amateur emissary, J. R. Pilling, a former British railroad entrepreneur in Turkey, to Switzerland to negotiate with the Porte, but not to present the proposal that he apparently did.[84] Whether such factors influenced Berlin to conclude on 27 October 1917 a new treaty with Turkey in which Germany agreed not to sign a peace that curtailed Ottoman sovereignty, is uncertain.[85]

Most British leaders correctly believed the Turkish approaches in Switzerland insincere and, according to Rumbold, "only meant to try to discover what is in our mind."[86] Still other officials, including Sykes in London and Wingate, the High Commissioner in Cairo, reacted with horror at the prospect of negotiating a separate peace with Turkey. They feared it would jeopardize Britain's position with the Arabs, who already suspected the Anglo-French dealing with them to be less than honest.[87]

Only in November did Sykes reverse himself. He suggested to the War Cabinet that the Turks, confronted with military and economic exhaustion, British military successes in Palestine and Mesopotamia, and the spread of the Arab uprising, would soon conclude peace.[88] During the weeks that followed the Foreign Office authorized Rumbold to enter peace negotiations with Turkey through Mukhtar Pasha, a delegate to the prisoner-of-war conference in Switzerland. Rumbold was directed to offer the Turks favorable financial treatment, abolition of the capitulations, and full recognition of Turkey's position as an independent power. In return Britain demanded the opening of the Straits and the independence of Armenia, Arabia, Mesopotamia, Syria, and Palestine.[89]

Rumbold met Mukhtar Pasha several times. The Foreign Office acted in typical fashion: publicly it denied the meetings, while privately it urged Rumbold to acquire a counter-proposal from the Turks.[90] In the event, the British courting of the Turks dragged on and resulted in little but meetings. Mukhtar, Rumbold told the Foreign Office, was kept in Switzerland to push for concessions in the German-Russian peace talks at Brest Litovsk.[91] Peace in the Middle East would have to await the new year and final Allied military triumph.

10 Epilogue
The War's
End, 1918

During the last months of the war the fortunes of both sides ebbed back and forth until in September and October 1918 the superior military resources of the Anglo-French and Americans prevailed. Notwithstanding, as 1918 began, optimism dominated German military and political circles. In March the new Bolshevik regime in Russia surrendered, and the German army began a massive new offensive in France. In contrast, however, in the Middle East the fortunes of Germany and Turkey declined steadily. During February Allenby's EEF pushed further into Palestine, capturing Jericho and the west bank of the Jordan River. Arab forces allied to Britain liberated Transjordan and later joined the EEF to complete the freeing of Palestine and then Syria from Turkish rule. Germany, stung since June 1916 by the Arab revolt but still attempting to wage war by inciting native revolts in the Middle East and India against the British, hoped the Turks would soon reconcile themselves with the Arabs.

"A Movement of Revolt That Grows More and More Menacing"

Not surprising, therefore, discussions increased between the Germans and Turks and among the Turks themselves over what to do about the growing Arab influence in the war. In January 1918 Talaat Pasha voiced doubts to Bernstorff that the Turks could suppress the Arab revolt militarily. He also spoke of the need for Turkey to offer autonomy to the Arabs. But, the ambassador reported to the foreign ministry, some Young Turks, including Jemal Pasha, would not give the Arabs even the slightest concession.[1]

Also, the fanatical pan-Turanian ambitions of Enver Pasha and Talaat Pasha—which were symbolized by the Ottoman attack on Transcaucasia—lessened the Young Turks' interest in holding Palestine and Syria against the British and in responding to German wishes that they reach a settlement with the Arabs.[2] Niedermayer, the German officer assigned to Palestine with orders to bribe the rebel Arab leader, Faysal, to rejoin the Turks, recognized the growing interest of both Turkey and Germany in Asia. Because of the Porte's pan-Turanism and "the ethnographic situation in Central Asia," he wrote in a memo after returning to Germany, "we are forced to cooperate with the Turks, for whom we must produce substitutes for the many losses in Europe and Arabia."[3]

Despite this relative lack of interest of Constantinople in its Arab provinces, stiff Turkish and German resistance stopped a series of Anglo-Arab offensives into Transjordan. The attacks aimed at Amman and Maan on the Hijaz railway; Allenby, the commander of the British EEF, hoped to destroy the railroad and leave the Ottoman garrison in Medina isolated and incapable of intervening in the fighting to the north. However, the British War Cabinet ordered Allenby to transfer some of his best units, totaling sixty thousand troops, to France; until September this loss restricted the EEF to only minor operations.

Meanwhile, the Arab army led by Faysal remained a constant drain on the Turks. In Transjordan the rebels, assisted by T. E. Lawrence and other British officers as well as by small British armored car units and light guns, increased their destructive raids on the Hijaz railroad. They kept more than twenty-two thousand Turkish troops pinned down at Medina, Maan, and other posts north along the railway. In March the Turks tried and failed to evacuate Medina; by then their casualties from the Arab revolt numbered 4,800 killed, 1,600 wounded, and eight thousand captured.[4]

The Turks and Germans seemed unable to reverse the increasingly favorable Anglo-Arab position. They replaced Falkenhayn, the supreme commander of Army Group F ("Yilderim"), with Liman von Sanders, who had led the successful defense of the Dardanelles. But Liman's effectiveness, much like that of his predecessor, was hurt by bitter differences with Turkish military leaders, by insufficient troops, weapons, and food, and by the diversion by the Turks of both troops and supplies from the Palestine and Syrian fronts to Transcaucasia.[5]

In May, the Arab army expanded its attacks in Transjordan, and pressure mounted on the Porte to respond, but neither Jemal Pasha, the Young Turk leader who had the most contact with the Arab rebels, nor Enver Pasha was persuaded that Turkey needed to bring the Arabs to their side. For example, Franz von Papen, the German chief of staff of the Turkish Fourth Army in Syria and former military attaché in the United States, informed Bernstorff that while Jemal favored a policy of conciliation in the Arab question, he and Enver Pasha could not make up their minds about concessions to the Arabs.[6] Jemal, said Papen, believed it enough to grant the Sharif of Mecca an autonomous position in the Hijaz, without settling the caliphate question. Papen concluded that the "[Arab] question presses for a solution from every side," inasmuch as the Fourth Army was "fighting with its front towards the English, and defending its rear with half-hearted and inadequate measures against a movement of revolt that grows more and more menacing." He urged the ambassador to convince the Porte to adopt a pro-Arab policy.[7] Bernstorff seemed helpless in the matter; he replied on 14 June that in his meetings with CUP leaders he never missed a chance "to preach reconciliation between Turks and Arabs."[8]

For a moment, however, several weeks later, the Germans thought the enemy might provide the needed impetus for an agreement. Papen reported, clearly surprised, that Faysal had proposed negotiations between him and the Turks.[9] Faysal's action may have arisen from the anger of his father, Husayn, who had now learned of both the Sykes-Picot Agreement and the Balfour Declaration. But the interpretation of postwar historians that Husayn's unhappiness over the matter, coupled with the growing hostility between him and Ibn Saud, the amir of Najd, caused widespread anxiety in Cairo and London seems overdrawn.[10]

As early as January 1918, the Arab Bureau in Cairo had received word that Husayn had instructed Faysal not to correspond further with the Turks.[11] Still other evidence makes problematical Faysal's approach to the enemy, especially the issue of whether he represented his father. Within the sharifian camp, conflicts existed between the son, who was physically cut off from the Hijaz and had moved north into the British orbit, and Husayn.[12]

In London, concern about the issue in the War Cabinet focused less on assuaging Husayn's hostility than on protecting Britain's postwar position in the Middle East against France. The French, hoping to gain control of most, or a large part, of postwar Syria, had turned their attention toward the influential Faysal and away from his father. France's eventual understanding with Britain, according to which France agreed to dominant British influence in the Arabian Peninsula, also resulted in the reduction of France's interest there.[13]

The Germans apparently knew little of Husayn's anger toward his allies. On 19 July, however, Bernstorff informed Berlin that his Arab sources held the view that the sharif was not entirely pro-English. The ambassador surveyed the sporadic and unsuccessful Turkish efforts at approaching Husayn and relayed the opinion of the ex-khedive, Abbas Hilmi, who had discussed the issue with Prüfer, the chief agent of the Information Service for the East in Constantinople. The sharif, the ex-khedive told Prüfer, knew he could not possibly trust the Young Turks, which made reconciliation moot.[14] Meanwhile, Oppenheim in Berlin added a further pessimistic voice: he reminded the foreign ministry of Arab hatred for the Turks stemming from Jemal Pasha's persecutions in Syria, and of the problem of supplying food to the hunger-ridden Hijaz, which the Turks could not undertake at the moment.[15]

The Germans appeared even more discouraged about the Turkish attitude when Papen reported that Faysal had offered a second time to negotiate with the Turks. Bernstorff, responding to the foreign ministry's directive to press Talaat Pasha to make peace with the Arabs, reported, first, an erroneous claim of the demise of Sharif Husayn, and second, a power struggle between the sultan's palace and the Porte. He doubted that the Turks would oblige Faysal: "The Grand Vizier said that Faysal demands too much. He demands a position 'like Bavaria in the German Empire.' That much the Turkish government cannot promise."[16]

German pressure on the Turks to reach a settlement with the Arabs began to peak at the end of August. Papen and other officers of the Turkish Fourth Army feared that with the arrival of the rainy season in several weeks the British would resume their offensive in Palestine, and that soon the Hijaz railroad would fall to the Arabs. "Accordingly," Papen argued, "it is of the highest priority for the entire Palestine front that, as soon as possible, an agreement with Sharif Faysal is achieved and the rear of the 4th Ottoman Army is relieved."[17] Such a pact, he advised, would also improve Turkey's relationship to the tribes of the Hauran, the grain-producing region east of Damascus, thereby assisting the Turks in acquiring the local harvest, which they badly needed to feed their troops.[18]

Even General Erich Ludendorff, the chief of the German high command, urgently suggested to the foreign ministry that "for relieving the Syrian front . . . an understanding with Sharif Faysal would be especially effective." But unfortunately, he continued, the Turkish government still appeared unable to recognize the seriousness of the situation;[19] he urged the ministry to raise the issue again with Bernstorff and Talaat. Meanwhile, renewed negotiations between Faysal and the Turks faltered. On 4 September General Hans von Seeckt, the deputy commander of the German military mission in Turkey, reported to Bernstorff that Faysal had demanded postwar rule over Palestine and Syria, which the new Ottoman sultan, Mehmed VI, had rejected. Instead, the Turks proposed to make Faysal governor-general of the Hijaz which, as Seeckt prophesied, Faysal soon refused.[20]

Even had the desperate German campaign to achieve a rapprochement with Faysal succeeded, it would have made little difference to the outcome of the war in the Middle East. Allenby, now reinforced by Indian regiments and air power, launched his surprise cavalry offensive at Megiddo, in northern Palestine. The Turkish troops and German Army Group F—poorly supplied, plagued by widespread desertions, and lacking either adequate reinforcements or air support—soon dissolved. On 1–2 October Allenby authorized Faysal, Lawrence, and the Arab forces to enter Damascus; from there the EEF, which included a portion of Faysal's Arab army, chased the remnants of the enemy's troops further northward toward Anatolia.[21]

In Mesopotamia, Anglo-Indian cavalrymen advanced rapidly up the Tigris River against the Turks and Germans. The British capture in March of the notorious German agent Preusser had lessened much of the anti-British agitation among local Arabs. Most important for Britain's success, however, the Ottoman army facing the British remained wholly inadequate in numbers of troops and weapons.[22]

The Remnants of *Weltpolitik* in Defeat

Even as Turkey in the Middle East, and Germany in France, collapsed militarily, the German army, navy, colonial ministry, and many other reactionary groups, including the pan-Germans and new Fatherland party, still dreamed of final victory and global power.[23] Among German officials in Turkey, such as Bernstorff and an embassy subordinate, Werner Otto von Hentig, rumors circulated about a British peace offer to divide the Middle East with Germany and Turkey. At least one other German official in Turkey, Prüfer, suggested that Germany gain from the war in the Middle East by ending its alliance with Turkey and dividing that state with Britain.[24]

Similarly, at the war's end an aura of unreality and zealotry in support of German expansionism characterized Germany's feverish search for Muslim support in Egypt and Libya and for revolutionary influence in India. Berlin still viewed the ex-khedive, Abbas Hilmi, as its future ally in Egypt once the Reich had defeated and ousted Britain. Both the Turks and Germans had agreed to return him to the Egyptian throne once the war ended in victory. On 31 July 1918 Wilhelm II met with Abbas Hilmi at Spa in the hope of ensuring his loyalty to Germany after the war.[25]

An air of fantasy likewise existed with respect to Libya. At the end of September the visit to Constantinople of the deposed Libyan Shaykh al-Sanussi, Sayyid Ahmad, raised hopes in Berlin that the shaykh would visit Germany and, upon returning home, restoke the fire of Sanussi revolt against the British in Egypt.[26] But that did not happen; Germany and Turkey had lost completely their former influence in Libya. Two months later the last German agents in Tripolitania, Todenwarth and fourteen other officers and men, returned to Europe by submarine.[27]

Regarding India at least the Germans no longer held illusions about causing trouble for Britain. The relationship between the Germans and Indian revolutionary committees in Berlin and Stockholm had collapsed. The Berlin committee, insulted at the end of 1917 by Germany's refusal to issue a public statement supporting India's independence, believed that among the major European states only the new Bolshevik regime favored postwar freedom for Indians and other Asians.[28] But the Germans refused to permit Indian agents to visit Russia, fearing that to do so would be, in Wesendonk's words, "clearly dangerous."[29]

The Indians responded angrily, as they did to the unabashed imperialism of the German colonial secretary, Solf. Solf, echoing similar demands from the German high command and statements he had made previously, had called in January 1918 for Germany to use the war to acquire a central African empire and possessions in Asia and the Pacific Ocean. The foreign ministry tried unsuccessfully to mend fences with the Indians by claiming that Solf had referred only to colonies "with inferior populations, but not to regions with particularly superior culture, as with India or Egypt."[30] However, relations between the Indians and German government worsened.[31] When Mahendra Pratap Singh, the Indian prince-revolutionary who had accompanied the Hentig mission to the amir of Afghanistan, returned to Germany, he charged that the foreign ministry had mistreated him and that Hentig had bungled the mission. Pratap, like the other Indian revolutionaries, now believed Bolshevik Russia would be India's future salvation from British rule.[32]

Thus the remnants of German imperial ambitions lingered, but the surrender of both Austria-Hungary and Bulgaria in the fall of 1918 worsened seriously the situation of Germany and Turkey. The route through the Balkans now lay open for the Allies, and an attack on Constantinople seemed a possibility. Nothing remained for the Ottoman government and high command but to accept Germany's sudden decision, forced by the defeat of its exhausted armies in France, to sue for the cessation of hostilities and initiate peace talks. A new Turkish regime replaced the CUP leadership of Enver, Talaat, and Jemal, whose policies had led to the Turkish defeat. On 31 October, at Mudros, the Porte signed the armistice—an ending to the war very different from what the Young Turks had envisioned in November 1914, when they declared the jihad.[33]

Immediately the roughly twenty thousand German troops and officers in Turkey were evacuated across the Black Sea; with them were Enver, Talaat, and Jemal, who fled to Germany. The last of the German forces left Turkey in January 1919, often amid scorn and resentment heaped on them by the Turkish population, which blamed Germany for the defeat and the economic misfortune of their country. For the first time in eighty-four years, Turkey had no German military mission or presence. Indeed, Germany's once-formidable position in the Ottoman Empire, and especially its rivalry with Britain, had disappeared.[34] The Versailles Treaty of June 1919 made this situation official. Germany, by signing the treaty liquidated its investments overseas (article 119), specifically in the former Ottoman Empire (articles 155 and 434) and Egypt (articles 147–54).[35]

During the 1920s the Orient was to play almost no role in the foreign policy of the new Weimar Republic. With its investments and trade destroyed and no navy to exert political influence in the Middle East, Germany clearly viewed that area as peripheral to its immediate sphere of national interest. Berlin focused during the 1920s on revising the Versailles settlement, which meant not antagonizing Britain and France in the Middle East lest they be given a reason to frustrate German efforts in Europe.[36]

Nevertheless, after the war ended both the German revolutionary and Weimar governments worked clandestinely to preserve the only postwar contacts in the Middle East that remained. The foreign ministry and Information Service for the East financially supported numerous Egyptians, Turks, Arabs, Afghans, and Indians who, because they had assisted the Reich during the war, could not return to their homelands. Much of this task fell to the Information Service, but not until after the foreign ministry had changed the organization's name to the more innocuous German Oriental Institute. The organization identified and arranged for Turks, Egyptian nationalists (including Shaykh al-Jawish and Muhammad Farid), and other pro-German Arabs (such as the Syrian Shekib Arslan), to obtain upon arrival from Turkey German passports and money with which to settle in neutral Switzerland.[37] The Germans also supported financially Aziz Ali al-Masri, the Egyptian-born former Ottoman army officer and chief of staff in the Arab rebel forces of the Sharif of Mecca.[38]

By September 1919 the Weimar government was paying subsidies to at least fifty Orientals, most of them living in Switzerland. Adolf Müller, Romberg's successor as German minister in Bern, urging the foreign ministry to continue supporting the refugees, explained the rationale for the policy: "Although it appears at the moment that the entire Orient is finally lost for Germany, things can change in a few years."[39]

A Triumph for the *Imperium Britannicum*?

How important was Britain's victory in the "war by revolution" it waged with its German rival in the Middle East between 1914 and 1918? Historians have criticized Germany's wartime alliance with Turkey for failing to trigger an anti-British, pan-Islamic revolution in Egypt and India. Most students of the war in the Middle East, however, have concluded that the Allied triumph there did not depend on the British-sponsored Arab revolt. Certainly the Arab military operations in Transjordan in the summer and fall of 1918 contributed significantly to Britain's victory over Turkey; Britain, however, would have defeated the Turks without the Arab campaign.

Would the reverse have been true? Could Britain and its allies have triumphed had Arabs followed the call of the sultan-caliph and waged jihad against the Entente? The answer must be pure conjecture; notwithstanding, and as this study has shown, the British before and during the world war greatly feared pan-Islamism and the possibility of a holy war directed against them. The British promoted the Arab revolt principally because they were worried by 1915 that the Turks, assisted by a powerful Germany, were about to raise the Muslim world from North Africa to Afghanistan in a fanatical insurrection against Britain. Even before the world war, visions of pan-Islamism inciting widespread native and anti-British revolts in Egypt, the Persian Gulf, and India had horrified British officials. This anxiety, heightened during the war by the disastrous British campaigns at the Dardanelles and in Mesopotamia, forced Britain to keep nearly a half-million troops in the Middle East throughout much of the war.[40] One can only speculate on the impact these forces might have had on the course of the fighting in France.

Furthermore, the numerous secret agreements and overt promises on the Middle East concluded by Britain during the war with the French, Arabs, and Jews, while they helped swing the military outcome in Britain's favor, contained basic contradictions, some of which have not yet been resolved. These decisions formed the basis of the postwar settlements in the Middle East, a series of actions, signed agreements, and documents dating principally from 1921 and 1922. The settlements dismantled the Ottoman Empire. In 1922 a Turkish national assembly abolished the sultanate and caliphate and established a new Turkish national state that included only the Turkish-speaking portion of the dissolved empire; Britain and France partitioned between them the remainder. France received from the League of Nations a mandate to rule Syria and Lebanon, and Britain to rule Palestine, including Transjordan. In the Palestine portion of the mandate Britain had promised the Jews a "National Home," with full rights for non-Jews. Britain also established a protectorate in Iraq (Mesopotamia), a country the British created and upon whose throne they placed their own nominee, Faysal. Moreover, a new political entity, the Hijaz, acted as a British client; also, Ibn Saud governed farther north and east in Arabia with power that had been strengthened by the war.[41]

In the short term, then, Britain preserved its hold over Egypt and India and even expanded its empire in the Middle East. Few Englishmen, however, realized at the time the serious problems the war and the postwar settlements had created for Britain and the world. The announcement of the mandate system inflamed Arab nationalism: the mandates destroyed the Arab dream, encouraged during the war by Anglo-French promises and assurances, of a free Arab confederacy headed by Britain's wartime ally, Faysal.

Britain and France presided over the postwar dismemberment of the Ottoman Empire and the creation of the modern Middle East, producing thereby, in the words of the journalist David Fromkin in 1989, "a peace to end all peace." The Anglo-French diplomats were still concluding the settlement of 1921–1922 when the Arabs responded violently against Allied control of the Middle East. Faysal attacked French troops in Lebanon; an Arab rebellion then broke out in Iraq, costing the British £40 million and two thousand casualties and forcing them to confirm Faysal as king of the country. Henceforth Arab frustration and bitterness led to a pattern of widespread violence in the Middle East, resulting in heavy British losses—in both human and financial terms—in Egypt, Iraq, and Palestine.[42]

Thus in the long term the war undermined Britain's global empire. Britain depended heavily on troops from its Dominions and from India, many of whom fought in the Middle East. This dependence had major costs. At the Paris Peace Conference in 1919 were representatives from Canada, Australia, South Africa, New Zealand, and India. Here was a first internationally visible sign of one of the key consequences of the world war: the breakup of the European colonial empires into independent political entities. The Dominions had earned by their share in the fighting their autonomy and the right to participate at Paris on their own. Britain's promise during the war of changes leading to dominion status for India should be seen in the same light.[43]

Britain, forced by its triumph to focus much of its postwar attention and resources on preserving its position in the Middle East and elsewhere in its empire, had been weakened more in victory than Germany in defeat. World War II accelerated the decline. By the 1970s, according to Elizabeth Monroe, "Britain's moment in the Middle East," which had begun in 1914, had ended.[44]

Germany, in contrast, emerged from the war and the peace settlement of 1919 relatively stronger economically and demographically; having lost its former position in the Middle East, it could focus on rebuilding its power at home and in Europe. Only twenty-three years after the Central Powers' defeat in World War I, Nazi Germany, in control of most of Europe, directed its armies operating in southern Russia and North Africa to return to the Middle East to seize the vast oil supplies there. For Britain the Second World War completed what the first one had started and the interwar period confirmed—its demise as the world's premier power.

NOTES

PREFACE

1. The term "Middle East" raises problems of definition, but in this study the convention established in Western usage is (more or less) followed. That is, the Middle East is defined as the region bounded on the northwest by Turkey, on the southwest by Egypt, on the southeast by the Arabian Peninsula, and on the northeast by Persia (Iran). See Roy R. Andersen, Robert F. Seibert, and Jon G. Wagner, *Politics and Change in the Middle East: Sources of Conflict and Accommodation,* xii–xiii. Where necessary, bordering regions like Libya, Abyssinia, the Sudan, Afghanistan, and India, which often influenced events in the Middle East, are discussed.

2. See his classic account of the revolt, originally published in 1926 in a private edition, *Seven Pillars of Wisdom: A Triumph,* 56–57. For an analysis of the book and its author, note Eugene Goodheart, "A Contest of Motives: T. E. Lawrence in *Seven Pillars of Wisdom,*" in *T. E. Lawrence: Soldier, Writer, Legend,* ed. Jeffrey Meyers, 110–27.

3. The anglo-centric nature of historical writing on World War I in the Middle East is evident in the vast list of books on British policies there presented in Ritchie Ovendale, *The Longman Companion to the Middle East since 1914,* 309–10; M. E. Yapp, *The Making of the Modern Near East, 1792–1923,* 370–73; Albert Hourani, *A History of the Arab Peoples,* 520–23; and C. Ernest Dawn, "The Influence of T. E. Lawrence on the Middle East," in *T. E. Lawrence: Soldier, Writer, Legend,* ed. Jeffrey Meyers, 58–86, 189–99.

4. Most of the writing on Germany and the Middle East has focused on German relations with Turkey (and Morocco, on the periphery) and particularly on German economic ambitions in the region. See Gregor Schöllgen, *Imperialismus und Gleichgewicht. Deutschland, England und die orientalische Frage 1871–1914;* Ulrich Trumpener, *Germany and the Ottoman Empire, 1914–1918,* 3–20; and Frank G. Weber, *Eagles on the Crescent: Germany, Austria, and the Diplomacy of the Turkish Alliance, 1914–1918,* chapter 1.

5. A theme noted, but not fully explored, in Lawrence James, *The Rise and Fall of the British Empire,* 359–60; Herbert Landolin Müller, *Islam, gihad ("Heiliger Krieg") und Deutsches Reich. Ein Nachspiel zur wilhelminischen Weltpolitik im Maghreb 1914–1918,* 180–82; Jacob Landau, *The Politics of Pan-Islam: Ideology and Organization,* 42–43; and John Esposito, *The Islamic Threat: Myth or Reality,* 37–51.

6. Accounts of the visit include Wolfgang J. Mommsen, *Der autoritäre Nationalstaat. Verfassung, Gesellschaft und Kultur des deutschen Kaiserreiches,* 159; Schöllgen,

108-11, 159; Landau, 46-47; Neil Asher Silberman, *Digging for God and Country: Exploration, Archeology, and the Secret Struggle for the Holy Land, 1799-1917,* 161-63; Lothar Rathmann, *Berlin-Bagdad. Die imperialistische Nahostpolitik des kaiserlichen Deutschlands,* 48-50; and Ulrich Trumpener, "Germany and the End of the Ottoman Empire," in *The Great Powers and the End of the Ottoman Empire,* ed. Marian Kent, 112.

7. An important point made by Roger Adelson, *Mark Sykes: Portrait of an Amateur,* 196-97.

8. See, for instance, Joseph Heller, *British Policy towards the Ottoman Empire, 1908-1914,* 34-39, 49; Stuart A. Cohen, *British Policy in Mesopotamia, 1903-1914,* 211, 236; and C. Ernest Dawn, *From Ottomanism to Arabism: Essays on the Origins of Arab Nationalism,* 61-63.

9. The rapprochement was part of "a certain calm [that] had descended on Europe," and particularly on Anglo-German relations after 1910; Holger H. Herwig, *The First World War: Germany and Austria-Hungary, 1914-1918,* 7. Also note Cohen, 249-62; and Fritz Fischer, *War of Illusions: German Policies from 1911 to 1914,* trans. Marian Jackson, 300-7.

10. In the words of David Fromkin, *A Peace to End All Peace: The Fall of the Ottoman Empire and the Creation of the Modern Middle East.*

11. During the 1960s, Fritz Fischer, in his famous study, *Germany's Aims in the First World War,* 120-55, provided the initial broad outlines of this "revolutionary" German policy. The most significantly researched examples of the policy deal with Germany's application of it outside the Middle East, namely toward Russia, Ireland, Morocco, Algeria, Persia, Afghanistan, and India. Regarding Russia, see Seppo Zetterberg, *Die Liga der Fremdvölker Russlands 1916-1918. Ein Beitrag zu Deutschlands antirussischem Propagandakrieg unter den Fremdvölkern Russlands im ersten Weltkrieg;* Egmont Zechlin, "Friedensbestrebungen und Revolutionierungsversuche," *Aus Politik und Zeitgeschichte. Beilage zur Wochenzeitung 'Das Parlament,'* B25(21 June 1961):341-60; Willi Gautschi, *Lenin als Emigrant in der Schweiz;* Z. A. B. Zeman, *Germany and the Revolution in Russia, 1915-1918: Documents from the Archives of the German Foreign Ministry;* George Katkov, "German Political Intervention in Russia during World War I," in *Revolutionary Russia: A Symposium,* ed. Richard Pipes, 80-112; and Werner Hahlweg, *Lenins Rückkehr nach Russland 1917. Die deutschen Akten.* For Ireland, the standard work is Reinhard Doerries, "Die Mission Sir Roger Casements im Deutschen Reich 1914-1916," *Historische Zeitschrift,* 222 (1976):578-625. For the French colonies, Morocco and Algeria, note Müller's book on German policy in the Maghreb; Edmund Burke, "Moroccan Resistance, Pan-Islam, and German War Strategy, 1914-1918," *Francia. Forschungen zur West- europäischen Geschichte,* 3(1975):434-64; and Andre Nouschi, *La Naissance du nationalisme algérien,* 24-28. For Persia and Afghanistan, the most important studies are Ulrich Gehrke, *Persien in der Deutschen Orientpolitik während des Ersten Weltkrieges;* Renate Vogel, *Die Persien-und Afghanistan expedition Oskar Ritter v. Niedermayers 1915/16;* and Imperial War Museum [hereafter IWM], *Operations in Persia, 1914-1919.* For India, see Thomas G. Fraser, "Germany and Indian Revolution, 1914-18," *Journal of Contemporary History,* 12 (1977):255-72; Reinhard Doerries, *Imperial Challenge: Ambassador Count Bernstorff and German-American Relations, 1908-1917,* 146-55; and Milan Hauner, *India in Axis Strategy:*

Germany, Japan, and Indian Nationalists in the Second World War, chapter 1.

12. Brief summaries are in Martin Kröger, "Revolution als Programm. Ziele und Realität deutscher Orientpolitik im Ersten Weltkrieg," in *Der Erste Weltkrieg. Wirkung, Wahrnehmung, Analyse,* ed. Wolfgang Michalka, 366–91; Fischer, *Germany's Aims,* 120–21, 126–31; Lothar Rathmann, *Stossrichtung Nahost 1914–1918. Zur Expansionspolitik des deutschen Imperialismus im ersten Weltkrieg,* 81–86; and Zechlin, "Friedensbestrebungen und Revolutionierungsversuche," B20(17 May 1961):280–88, B24(14 June 1961):325–37.

13. Waging "war by revolution" was nothing new to the West. For example, for nearly sixty years after 1688 the French monarchy had supported uprisings by Scottish and Irish Jacobites hoping they would undermine or divert British power. During the 1770s and 1780s, France, seeking to avenge its defeat to Britain in the Seven Years' War, had assisted the North American colonies in their "revolutionary war" to free them from British rule. As the present study illustrates, as early as 1866, during the Austro-Prussian war, the Prussian government established contacts with nationality groups in Austria, including Slavs and Hungarians, with the aim of inciting them to revolt against the Vienna government. See below, chapter 1.

14. Note the title of the German edition *(Griff nach der Weltmacht),* published in 1961, of Fischer's *Germany's Aims.* See also Herwig, *First World War,* 19.

15. According to Paul M. Kennedy, *Preparing for the Twenty-First Century,* 211, "the West may have played more of a role in turning the Muslim world into what it is today than outside commentators are willing to recognize." Also, see Edwin G. Corr and Stephen Sloan, eds., *Low-Intensity Conflict: Old Threats in a New World.*

16. See Esposito; Steven Barboza, ed., *American Jihad: Islam after Malcolm X,* 3–20; and "Many Varieties of Fundamentalism," *New York Times,* 8 Mar. 1993.

1. INTRODUCTION: BRITAIN, GERMANY, AND THE MIDDLE EAST, 1871–1904

1. Quoted from Lt. Col. Mark Sykes, "Memorandum," 28 Oct 1915, in Sykes to Major Gen. C. B. Callwell (director of military operations in the War Office, London [hereafter WO]), 15 Nov. 1915, Public Record Office, London [hereafter PRO]/Foreign Office Series [hereafter FO] 882 (Arab Bureau Papers)/volume 13/document no. MIS/15/16. The best account of Sykes and his role in the war is Adelson's biography.

2. Sykes, "Memorandum," 28 Oct. 1915, PRO/FO 882/13/MIS/15/16.

3. Extensive statistics are in M. Larcher, *La guerre turque dans la guerre mondiale,* 10. Basic surveys of the aspects of the British Empire mentioned include S. M. Burke and Salim Al-Din Quraishi, *The British Raj in India: An Historical Overview,* 9–50; James, *Rise and Fall of the British Empire,* particularly 169–349; Ronald Robinson and John Gallagher, *Africa and the Victorians: The Official Mind of Imperialism,* 84–87, 462–67; Paul M. Kennedy, *The Rise and Fall of the Great Powers: Economic Change and Military Conflict from 1500 to 2000,* 154–55, 224–27; David K. Fieldhouse, *Die Kolonialreiche seit dem 18 Jahrhundert,* 230–40; and Elizabeth Monroe, *Britain's Moment in the Middle East, 1914–1971,* 16–17. The head start which Britain had over Germany in Africa, Asia, and the Middle East is discussed in Zara Steiner, *Britain and the Origins of the First World War,* 62–63.

4. IWM, *Operations in Persia,* 31, 34; Briton Cooper Busch, *Britain and the Persian Gulf, 1894–1914,* chapter 1; H. C. G. Matthew, "The Liberal Age (1851–1914)," in

The Oxford History of Britain, ed. Kenneth O. Morgan, 562-63; and Monroe, 12-14.

5. See Peter Hopkirk, *The Great Game: The Struggle for Empire in Central Asia;* Fromkin, chapter 2; James, *Rise and Fall of the British Empire,* 176, 180-82, 214-15; Kennedy, *Rise and Fall,* 190-91, 227; Steiner, *Origins of the First World War,* 79-80; and James Joll, *The Origins of the First World War,* 176.

6. A discussion of the doctrine's development is in Landau, 9-70. Also, note the definitions of it in Yapp, 181-83; Landau, 37; and Hourani, *History of the Arab Peoples,* 313-14.

7. Yapp, 182; Landau, 11-13, 68-70, 86, 122-23; and Hourani, *History of the Arab Peoples,* 314.

8. For example, most of the hundreds of British soldiers, diplomats, civil servants, scholars, and missionaries who served in the Middle East and India by the end of the nineteenth century, following the mores of their time and social class, thought kindlier of animals than of the lower classes there and frequently treated the latter accordingly; see Derek Hopwood, *Tales of Empire: The British in the Middle East,* 1880-1952, especially xiii, 17, 19, 40, 56. Maxime Rodinson, *Europe and the Mystique of Islam,* trans. Roger Veinus, 60, observes that such views on the part of Europeans form "the origin of the *homo islamicus,* a notion widely accepted even today" in the West. Also on the European response, note Edward W. Said, *Culture and Imperialism;* Joll, 178-79; William Montgomery Watt, *Muslim-Christian Encounters: Perceptions and Misperceptions,* 85-87, 92-93, 104-5; Burke and Quraishi, 56-57; Esposito, 37-51; and Fieldhouse, 234-35.

9. See Burke and Quraishi, 74-75, 143-44, which emphasizes that in the war of 1877, "many" Muslims in Calcutta mosques "expressed a desire to fight in the ranks of their Turkish comrades. Similar feelings were roused during the Greco-Turkish war of 1897. Henceforth, all Turkish causes evoked agitation in India." According to Yapp, 182-83, 206, "Under Abd ul-Hamid the new theory of the caliphate became a powerful diplomatic weapon against all European powers which ruled over substantial numbers of Muslims, in particular Russia, France and Britain." According to James, *Rise and Fall of the British Empire,* 230, the rebellion of 1857 "was a civil war."

10. The figure is in Larcher, 10. See also Lothar Rathmann, *Berlin-Bagdad,* 12; Monroe, 16; and Helmuth Stoecker, "German East Africa 1885-1906," in *German Imperialism in Africa: From the Beginnings until the Second World War,* ed. Helmuth Stoecker, trans. Bernd Zöllner, 93-113.

11. Accordingly, for example, he favored Britain's occupation of Egypt after 1882, thereby encouraging Anglo-French differences over the "Egyptian question" and using it to extract colonial concessions from Britain. See Schöllgen, 15-30; Hans-Ulrich Wehler, *Das Deutsche Kaiserreich 1871-1918,* 172-75; and Paul M. Kennedy, *The Rise of the Anglo-German Antagonism, 1860-1914,* 161, 167-75. According to Holger H. Herwig, *Hammer or Anvil? Modern Germany, 1648-Present,* 131, "Overseas competition was simply the extension of Bismarck's European security policy to the periphery." In the words of George O. Kent, *Bismarck and His Times,* 109, "Germany needed both Russia and Austria, and could therefore not afford to become involved in the Near East or the Balkans."

12. Michael Fröhlich, *Imperialismus. Deutsche Kolonial- und Weltpolitik 1880-1914,* 1994), 34-42; Kennedy, *Anglo-German Antagonism,* 175-82; Raymond James Sontag, *Germany and England: Background of Conflict, 1848-1894,* 186, 196-99, 201,

218–19; Schöllgen, 28–29; Wehler, 175–76; Herwig, *Hammer or Anvil?* 131; and Volker R. Berghahn, *Imperial Germany, 1871–1914: Economy, Society, Culture and Politics*, 266.

13. For a time during the 1830s Prussia had sent officers to advise the sultan's army, and it had opened a consulate in Jerusalem. Also, Swabian religious dissidents, the Templars, had founded settlements in the Holy Land, and beginning in the 1870s German engineers, surveyors, and railroad construction companies had worked in Asia Minor. See Trumpener, "Germany and the End of the Ottoman Empire," 112; and Jehuda L. Wallach, *Anatomie einer Militärhilfe. Die preußisch-deutschen Militärmissionen in der Türkei 1835–1919*, 15–33.

14. Schöllgen, 32–47; and Rathmann, *Berlin-Bagdad*, 13–32. On the military mission, note Wallach, *Anatomie*, 34–108; and Reeva S. Simon, "The Education of an Iraqi Ottoman Army Officer," in *The Origins of Arab Nationalism*, eds. Rashid Khalidi, Lisa Anderson, Muhammad Muslih, and Reeva S. Simon, 155–61. Regarding Bismarck's policy, as reflected in the Russo-Turkish war and Berlin Congress of 1877–78, see Kent, *Bismarck*, 110–12.

15. A discussion on the German attitude toward Egyptians and other peoples in the Middle East between 1870 and 1914 is in Mommsen, particularly 141–42, 144–45. Regarding the government's contempt for the minorities in Germany, such as Catholics, Jews, Poles, Danes, and Alsace-Lorraineans, note Berghahn, 97–123; and Herwig, *Hammer or Anvil?* 138. In Kent, *Bismarck*, 112, the author observes of Bismarck's role in the settlement at the Congress of Berlin in 1878, "For the Balkan people he showed no concern whatever." Portions of this chapter, as well as parts of the second, are discussed in Donald M. McKale, "Germany and the Arab Question before World War I," *The Historian*, 59 (1997): 311–26.

16. Johann Fück, *Die Arabischen Studien in Europa bis in den Anfang des 20. Jahrhunderts*, 234.

17. Some of these ideas the Germans had learned from Napoleon III's threat, during his brief war against Austria in 1859, to incite the different nationalities in the Hapsburg empire to revolt against Vienna. See Zechlin, "Friedensbestrebungen," B24 (14 June 1961): 325–37; and Gottfried Hagen, *Die Türkei im Ersten Weltkrieg. Flugblätter und Flugschriften in arabischer, persischer und osmanisch-türkischer Sprache aus einer Sammlung der Universitätsbibliothek Heidelberg eingeleitet, übersetzt und kommentiert*, 30.

18. Hagen, 31–34.

19. Nationalist and economic groups, which included the Pan-German League, demanded that Germany expand its colonial interests overseas; also, the Berlin government hoped to blunt socialist opposition to the government by unifying the nation around the ideal of the Reich's military might and world influence. Standard accounts include Wehler, 171–92; Berghahn, 270–77; Herwig, *Hammer or Anvil?* 171–75; Helmut Stoecker, "The Quest for 'German Central Africa,'" in *German Imperialism in Africa: From the Beginnings Until the Second World War*, ed. Helmuth Stoecker, trans. Bernd Zöllner, 250–52; Kennedy, *Anglo-German Antagonism*, passim; and Roger Chickering, *We Men Who Feel Most German: A Cultural Study of the Pan German League*, especially the section on the league's ideology, 74–125.

20. Regarding the Franco-German conflict over Morocco, the Germans were interested in acquiring raw materials, like iron ore. German armaments and mining companies, namely Krupp and Mannesmann, had representatives in Morocco who

actively opposed with the Moroccan sultan and among ruling circles France's move toward establishing a protectorate there; note Helmuth Stoecker and Helmut Nimschowski, "Morocco 1898–1914," in *German Imperialism in Africa: From the Beginnings until the Second World War*, ed. Helmuth Stoecker, trans. Bernd Zöllner, 230–35. In 1898, moreover, the kaiser tried, unsuccessfully, to encourage a war between Britain and France during their confrontation at Fashoda in the Sudan; see Jamie Cockfield, "Germany and the Fashoda Crisis, 1898–99," *Central European History*, 16 (1983): 256–75. Also, see Fröhlich, 57–89; Paul M. Kennedy, *The Samoan Triangle: A Study in Anglo-German-American Relations*, 25–51, 76–87, 108–45, 178–98; Schöllgen, 51–76; Holger H. Herwig, *"Luxury" Fleet: The Imperial German Navy 1888–1918*, chapter 3; Wehler, 165–70; Imanuel Geiss, *Das Deutsche Reich und die Vorgeschichte des Ersten Weltkriegs*, 28–53; and Berghahn, 276–77.

21. Trumpener, "Germany and the End of the Ottoman Empire," 122, discusses the inconsistency and lack of direction in the German policy toward Turkey. Rathmann, *Stossrichtung Nahost*, 22–26, provides a Marxist interpretation of the relationship and emphasizes that Germany sought complete control over Turkey, mainly to exploit the Turkish economy for raw materials and markets.

22. See, in this regard, "The Panislamic Movement," *The Times* (London) 22 Sept. 1897; Arthur Hirtzel (political secretary, India Office), "The War with Turkey: Memorandum by Political Department, India Office," 25 May 1916, PRO/FO 371 (General Correspondence, Political from 1906)/piece no. 2778/file 130553; Schöllgen, 69–86; and Burke and Quraishi, 144.

23. According to C. C. Davies, "The North-West Frontier, 1843–1918," in *The Cambridge History of India, The Indian Empire*, ed. H. H. Dodwell, 460–67, violent tribal uprisings on the Indian-Afghan border occurred during 1897 and 1898: "Contemporary opinion, especially that of [British] officers and officials in the war zone, favored [religious] fanaticism as the chief cause of the outbreak, but they have ever been ready to confuse fanaticism with the natural desire of the tribesmen for independence." Also, see Burke and Quraishi, 144. On the history of Krupp to the Afghan regime, note Friedrich Krupp Company (Essen) to Gustav Krupp von Bohlen und Halbach, 20 Oct. 1914, National Archives and Records Administration, Washington, D.C. [hereafter NARA]/microcopy T-137 (German Foreign Ministry Archives, 1867–1920, microfilmed by the University of Michigan)/reel 139/frames 0799–0802.

24. M. S. Anderson, *The Eastern Question, 1774–1923: A Study in International Relations*, 247–48, 251; and Hourani, *History of the Arab Peoples*, 313.

25. Steiner, *Origins of the First World War*, 22; and James, *Rise and Fall of the British Empire*, 344–45.

26. Bernhard Prince von Bülow, *Memoirs of Prince von Bülow*, 1:292.

27. Regarding the kaiser's view that the Muslims formed a monolithic force under Abd ul-Hamid, note his letter to "Nicky," his cousin Nicholas II, the czar of Russia, from Constantinople, 20 Oct. 1898, in Isaac Don Levine, ed., *Letters from the Kaiser to the Czar: Copied from Government Archives in Petrograd Unpublished Before 1920*, 55–58. According to Vahakn N. Dadrian, *The History of the Armenian Genocide: Ethnic Conflict from the Balkans to Anatolia to the Caucasus*, 253, "In fact [Wilhelm II] regarded Turkey as the Prussia of the Orient; he compared the Islamic attributes of self-denial to his notions of Prussian puritanism." Also, note Edward W. Said, *Orientalism*, 19; and Mommsen, 159.

28. Lamar Cecil, *Wilhelm II: Prince and Emperor, 1859–1900*, 321–22, 281, 137–38. Despite Germany's increased commerce with Turkey, Britain and France still dominated Ottoman foreign trade. The standard works are Mommsen, 156–57; and Trumpener, "Germany and the End of the Ottoman Empire," 111–12.

29. Schöllgen, 107.

30. See William Ochsenwald, *The Hijaz Railroad*, 22–23; Pinhas Walter Pick, "German Railway Constructions in the Middle East," in *Germany and the Middle East, 1835–1939*, ed. Jehuda L. Wallach, 74–76; Edward Mead Earle, *Turkey, the Great Powers, and the Bagdad Railway: A Study in Imperialism*, 64–65. Emphasizing the economic motives behind Germany's interest in the construction of the Ottoman railroads are, along with Earle, Trumpener, *Germany and the Ottoman Empire*, 7–9; Rathmann, *Berlin-Bagdad*, 21–46; and Kurt Grunwald, "Pénétration Pacifique—The Financial Vehicles of Germany's 'Drang nach Osten,'" in *Germany and the Middle East, 1835–1939*, ed. Jehuda L. Wallach, 90–95.

31. For example, he provided the kaiser with an imperial bodyguard of two Syrian soldiers, who, according to Wilhelm, would "cut down anyone who might look askance at the German Emperor, the Khalif's friend." See Bülow, 1:290, 299–300.

32. Note "Willy" to "Dearest Nicky," 9 Nov. 1898, in Levine, 61.

33. Quoted in Bülow, 1:300. Discussion of the speech is also in Schöllgen, 111; Fischer, *Germany's Aims*, 121; Trumpener, "Germany and the End of the Ottoman Empire," 112; and Joll, 186–87.

34. Indeed, Wilhelm even encouraged them; for instance, he wrote to Nicholas II from Damascus "that if I had come [to Jerusalem] without any Religion at all I certainly would have turned Mahommetan!" Note "Willy" to "Dearest Nicky," 9 Nov. 1898, Levine, 62. Secondary accounts of the kaiser's visit to Turkey include Mommsen, 159; Landau, 46–47; Silberman, 161–63; Rathmann, *Berlin-Bagdad*, 48–50; Schöllgen, 108–111, 159; and Trumpener, "Germany and the End of the Ottoman Empire," 112.

35. Silberman, 162; Rathmann, *Stossrichtung Nahost*, 25–27; and Landau, 47. The kaiser's remarks in Jerusalem were also edited for the press by Bülow, because Wilhelm had "toasted his host, the Sultan, the Mohammedans and Islam, with such enthusiasm." Note Bülow, 1:298.

36. In his letter from Damascus to Nicholas II he reported gleefully, "The hatred of the English is strong and growing more and more intense—no wonder—whilst in the same time apace with it grows the open contempt of France, which has lost all the respect it once possessed of old!" Note "Willy" to "Nicky," 9 Nov. 1898, Levine, 62–63.

37. "Willy" to "Nicky," 20 Oct. 1898, Levine, 57, recalling his visit to St. Petersburg the previous year. His remark in 1896 to a Russian is noted in Hagen, 31.

38. Müller, 163–68.

39. Fück, 239–45, 260–65, 269–73, 290–92, 313–18; and Gustav Pfannmüller, ed., *Handbuch der Islam-Literatur*, passim. In 1845, the Deutsche Morgenländische Gesellschaft was founded; note Rudi Paret, *The Study of Arabic and Islam at German Universities: German Orientalists since Theodor Nöldeke*, 8.

40. According to Lamar Cecil, *The German Diplomatic Service, 1871–1914*, 101–2, before World War I, only one Jew, Albert von Goldschmidt-Rothschild, achieved entry into the diplomatic service and was assigned abroad; other Jews from distinguished families (like Oppenheim) tried to win entry into the service, but failed. Note

further, Kröger, 368; Wilhelm Treue, "Max Freiherr von Oppenheim—Der Archäologe und die Politik," *Historische Zeitschrift,* 209 (1969): 39–49; and R. L. Melka, "Max Freiherr von Oppenheim: Sixty Years of Scholarship and Political Intrigue in the Middle East," *Middle Eastern Studies,* 9 (1973): 81. Some portions of this study regarding Oppenheim are discussed in Donald M. McKale, "'The Kaiser's Spy': Max von Oppenheim and the Anglo-German Rivalry before and during the First World War," *European History Quarterly,* 27 (1997): 199–220. Also, see Ernest Gellner, *Anthropology and Politics: Revolutions in the Sacred Grove,* particularly 11–27, on the use of archaeologists and other scholars to collect foreign political and intelligence information.

41. Treue, 47–49; and Kröger, 368.

42. Treue, 48–49, 53.

43. On the funding of his work, see Treue, 54; and Major J. Ramsay (British resident in Baghdad) to Secretary to Government of India, 19 Nov. 1906, PRO/FO 371/245/1150. Ramsay claimed to have learned from the German consul in Baghdad that Oppenheim lived on £3000 annually from his family, plus £400 from the German foreign ministry (*Auswärtiges Amt,* AA).

44. Treue, 50.

45. Müller, 194–95. For Abduh's ideology, see n. 47 below.

46. See Oppenheim to Prince Chlodwig zu Hohenlohe-Schillingsfürst (German chancellor), 23 Apr. 1897; Oppenheim, memo ("Die Panislamische Bewegung"), 5 July 1898, both in *Politisches Archiv,* Bonn [hereafter PA], and cited in Landau, 96.

47. While Abduh and other Arab writers, such as Jamal ad-Din al-Afghani, preached a reawakening and reform of Islam, Abduh believed that for such a task even the presence of the British in Egypt could be of use. Oppenheim once described Abduh as "a bellicose Egyptian shaykh, orthodox but also inclined toward innovation, who could get along neither with Lord Cromer nor with the khedive, but is beloved by the Egyptian youth." See Müller, 60–61. More specifically Abduh renounced his radical views, which he had held after 1882, advocating a Muslim uprising against British rule. By the 1890s he preached Egyptian patriotism, a loyalty owed to Egypt equally by Muslims and non-Muslims. In learning and religion he increasingly favored pan-Islamism. His views are in Albert Hourani, *Arabic Thought in the Liberal Age, 1798–1939,* chapter 6; Landau, 25; and Yapp, 239.

48. Zechlin, "Friedensbestrebungen," B25 (21 June 1961): 354 n. 229.

49. According to Fischer, *Germany's Aims,* 123, Oppenheim's memo of 5 July 1898 "inspired the Emperor to his Damascus speech." But Oppenheim's biographer, Treue, 53 n. 6, notes that while the consular official's reports were given to William II, Oppenheim never wrote or talked directly to the kaiser, nor did he receive acknowledgment for having assisted preparations for the emperor's visit. Regarding Oppenheim's prewar career in Cairo, Trumpener, "Germany and the End of the Ottoman Empire" 121, observes: "It appears . . . that his influence was actually quite limited."

50. Kröger, 371; Trumpener, "Germany and the End of the Ottoman Empire," 122; Hagen, 33–34; and Rathmann, *Berlin-Bagdad,* 46–47.

51. Hagen, 33; Kennedy, *Anglo-German Antagonism,* 317; and Treue, 52. Rosen served before World War I at Tangier and in Rumania and Portugal; see G. P. Gooch, *Recent Revelations of European Diplomacy,* 61–62.

52. Schöllgen, 125–63; Rathmann, *Berlin-Bagdad*, 47–62; and Busch, *Britain and the Persian Gulf*, chapter 7.

53. Busch, *Britain and the Persian Gulf*, 106, 353–54.

54. One of the best brief discussions, although an old one, of the strategic and economic value of Turkey to the Great Powers remains W. W. Gottlieb, *Studies in Secret Diplomacy*, 19–33.

55. Schöllgen, 155–56.

56. Once the Ottomans learned the details of the agreement, a crisis ensued when they attempted, without success, to use military pressure to force Mubarak to break it. See Yapp, 176; Hourani, *History of the Arab Peoples*, 280–81; and Gottlieb, 186–234.

57. The standard account is Kennedy, *Anglo-German Antagonism*, 251–90, 415–31. Also, note Herwig, *Hammer or Anvil?* 176–77; Berghahn, 277–78; Geiss, 69–71; and Gordon A. Craig, *Germany, 1866–1945*, 303–14.

58. Regarding the German perception of "encirclement," see Herwig, *First World War*, 18–19. The many issues leading to Britain's decision for the major diplomatic realignment are discussed in a vast literature. Two useful analyses are Steiner, *Origins of the First World War*, chapters 2 and 4; and David Reynolds, *Britannia Overruled: British Policy and World Power in the Twentieth Century*, 67–77.

59. Kennedy, *Anglo-German Antagonism*, 269; Thomas W. Kramer, *Deutsche-ägyptische Beziehungen in Vergangenheit und Gegenwart*, 55–56; and regarding the general nature of the entente cordiale, Pierre Guillen, "The Entente of 1904 as a Colonial Settlement," in *France and Britain in Africa: Imperial Rivalry and Colonial Rule*, ed. Prosser Gifford and William Roger Louis, 358–66.

2. THE SPECTER OF MUSLIM UNREST AND GERMAN SUPPORT, 1905–1914

1. The letter is noted in Bülow, 1: 218. Later, in 1906 and 1908, during the international crises over Morocco and Bosnia, the emperor stressed the same theme. "The British," he wrote, "had better realize that war with Germany means the loss of India, and therewith the World War." See Fischer, *Germany's Aims*, 121.

2. Regarding the British, Fromkin, 96–97, observes: "[Lord] Kitchener, like most Britons who had lived in the East, believed that in the Moslem world religion counts for everything. . . . They believed that [Islam] obeyed its leaders." In 1911, Sir John A. Fisher, the former head of the Royal Navy, remarked, "The world has yet to learn what the Mohammedans can do if once their holy fervour seizes them." See James, *Rise and Fall of the British Empire*, 359.

3. The best account is D. A. Farnie, *East and West of Suez: The Suez Canal in History, 1854–1956*, 499–502.

4. See Ochsenwald, *Hijaz Railroad*, 18–23, 60–61; Pick, "German Railway Constructions," 74–79; and Rashid Ismail Khalidi, *British Policy towards Syria & Palestine, 1906–1914: A Study of the Antecedents of the Hussein–McMahon Correspondence, the Sykes-Picot Agreement, and the Balfour Declaration*, 20–21.

5. Between 1903 and 1907, forty engineers were employed on the railroad, of which one-half were foreigners, mostly German, including the lead engineer, Heinrich August Meissner; Ochsenwald, *Hijaz Railroad*, 32–33. Also, the Hijaz railway encouraged a German idea for a Beirut-Maan-Aqaba line to compete with the Suez Canal; see Farnie, 499.

6. Khalidi, *British Policy*, 25, 31, 37–40; and Robert L. Tignor, *Modernization and British Colonial Rule in Egypt, 1882–1914*, 278.

7. See Cromer to Foreign Office, London [hereafter FO], 12 Apr. 1906, PRO/FO 371/65/12624. Müller, 196, mentions Oppenheim's involvement in the Aqaba incident but does not define what it was.

8. Kramer, 61; and Major J. Ramsay to Secretary to Government of India, 19 Nov. 1906, noting information about Oppenheim he had gleaned from the local German consul, Richarz, in PRO/FO 371/245/1150. Richarz, said Ramsay, "seemed to think that Baron Oppenheim had very little authority from the German Government, but without appearing too interested I could not discover why the German Government paid him £400 a year."

9. Khalidi, *British Policy*, 42–43.

10. Ibid., 58–73.

11. See Ibid., 3–10; P. J. Vatikiotis, *The History of Modern Egypt: From Muhammad Ali to Mubarak*, 173–76; and Tignor, chapter 8.

12. In another part of his speech, Grey used the word "fanaticism"; Landau, 27–28.

13. See, for instance, German press articles that mentioned the subject, "Arabische Hochzeitsgebräuche," *Der Tag*, 4 Aug. 1907; "Haremsleben in Egypten," *Berliner Lokal-Anzeiger*, 31 July 1908; "Ägyptischer Aberglaube," *Berliner Lokal-Anzeiger*, 31 August 1908; Kramer, 189–90; and Grunwald, "Pénétration Pacifique," 96–97.

14. Lascelles to Grey, 11 Apr. 1907, PRO/FO 371/248/11874; and Bernstorff to Bülow ("Inhalt: Unterredung mit Lord Cromer"), 7 Apr. 1907, NARA/T-137/31/0771-72.

15. Bernstorff to Bülow ("Inhalt: Die Haltung des Khedive."), 28 Dec. 1906, NARA/T-137/31/0725-26; and German embassy Therapia to Bülow, 3 June 1905, NARA/T-137/28/0124-25.

16. Note Donald M. McKale, "*Weltpolitik* Versus *Imperium Britannica*: Anglo-German Rivalry in Egypt, 1904–14," *Canadian Journal of History* 22 (1987): 197–205; and AA to Bernstorff, 25 Mar. 1907, NARA/T-137/31/0753.

17. Donald M. McKale, *Curt Prüfer: German Diplomat from the Kaiser to Hitler*, 13–14; and Ronald Storrs, *Orientations*, 121.

18. See the Egyptian government memorandum, "Note confidentielle è Son Excellence le President du Conseil des Ministres," 11 Nov. 1911, PRO/FO 371/1114/44628.

19. Oppenheim to Bülow, 26 May 1908, NARA/T-137/32/0100; and Oppenheim to Bülow, 31 July 1906, NARA/T-137/31/0661.

20. Landau, 97.

21. See Oppenheim's memo, "Berlin, den 28. Juli 1918.," PA/*Türkei* 165 (*Arabien*)/Bd. 42. The British noted only much later the meeting between Husayn and Oppenheim; note D. G. Hogarth, "Germans in Hejaz," *Arab Bulletin*, No. 77 (27 Jan. 1918): 6, in PRO/FO 882/volume 27. Husayn arrived as sharif in the Hijaz in Dec. 1908; see Robert Lacey, *The Kingdom: Arabia and the House of Sa'ud*, 85.

22. "The Foreign Legion in Algeria," *The Times* (London), 17 Dec. 1908; Landau, 96–97; and Müller, 194.

23. Oppenheim to Bülow, 28 May 1909, NARA/T-137/28/0365-66.

24. Count J. de Salis (counselor at the British embassy in Berlin) to Grey, 8 July 1908, PRO/FO 371/452/24070; and Oppenheim to Bülow, 28 May 1909, NARA/T-137/28/0365, noting Abbas Hilmi's opposition to a constitution.

25. McKale, *"Weltpolitik,"* 198–99; Vatikiotis, 210–11, 216–18; Hourani, *Arabic Thought,* 170–82, 193–209; and Tignor, 291–97.

26. Marschall von Bieberstein to Bethmann Hollweg, 4 Jan. 1910, doc. no. 9989, *Die Grosse Politik der Europäischen Kabinette 1871–1914. Sammlung der Diplomatischen Akten des Auswärtigen Amtes* [hereafter *GP*], ed. Johannes Lepsius, Albrecht Mendelssohn Bartholdy, Friedrich Thimme, 27: 611; Lukasz Hirszowicz, "The Sultan and the Khedive, 1892–1908," *Middle Eastern Studies* 8 (1972): 303–6; James Jankowski, "Egypt and Early Arab Nationalism, 1908–1922," in *The Origins of Arab Nationalism,* ed. Rashid Khalidi, Lisa Anderson, Muhammad Muslih, and Reeva S. Simon, 246–47; Israel Gershoni and James P. Jankowski, *Egypt, Islam and the Arabs: The Search for Egyptian Nationhood, 1900–1930,* 18–19; Elie Kedourie, *Arabic Political Memoirs and Other Studies,* 107–111; Philip S. Khoury, *Urban Notables and Arab Nationalism: The Politics of Damascus, 1860–1920,* 62; and Vatikiotis, 218–19. Another witness to the khedive's much-publicized Islamic practices was an American officer who had visited Egypt before World War I; note Military History Institute, U.S. Army War College, Carlisle Barracks, Pa./Edward Davis Papers/book 4, p. 104.

27. Müller, 195; Cromer to FO, 12 Apr. 1906, PRO/FO 371/65/12624; and Bernstorff to Bülow, 30 May 1908, NARA/T-137/32/0102-03.

28. Alfred von Kiderlen-Wächter (German foreign secretary) to Wilhelm II, 24 Sept. 1911, doc. no. 10830, *GP,* 30: 49–50; Bernstorff to Bülow, 26 Apr. 1907, NARA/T-137/28/0213-14; and Bernstorff to Bülow, 11 Feb., 30 May, 1 July, and 17 Nov. 1908, NARA/T-137/32/0069, 0102-04, 0110-12, 0138-40.

29. Oppenheim to Bülow, 19 Dec. 1908 and 12 Feb. 1909, NARA/T-137/28/0306-07, 0309-10.

30. The revolution, which began in Macedonia, forced Abd ul-Hamid to restore the 1876 constitution and recall the parliament, which had been dissolved in 1877. The Young Turk movement had emerged in the 1880s and spread particularly among intellectuals and younger army officers. See Feroz Ahmad, *The Young Turks: The Committee of Union and Press in Turkish Politics, 1908–1914,* chapter 1; Ernest Edmondson Ramsaur, Jr., *The Young Turks: Prelude to the Revolution of 1908;* Lord Kinross, *The Ottoman Centuries: The Rise and Fall of the Turkish Empire,* 572–76; and Hourani, *History of the Arab Peoples,* 281.

31. Ahmad, *Young Turks,* 24–91; and C. J. Lowe and M. L. Dockrill, *The Mirage of Power,* vol. 1, *British Foreign Policy, 1902–14,* 80–86. Austria-Hungary had completed its annexation of the Ottoman provinces of Bosnia and Herzegovina during the Bosnian crisis, and Russia threatened to secure changes in its favor in the Ottoman administration of the Black Sea straits. According to previous international treaties, the straits were open to commercial navigation but closed to all non-Turkish warships. Also during the Bosnian crisis, Bulgaria declared its independence from Turkey, and Crete proclaimed its decision to unite with Greece.

32. Curiously, under the guidance of Lowther and the dragoman at the embassy, Gerald Fitzmaurice, British officials viewed the Young Turks as influenced by Freemasons and Jews engaged in a conspiracy to impose on the Ottoman Empire an alien system of ideas. Note Fromkin, 41–44; and Yapp, 183–84.

33. Heller, 34–37. In reality, according to Landau, 73–74, 86–88, before World War I pan-Islamism enjoyed only lukewarm support from the Young Turks. Above all,

they were uneasy about a supra-national ideology like pan-Islamism in an age of surging nationalisms, including their own.

34. Quoted in Heller, 39.

35. Ibid., 39–40; and the prewar views toward pan-Islamism detailed in Sir Arthur Hirtzel (political secretary in the India Office [hereafter IO]), "The War with Turkey: Memorandum by Political Department, India Office," 25 May 1916, PRO/FO 371/2778/130553.

36. Heller, 39–40. Most Muslims, including the Turks, were Sunnis, who followed the *Sunna,* or traditions of the Prophet Muhammad, and who accepted the orthodox successors or caliphs to Muhammad. The Shiites claimed that the divinely guided leaders of Islam descended from Ali ibn Abi Talib, Muhammad's cousin and husband of his daughter Fatima, and father of the Prophet's only grandchild. Although Shiite Islam was much the same in practice as Sunni orthodox Islam, Shiite jurists qualified to interpret Islamic law, the *Sharia,* held greater power and could change the applications of the law as spokesmen of Ali. Brief, but useful, definitions are in Ovendale, 221–23.

37. Ahmad, *Young Turks,* 153.

38. The details are in Hermann Count von Hatzfeldt (German consul general in Cairo) to Bethmann Hollweg, 15 Nov. 1911, NARA/T-137/28/0456-58. Also see Ahmad, *Young Turks,* 153; and Khalidi, *British Policy,* 234, which notes that the Arab dissatisfaction with the Ottoman defeat in Libya was reported extensively by British consuls in Syria.

39. Yapp, 175.

40. Hirszowicz, "Sultan and the Khedive," 303–6; Jankowski, "Egypt and Early Arab Nationalism," 246–47; Kedourie, *Arabic Political Memoirs,* 107–111; and Khoury, 62.

41. A multitude of studies exists on this subject. The first historical-scholarly treatment was George Antonius, *The Arab Awakening: The Story of the Arab National Movement.* It argued that before World War I Arabs of differing origin in the Ottoman Empire had, because of the rediscovery of Arabic culture, resolved to recreate a society in which Arabs could live together and rule themselves. A reform of the empire that would enable Arabs to continue living in it was impossible. Subsequent historians have attacked this view, arguing that before 1914 most Arab nationalists sought some form of influence or autonomy within the empire. An excellent analysis of the differing interpretations is Albert Hourani, "*The Arab Awakening* Forty Years After," in *Studies in Arab History: The Antonius Lectures, 1978–87,* ed. Derek Hopwood, 21–40.

42. These issues are covered extensively in Dawn, *From Ottomanism to Arabism,* 57–58; Elie Kedourie, *England and the Middle East: The Destruction of the Ottoman Empire,* chapters 1–2; Zeine N. Zeine, *The Emergence of Arab Nationalism: With a Background Study of Arab-Turkish Relations in the Near East,* 72–100; Khoury, 54–72; Antonius, chapters 4–6; Gottlieb, 48–51; Anderson, *Eastern Question,* 269–304; Hourani, "*The Arab Awakening* Forty Years After," 28–32; and the numerous excellent articles in *The Origins of Arab Nationalism,* ed. Rashid Khalidi, Lisa Anderson, Muhammad Muslih, and Reeva S. Simon.

43. This is particularly stressed by Mahmoud Haddad, "Iraq Before World War I: A Case of Anti-European Arab Ottomanism," in *The Origins of Arab Nationalism,* ed. Rashid Khalidi, Lisa Anderson, Muhammad Muslih, and Reeva S. Simon, 120–

50; and Elie Kedourie, *The Chatham House Version and Other Middle-Eastern Studies,* 255.

44. See the study of Arab influence in the Turkish parliament, Sabine Prätor, *Der arabische Faktor in der jungtürkischen Politik. Eine Studie zum osmanischen Parlament der II. Konstitution (1908–1918),* 2. Also, note Dawn, *From Ottomanism to Arabism;* and Hourani, *"The Arab Awakening Forty Years After,"* 28–31.

45. Regarding the policy toward Britain, see Fischer, *War of Illusions,* especially chapter 4; Geiss, 71; Craig, 333–37; and Andreas Hillgruber, *Germany and the Two World Wars,* trans. William C. Kirby, chapter 3. This German policy was part of what Herwig, *First World War,* 7, observes was "[a] certain calm" in Europe after 1910, which included London and Berlin "amicably discussing" a number of important issues that had been sources of tension between them previously.

46. Note W. G. Hesse (German consul Baghdad) to Bülow, 18 Mar. 1908; and Constantinople embassy to Bülow, 17 Apr. 1908, PA/*Türkei* 165/Bd. 29. Also in the same collection, Bd. 28, see Richarz (German consul Baghdad) to Bülow, 6 June 1907; von Strempel (German military attaché in Constantinople) to German war ministry ("Militärbericht 36. Lage im Yemen"), 3 July 1907; and Bernstorff to Bülow, 13 Mar. 1908.

47. Padel to Bethmann Hollweg, 30 Sept. 1910, PA/*Türkei* 165/Bd. 32.

48. Ibid.

49. Hesse to Bethmann Hollweg, 24 Mar. 1910, PA/*Türkei* 165/Bd. 32.

50. Hesse to Bethmann Hollweg, 14 Aug. 1911, PA/*Türkei* 165/Bd. 34.

51. Hesse to Bethmann Hollweg, 19 Sept. 1910, PA/*Türkei* 165/Bd. 32; Prätor, 281; and Busch, *Britain, India, and the Arabs, 1914–1921,* 11–12.

52. Strempel and other Germans reminded the Young Turks that their real control over Yemen would only be achieved when they extended the Hijaz railroad to Mecca and Aqaba. See Strempel to war ministry, 24 June 1907 ("Militärbericht Nr. 34"); and Strempel to war ministry, 3 July 1907 ("Militärbericht 36. Lage im Yemen."), PA/*Türkei* 165/Bd. 28. See also, "Türkei. Aus Yemen und Hedschas," *Kölnische Zeitung,* 25 July 1907. On the role of the sharif in assisting the Ottomans in halting the Yemen revolt, note Dawn, *From Ottomanism to Arabism,* 10–12.

53. The khedive's pilgrimage to Mecca at the end of 1909 prompted vigorous criticism from the German embassy in Constantinople; Marschall von Bieberstein to Bethmann Hollweg, 4 Jan. 1910, doc. no. 9989, *GP,* 27: 611. Regarding the khedive's ambitions, note Dawn, *From Ottomanism to Arabism,* 148–57; Vatikiotis, 218; Jankowski, "Egypt and Early Arab Nationalism," 246; Kedourie, *Chatham House Version,* 255; Khoury, 53–73; Zeine, 73–100; and Antonius, chapters 5–6.

54. Oppenheim to Bülow, 6 June 1909, PA/*Türkei* 165/Bd. 31; and "Die Lage in Arabien," *Dresdner Anzeiger,* 18 Feb. 1911.

55. Hesse to Bethmann Hollweg, 24 Mar. 1910 and 14 Aug. 1911, PA/*Türkei* 165/Bd. 34.

56. Hesse to Bethmann Hollweg, 25 July 1912, PA/*Türkei* 165/Bd. 34.

57. Heinrich von Tschirschky (German ambassador in Vienna) to Bethmann Hollweg, 17 Oct. 1911, PA/*Türkei* 165/Bd. 34. Also, see Karl Johannes Bauer, *Alois Musil. Wahrheitssucher in der Wüste,* chapter 7; and Erich Feigl, *Musil von Arabien: Vorkämpfer der islamischen Welt,* chapter 9.

58. According to Lorimer, the pan-Islamic campaign appeared designed to provoke anti-British agitation among Shiites in southern Persia. This, Hesse concluded,

"through lack of success [could] damage our reputation and prompt great annoyance in British circles." See Hesse to Bethmann Hollweg, 20 Jan. 1911, PA/*Türkei* 165/ Bd. 33.

59. Dawn, *From Ottomanism to Arabism*, 62 n. 27; and the emperor's marginalia on Kiderlen-Wächter to Wilhelm II, 24 Sept. 1911, doc. no. 10830, *GP*, 30: 50–51.

60. Khalidi, *British Policy*, 207, 225–26.

61. Something that angered the French, who still hoped to realize their claims to Syria. The quotes are in ibid., 225.

62. Rida had also attempted to recruit several Arab princes in Arabia and the Persian Gulf; Dawn, *From Ottomanism to Arabism*, 57–58.

63. "The Coming of a New Empire," *Pall Mall Gazette*, 13 May 1908; and "An Independent Arabia," *The Pioneer*, 29 June 1908.

64. Dawn, *From Ottomanism to Arabism*, 61; and Khalidi, *British Policy*, 91–92, 100–3.

65. Dawn, *From Ottomanism to Arabism*, 62.

66. An extensive discussion of Kitchener's views is in Khalidi, *British Policy*, chapter 6; ibid., 58–60, 62; and Kedourie, *England and the Middle East*, 32–36.

67. McKale, *"Weltpolitik,"* 199–201.

68. By 1913 Jawish had taken refuge in Constantinople, where the Turkish prime minister *(grand vizier)*, Said Halim, encouraged his pan-Islamism; Farid, another pan-Islamist, settled in Switzerland. See Tignor, 307–15; Landau, 130–33; Vatikiotis, 211–29; Hourani, *Arab Thought*, 208–9; and Kitchener to Grey, 30 Sept. 1911, PRO/FO 371/ 1114/39288.

69. The episode, which involved the highest levels of the two governments, including Grey and the German ambassador in London, Paul Graf Wolff-Metternich zur Gracht, is discussed in McKale, *Curt Prüfer*, 21–23. Appointed the new director of the library was Ahmad Lutfi al-Sayyid, a leader of the moderate nationalist party. Regarding the number of troops in the prewar peacetime garrison, note Antonius, 136.

70. Hatzfeldt to Bethmann Hollweg, 15 Nov. 1911, NARA/T-137/28/0457, which emphasizes the key role played in the recruitment of Egyptians by the dragoman Prüfer. Also, see Kiderlen-Wächter to Wilhelm II, 24 Sept. 1911, doc. no. 10830, *GP*, 30:49–50. The war provided Germany with a dilemma as to which of its allies to support; on this issue, see W. D. Wrigley, "Germany and the Turco-Italian War, 1911–1912," *International Journal of Middle East Studies* 11 (1980): 313–38.

71. Note Klein, "Die Befestigung des Sinai und seine Vorgeschichte," n.d., in Hatzfeldt to Bethmann Hollweg, 23 Apr. 1912, PA/*Türkei* 165/Bd 34.

72. Accounts of the triumvirate's takeover, which was completed during 1913, are in Ahmad, *Young Turks*, 119–30; Kinross, 590–98; and Yapp, 192–95.

73. According to Ahmad, *Young Turks*, 133, 153–54: "The Turks reacted to these changes by becoming more ethnocentric, and they began to give a more definite form to their own nationalism. At first this was of the Pan-Turanian variety, partly because Pan-Turanism was sufficiently vague to be easily reconciled with Pan-Islam. . . . Furthermore, Pan-Turanism, like Pan-Islam, was an expansionist ideology which suited the mood of the Young Turks, then in full retreat at the opposite front."

74. Moreover, Husayn would receive money to buy off the local tribes, he would control one-third of all revenues derived from the railway, and he would have total

command over the force needed to finish the project. See Ahmad, *Young Turks,* 134–37, who contradicts the widespread view (fostered by Antonius, Zeine, and others) that extreme Young Turk nationalism was most responsible for Arab nationalism, particularly in Syria, and hatred of the Turks by other non-Turkish peoples in the Ottoman Empire. A good summary of the evidence and differing scholarly views on the issue is in Yapp, 207. On Said Halim, note Landau, 84–86.

75. For the impact of the mission on Great Power relations, see Heller, 112–16; Craig, 337; Hillgruber, 21; and Rathmann, *Stossrichtung Nahost,* 27.

76. Heller, 101–6; and Lowe and Dockrill, 1:108.

77. See Heller, 40–52; Marian Kent, "Constantinople and Asiatic Turkey, 1905–1914," in *British Foreign Policy Under Sir Edward Grey,* ed. F. H. Hinsley, 148–55; Busch, *Britain and the Persian Gulf,* 376–83; and Schöllgen, 317–28, 375–92.

78. Key quotes are in Heller, 49; and Cohen, 211. According to Cohen, 236, both the Indian and British authorities agreed in 1913 that, in deference to Muslim opinion, "every effort should be made to avoid actions likely to lead to [Ottoman] partition either now or in the future." Also, note Herwig, *First World War,* 7.

79. The nationalists bitterly opposed the India government's partition of the huge province of Bengal in October 1905. The division had created two new provinces: Bengali Hindus formed a minority in both and Muslims a majority in one. A wave of extremist agitation had exploded into violence, including the later near-assassinations of Hardinge and his wife in December 1912. Muslim leaders had disapproved of the partition, fearing Hindu domination as much or more than British rule. By 1908, Muslims had established their own political organization, the All-India Muslim League, led initially by Aga Khan, to represent them to the government. Note Burke and Quraishi, 109–35; Stanley Wolpert, *A New History of India,* 275–80; Vincent A. Smith, *The Oxford History of India,* 771–72; and on the number of Muslims in India, Larcher, 8. According to Landau, 197, Indian pan-Islamism "was a potentially significant political force if these Muslims supporting it could be organized."

80. Cohen, 262–63, provides important quotes, including Crewe's that there was "no solid ground" for a "German-Turkish-Pan Islamic scare."

81. The British aimed at confirming the Government of India's domination of Kuwait, which had existed since the secret agreement with the Shaykh of Kuwait in 1899 and extended in October 1907. See Busch, *Britain and the Persian Gulf,* 330–36. According to Cohen, 227, the Anglo-Turkish and Anglo-German agreements of 1913–1914 subordinated the implementation of Britain's Mesopotamian policy to the defense of its Gulf interests.

82. See Lacey, chapter 10; and H. V. F. Winstone, *Leachman: 'OC Desert': The Life of Lieutenant-Colonel Gerard Leachman D.S.O.,* 120–36.

83. Busch, *Britain and the Persian Gulf,* 380–82; and Yapp, 262–64.

84. Regarding the Gulf and Abu Musa affair, note Busch, *Britain and the Persian Gulf,* 353–57, 369–72; and IWM, *Operations in Persia,* 31–32.

85. See, for example, the reports to the AA by Wassmuss and the other German agent at Bushire, Dr. Helmut Listemann, in PA/*Türkei* 165/Bde. 29–31.

86. Mallet, then in the FO, compared the German activity in Persia to Berlin's previous policy regarding Morocco, in which "the object is the same"—in this instance to divide Britain and Russia, whose alliance of 1907 had not removed all conflicts between London and St. Petersburg, and to enhance Berlin's influence in Persia. Note

Schöllgen, 318–28; and Ulrich Gehrke, "Germany and Persia up to 1919," in *Germany and the Middle East, 1835–1939,* ed. Jehuda L. Wallach, 109–12.

87. Lowther to Grey, 8 Aug. 1911, PRO/FO 371/1261/31881; and report of the British consulate general in Baghdad, "Summary of events in Turkish Iraq for the month of November 1911," 4 Dec. 1911, PRO/FO/ 371/1490/3025.

88. Fück, 291; and Pfanmüller, 369–70, 373–74.

89. Bauer, chapter 6; Feigl, chapter 10; Georg Sauer, "Alois Musil's Reisen nach Arabien im Ersten Weltkrieg," *Archiv Orientální,* 37 (1969): 245; and Robin Bidwell, *Travellers in Arabia,* 156. Also on Musil's 1909 visit to Ibn Shaalan, note Feigl, 118–51; and H. V. F. Winstone, *The Illicit Adventure: The Story of Political and Military Intelligence in the Middle East from 1898 to 1926,* 37–41. Further, Winstone, 92–93, discusses the 1912 journey.

90. Cohen, 249–62, has an extensive discussion. Also useful for the British side is Fischer, *War of Illusions,* 302–6. The Anglo-Turkish agreement of July 1913 is covered in Busch, *Britain and the Persian Gulf,* 336–40.

91. Fischer, *War of Illusions,* 300–6; Geiss, 69–71; Herwig, *Hammer or Anvil?* 177–80; and Berghahn, 278–79.

92. Rathmann, *Stossrichtung Nahost,* 21–22, 27–29, 44–46; and on the role of such pressure groups in general, Herwig, *Hammer or Anvil?* 171. On Jagow's imperialism, note Herwig, "Imperial Germany," in *Knowing One's Enemies: Intelligence Assessment before the Two World Wars,* ed. Ernest R. May, 85.

93. See Marian Kent, *Oil and Empire: British Policy and Mesopotamian Oil, 1900–1920,* 59–94; and Fischer, *War of Illusions,* 306–7.

94. A point made by Trumpener, "Germany and the End of the Ottoman Empire," 119, 122; and Mommsen, 156–57.

95. Hesse to Bethmann Hollweg, 27 June 1914; and Lichnowsky to Bethmann Hollweg ("England und Persische Golf."), 3 Apr. 1914, PA/*Türkei* 165/Bd. 36.

96. Cohen, 235–36, 264–67.

97. Fromkin, 97–98; Khalidi, *British Policy,* chapter 6; Dawn, "Influence of T. E. Lawrence," 58–62, which is convincing in arguing that Hogarth and Lawrence were not British spies; Kedourie, *England and the Middle East,* 34, 89–96; and Metternich (German ambassador in London) to Bethmann Hollweg, 8 Feb. 1912, PA/*Türkei* 165/Bd. 34.

98. Dawn, *From Ottomanism to Arabism,* 61–63; Fromkin, 98–99; Mary C. Wilson, "The Hashemites, the Arab Revolt, and Arab Nationalism," *The Origins of Arab Nationalism,* ed. Rashid Khalidi, Lisa Anderson, Muhammad Muslih, and Reeva S. Simon, 211–12; Gottlieb, 49–50; Zeine, 100–16; Antonius, 124–30; Khalidi, *British Policy,* chapter 4; Heller, 127–30; and Ochsenwald, *Hijaz Railroad,* 198–99.

99. Miquel to Bethmann Hollweg, 1 Apr. 1913 ("Arabische Unabhängigheits-Bestrebungen"), PA/*Türkei* 165/Bd. 35.

100. Wangenheim to Bethmann Hollweg, 17 and 19 Nov. and 20 and 31 Dec. 1912; and Wangenheim to Bethmann Hollweg, 14 June and 7 July 1913, all in PA/*Türkei* 165/Bd. 35. Also, note Wangenheim to Bethmann Hollweg, 22 Mar. 1914, PA/*Türkei* 165/Bd. 36.

101. Wangenheim to Bethmann Hollweg, 18 Jan. 1913; Wangenheim to AA, 25 Feb. 1913; Jagow to German embassy London, 3 Mar. 1913, PA/*Türkei* 165/Bd. 35; Haddad, "Iraq Before World War I," 127, 134–38; and Kedourie, *Chatham House Version,* 255.

102. Gerhard Mutius (Beirut) to Bethmann Hollweg, 3 May 1913, PA/*Türkei* 165/ Bd. 35.

103. AA to London and Constantinople embassies, 25 Jan. 1914; and Wangenheim to Bethmann Hollweg, 9 Mar. 1914, PA/*Türkei* 165/Bd. 36. Also, in the same volume, note Mutius (Constantinople) to Bethmann Hollweg, 6 Jan. 1914. Apparently, the British had heard of a projected congress for Mar. 1914 at Kuwait of Arab chiefs that did not take place; Heller, 129.

104. Miquel to Bethmann Hollweg, 11 Mar. 1914, PA/*Türkei* 165/Bd. 36; and Dawn, *From Ottomanism to Arabism,* 63.

105. Wangenheim to Bethmann Hollweg, 28 Mar. 1914, PA/*Türkei* 165/Bd. 36.

106. Wangenheim to Bethmann Hollweg, 22 May 1914, PA/*Türkei* 165/Bd. 36. The Arab officer, al-Masri, had played a role in the CUP until 1909. Later he joined Arab secret societies working for autonomy within the Ottoman empire; prior to his arrest he had founded a new society, al-Ahd, or the Covenant. To say the least, the Porte was suspicious of al-Masri's activities. It had learned that he was in the pay of the khedive of Egypt, Abbas Hilmi, who wanted al-Masri to persuade the Sanussis in Libya to make peace with the Italians. The Turks, who were at peace with Italy, could not object openly to such action on the part of al-Masri, but they resented the khedive's intrigues. See Ahmad, *Young Turks,* 138–39; and Khalidi, *British Policy,* 341–45.

107. Hesse to Bethmann Hollweg, 16 July 1914, PA/*Türkei* 165/Bd. 37. Ajaimi's hatred for Talib centered around the latter's assistance in the Ottoman arrest and execution of Ajaimi's father, Sadhun Pasha.

108. Apparently the German embassy in Constantinople had received numerous requests as late as March and June 1914 from Arab and Ottoman circles for assistance against Britain and France, which were turned down because of the Reich's policy toward Britain. See Wangenheim to AA, 26 Aug. 1914, NARA/T-137/143/0025.

109. According to Fischer, *War of Illusions,* 306–7.

110. Müller, 239, 281–82. According to Hagen, 33, Wangenheim had always had little enthusiasm for pan-Islamism.

111. Fischer, *War of Illusions,* 307–8.

112. The details are in Ibid., 308; and Zara Steiner, *Origins of the First World War,* 108–9.

3. GERMANY AS WARTIME "REVOLUTIONARY," FALL 1914

1. A theme emphasized by German officials themselves at the war's beginning. See, for example, Wangenheim to AA, 26 Aug. 1914; and Jäckh to Zimmermann, 3 Jan. 1915, NARA/T-137/143/0025, 0153-57.

2. Herwig, *"Luxury" Fleet,* 92, 144–49. Germany's only war plan was that initially drafted in 1905 and 1906 by the chief of the German General Staff, Field Marshal Alfred Count von Schlieffen, designed to defeat France quickly and then Russia.

3. See above, chapter 2.

4. Hagen, 32; Trumpener, *Germany and the Ottoman Empire,* 12–15; and Joll, 188–89.

5. Fischer, *Germany's Aims,* 121.

6. Ibid., 120–21.

7. See ibid., 121; and Kröger, 371.

8. Kroger, 371; Carl Mühlmann, *Das Deutsch-Türkische Waffenbündnis im Weltkriege*, 25; Trumpener, *Germany and the Ottoman Empire*, 15–17; Fischer, *Germany's Aims*, 126; and Zechlin, "Friedensbestrebungen," B24(14 June 1961):329 and B25(21 June 1961):360–61. On Zimmermann, the so-called "strong man" in the AA, note Fischer, *Germany's Aims*, 187–88. A copy of the German-Ottoman treaty is in Larcher, 36–38.

9. Accounts from the German side include Trumpener, *Germany and the Ottoman Empire*, 21–61; and Rathmann, *Stossrichtung Nahost*, 113–15. For Britain's negotiations with the Porte, see Heller, chapter 7; and Marian Kent, "Asiatic Turkey, 1914–1916," in *British Foreign Policy under Sir Edward Grey*, ed. F. H. Hinsley, 436–38.

10. Moltke's telegrams to Liman are discussed in Rathmann, *Stossrichtung Nahost*, 120.

11. Mühlmann, 24–25; and on the estimates of prewar German intelligence on the enemy's colonial forces, Herwig, "Imperial Germany," 68.

12. Ali Bas Hamba was expelled by the French from Tunisia in March 1912 and settled in Constantinople, where he established ties to the CUP and Enver. See Müller, 238–46; and Wallach, *Anatomie*, 192. According to Farnie, 531, Enver Pasha ordered preparation of a plan for an attack on the Suez Canal on 3 August 1914.

13. Both the Sektion Politik and the AA appointments are discussed in Kröger, 368; Rathmann, *Stossrichtung Nahost*, 121; Fischer, *Germany's Aims*, 123–25; and Treue, 57.

14. Ernst Freiherr Langwerth von Simmern (assistant director of the AA's political department) to General Staff, 16 Aug. 1914, in Zechlin, "Friedensbestrebungen," B25(21 June 1961):363–64. Regarding the prewar Mannesmann activities in Morocco, note Stoecker and Nimschowski, "Morocco," 242–44; and "Der Reichskanzler von Bethmann Hollweg, z.Z. in Hohenfinow, an Kaiser Wilhelm II., z.Z. in Stettin," 29 Aug. 1911, doc. no. 10728, *GP*, 29:349–50.

15. Amir Said to AA, 5 Aug. 1914, PA/*Aktenzeichen Weltkrieg* (hereafter *WK*) Nr.11g (*Ägypten, Syrien und Arabien*)/Bd. 1. For background on the Abd al-Qadir family in Syria, see Müller, 310–12.

16. "If widespread unrest occurs in this region," he declared, "Britain would be forced to send a large part of its fleet into Indian waters to protect Britain's numerous interests, its many people, and its global position." See Oppenheim to Bethmann Hollweg, 13 Aug. 1914, NARA/T-137/143/0016-19; and on the meeting in the AA's political department, Müller, 239 n. 17.

17. Langwerth von Simmern to General Staff, 16 Aug. 1914, in Zechlin, "Friedensbestrebungen," B25(21 June 1961):363–64.

18. Oppenheim to Bethmann Hollweg, 18 Aug. 1914, NARA/T-137/143/0022-23.

19. Ibid.

20. Farnie, 530.

21. See Pannwitz to Bethmann Hollweg ("Ganz geheim! Inhalt: Mißglückte Versuche, den Suezkanal zu sperren."), 26 Sept. 1914, PA/*WK* Nr.11g/Bd. 2; state secretary of the Imperial naval office to state secretary of the AA, 20 Aug. 1914, PA/*WK* Nr.11g/Bd. 1; and Farnie, 530.

22. On Mors, see below, in this chapter, 55, 57. Also note Reich naval office (intelligence bureau) to Langwerth von Simmern, 28 Aug. 1914, PA/*WK* Nr.11g/Bd. 1; and Egmont Zechlin, "Cabinet versus Economic Warfare in Germany: Policy and Strategy

during the Early Months of the First World War," in *The Origins of the First World War: Great Power Rivalry and German War Aims*, 231–32.

23. See FO, "Memorandum on the Deposition of Khedive, Abbas Hilmi Pasha, and the Liquidation of his Property in Egypt," 15 Jan. 1924, PRO/FO 371/14638/E11646; and Storrs, 124.

24. Note the extensive report by the ex-khedive's Austrian confidant, Dr. Rudolf Amster, in Zimmermann to the German embassy in Constantinople, 26 Oct. 1915, NARA/T-137/136/0711-13.

25. Wangenheim to AA, 22 Aug. 1914, PA/*WK* Nr.11g/Bd. 1.

26. Memo, Austro-Hungarian embassy in Berlin, 3 Sept. 1914, NARA/T-137/136/0390; and Wangenheim to AA, 28, 29 Aug. and 4 Sept. 1914, PA/*WK* Nr.11g/Bd. 1.

27. See Grant Duff (British minister in Bern) to Grey, 28 Nov. 1914, PRO/FO 371/1966/78320; Oppenheim, "G. A.," 23 Nov. 1914; AA to Wangenheim, 7 Oct. 1914, PA/*WK* Nr.11g/Bd. 3; Romberg to AA, 28 Aug. 1914, PA/*WK* Nr.11g/Bd. 1; and Gershoni and Jankowski, *Egypt, Islam, and the Arabs*, 25.

28. Subsequently Wangenheim informed the AA that only the sons of the shaykhs, not the shaykhs themselves, had delivered the gifts and messages. Note Wangenheim to AA, 3, 4, and 5 Sept. 1914; Athens legation to AA, 2 Sept. 1914, PA/*WK* Nr.11g/Bd. 1; Dr. Paul Krückmann to Zimmermann, 23 Sept. 1914, PA/*WK* Nr.11g/Bd. 2; and Müller, 240–41.

29. Bethmann Hollweg to AA, 4 Sept. 1914, NARA/microcopy T-149 (German Foreign Ministry Archives, 1867–1920, American Historical Association Committee for the Study of War Documents)/reel 397/frame 0326; and Zechlin, "Cabinet versus Economic Warfare," 238.

30. Bethmann Hollweg to Constantinople embassy, 7 Sept. 1914, Yale University Library, Manuscripts and Archives (Sterling Memorial Library), New Haven, Conn. (hereafter YUL)/Ernst Jäckh Papers/box 1/folder 10.

31. Konrad H. Jarausch, *The Enigmatic Chancellor: Bethmann Hollweg and the Hubris of Imperial Germany*, 196; Herwig, *First World War*, 19, 117; Fischer, *Germany's Aims*, 104, 109–10; Rathmann, *Stossrichtung Nahost*, 99–101; and David Stevenson, *First World War and International Politics*, 90–91.

32. Zimmermann to German embassy Constantinople, 25 Aug. 1914; AA to embassy, 28 Aug. 1914, PA/*WK* Nr.11g/Bd. 1; and Prüfer's war diary, "Krieg, 1914–1918," Hoover Institution on War, Revolution, and Peace, Stanford University, Palo Alto, Calif. (hereafter HIWRP)/Curt Prüfer Papers. See also, McKale, *Curt Prüfer*, 28–33.

33. Prüfer, "Krieg," entry for 4 Sept. 1914, HIWRP/Prüfer Papers. Many of the divisions, rivalries, and fears which Prüfer noted and that characterized the German alliance with Turkey and war effort in the Middle East are discussed in Trumpener, *Germany and the Ottoman Empire*, 22–37 (and especially between Wangenheim and Liman, 73–79).

34. See Prüfer, "Krieg," entries for 5–6 Sept. 1914, HIWRP/Prüfer Papers; and "Further Interrogation of Lieutenant Mors," n.d., Great Britain, FO, *Correspondence Respecting Events Leading to the Rupture of Relations with Turkey, November 1914*, 73–74 (doc. no. 181).

35. Prüfer, "Krieg," entry for 6 Sept. 1914, HIWRP/Prüfer Papers.

36. Ibid., entry for 7 Sept. 1914; and Prüfer's report, German embassy Constantinople to AA, 7 Sept. 1914, PA/*WK* Nr.11g/Bd. 2.

37. Bethmann Hollweg to Constantinople embassy, 7 Sept. 1914, YUL/Jäckh Papers/1/10.

38. Wangenheim to AA, 9 Sept. 1914, NARA/T-137/136/0403; and Trumpener, *Germany and the Ottoman Empire*, 37–38.

39. Mannesmann's approach to the Arabs not only produced protests to Berlin from Italy and Austria-Hungary, which worried about the neighboring Italians joining the Entente, but also drew the attention of the British. See FO to Sir Rennell Rodd (ambassador in Rome), 24 Sept. 1914, PRO/FO 371/1971/52791; and Austro-Hungarian embassy Berlin, "Notiz," 3 Sept. 1914, NA/T-137/5/0331. Also note Sektion Politik, "Der K. Militärattaché in Rom telegraphiert an Stellv. Grossen Generalstab.," 3 Sept. 1914; and Flotow to AA, 29 Aug. 1914, NARA/T-137/143/0400, 0385, respectively. Regarding the perpetual Italian-Sanussi hostilities, see E. E. Evans-Pritchard, *The Sanusi of Cyrenaica*, 115–21.

40. Prüfer, "Krieg," entries for 8, 12, and 13 Sept. 1914, HIWRP/Prüfer Papers; and "Further Interrogation of Lieutenant Mors," n.d., FO, *Correspondence*, 73 (doc. no. 181).

41. Prüfer, "Krieg," entry for 8 Sept. 1914, HIWRP/Prüfer Papers; and A. P. Wavell, *The Palestine Campaigns*, 24–25.

42. Rathmann, *Stossrichtung Nahost*, 120; and Bethmann Hollweg to AA, 14 Sept. 1914, NARA/T-137/136/0413.

43. Jagow to Zimmermann, 12 Sept. 1914, PA/*WK* Nr.11g/Bd. 2; Trumpener, *Germany and the Ottoman Empire*, 37–38; and Wallach, *Anatomie*, 165.

44. Jagow to Zimmermann, 6 Sept. 1914, NARA/T-137/5/0335; and Jagow to Zimmermann, 15 Sept. 1914, PA/*WK* Nr. 11g/Bd. 2.

45. Wallach, *Anatomie*, 191–92; Friedrich Freiherr Kress von Kressenstein, *Mit den Türken zum Suezkanal*, 27–41; Ulrich Trumpener, "German Officers in the Ottoman Empire, 1880–1918: Some Comments on Their Backgrounds, Functions, and Accomplishments," in *Germany and the Middle East, 1835–1939*, ed. Jehuda L. Wallach, 38–43; and on the appointment of Kressenstein and Prüfer to VIII Corps, Wangenheim to AA, 20 Sept. 1914, PA/*WK* Nr.11g/Bd. 2.

46. Note the request for the maps in Reich naval office to Langwerth von Simmern (AA), 16 Sept. 1914, PA/*WK* Nr. 11g/Bd. 2.

47. Prüfer, "Krieg," entries for 20 Sept. through 19 Oct. 1914, HIWRP/Prüfer Papers; and on the numerous contacts mentioned by Prüfer, Djemal Pasha, *Memories of a Turkish Statesman, 1913–1919*, 137–49.

48. AA to Wangenheim, 14 Oct. 1914, PA/*WK* Nr.11g/Bd. 2; and Prüfer, "Krieg," entries for 4–5, 8, 15, 23, 25–27, 29 Oct. and 1 Nov. 1914, HIWRP/Prüfer Papers.

49. Jagow to the Prussian minister of culture, 12 Sept. 1914, NARA/T-137/143/0036, asking for the cultural ministry to provide suitable German and foreign persons to do translations. Note also Rathmann, *Stossrichtung Nahost*, 184.

50. Regarding the close ties developed before the war by German agents in Abyssinia to the young pro-Muslim emperor, Lij Iyasu, see von Syburg (German minister in Addis Ababa) to AA, 20 Dec. 1913, NARA/T-137/14/0041; Harold G. Marcus, *A History of Ethiopia*, 113–14; Richard Greenfield, *Ethiopia: A New Political History*, 134; and Robert L. Hess, *Ethiopia: The Modernization of Autocracy*, 62.

51. See above, chapter 2.

52. As examples, note Julius Loytved Hardegg (German consul in Haifa and ad-

ministrator of the consulate in Damascus) to Bethmann Hollweg, 1 Oct. 1914, NARA/ T-137/143/0553; and Wangenheim to AA, 6 Sept. 1914, NARA/T-149/397/0330.

53. Oppenheim, "Zu Telegramm 425 aus Athen vom 13. September.," 14 Sept. 1914; and Quadt to AA, 13 Sept. 1914, PA/*WK* Nr.11g/Bd. 2. For the duties and position of Shaykh al-Islam, see Yapp, 377.

54. Oppenheim, "G. A.," 25 Oct. 1914, NARA/T-137/138/0376-77; Moritz to Georg Graf von Wedel (acounselor in the AA's political department and aide-de-camp of the kaiser), 30 Oct. 1914, PA/*WK* Nr.11g/Bd. 3; and Prüfer, "Krieg," 30 Oct. 1914, HIWRP/ Prüfer Papers. Also see Donald M. McKale, "German Policy toward the Sharif of Mecca, 1914-1916," *The Historian*, 55(1993):306.

55. See Sektion Politik to its command unit in the VI Army Corps (Breslau), 5 Feb. 1915, NARA/T-137/23/0645; Kröger, 382; and Hans Dumreicher (a lawyer from Cairo living in Darmstadt), "Betrifft: Reise Rohloff.," 17 Sept. 1914, PA/*WK* Nr.11g/Bd. 2. According to Müller, 369, Roloff received two hundred thousand gold marks.

56. Note AA to Rome embassy, 25, 30 Sept. 1914; and Oppenheim, "G. A.," 10 Oct. 1914, NARA/T-137/143/0456-57, 0475, 0521, respectively. Also, see Prüfer, "Krieg," entries for 5, 13 Sept. 1914, HIWRP/Prüfer Papers; and Evans-Pritchard, 125-27.

57. Moritz to Wedel, 30 Oct. 1914; Wangenheim to AA, 15 Oct. 1914, PA/*WK* Nr.11g/ Bd. 3; and Wangenheim to AA, 28 Sept. 1914, PA/*WK* Nr.11g/Bd. 2, noting Enver Pasha's agreement with Moritz's mission. Also, see Prüfer, "Krieg," entries for 25, 27 Oct. 1914, HIWRP/Prüfer Papers.

58. Such problems are discussed in Syburg to AA, 27 June 1915, NARA/T-137/14/ 0091. Also, note Wangenheim to AA, 27 Nov. 1914, NARA/T-137/138/0424.

59. See Prüfer, "Krieg," entry for 19 Oct. 1914, HIWRP/Prüfer Papers. Although Kressenstein, 55, denigrated Hilgendorf's scheme, he later urged using German colonists in Palestine in the upcoming Egyptian expedition; note Wangenheim to AA, 19 Nov. 1914, NARA/T-137/23/0181. More than likely, Hilgendorf's group was the same one mentioned in Sir George Macmunn and Capt. Cyril Falls, *The History of the Great War Based on Official Documents: Military Operations Egypt & Palestine: From the Outbreak of War with Germany to June 1917*, 15.

60. Nadolny (Sektion Politik) to AA, 22 Dec. 1914; Prüfer to Oppenheim, 31 Dec. 1914, NARA/T-137/23/0408, 0637-38; and Wallach, *Anatomie*, 168.

61. Nevertheless, later, during the spring of 1915, the British suspected Gondos of bombing one of their coastal stations, at Abu Zanima on the Sinai Peninsula side of the Gulf of Suez. Note "Intelligence Bulletin," 20 Apr. 1915, PRO/War Office Series (hereafter WO) 157 (Intelligence Summaries, 1914-1921)/file 690; Prüfer to Oppenheim, 31 Dec. 1914, NARA/T-137/23/0637-38; Prüfer, "Krieg," entry for 19 Oct. 1914, HIWRP/ Prüfer Papers; and Kress, 55-56.

62. Note Robin Bidwell, *Travellers in Arabia*, passim; Schwabe to AA, 13 May 1915, NARA/microcopy T-120 (Records of the German Foreign Ministry Received by the United States Department of State)/reel 4951/frame L367448; Col. Otto von Lossow (military attaché at the Constantinople embassy beginning in July 1915) to Sektion Politik, 13 Nov. 1915, NARA/T-137/25/0076-86; Wallach, *Anatomie*, 168; and "Intelligence Summary," 7 Dec. 1915, PRO/WO 157/698. On Neufeld's prewar activity in the Sudan, note Macmunn and Falls, *Military Operations Egypt & Palestine*, 228-29.

63. Moritz to AA, 8, 16 Jan. 1915, PA/*Türkei* 165/Bd. 37.

64. German embassy Constantinople to Abyssinian government, n.d., NARA/T-137/

137/00713; Fischer, *Germany's Aims*, 129–30; and Jäckh to Zimmermann ("Bericht über die Organisation in Konstantinopel zur Revolutionierung feindlicher Gebiete."), 3 Jan. 1915, NARA/T-137/0156-57.

65. See Frobenius, "Bericht V. durch das ksl. Deutsche Konsulat in Damas.," 6 Feb. 1915, NARA/T-137/138/0588-91.

66. Musil, "Eure Exzellenz! Hochverehrter Herr Botschafter!" 13 Oct. 1914, contained in German embassy Vienna to AA, 14 Oct. 1914, NARA/T-137/138/0359-62; Fiegl, 290–93; Bauer, 205–6; and Sauer, 245–6.

67. Musil, "Eure Exzellenz! . . . ," 13 Oct. 1914, NARA/T-137/138/0361; and Fiegl, 292–93.

68. Oppenheim, "G. A.," 25 Oct. 1914, NARA/T-137/138/0376-77; Fiegl, 293; and Bauer, 207.

69. "Abschrift eines Briefes des Hofrats Musil an Seine Exzellenz den Herrn Minister ddo. Damaskus, 1 Dezember 1914.," NARA/T-137/138/0511.

70. Ibid.; Fiegl, 310–11; Bauer, 208–9; and Joseph Pomiankowski, *Der Zusammenbruch des Ottomanischen Reiches. Erinnerungen an die Türkei aus der Zeit des Weltkrieges*, 171–72.

71. The memo, titled "Die Revolutionierung der Islamischen Gebiete Unsere Feinde," a copy of which is in YUL/Jäckh Papers/2/47, comprised 136 typewritten pages. Good summaries and analyses of the memo are in Kröger, 368–70; and Müller, 193, 196–204.

72. See Zimmermann to Sektion Politik and war ministry, 10 Jan. 1915, NARA/T-149/365/0011-13.

73. Summaries of the *Nachrichtenstelle für den Orient* (NfdO) are in Kröger, 373–76; Müller, 204–9, 211–12; and Landau, 105–6.

74. See Wangenheim to AA, 12 Sept. 1914, YUL/Jäckh Papers/1/10; Oppenheim, "G. A.," 14 Sept. 1914; Oppenheim, memo ("Benutzung der Kriegsgefangene Muhammedaner."), 2 Oct. 1914; Wesendonk, "G. A.," 13 Oct. 1914, NARA/T-137/143/0423-24, 0489-96, 0523; and Kröger, 374.

4. THE THICKENING PLOT AND HOLY WAR, FALL 1914

1. The best analysis is Heller, chapter 7.

2. During the fall of 1914, as rumors spread of an impending Turkish assault on the Suez Canal, one heard in Cairo references praising the anticipated triumphant arrival of an Ottoman army symbolically led by the khedive: "God lives. . . . Abbas is coming." But a much more narrowly Egyptian motive for wishing a Turkish victory overlapped this religious loyalty to the Ottomans: the expectation that it would end the British occupation of Egypt. See Gershoni and Jankowski, *Egypt, Islam, and the Arabs*, 23–25; Storrs, 132–33; and WO, intelligence news, "22/IX/14.," PRO/WO 157/698.

3. Storrs, 130–31.

4. Pannwitz to Bethmann Hollweg, 26 Sept. 1914, PA/WK Nr.11g/Bd. 2; and Gershoni and Jankowski, *Egypt, Islam, and the Arabs*, 25.

5. Cheetham to Grey, 28 Aug. 1914, India Office Library and Records, London (hereafter IOLR)/File L/Political and Secret (hereafter P&S)/10/464.

6. As examples, note Mallet's telegrams to Grey in Great Britain, FO, *Correspondence*, 16 (entry for 1 Sept. 1914), 32 (25 Sept. 1914), 34 (2 Oct. 1914), 40 (10 Oct. 1914), 43,

48 (14 Oct. 1914), 48 (15 Oct. 1914); and Cheetham's telegrams to Grey, 21 (8 Sept. 1914), 28 (21 Sept. 1914), 31 (25 Sept. 1914).

7. Cheetham to Grey, 28 Oct. 1914, PRO/FO371/1971/64465.

8. MacMunn and Falls, *Military Operations Egypt & Palestine*, 14–15.

9. See the account of the interrogation of Mors on 10 Oct. 1914, "Mulazim Awal Robert Mors recalled and re-examined, states," IOLR/L/P&S/10/464. Note, moreover, "Interrogatories of Lieutenant Mors" and "Further Interrogatories of Lieutenant Mors," FO, *Correspondence*, 43–45 (28 Sept. 1914), 73–74 (n.d.); Mors received a sentence of life imprisonment, an unusual one in that most such prisoners were executed, particularly by the Germans.

10. Grey to Mallet, 24 Oct. 1914; Mallet to Grey, 29 Oct. 1914, FO, *Correspondence*, 69, 71; and Kress, 53.

11. This drew a vigorous protest from the consular leaders—unheeded by the government—which claimed that the action violated Egyptian neutrality and laws (capitulations) protecting Europeans. See Cheetham to Grey, 9 Oct. 1914, PRO/FO 371/1971/57810; Storrs, 130; MacMunn and Falls, *Military Operations Egypt & Palestine*, 15; and Egyptian ministry of interior, "General Situation in Egypt," 27 Dec. 1914, PRO/FO 371/2355/4307.

12. Farnie, 531.

13. Ibid.; Macmunn and Falls, *Military Operations Egypt & Palestine*, 14–15; and Kress, 52–53.

14. Macmunn and Falls, *Military Operations Egypt & Palestine*, 14–15.

15. See above, chapter 2.

16. FO to Cheetham, 11 Aug. 1914; and Cheetham to Grey, 9 Aug. 1914, IOLR/L/P&S/10/464.

17. Fromkin, 100–1, which views this document as crucial to future British policy, mentions nothing about Clayton's assertion that the Turks had success in attracting the Arabs; and Jankowski, "Egypt and Early Arab Nationalism," 256.

18. See WO Cairo, intelligence department, "Appreciation of Situation in Arabia," 6 Sept. 1914, PRO/FO 882 (Arab Bureau Papers)/13/MIS/14/1.

19. Ibid.

20. Ibid.

21. The main initiatives to unite them behind the Turks began only later, during November and December, when the Porte contacted the Arab leaders, as did the Austrian Orientalist Musil.

22. Heller, 139–41.

23. Cohen, 306; and Heller, 210 n. 62.

24. Quoted in Cohen, 306. Also, note Busch, *Britain, India, and the Arabs*, 56–57, 61–62, 220. In one instance the British practiced such caution. When the Arab leader of Basra, Sayyid Talib, approached the local British consul about an alliance against the Turks, the British refused, mainly out of a deep, and justifiable, mistrust of Talib. Regarding the popular belief in British officialdom, especially in Constantinople and Cairo, that Jews and Freemasons controlled the Porte, see Fromkin, 41–44.

25. Note FO to Cheetham, 24 Sept. 1914, IOLR/L/P&S/10/387; Fromkin, 100–1; Heller,146; Kedourie, *England and the Middle East*, 49; and Busch, *Britain, India, and the Arabs*, 57–58.

26. See Cohen, 303; and Busch, *Britain, India, and the Arabs*, 56–63.

27. Heller, 146–49; Busch, *Britain, India, and the Arabs,* 232; and Lacey, 114. On Shakespear's numerous visits to Ibn Saud before World War I, see Lacey, chapter 10.

28. Heller, 148–49; and Busch, *Britain, India, and the Arabs,* 216–20.

29. Dan Eldar, "French Policy towards Husayn, Sharif of Mecca," *Middle Eastern Studies,* 26(1990):330. According to Jukka Nevakivi, *Britain, France and the Arab Middle East, 1914–1920,* 27, "The French nevertheless later complained that they had been kept in the dark as to the [British] correspondence with the sharif. . . . Meanwhile, having learnt that a French representative in Cairo had also been in contact with Arab leaders, Grey instructed his ambassador in Paris to ask the French government to discourage such activity."

30. Dawn, *From Ottomanism to Arabism,* 26; and Heller, 149.

31. Kedourie, *England and the Middle East,* 52; and Dawn, *From Ottomanism to Arabism,* 26.

32. Grey to Mallet, 29 Sept. 1914, FO, *Correspondence,* 33.

33. Grant Duff (British minister in Bern) to Grey, 24 Oct. 1914, PRO/FO 371/2109/66727.

34. Germany was India's second-largest export market; Wolpert, 291.

35. See Doerries, *Imperial Challenge,* 147–48, who observed, "The mere fact that many Indians were quite willing to rebel against British rule was no indication that they wished to surrender to German colonialist ambitions."

36. Burke and Quraishi, 148–53; L. F. Rushbrook Williams, "India and the War," *The Cambridge History of India,* ed. H. H. Dodwell, vol. 6, *The Indian Empire, 1858–1918,* 478–85; Doerries, *Imperial Challenge,* 291–93; James, *Rise and Fall of the British Empire,* 360; Richard Burn, "Political Movements, 1909–1917," *The Cambridge History of India,* ed. H. H. Dodwell, vol. 6, *The Indian Empire, 1858–1918,* 574, 582–85; and Smith, *Oxford History of India,* 779–80. Regarding the Aga Khan, see below, 92.

37. On 22–23 September 1914, the *Emden* shelled the oil tanks of the Anglo-Persian Oil Company at Madras. See Edwin P. Hoyt, *The Last Cruise of the Emden,* 108–10; and Wolpert, 290–91.

38. As examples, note Wangenheim to AA, 11 Sept. 1914; and AA, "Telegramm aus Berlin vom 26. September 1914," sent to Constantinople, YUL/Jäckh Papers/1/10, 11.

39. See the section on India in his lengthy memo, "Die Revolutionierung der Islamischen Gebiete Unsere Feinde.," written at the end of Oct. 1914, YUL/Jäckh Papers/2/47; and Fraser, 259.

40. Landau, 190–94, 198–202; and Burn, 577–78.

41. On the formation of the Indian committee, see its memo, "Eine kurze Zusammenfassung der Pläne des indischen Committees in Berlin," Dec. 1914, NARA/T-149/397/0461-65.

42. Fraser, 256–59; and Burke and Quraishi, 155.

43. See Helmut von Glasenapp, *Meine Lebensreise. Menschen, Länder und Dinge, die ich sah,* 75–77; and Don K. Dignan, "The Hindu Conspiracy in Anglo-American Relations during World War I," *Pacific Historical Review,* 40(1971):62.

44. Horst Krüger, "Har Dayal in Deutschland," *Mitteilungen des Instituts für Orientforschung,* 10(1964):145–49; and Wangenheim to AA, 15 Oct. 1914, NARA/T-149/397/0379.

45. Note Wesendonk, memorandum ("Die Frage der Beschaffung von Waffen und Munition in Amerika zur Verschiffung nach Indien."), 18 Oct. 1914; Papen to

AA, 20 Oct. 1914, NARA/T-149/397/0390, 0420; and Doerries, *Imperial Challenge,* 151.

46. Kröger, 380; and Franz von Reichenau (German minister in Stockholm) to Zimmermann, 25 Aug. 1914, NARA/T-137/139/0471.

47. Apparently the Germans first discovered this Turkish mission at the end of Aug. 1914; see Wangenheim to AA, 30 Aug. 1914; and AA to Hamburg legation, 19 Aug. 1914, NARA/T-137/139/0472, 0454, respectively. Also, note Gehrke, *Persien,* vol. 1:pt. 1:22–23, 60; and Vogel, 49.

48. Wallach, *Anatomie,* 169.

49. Friedrich Wilhelm von Prittwitz-Gaffron (an official in the AA), "Protokoll. Sitzung am 4. September 1914;" AA, "Personalbogen," n.d.; Wesendonk, "G. A.," 22 Sept. 1914, NARA/T-137/139/0482, 0484-85, 0578-79; Gehrke, *Persien,* 1:1:24; and Christopher Sykes, *Wassmuss: "The German Lawrence,"* 45–47. Especially on Wassmuss's return to Berlin in Aug. 1914, note Dagobert Mikusch, *Wassmuss der deutsche Lawrence,* 29–30.

50. Oppenheim to Bethmann Hollweg, 7 Sept. 1914; Wassmuss, "Gehorsame Meldung zu dem geplanten Zuge türkischer Offiziere nach Afganistan unter beteiligung von Deutschen.," 5 Sept. 1914, NARA/T-137/139/0538-39, 0511-12, respectively; and Gehrke, *Persien,* 1:1:38–39, 62–63.

51. Mikusch, 59; Rathmann, *Stossrichtung Nahost,* 128; Sykes, 50; and on the Rumanian problem for Germany, Gerard E. Silberstein, *The Troubled Alliance: German-Austrian Relations, 1914–1917,* chapter 2.

52. Wesendonk, "G. A.," 20, 22 Sept. 1914, NARA/T-137/142/0210-11, 0213-14; and Gehrke, *Persien,* 1:1:24.

53. See "Abschrift. Bestimmungen für die Teilnehmer an der Expedition.," 2 Oct. 1914; "Abschrift," 9 Oct. 1914, signed by the unhappy members, NARA/T-137/140/0423, 0421-22, respectively; Wassmuss to Bethmann Hollweg, 1, 6 Oct. 1914; Hermann Consten to Reinhard Mannesmann, 2 Oct. 1914, NARA/T-137/139/0794-96, 0797, 0721-25, respectively; Vogel, 51; and Sykes, 53–54.

54. See AA to Constantinople embassy, 21 Oct. 1914, NARA/T-137/139/0790. The gifts and letter were suggested by Oppenheim, "G. A.," 17, 18 Sept. 1914, frames 0568, 0563-64, respectively. Jagow, however, had "serious reservations" about sending the letter; Jagow to Zimmermann, 10 Oct. 1914, frame 0736. For a copy of part of the letter, see Fischer, *Germany's Aims,* 120.

55. Wassmuss to Bethmann Hollweg, 1 Oct. 1914, NARA/T-137/139/0794-96.

56. Niedermayer to Wesendonk, 18 Oct. 1914, NARA/T-137/139/0806-11.

57. Wangenheim to AA, 29 Oct., 11 Nov. 1914, NARA/T-137/140/0007, 0021; Romberg (German minister in Switzerland) to Bethmann Hollweg, 30 Sept. 1914; Wangenheim to AA, 4 Oct. 1914, NARA/T-137/139/0670, 0669, respectively; Gehrke, *Persien,* 1:1:39–40; and Kröger, 376–77.

58. Wesendonk, "G. A.," 22 Sept. 1914, NARA/T-137/142/0215.

59. Listemann to Bethmann Hollweg, 22 Aug. 1914; and Ehlow (Basra) to Hesse (German consul in Baghdad), 4 Sept. 1914, PA/*Türkei* 165/Bd. 37. According to Brig.-Gen. F. J. Moberly, *History of the Great War Based on Official Documents: The Campaign in Mesopotamia, 1914–1918,* 1:77–79, the British considered for a brief time sending a warship and a hundred Indian soldiers from Bushire to Abadan to defend against a Turkish attack. The operation was not carried out, however, for fear that it might

precipitate a collision with the Turks and also with the Shaykh of Muhammarah.

60. See Wesendonk, "G. A.," 13 Oct. 1914, containing Ballin's memo of the same day ("Ganz Geheim!"); Oppenheim, "Anschalg auf die Ölquellen am Karun.," 30 Sept. 1914; Oppenheim, "G. A.," 1 Oct. 1914; and Oppenheim, "G. A.," 8 Oct. 1914, NARA/T-137/142/0241-43, 0221, 0228, respectively.

61. Wangenheim to AA, 17 Oct. 1914; and Jagow to Constantinople embassy, 8 Oct. 1914, NARA/T-137/142/0246, 0229, respectively.

62. Jagow (at General Staff headquarters) to AA, 4 Nov. 1914; Jagow, "G. A.," 20 Oct. 1914; and AA to Constantinople embassy, 27 Oct. 1914, NARA/T-137/142/0268, 0247-48, 0253, respectively. The major accounts of the formation of the Klein mission do not discuss the group's origins; see Gehrke, *Persien*, 1:1:27-28; and Kröger, 378-79.

63. On Shakespear, see Busch, *Britain, India, and the Arabs*, 232; and Lacey, 114. Also note Moberly, 1:87; Llewellyn Woodward, *Great Britain and the War of 1914–1918*, 99-101; and Paul Guinn, *British Strategy and Politics, 1914-1918*, 43-44.

64. The debate is outlined in Cohen, 298-300, 303-4, which also provides the best brief account of the landing of the IEF D in Mesopotamia. See, too, on Britain's motives for sending the force to the Gulf, Busch, *Britain, India, and the Arabs*, 3-8, 10-12.

65. See above, chapter 2.

66. Wesendonk, "G. A.," 10, 11 Nov. 1914, NARA/T-137/142/0296, 0266, 0304, respectively. The AA provided four hundred thousand marks for Klein's expedition. Also, note Gehrke, *Persien*, 1:1:27-28.

67. The literature here is extensive; the best includes Geoffrey Lewis, "The Ottoman Proclamation of Jihad in 1914," 157-63; Hagen, 3-4; Landau, 99-100; Trumpener, *Germany and the Ottoman Empire*, 50-62, 117-18; Larcher, 44-48; and Antonius, 140-41.

68. Gehrke, *Persien*, 1:1:33; and for the definition of *ulama*, Ovendale, 303.

69. Wallach, *Anatomie*, 167-68; Djemal Pasha, 137-38; and Prüfer, "Krieg," entry for 20 Nov. 1914, HIWRP/Prüfer Papers.

70. Fischer, *Germany's Aims*, 184-88.

71. Quoted in Trumpener, *Germany and the Ottoman Empire*, 118. Also note Lt. von Janson (Constantinople) to Jäckh, 13 Oct. 1914, YUL/Jäckh Papers/1/4, which claimed the holy war would end Britain's "world domination"; and Wangenheim to Bethmann Hollweg, 30 Nov. 1914, NARA/T-137/23/0296.

72. Landau, 126-27.

73. Oppenheim, "Vorschläge wegen Besetzung der in meiner Denkschrift erwähnten neuen oder neu zu besetzenden Posten für den Nachrichtendienst etc.," 20 Nov. 1914; and Oppenheim to Zimmermann, 13 Nov. 1914, NARA/T-120/4949/L365619-620, L365475-476, respectively.

74. Dr. Theodor Weber (dragoman at the Constantinople embassy), "Abschrift, 31.12.14.," YUL/Jäckh Papers/1/18; and Quadt (ambassador to Greece) to AA, 28 Dec. 1914, NARA/T-137/23/0438.

75. War ministry to Reich treasury office, 6 Dec. 1914; and Zimmermann to Constantinople embassy, 10 Dec. 1914, NARA/T-137/23/0287, 0315.

76. Trumpener, *Germany and the Ottoman Empire*, 70-71.

77. Weber to Oppenheim, 6 Dec. 1914, NARA/T-137/143/0057.

78. As noted, for example, in Humann, "Vertrauliche Mitteilungen vom 16. Oktober 1914.," YUL/Jäckh Papers/1/14; and Austro-Hungarian embassy Berlin, "Notiz," 3 Sept. 1914, NARA/T-137/5/0331.

79. Wangenheim to AA, 26 Oct. 1914; and Jagow to AA, 25 Oct. 1914, NARA/T-137/5/0338, 0337, respectively. According to Trumpener, "German Officers in the Ottoman Empire," 37, Bentheim had served as Enver Pasha's adjutant from 1911 to 1914, including in Libya during the Ottoman war against Italy.

80. Flotow to AA, 1 Nov. 1914, NARA/T-137/5/0347.

81. Humann, "Besprechung mit Enver Pascha.," 3 Nov. 1914, YUL/Jäckh Papers/1/17. Also on Enver's determination to dispatch Nuri to Libya, see Trumpener, *Germany and the Ottoman Empire*, 119–20.

82. Flotow to AA, 1 Dec. 1914; and Wangenheim to AA, 28 Nov. 1914, NARA/T-137/5/0365, 0363. The Italians in Tripoli also encouraged Mannesmann to focus his revolutionary activities westward toward the French colonies of Algeria and Tunisia and away from Libya. He sent emissaries to Arab tribal chiefs in Algeria and Tunisia, promising to support their rebellions against French rule with weapons. But Nadolny and the Sektion Politik failed to dispatch former German members of the French Foreign Legion through Italy and Spain to Algeria to provoke a mutiny of the legionnaires. See Weber to Oppenheim, 11 Dec. 1914; Wesendonk, "G. A.," 7 Dec. 1914; "Telegramm vom Grossen Hauptquartier., 2.X.[1914]"; Wesendonk, "G. A.," 15 Sept. 1914, NARA/T-137/143/0690, 0630, 0483, 0462; Mannesmann, "Retiro," 16 Dec. 1914, NARA/T-120/4950/L365838-841; and Müller, 371–72.

83. Consulate Tripoli (Mannesmann) to AA, 16 Dec. 1914, containing a copy of the letter, "Übersetzung. An Senussi," NARA/T-137/23/0430-31.

84. Wangenheim to Bethmann Hollweg, 18 Dec. 1914; Wesendonk, memo, 18 Dec. 1916; and Nadolny to AA, 22 Dec. 1914, NARA/T-137/23/0413, 0388-89, respectively.

85. Humann, "Vertrauliche Mitteilungen vom 26. November 1914.," YUL/Jäckh Papers/1/18; and Wangenheim to AA, 2 Dec. 1914, NARA/T-137/23/0261.

86. For the khedive's deposition and other changes in Egypt, see below, 92. Also note FO to Rennell Rodd (British ambassador in Rome), 28 Nov. 1914; and Rodd to FO, 27 Nov. 1914, PRO/FO 371/1972/76163.

87. Wangenheim to AA, 14 Dec. 1915; Wesendonk, "G. A.," 16 Dec. 1914; and Oppenheim, memo, 22 Jan. 1915, NARA/T-137/23/0356, 0366, 0552-61.

88. Wesendonk, "G. A.," 29 Dec. 1914, NARA/T-137/23/0439.

89. Prüfer to Oppenheim, 31 Dec. 1914, NARA/T-137/23/0635-42; and McKale, *Curt Prüfer*, 31–33. Wahib Bey's assignment to Mecca at the beginning of 1914 to increase Ottoman authority is in Dawn, *From Ottomanism to Arabism*, 58.

90. See "Abschrift eines Schreibens Hofrates Musil. Zwischen Al-Hegm und al Bark E.VI.29/XII 1914.," NARA/T-137/138/0579; Feigl, 318–19; Bauer, 210–27; and Sauer, 249.

91. Burke and Quraishi, 149.

92. Egyptian interior ministry, "General Situation in Egypt," 27 Dec. 1914, PRO/FO 371/2355/4307; and Cheetham to Grey, 12 Dec. 1914, PRO/FO 371/1972/87392.

93. Egyptian interior ministry, "General Situation in Egypt," 27 Dec. 1914, PRO/FO 371/2355/4307; and Farnie, 532.

94. "Proclamation," 19 Dec. 1914, *Journal Officiel du Gouvernement Egyptien*, no. 171, PRO/FO 371/2353/599; Cheetham to Grey, 4 Dec. 1914, IOLR/L/P&S/10/464; and Landau, 126–27.

95. See the interesting memo, "Note by the Aga Khan and M. A. Ali Baig on the Situation in Egypt," 12 Jan. 1915, IOLR/L/P&S/10/464; and Macmunn and Falls, *Military Operations Egypt & Palestine,* 19–25.

96. These and other measures are discussed in WO, "Sudan Intelligence Report," 244 (Nov. 1914) and 245 (Dec. 1914), PRO/FO 371/2349/9692, 17709.

97. FO to Rodd, 24 Sept. 1914; Rodd to Grey, 6 Oct. 1914, PRO/FO 371/1971/5279, 56623; and "Clear of telegram No. 15 dated 20th. September 1914 from Bimbashi Royle Salloom to Sawahil Alexandria.," PRO/WO 157/687.

98. As examples, note Cheetham to Grey, 18 Oct. and 3 Nov. 1914, PRO/FO 371/1971/60770, 66798.

99. Cheetham to Grey, 14 Dec. 1914, PRO/FO 371/1971/87398; and Evans-Pritchard, 125.

100. WO, "Sudan Intelligence Report," 244 (Nov. 1914) and 245 (Dec. 1914), PRO/FO 371/2349/9692, 17709; and Busch, *Britain, India, and the Arabs,* 59, 220–22

101. WO, "Sudan Intelligence Report," 245 (Dec. 1914), PRO/FO 371/2349/17709.

102. Busch, *Britain, India, and the Arabs,* 217–22.

103. On the origins of this idea and on the debate over military strategy between "Easterners" and "Westerners," see Paul M. Kennedy, *The Realities behind Diplomacy: Background Influences on British External Policy, 1865–1980,* 179–83; and James, *Rise and Fall of the British Empire,* 357–58.

104. Nigel Steel and Peter Hart, *Defeat at Gallipoli,* 2–10; Alan Moorehead, *Gallipoli,* 84; B. H. Liddell Hart, *The Real War, 1914–1918,* 146–49; and Woodward, 63–66.

5. FAILED EXPECTATIONS ON BOTH SIDES, 1915

1. As examples, see Jäckh to Zimmermann, 3 Jan. 1915 ("Bericht über die Organisation in Konstantinopel zur Revolutionierung feindlicher Gebiete."), NARA/T-137/143/0153-57; and Humann, "Vertrauliche Mitteilungen vom 2. Januar 1915.," YUL/Jäckh Papers/1/20.

2. In this regard, Prüfer, "Krieg," entries for 27, 30 Oct. 1914, HIWRP/Prüfer papers, is revealing. For the number of British troops in Egypt in January, see MacMunn and Falls, *Military Operations Egypt & Palestine,* 48; and Wavell, 27. Also note above, 87, regarding the problem of collecting intelligence information in Egypt.

3. According to Kress, 67, 74: "We were very badly instructed on the situation of the enemy." For Prüfer's pessimistic view of the corps and its poor prospects for a successful attack on the canal, see his reports to Oppenheim, 3 Nov. and 31 Dec. 1914, NARA/T-137/23/0213-14, 0635-42.

4. Prüfer, "Krieg," entry for 11 Jan. 1915, HIWRP/Prüfer Papers; and McKale, *Curt Prüfer,* 34.

5. Oppenheim, memo, 22 Jan. 1915, NARA/T-137/136/00584.

6. Ibid.

7. The failed Turkish efforts to recruit them and British approaches to the same are in Antonius, 142–47; Dawn, *From Ottomanism to Arabism,* 24–25; Kedourie, *England and the Middle East,* 58; and Busch, *Britain, India, and the Arabs,* 216–25.

8. Shakespear to Sir Percy Cox (Resident in the Persian Gulf), 4 Jan. 1915, IOLR/R/15/2/31.

9. Ibid. London had received word of Shakespear's information from India by at

least the last week of January; see "Communicated by India Office, January 26, 1915. From Viceroy, 25th January 1915.," PRO/FO 882/8/IS/15/2, which mentioned recent telegrams "for information regarding intrigues of the Turks with Bin Saud and their result."

10. Shakespear to Cox, 4 Jan. 1915, IOLR/R/15/2/31.

11. "Copy of part of a letter from Captain W. H. I. Shakespear, I. A. Political Officer on Special Duty to the Persian Gulf Political Resident, January 19, 1915.," *Arab Bulletin*, 25 (7 Oct. 1916):336-38, PRO/FO 882/volume 25; and Cox to foreign department, Government of India, 16 Jan. 1915, IOLR/R/15/2/31. Regarding the "vague" responses of the Sharif of Mecca to the Turkish entreaties to him to join the jihad, note Dawn, *From Ottomanism to Arabism*, 25.

12. Lacey, 116-17; Busch, *Britain, India, and the Arabs*, 232-33; and Cox, "An account of the late Captain W. H. I. Shakespear's Mission to Ibn Saud. December 1914–January 1915.," PRO/FO 882/8/IS/15/1.

13. The German account of the march across the desert is in Mühlmann, 89-91; and Kress, 45-46, 85-90. The British version is in Macmunn and Falls, *Military Operations Egypt & Palestine*, 25-36; and Wavell, 26-30. Also see Farnie, 534-35.

14. Prüfer, "Krieg," entries for 18, 20, 22, 25-26, 28-30 Jan. 1915, HIWRP/Prüfer Papers. Also, note Kress, 71-74, discussing his conflicts with Jemal. The disagreements between the Germans and Jemal support the view of Trumpener, *Germany and the Ottoman Empire*, 69-70, that the influence of the Germans and Austrians on Ottoman military operations was limited. Also, note Farnie, 535.

15. Prüfer, "Krieg," entry for 3 Feb. 1915, HIWRP/Prüfer Papers; Wallach, *Anatomie*, 193; Woodward, 116; Rathmann, *Stossrichtung Nahost*, 122-24; and the other standard histories of the battle listed in n. 13 above, including Farnie.

16. This was later admitted by Kress, 75-76, who claimed that the Germans had been misled by agents of the Egyptian nationalists.

17. Prüfer to Oppenheim, 9 Feb. 1915, NARA/T-137/23/0868-69; and McKale, *Curt Prüfer*, 38. In a later report to Oppenheim, he denounced the Turkish officers for laziness and urged that Berlin remove them from the leadership of the next attack on the canal. See Prüfer to Oppenheim, 24 Feb. 1915, NARA/T-137/24/0274-77; and Kress, 97.

18. F. Elliot (British minister in Athens) to FO, 27 Feb. 1915, PRO/FO 371/2483/23234; Kress, 98-99; Mühlmann, 91; Farnie, 535; and Trumpener, *Germany and the Ottoman Empire*, 121-22.

19. Steel and Hart, 29-30, 32-33; and Farnie, 536.

20. Steel and Hart, 33; Moorehead, 43-89; and Liddell Hart, 150-58.

21. See, for instance, Martin Gilbert, *The First World War: A Complete History*, 136-37; and James, *Rise and Fall of the British Empire*, 358.

22. Yapp, 276-77; A. L. Macfie, *The Eastern Question 1774-1923*, 59; and Fromkin, 146-49.

23. The extensive literature includes Wallach, *Anatomie*, 187; Moorehead, 113-40, 241-73; Liddell Hart, 159-74; Guinn, 48-67; Woodward, 64-78; MacMunn and Falls, *Military Operations Egypt & Palestine*, 54-58; James, *Rise and Fall of the British Empire*, 358; and Herwig, *First World War*, 154-56.

24. Maxwell to Kitchener, 5 Mar. 1915, PRO/WO 33 (Reports and Miscellaneous Papers)/731.

25. Maxwell to Kitchener, 30 July 1915, PRO/WO 33/731.

26. MacMunn and Falls, *Military Operations Egypt & Palestine,* 58–59.

27. William Thompson (The Bath Club, London) to Sir George Arthur (WO), 28 Apr. 1915; and WO to under secretary of state for foreign affairs, 4 May 1915, PRO/FO 371/2356/54458.

28. McMahon to Grey, 6 May 1915, PRO/FO 371/2353/61642.

29. Lord Acton (British minister in Bern), "Memorandum," 12 Mar. 1915, PRO/FO 371/2355/30791.

30. McMahon to Grey, 23 May 1915, PRO/FO 371/2356/73973; and McMahon to Grey, 11 Apr. 1915, PRO/FO 371/2355/46702.

31. See Busch, *Britain, India, and the Arabs,* 62–65, 223–27. Shakespear's negotiations with Ibn Saud are noted above, 98–99.

32. Busch, *Britain, India, and the Arabs,* 218–27.

33. Togoland fell by the end of Aug. 1914; the Kamerun was occupied by an Anglo-French unit on 27 September. In German South-West Africa, inter-Allied conflicts and desertions of the British South African force slowed the British advance more than did German resistance. In German East Africa, German and native soldiers held out against overwhelming British and imperial troops until the end of the war. Surveys include A. Adu Boahen, *General History of Africa,* vol. 7, *Africa under Colonial Domination 1880–1935,* 132–33; and Byron Farwell, *The Great War in Africa, 1914–1918,* esp. chapters 1, 2, 7–9, 26.

34. See the comparisons of both navies at the war's beginning in Herwig, *"Luxury" Fleet,* 149–58; and John Keegan, *The Price of Admiralty: The Evolution of Naval Warfare,* 128–36.

35. Wesendonk, "G. A.," 28 Jan. 1915; Solf to AA, 4 Feb. 1915, NARA/T-137/138/0526, 0530-33; and Schellendorff to Bethmann Hollweg, 17 Feb. 1915, enclosing the memo, "Die Aufteilung Afrikas: Deutschland und Islam," 16 Feb. 1915, NARA/T-137/23/0753-59. Regarding Mecklenburg, see Fröhlich, 211.

36. Solf, "Ganz geheim! Anweisung Nr. I für die I. Staffel des Arabisch-Ägyptischen Erkundungskommandos.," 23 Feb. 1915, NARA/T-137/138/0551. The idea of acquiring a central African empire was widespread among German economic and political leaders, including the chancellor, Bethmann Hollweg, both before and during the war. Note Fischer, *War of Illusions,* 310–19; Stoecker, "Quest for 'German Central Africa,'" 249–62; Rathmann, *Stossrichtung Nahost,* 67–73; and Woodruf D. Smith, *The Ideological Origins of Nazi Imperialism,* 171–72.

37. McMahon to FO, 24 Feb. 1915; Wilfrid G. Thesiger (British minister in Abyssinia) to FO, 23 Feb. 1915, PRO/FO 371/22014, 22402; and Frobenius's reports to the AA in NARA/T-137/138/0583-86, 588-95, 0675, 0680-712.

38. German embassy Rome to AA, 10 Apr. 1915; Frobenius, "Bericht VIII," 23 Mar. 1915, NARA/T-137/138/0659, 0680-712; and the Anglo-Italian negotiations during Feb. and Mar., in PRO/FO 371/2227/21045-39613. Darfur was an independent state not effectively incorporated into the Anglo-Egyptian Sudan; Boahen, 23.

39. Fischer, *Germany's Aims,* 194–95; and Herwig, *First World War,* 149–51. Regarding Libya, note below, 145–51.

40. Hoyt, 208–36; and *Arab Bulletin,* 33(4 Dec. 1916):509–11, in PRO/FO 882/25.

41. Padel to Wangenheim, 20 Feb. 1915, YUL/Jäckh Papers/1/21; and McKale, "German Policy toward the Sharif of Mecca," 307.

42. Zimmermann to Constantinople embassy, 28 Mar. 1915, and the marginalia on Nadolny, NARA/T-137/138/0637. Also, see above, chapters 3–4, on doubts raised regarding the loyalty of the sharif and Arabs.

43. Zimmermann to embassy, 28 Mar. 1915, NARA/T-137/138/0637.

44. Humann, "Besprechung mit Enver Pascha am 11. April 1915.," NARA/T-137/23/0232-34.

45. Sauer, 250; and Friedrich Sarre (a German military liaison officer in Baghdad) to Nadolny, 20 Apr. 1915, NARA/T-137/140/0714-15. Lengthy discussions of Musil's mission are in Bauer, 227–46; and Feigl, chapter 13.

46. See Musil's extensive report on his mission to his government in Vienna, 26 Apr. 1916, contained in Tschirschky to Bethmann Hollweg, 5 May 1916, NARA/T-137/139/0141-64; and Sauer, 252–62. Subhan, claimed Musil, was receiving money from the British; note his memo to the Austro-Hungarian government written in Baghdad, 20–24 Apr. 1915, in Feigl, 346.

47. Note Musil's report, 26 Apr. 1916, NARA/T-137/139/0163-64; Feigl, 347; and Bauer, 255–56.

48. Konstantin von Neurath (Constantinople embassy) to AA, 18 July 1915, including Wesendonk's marginalia; Loytved Hardegg to Wangenheim, 28 June 1915; "Telegramm Damaskus vom 16. Juli 1915.," NARA/T-137/139/0074, 0075, 0078; and Bauer, 253–56.

49. Oppenheim, memo, 2 Mar. 1915, NARA/T-137/23/0828-29.

50. Oppenheim, "Abschrift. Fahrplan für die Fahrt nach Konstantinopel.," 15 Mar. 1915; Oppenheim to Langwerth von Simmern, 25 Mar. 1915, NARA/T-137/138/0630-31, 0629 respectively; Wangenheim to AA, 5 Mar. 1915, NARA/T-137/23/0843; and Rathmann, *Stossrichtung Nahost,* 189.

51. Humann, "Besprechung mit Enver Pascha am 6.IV.1915.," YUL/Jäckh Papers/1/23; Zechlin, "Friedensbestrebungen," B25(21 June 1961):355; and Landau, 92–94.

52. Wangenheim to Bethmann Hollweg, 2 Apr. 1915, NARA/T-137/24/0160-61; Wangenheim to Bethmann Hollweg, 3 Apr. 1915, containing the document, "Ins Arabische Artikel und Notizen," n.d.; and Constantinople embassy to AA, 4 Apr. 1915, NARA/T-120/4951/L366749-750, L366732, respectively.

53. Zechlin, "Friedensbestrebungen," B25 (21 June 1961):355.

54. Zimmermann to Constantinople embassy, 11 May 1915; and Wangenheim to AA, 5 May 1915, NARA/T-137/24/0400, 0378, respectively.

55. See Wangenheim to AA, 27 Apr. 1915, NARA/T-149/398/0068.

56. Oppenheim, memo, 15 May 1915, NARA/T-120/4951/L367241-256; and McKale, "German Policy Toward the Sharif of Mecca," 308. On Shaykh Salih's background, see Landau, 114.

57. Dawn, *From Ottomanism to Arabism,* 26–29; Kedourie, *England and the Middle East,* 51–52; Antonius, 149–50; and Zeine, 116. Regarding the plot by the Porte to remove the sharif, see above, 43.

58. Oppenheim, memo, 15 May 1915, NARA/T-120/4951/L367241-256.

59. Ibid.

60. Quoted in T. E. Lawrence, *Secret Despatches from Arabia by T. E. Lawrence,* 68 ("With the Northern Army [*Arab Bulletin,* 15 Feb. 1917]"). Also, see Oppenheim's memo, 15 May 1915, NARA/T-120/4951/L367241-256.

61. Wangenheim to Bethmann Hollweg, 22 May 1915, NARA/T-120/4951/L367234-238.

62. Dawn, *From Ottomanism to Arabism*, 30–31. Less informative are Kedourie, *England and the Middle East*, 62; and Antonius, 158–59.

63. Schabinger, "G. A.," 15 May 1915, with accompanying mailing lists *(Versandliste)* for propaganda materials to Turkey, NARA/T-149/365/0016-17, 19-47; Rathmann, *Stossrichtung Nahost*, 189; Wratislaw (Salonica) to FO, 1 July 1915, quoting a WO intelligence report; and H. Bax-Ironside (British minister in Sofia) to FO, 8 June 1915, PRO/FO 371/2489/87754, 74465. Also, see Dawn, *From Ottomanism to Arabism*, 29–31; Antonius, 152–59, 164; Kedourie, *England and the Middle East*, 62; and Zeine, 117.

64. Neurath (counselor at the Constantinople embassy), memo, 23 Oct. 1915, NARA/T-120/4952/L367824-826; Constantinople embassy to AA, 4 June 1915, NARA/T-120/4951/L367293; and McKale, *Curt Prüfer*, 45.

65. Isaiah Friedman, *Germany, Turkey, and Zionism, 1897–1918*, 215–26, 245–67; Egmont Zechlin, *Die Deutsche Politik und die Juden im Ersten Weltkrieg*, 288–325; and David Yisraeli, "Germany and Zionism," in *Germany and the Middle East, 1835–1939*, ed. Jehuda L. Wallach, 142–45.

66. The details on Weizmann are in McKale, *Curt Prüfer*, 40–43. Regarding Cohn's spying for the British, note WO, "Intelligence Summary," 21 Apr. 1915, PRO/WO 157/690.

67. The Turks started with the mass murder of Armenian intellectuals in the cities; soon spontaneous massacres of the rural population began, as did massive deportations by the Porte of the victims in death-ridden forced marches to Mesopotamia. The Armenians sought autonomy and sympathized with the enemies of the Turks in the war, which was hardly surprising given their repressed situation, but they rarely involved themselves on the Russian and British side. Among the vast number of studies of the subject, the most helpful are Lawrence S. Leshnik, "Vor den Augen es Waffenbruders. Das Massaker an den Armeniern im Ersten Weltkrieg und die deutsche Mitverantwortung," *Die Zeit*, 17(20 Apr. 1990):41-2; Christoph Dinkel, "German Officers and the Armenian Genocide," *Armenian Review*, 44(1991):77-133; Kröger, 383–85; Trumpener, *Germany and the Ottoman Empire*, chapter 7; Larcher, 95; and Wallach, *Anatomie*, 207.

68. The ambassador, for example, opposed the Armenians, his sentiments toward them ranging from simple antipathy to sheer hatred. Along with other Germans in Turkey, he accepted completely Turkish accusations that the Armenians were traitors who had conspired to subvert Ottoman military campaigns against the Russians. See Dadrian, 250–84; Dinkel, 77–133; "Auszug aus einem Brief des Deutschen Vicekonsul Kuckoff, Samsun, an die Deutsche Botschaft Konstantinopel vom 4. Juli 1915."; and "Auszug aus einem Brief des Auswärtigen Amtes an Herrn Dr. Faber, Magdeburg vom 4. Oktober 1915.," YUL/Jäckh Papers/2/49, 51. Especially on Jäckh, note Leshnik, 42.

69. Eugen Mittwoch of the NfdO criticized the media's "exaggeration" of the massacres. See Mittwoch, "G. A.," 9 Aug. 1915, NARA/T-149/365/0057; and Dadrian, 277-84. Note also "Die Armenier-Lügen der englischen Presse," *Neue Preussische Zeitung*, 14 Oct. 1915; and "Neuer Rekord englischer Heuchelei," *Hamburger Fremdenblatt*, 15 Oct. 1915.

70. According to Dadrian, 269, Wangenheim "had raised that avoidance to a level of firm policy." Also, note Leshnik, 42.

71. Note "Die Armenier-Lügen der englischen Presse," *Neue Preussische Zeitung*,

14 Oct. 1915; Dadrian, 278–79; and Rathmann, *Stossrichtung Nahost,* 139–40. Regarding Lepsius's protest to Enver Pasha, see "Von Dr. Paul Rohrbach, 21 September 1915," YUL/Jäckh papers/2/50. Especially interesting is the AA's criticism of Lepsius's lecture in Oct. 1915 denouncing the Armenian persecution; note "Auszug aus dem Vortrag des Dr. Johannes Lepsius vom 5.10.15 über die Lage der Türkischen Armenier.," YUL/Jäckh papers/2/51. On Metternich, see Pomiankowski, 176; Dadrian, 207; and Friedman, *Germany, Turkey, and Zionism,* 273.

72. See, for example, Thora v. Wedel-Jarlsberg and Eva Elvers, "Bericht über die Ereignisse in Ersingjan, Juni 1915."; and the unsigned report, "IV. Anlage," 18 July 1915, YUL/Jäckh Papers/2/49.

73. McMahon to Grey, 24 Oct. 1915, containing a memorandum, "Note on Propaganda, etc. on the part of Germans giving the impression that they or their Sovereign and Government had embraced Islam or were in sympathy with Anti-Christian Manifestations on the part of Ignorant or Fanatical Moslems.," n.d., PRO/FO 371/2354/163829; and WO, "Intelligence Summary.," 29 July and 14 Sept. 1915, PRO/WO 157/693, 695.

74. Henry Morgenthau (U.S. ambassador in Turkey) to Robert Lansing (U.S. secretary of state), 12 Aug. 1915, United States, *Papers Relating to the Foreign Relations of the United States,* 1915, Supplement to the World War, 985. According to Trumpener, "Germany and the End of the Ottoman Empire," 128, the Reich either opposed the Armenian persecution or adopted a policy of "diplomatic restraint."

75. See below, 177.

76. Weber, 182; Wangenheim to Bethmann Hollweg, 2 Apr. 1915, NARA/T-137/24/0160-61; Wesendonk, "G. A.," n.d. (but is Apr. 1915); Wangenheim to AA, 15 May 1915, NARA/T-120/4951/L366766-67, L367134; and Wangenheim to AA, 19 Apr. 1915, NARA/T-137/143/0166.

77. Many of the German accusations are in AA, memorandum, 5 Nov. 1915, NARA/T-120/4952/L367858-860. See also, Wallach, *Anatomie,* 194. Regarding prewar opposition of Germany to Jemal, note above, 29–30.

78. The meeting is discussed in AA, memorandum, 5 Nov. 1915, NARA/T-120/4952/L367858-860.

79. Oppenheim to Bethmann Hollweg, 9 Aug. 1915, NARA/T-137/24/0766-69; and Neurath to Bethmann Hollweg, 23 Aug. 1915, NARA/T-120/4952/L367614-615.

80. On 21 Aug. 1915, Jemal began the terror by executing eleven Arab leaders. He also killed Christians in Lebanon. See Kedourie, *England and the Middle East,* 63–64; Antonius, 186–87; and Dawn, *From Ottomanism to Arabism,* 32.

81. Of the Allies he inquired whether in exchange for his taking Syria and the Turkish Fourth Army out of the war, they would recognize him as the ruler of an independent state carved from the Arab provinces of the Turkish empire. Evidence from documents in the Russian archives is in Zeine, 113 n. 35.

82. Wesendonk, "G. A.," 3 May 1915; AA (Zimmermann) to German embassy Constantinople, 15 May 1915; and Wangenheim to Bethmann Hollweg, 30 May 1915, NARA/T-120/4951/L367061-062, L367113-15, 367298-99.

83. Regarding the approach of the Arab nationalists to Britain, note Fromkin, chapter 23; and Isaiah Friedman, *The Question of Palestine, 1914–1918: British-Jewish-Arab Relations,* 69–70. On al-Masri's career, see Fromkin, 99–101, 108, 177, 196, 220, 225–27, 318; and Majid Khadduri, *Arab Contemporaries: The Role of Personalities in Politics,* 7–18.

84. Tschirschky to Bethmann Hollweg, 21 Dec. 1914, NARA/T-137/23/0401.

85. Oppenheim, "Besuch Muhamed Bey Farids, des Praesidenten des egyptischen nationalistischen Komittees, und Muhamed Fehmis, des Vorstehers des Genfer Teilkomitees.," 4 Jan. 1915, NARA/T-137/136/0561-62; and Wesendonk, "G. A.," 4 Jan. 1915, NARA/T-137/23/0456.

86. It is unclear when the audience with Franz Joseph occurred. See Oppenheim, memo, 22 Jan. 1915, NARA/T-137/136/0584; and Wangenheim to AA, 12 Jan. 1915, NARA/T-137/23/0505.

87. Oppenheim, memo, 22 Jan. 1915, NARA/T-137/136/0584; and Gershoni and Jankowski, *Egypt, Islam and the Arabs,* 27–28. On the wartime disagreements between Germany and the Ottomans, which covered a variety of military and economic issues, and in which the Ottomans often prevailed, note Trumpener, *Germany and the Ottoman Empire,* esp. chapters 4, 7–9.

88. See above, 100–101.

89. See Dr. Rudolf Amster, memo, contained in Zimmermann to German embassy Constantinople, 26 Oct. 1915, NARA/T-137/136/0711-13. Regarding Enver Pasha's continued hostility toward the ex-khedive, see Wesendonk, "G. A.," 21 Oct. 1915, NARA/T-137/25/0026-27; Wangenheim to AA, 6 June 1915, NARA/T-137/138/0064; and German embassy Vienna to AA, 17 June 1915, NARA/T-137/24/0615-16.

90. See above, 110. Also, note Wangenheim to Bethmann Hollweg, 2 Apr. 1915, NARA/T-137/24/0160-61; Oppenheim, memo, 15 May 1915, NARA/T-120/4951/L367242-256; and Gershoni and Jankowski, *Egypt, Islam, and the Arabs,* 31.

91. Klaus Epstein, *Matthias Erzberger and the Dilemma of German Democracy,* 103–4; German legation Copenhagen to Bethmann, 16 Oct. 1915, NARA/T-120/4952/L367779-781; Erzberger, memo, 10 Nov. 1916, NARA/T-137/137/0254; and British memo, source unknown, distributed to the FO, IO, and military intelligence, "Ex-Khedive of Egypt.," 13 Dec. 1916, IOLR/L/P&S/10/467.

92. Wesendonk, memo, 29 Oct. 1916, NARA/T-137/137/0208.

93. Jacoby had three thousand marks monthly to spend, plus an extra fund of ten thousand marks; see AA to German legation Bern, 27 July 1915; Jacoby to Wesendonk, 14 Aug. 1915, NARA/T-149/402/0574-75, 0577-78; and Müller, 209–10. Also, note Duff to Grey, 21 Sept. 1915, PRO/FO 395 (Consular Papers)/piece no. 846/file no. 137963; and Christopher Andrew, *Her Majesty's Secret Service: The Making of the British Intelligence Community,* 148–52.

94. As examples, note German legation Bern to AA, 10 Apr. 1915, NARA/T-120/4951/L366793-794; and Wesendonk, "G.A.," 17 Oct. 1915, NARA/T-120/4952/L367764-767. Also see Romberg to AA, 14 Oct. 1915, NARA/T-137/24/0878.

95. See WO to Director Military of Operations (hereafter DMO), 21 Nov. 1915, containing a memo, "Note on Arab Movement," PRO/FO 882/2/AP/15/8; and Hirtzel to Sir George R. Clerk (senior clerk in the FO), 26 Oct. 1915, PRO/FO 371/2357/159028.

96. Kitchener to Maxwell, 4 Nov. 1915, PRO/FO 882/13/MIS/15/15/A. The extensive literature on the negotiations of McMahon with the Sharif of Mecca is discussed in Ovendale, 309–10.

97. German embassy Constantinople to AA, 7 Nov. 1915, NARA/T-137/136/0757; and German legation Bern to AA, 29 Nov. 1915, NARA/T-137/137/0003.

98. McMahon to FO, 11 Dec. 1915, PRO/FO 371/2357/189454.

99. Duff to Grey, 17 Dec. 1915, PRO/FO 371/2357/196626.

100. FO to Duff, 3 Jan. 1916; and FO to McMahon, 3 Jan. 1916, PRO/FO 371/2357/196626.

101. McMahon to FO, 20 May 1916, PRO/FO 371/2672/96750.

102. Romberg to Bethmann Hollweg, 14 Dec. 1915, NARA/T-149/402/0673; and Romberg to Bethmann Hollweg, 13 Dec. 1915, NARA/T-137/137/0023-25, which contains Jacoby's reports asserting the ex-khedive's loyalty to the Central Powers.

103. Romberg to Bethmann Hollweg, 14 Dec. 1914, NARA/T-149/398/0414-5, containing Jacoby's report in English on Maugham; and Andrew, 148–50.

6. THE GERMAN THREAT ON THE PERIPHERY

1. See, for example, the report from Salonica of the WO official Sir Mark Sykes (a major figure in Britain's Middle Eastern policy who had started a fact-finding tour for Kitchener of the Middle East and India), "Intelligence Summary," 4 July 1915, PRO/WO 157/693. Also, see Rodd (British ambassador in Rome) to FO, 29 May 1915, PRO/FO 371/2489/68849; and Adelson, 180–82.

2. Nadolny to war ministry, 7 Jan. 1915; Mansur Ahmad (Indian committee member) to AA, 1 Jan. 1915; and Oppenheim, memo, 9 Jan. 1915, NARA/T-149/397/0550, 0542, 0563 respectively.

3. Wilhelm Salomon to AA, 11 June 1915, NARA/T-149/398/0160; Fraser, 258; and Wesendonk, memo, 5 Feb. 1915, NARA/T-149/397/0614.

4. Wesendonk, "G. A.," 27 Feb. 1915, NARA/T-149/397/0760.

5. Dignan, 64, 66; German legation Stockholm to AA, 9 Jan. 1915; German embassy Rome to AA, 18 Jan. 1915; AA to Stockholm legation, 4 Feb. 1915, NARA/T-149/397/0562, 0590, 0662; and Burke and Quraishi, 157.

6. A point emphasized most recently and effectively by Gerhard L. Weinberg, *A World at Arms: A Global History of World War II*, 12. For the Indian contribution to the war effort and the report, see Burke and Quraishi, 149–50; James, *Rise and Fall of the British Empire*, 367; and Rushbrook Williams, 481–82.

7. A good analysis of such problems in the United States is Doerries, *Imperial Challenge*, 153–55.

8. Still, nowhere near all Punjabis were revolutionaries. Altogether, the Punjab recruited during the war nearly a half-million troops for the Indian army. Among them, the Muslims and Sikhs were preeminent, the former with 136,000, the latter with 88,000. See Rushbrook Williams, 481, 485; Arnold Fletcher, *Afghanistan: Highway of Conquest*, 180; and Gilbert, *First World War*, 130–31.

9. Military Intelligence [hereafter MI], "Memorandum on German Literary Propaganda as Regards India and the Orient," June 1916, IOLR/L/P&S/11/88; Government of India to T. W. Holderness (under secretary of state for India), 13 May 1915, PRO/FO 371/2493/91242; and Government of India to Holderness, 22 July 1915, PRO/FO 371/2572/166568.

10. On Papen, see above, 79.

11. Wesendonk, "G. A.," 18 Jan. 1915; and Oppenheim, memo ("Betr. Waffenfrage."), 9 Jan. 1915, NARA/T-149/397/0563, 0588-89, 0563.

12. Bernstorff (via Stockholm legation) to AA, 3 Feb. 1915; and Zimmermann to Stockholm legation, 8 Feb. 1915, NARA/T-149/397/0658, 0688.

13. AA to Constantinople, 9 June 1915, NARA/T-149/398/0146; a 1918 memoran-

dum, "Aufzeichnung über die Tätigkeit der Etappe Manila vom Beginn des Krieges bis zum Abbruch der Beziehungen zu den Vereinigten Staaten von Amerika.," NARA/ T-149/400/0597; and Doerries, *Imperial Challenge,* 149–50.

14. The remaining Indian revolutionaries in Siam, most of them disheartened, fled to China. See Fraser, 266–67; and Erwin Remy to Reich chancellor Georg von Hertling, 11 Nov. 1917, NARA/T-149/400/0142-54.

15. MI, "Memorandum on German Literary Propaganda As Regards India and the Orient," June 1916, IOLR/L/P&S/11/88; and Hirtzel (IO) to secretary, Board of Trade, 11 Oct. 1915, PRO/FO 371/2496/149282.

16. Doerries, *Imperial Challenge,* 151–52; and Fraser, 261–63.

17. Fraser, 263–65.

18. General Officer Commanding (hereafter GOC) Straits Settlements to WO, 4 Aug. 1915, PRO/FO 371/2590/108941; IO, "German Schemes for Raising Revolt in India. Summary of Information 17/8/1915," IOLR/L/P&S/11/103; and Indian Independence Committee, Berlin, "Herr Kraft of Sumatra," 28 Apr. 1915, NARA/T-149/398/ 0072.

19. On Papen's expulsion, note Doerries, *Imperial Challenge,* 75. Also see Dignan, 59, 62–63, 66–73, who emphasizes how the FO and British ambassador in Washington, Sir Cecil Spring-Rice, differed on approaching the United States with the issue. Also note Spring-Rice to Grey, 6 Sept. 1915, PRO/FO 371/2495/135728; the military intelligence report, FO to Spring-Rice, 10 Dec. 1915, PRO/FO 371/2496/170278; and "Lahore Conspiracy Case, German Connection with the Revolutionists. Interesting New Evidence," *The Civil and Military Gazette,* 5 Dec. 1916.

20. For examples that did not, see Wesendonk's marginalia on AA to Budapest consul general, 18 Mar. 1915; Wangenheim to AA, 17 Mar. 1915, NARA/T-149/397/0861, 0860, respectively; and Wesendonk, "G. A.," 16 Apr. and 27 Mar. 1915, NARA/T-149/ 398/0054, 0025, respectively.

21. Note Oppenheim, "Auszugsweise Abschrift.," 3 Sept. 1915; and summaries of the numerous divisions between the Indians in Turkey, Hohenlohe-Langenburg (Constantinople embassy) to Bethmann Hollweg, 1 and 3 Sept. 1915, NARA/T-149/ 398/0331, 0315-16, 0318-19, respectively.

22. Hesse to Bethmann Hollweg, 22 Sept. 1915, NARA/T-149/398/0353-54.

23. Note "Suggestions for the Admiralstab," 14 Nov. 1915, NARA/T-149/398/0366-67.

24. Indian Independence Committee (Chattopadhyaya) to Jagow, 17 Dec. 1915, NARA/T-149/398/0406-07.

25. Jagow to Chattopadhyaya, 19 Dec. 1915, NARA/T-149/398/0408-09.

26. His biography is in "Kumar Mahendra Pratap," 8 Apr. 1918, apparently produced by the Indian committee, NARA/T-149/400/0487. Also note the committee to Jagow, 17 Dec. 1915, NARA/T-149/398/0406-07.

27. Gehrke, *Persien,* 1:1:146–47; Larcher, 463–64; Vogel, 66; Wesendonk to Karl Georg Treutler (a representative of the AA at General Staff headquarters), 29 Mar. 1915, NARA/ T-137/142/0195-96; Wesendonk, "G. A.," 25 Feb. 1915, NARA/T-140/0298-99; and Werner Otto von Hentig, *Mein Leben eine Dienstreise,* 91–94.

28. Gehrke, *Persien,* 1:1:146–47; Hentig, 100–09; Vogel, 66–67; and Bethmann Hollweg to Pratap, 17 Apr. 1915, NARA/T-137/142/0199, which contains copies of the letters to the amir and princes (frames 0165–0192). Also, see above, 80–82.

29. Nadolny to AA, 21 Feb. 1915; and AA to Constantinople, 13 Apr. 1915, NARA/T-137/140/0307-08, 0602-03.

30. Vogel, 55–57, 61–62; Gehrke, *Persien*, 1:1:25–26; and Oskar Ritter von Niedermayer, *Im Weltkrieg vor Indiens Toren. Der Wüstenzug der deutschen Expedition nach Persien und Afganistan*, 3rd ed. 18–23.

31. Rathmann, *Stossrichtung Nahost*, 129; and Gehrke, *Persien*, 1:1:54–56, 66–70, 99. Regarding the Klein expedition, see below in this chapter, 131–33.

32. The meeting is discussed in Wangenheim to Bethmann Hollweg, 13 Feb. 1915; Nadolny to AA, 21 Feb. 1915, NARA/T-137/140/0282-83, 0307-08; and Gehrke, *Persien*, 1:1:84–86, which discusses particularly the differences between the AA and General Staff. Regarding the Turkish mistreatment of Persians in Azerbaijan and its effects, note Constantinople embassy to AA, 1 Feb. 1915; and AA to Constantinople embassy, 19 Feb. 1915, NARA/T-137/140/0157-58, 0289-90.

33. Sarre left for his appointment in mid-February 1915; AA to Constantinople embassy, 18 Feb. 1915, NARA/T-137/140/0276. For background on Sarre, who had made numerous archaeological excavations along the Tigris and Euphrates rivers and was a brother-in-law of Humann, the German naval attaché in Constantinople, note Rathmann, *Stossrichtung Nahost*, 130; and Fück, 291–92.

34. Niedermayer, "Gruppe 1: Schuenemann," 12 Jan. 1915; Niedermayer, "Befehl für Gruppe 2: Zugmayer. Streng geheim!" 21 Feb. 1915; Niedermayer, "Befehl für Gruppe 3: P. Paschen," 23 Feb. 1915; Niedermayer, "Bericht II.," 27 Feb. 1915, NARA/T-137/140/0545, 0553, 0554, 0546-52, respectively; Rathmann, *Stossrichtung Nahost*, 130–32; Gehrke, *Persien*, 1:1:123; and Vogel, 57–58.

35. For example, note Schuenemann (Kermanshah) to the embassy, 18 Mar. 1915, NARA/T-137/140/0515.

36. Wangenheim to AA, 11 Mar. 1915, NARA/T-137/140/0392; Sykes, 68–70; and Dagobert Mikusch, *Wassmuss der deutsche Lawrence*, 80–94. A code designated 13040, seized from Wassmuss by the British, was one of the two codes used by Germany for communication between Berlin and Washington, and between Berlin and all German diplomatic missions in the Western Hemisphere; Barbara W. Tuchmann, *The Zimmermann Telegram*, 3, 16–19.

37. IWM, *Operations in Persia*, 55–56; and Gehrke, *Persien*, 1:1:78–83.

38. Chief of the General Staff [hereafter CGS], India to Chief of Imperial General Staff [hereafter CIGS], 16 Mar. 1915, PRO/WO 33/731.

39. Colonel Erich von Leipzig (German military attaché in Constantinople) to Sektion Politik and AA, 6 Mar. 1915, NARA/T-137/140/0448-51, described Klein's visit as "a severe tactical mistake that caused bad blood for us" among the Turks. See also, Humann, "Besprechung mit Enver Pascha vom 9 Februar 1915.," YUL/Jäckh Papers/1/21; Gehrke, *Persien*, 1:1:56–57; Klein's report in Wangenheim to AA, 29 Jan. 1915; and entries for 20–31 Jan. 1915 in "Kriegstagebuch der Karun-Expedition von Major Klein, 1914/1915," NARA/T-137/142/0384, 0449-53.

40. See the entries for 6 February–11 March 1915 in "Kriegstagebuch der Karun-Expedition von Major Klein, 1914/1915.," NARA/T-137/142/0454-61.

41. Wangenheim to AA, 6 Feb. 1915, NARA/T-137/140/0203, 0205; IWM, *Operations in Persia*, 53; Moberly, 1:160–88; and Gehrke, *Persien*, 1:1:91–93.

42. Nadolny to Langwerth von Simmern (AA), 22 Feb. 1915.

43. Hans Lührs, *Gegenspieler des Obersten Lawrence*, 9th ed., 49–103.

44. Moberly, 1:198–219; Wangenheim to AA, 19 Apr. 1915; and entries for 15 March–16 April 1915, "Kriegstagebuch der Karun-Expedition von Major Klein, 1914/1915.," NARA/T-137/142/0425, 0461-72.

45. Britain claimed that the damage was considerable; engineers burned thirty-six million gallons of oil to prevent its overflow into the Karun River. See Gehrke, *Persien*, 1:1:94-95.

46. Wangenheim to AA, 10 Oct. 1915, NARA/T-137/141/0364; and Moberly, 1:193, 350-56.

47. See "Tagebuch des Verbindungsoffiziers für Persien, Rittmeister der Reserve Sarre vom 1. Mai bis 17. Juli 1915;" Kardorff (Teheran legation) to Constantinople embassy, 22 Apr. 1915; Sarre to Nadolny, 20 Apr. 1915, NARA/T-137/140/0330, 0674, 0712-13; and Niedermayer, "Bericht: IV," 30 Apr. 1915, NARA/T-137/141/0087-88.

48. Gehrke, *Persien,* 1:1:110-11.

49. AA to Constantinople embassy, 7, 10, and 16 Apr. 1915, NARA/T-137/140/0576, 0595, 0611-12; and Gehrke, *Persien,* 1:1:133-34.

50. IWM, *Operations in Persia,* 62; Vogel, 63–64; Gehrke, *Persien,* 1:1:104; and Niedermayer, "Bericht: IV," 30 Apr. 1915, NARA/T-137/141/0087-88.

51. Gehrke, *Persien,* 1:1:63, 100, 105. Reuss had been on vacation in Germany when the war began, and he was sent to Belgium; when Germany became interested in Persia, the AA returned him there.

52. IWM, *Operations in Persia,* 62–64.

53. These issues are discussed in Rathmann, *Stossrichtung Nahost,* 130; and Gehrke, *Persien,* 1:1:111-18.

54. Wangenheim to AA, 8 May 1915, NARA/T-137/142/0684; Niedermayer, "Bericht: IV," NARA/T-137/141/0089; and Wangenheim to AA, 10 May 1915, NARA/T-137/140/0695.

55. Nadolny to AA (for Kanitz), 21 May 1915; and Wangenheim to AA, 12 May 1915, NARA/T-137/140/0727-28, 0699, respectively.

56. Regarding Rauf's brutal attack on Karind, note the entry for 5 July 1915 in "Tagebuch des Verbindungsoffiziers für Persien, Rittmeister der Reserve Sarre vom 1. Mai bis 17. Juli 1915.," NARA/T-137/141/0341.

57. See his report in Wangenheim to Bethmann Hollweg, 14 June 1915, NARA/T-137/142/0483-84. Regarding the Shiite rebellion, caused in part by Turkish attempts to confiscate treasures from the mosques in the holy cities, note Wangenheim to AA, 26 June 1915; Baghdad consulate (Hesse) to Constantinople embassy, NARA/T-137/140/0816, 0840; and Sarre to Constantinople embassy, 8 July 1915, NARA/T-137/141/0115.

58. Humann, "Besprechung mit Enver Pascha vom 4. Juli 1915.," YUL/Jäckh Papers/1/25; and Wangenheim to AA, 17 and 20 June 1915, NARA/T-137/140/0795, 0788, respectively.

59. Gehrke, *Persien,* 1:1:165-67; AA to Constantinople, 15 June 1915; and Wangenheim to AA, 11 June 1915, NARA/T-137/140/0765, 0757, respectively.

60. The expedition members remained subordinate to Niedermayer. Note Wangenheim to Bethmann Hollweg, 14 July 1915, NARA/T-137/140/0863; and Reuss, "Abschrift. Entzifferung.," 8 Sept. 1915, NARA/T-137/141/0232.

61. This account of their activities and advance into Afghanistan is based on the large literature on the subject. See, for example, Vogel, 71–74; Gehrke, *Persien,* 1:1:148–

49; Kröger, 381; Niedermayer, *Im Weltkrieg vor Indiens Toren,* 48–90, 108–09; and Hentig, 116–38.

62. Only later did the Indian Government reinforce its troops in East Persia; note IWM, *Operations in Persia,* 85–96, 114–15.

63. Kröger, 381; Niedermayer, *Im Weltkrieg vor Indiens Toren,* 93–107; Vogel, 80; and Landau, 103, which erroneously notes that the Germans arrived in Kabul on 1 August 1915.

64. See, for example, Reuss, "Abschrift. Entzifferung.," 8 Sept. 1915; and Hohenlohe-Langenburg (Constantinople embassy) to AA (enclosing a report from Reuss), 11 Sept. 1915, NARA/T-137/141/0232-33, 0218, respectively.

65. The activities in Kermanshah as well as in Isfahan and Kerman, which are discussed in the next paragraphs, are chronicled in Gehrke, *Persien,* 1:1:149–56, 158–64, 225; and Vogel, 102–7, 112–13.

66. Seiler admitted to instigating the attempt to murder the consul, in a letter seized by the British and contained in J. E. Shuckburgh (IO) to L. Oliphant (FO), 23 Nov. 1917, IOLR/L/P&S/10/477.

67. Gehrke, *Persien,* 1:1:158–59.

68. Ibid., 156–57.

69. Examples are Constantinople embassy to AA, 13 Aug. and 4 Oct. 1915, NARA/T-137/141/0068, 0353. Also, see Gehrke, *Persien,* 1:1:157; Mikusch, 142–43; and Sykes, 95–96.

70. Gehrke, *Persien,* 1:1:157–58; and Mikusch, 103–6. According to Wassmuss, the tribal attack on Bushire had to be ended because of a lack of munitions; see Hohenlohe-Langenburg to AA, NARA/T-137/141/0068.

71. Mikusch, 150–58, 166–77; Sykes, 95–96, 103–10, 114–26; and IWM, *Operations in Persia,* 98–102.

72. See Reuss's report in Constantinople embassy to AA, 11 Sept. 1915; Reuss, "Abschrift. Entzifferung.," 8 Sept. 1915, NARA/T-137/141/0218, 0232; and Gehrke, *Persien,* 1:1:172–77. Regarding Bulgaria's entry into the war and Serbia's defeat, note Herwig, *First World War,* 157–59.

73. Rathmann, *Stossrichtung Nahost,* 132; Wallach, *Anatomie,* 184; Trumpener, "German Officers," 33-34; and Gehrke, *Persien,* 1:1:188–89. Wangenheim first informed the AA of the arrival of the Germans in Afghanistan on 7 October 1915, NARA/T-137/141/0358.

74. Kanitz's reports are in Hohenlohe-Langenburg to AA, 13 Aug. 1915; and Constantinople embassy to AA, 25 Aug. 1915, NARA/T-137/141/0068, 0171-71.

75. Lossow (military attaché at the Constantinople embassy) to AA, 13 Sept. 1915, NARA/T-137/141/0240-41, enclosing Kanitz's report; and Gehrke, Persien, 1:1:198–99.

76. Note Klein's report in Wangenheim to AA, 10 Oct. 1915; Sarre's report in Constantinople embassy to AA, 1 Oct. 1915; and Lossow to AA, 13 Sept. 1915, NARA/T-137/141/0364, 0324-25, 0240-41.

77. Kariabachi (unidentified) to Constantinople embassy, 6 Aug. 1915, discussing Kanitz's plan for the prisoners of war; AA to Constantinople, 12 Aug. 1915; and AA to German embassy Vienna, 7 Sept. 1915, NARA/T-137/141/0063, 0059, 0208, respectively.

78. IWM, *Operations in Persia,* 119–25; and Gehrke, *Persien,* 1:1:201–6.

79. Gehrke, *Persien,* 1:1:204–5, 208–10, 215–18; and IWM, *Operations in Persia,* 133–38.

80. IWM, *Operations in Persia,* 133; and Gehrke, *Persien,* 1:1:212–15.

81. Mikusch, 175–77, 193–97, 203–4; Vogel, 120–21; and Wustrow, "Bericht," 7 Sept. 1915, NARA/T-137/141/0550.

82. Seiler, "Reisebericht der Hauptgruppe Persien der Afganistan-Expedition," 27 Dec. 1916, NARA/T-137/141/0745-59, written while he was imprisoned in Kermanshah; Zugmayer, "Bericht über die Tätigkeit der Balutschistan Gruppe der deutschen Afganistan Expedition.," 7 Mar. 1918; "Bericht der Tätigkeit des Mitgliedes Erik Bohnstorff der Afganistan-Expedition.," 18 June 1918, NARA/T-137/142/0078-79, 0116-20; and Wallach, *Anatomie*, 184.

83. Gehrke, *Persien*, 1:1:215–17, 227–28.

84. Most of the Germans were imprisoned in Shiraz and then in 1917 taken to Russian prisoner of war camps. See Zugmayer, "Bericht. . . ," 7 Mar. 1918; "Bericht der Tätigkeit des Mitgliedes Erik Bohnstorff. . . ," 18 June 1918, NARA/T-137/142/0079-81, 0120; and Seiler, "Reisebericht. . . ," 27 Dec. 1916, NARA/T-137/141/0760-61. Useful for the British, both in the informational and propaganda senses, was their capture of Griesinger's diary, which they later published as *German Intrigues in Persia. The Diary of a German Agent. The Niedermayer Expedition through Persia to Afghanistan and India.*

85. IWM, *Operations in Persia*, 139; Landau, 104; and the interesting British document on Wassmus's "considerable influence," GHQ MEF, "Daily Situation Summary, 2nd Oct. 1917," PRO/WO 157/804. Also, note Gehrke, *Persien*, 1:1:269–71; and the interpretation of Wassmuss contained in the biographies by Mikusch and Sykes.

86. The meeting occurred on 26 Oct. 1915. Note Niedermayer, *Im Weltkrieg vor Indiens Toren*, 114–16; and Vogel, 84–85.

87. IWM, *Operations in Persia*, 91.

88. Ibid., 91, 96; and Fletcher, 179–80.

89. Note Vogel, 94–96; and Reuss (Teheran) to Constantinople embassy, 19 Mar. 1916 [received 10 July], NARA/T-137/141/0506, containing the intial agreements of the amir on 26–27 December 1915 to the treaty. Fletcher, 180–81, provides a useful discussion of the anti-British group at the amir's court and of Habibullah's view that the Allies would win the war and show their gratitude to Afghanistan for its neutrality.

90. The right to be represented at the peace conference was written into the draft treaty with Germany; see Gehrke, *Persien*, 1:1:227–29, 239–61, 291–93.

91. Niedermayer, "Afganistan-Expedition. Afganistan-Gruppe Reise-Bericht.," 1 Oct. 1916, NARA/T-137/141/0619-21; and Hentig, 161-200. Gehrke, *Persien*, 1:1:137–272, provides an extensive analysis of the reasons for the German failures in Persia and Afghanistan.

92. Fletcher, 182; and Wesendonk, "G.A.," 11 July 1917, NARA/T-149/399/0847-48. Pratap returned to Germany in 1918; see below, 226.

93. IWM, *Operations in Persia*, chapters 4-5; and Gehrke, *Persien*, 1:1:209–11, 233–34.

94. Regarding Nuri Bey's arrival in Libya, note Gumppenberg, "Bericht Nr. 2," 17 Apr. 1915, NARA/T-120/4951/L366984; Lisa Anderson, "The Development of Nationalist Sentiment in Libya, 1908-1922," in *The Origins of Arab Nationalism*, ed. Rashid Khalidi, Lisa Anderson, Muhammad Muslih, and Reeva S. Simon, 233; and Evans-Pritchard, 125.

95. Bülow (Rome embassy) to AA, 15 and 16 Mar. 1915, NARA/T-137/144/0093, 0099. Regarding the encampment of the Shaykh al-Sanussi near the frontier, note MacMunn

and Falls, *Military Operations Egypt & Palestine,* 104; and Evans-Pritchard, 125.

96. Wesendonk, "G. A.," 30 Mar. 1915, NARA/T-120/L3666701.

97. Evans-Pritchard, 122; and Anderson, "Development of Nationalist Sentiment," 233. According to Farnie, 540–41, the German submarines operating along the Libyan coast and in the eastern Mediterranean "employed Germany's best commanders and inflicted heavy losses [on Allied shipping] out of all proportion to their small numbers." Regarding the naval bases, note Herwig, *First World War,* 156.

98. McMahon to Grey, 6 May 1915; and McMahon to FO, 26 Feb. 1915, PRO/FO 371/2353/61642, 21896, respectively; WO, "Sudan Intelligence Report," Feb. 1915, PRO/FO 371/2349/44359; and Evans-Pritchard, 126.

99. Maxwell to Kitchener, 7 May 1915, PRO/WO 33/731; and FO to McMahon, 23 Apr. 1915, PRO/FO 371/2353/46335.

100. McMahon to FO, 3 June 1915, PRO/FO 371/2353/71610.

101. Ibid.; and MacMunn and Falls, *Military Operations Egypt & Palestine,* 104.

102. For example, AA to German legation Athens, 29 Mar. 1915; Nadolny to AA, 11 June 1915; and Mannesmann, "Abschrift. Retiro-Abteilung IIIb. Nadolny," 5 June 1915, NARA/T-120/4951/L366685-87, L367354. L367428-32.

103. The first of such shipments is discussed in Kalle (military attaché at the German embassy in Madrid) to Sektion Politik, 15 Mar. 1917, NARA/T-137/145/0259-60.

104. Count N. von Mirbach-Harff (Athens legation) to AA, 28 June 1915, containing a message from Gumppenberg of 20 May, NARA/T-120/4951/L367455-56.

105. On the Turks' need of German naval support and on the Ottoman view that Libya belonged to Turkey, note Müller, 241–42. Germany even felt compelled to inform the Turks that it had no political aims in Libya; see Zimmermann to Constantinople embassy, 17 Nov. 1915, NARA/T-137/144/0684.

106. Humann, "Besprechung mit Enver Pascha vom 4. Juli 1915.," YUL/Jäckh Papers/1/25; and Wangenheim to AA, 4 July 1915, NARA/T-120/4951/L367477-78.

107. Mannesmann, "Dfna, den 2. Juli 1915" NARA/T-137/141/0436-41. Details of Gumppenberg's capture are in WO, "Intelligence Summary," 7 Aug. 1915, PRO/WO 157/694.

108. Mannesmann, "Dfna, den 24. Aug. 1915.," NARA/T-137/5/0448-49; and MacMunn and Falls, *Military Operations Egypt & Palestine,* 104–5.

109. Mannesmann, "Senussenlager 3 km westlich Solum.," 22 Sept. 1915, NARA/T-137/5/0504-05; and Evans-Pritchard, 125–27.

110. Mannesmann, "Dfna, den 3. September 1915," NARA/T-137/5/0447; and Evans-Pritchard, 126.

111. Mannesman, memo, n.d. (but is mid-Oct. 1915); Nadolny to AA, n.d. (but is Nov. 1915), containing Mannesmann's report; Constantinople embassy to Sektion Politik, n.d. (but is Nov. 1915), NARA/T-137/5/0475-76, 0503, 0509; and Boahen, 23.

112. FO to McMahon, 29 Oct. 1915, PRO/FO 371/2354/160694; and MacMunn and Falls, *Military Operations Egypt & Palestine,* 105.

113. FO to Rodd (British ambassador in Rome), 29 Sept. 1915; and Rodd to FO, 29 Sept. 1915, PRO/FO 371/2354/139604, 141029.

114. See Snow's report in Maxwell to WO, 5 Oct. 1915, PRO/FO 371/2354/156263; and GOC Egypt to WO, 21 Nov. 1915, PRO/WO 33/747.

115. Maxwell to WO, 18, 20, and 21 Nov. 1915, PRO/WO 33/747; McMahon to FO, 22 Nov. 1915, PRO/FO 371/2354/175772; MacMunn and Falls, *Military Operations Egypt*

& *Palestine*, 106–7; and "Engländer im Senussi Gefangenschaft," *Vossische Zeitung*, 28 Jan. 1916.

116. According to MacMunn and Falls, *Military Operations Egypt & Palestine*, 110–18, at least several hundred Arabs died in the clashes. Also, note McMahon to FO, 14 Dec. 1915, PRO/FO 371/2357/191226; and the telegrams from GOC Egypt to the WO and CIGS, 26–31 Dec. 1915, PRO/WO 33/760.

117. Six tons of armaments and munitions were delivered by the submarine; note "Ganz geheim! Auszug aus dem Kriegstagebuch von S.M. Unterseeboot 'U 38.' Kommandant: Kapitänleutnant Max Valentiner.," NARA/T-120/4196/K202392-93.

118. Max Valentiner (commander of submarine U-38), "Abschrift 'U 38.' Bericht über meinen Eindruck bei den Senussen;" Pröbster, memo, 9 Mar. 1916, NARA/T-137/5/0562, 0593-602; and Nadolny to AA, 20 Nov. 1915, NARA/T-120/4196/K202279-84.

119. See Neurath (Constantinople embassy) to AA, 7 Nov. 1915, YUL/Jäckh Papers/1/28; Falkenhayn's message to Enver in Werner Otto Freiherr von Grünau (the AA's liaison at German high command headquarters) to AA, 11 Nov. 1915; Zimmermann to Constantinople embassy, 17 Nov. 1915; and Lossow to Enver, 6 Dec. 1915, NARA/T-137/144/0679, 0684, 0730.

120. McMahon to FO, 21 Dec. 1915, PRO/FO 371/2357/196053.

7. A SENSE OF CRISIS ON BOTH SIDES, FALL 1915

1. Less so Grey than Kitchener; see above, 32–33, 41.

2. Dawn, *From Ottomanism to Arabism*, 31; Kedourie, *England and the Middle East*, 55–57; Friedman, *Question of Palestine*, 69, 73; Antonius, 169–70; Fromkin, 182–84; Zeine, 108, 116; and Yapp, 275–76.

3. See the telegrams and intelligence reports for 10, 26, 30 Apr. and 8, 17, 19 May 1915, in PRO/WO 157/776; WO, "Intelligence Summary, 10 Apr. 1915; and WO, "Intelligence Bulletin," 13 Apr. 1915, PRO/WO 157/690.

4. Fromkin, 176–79; Gilbert, *First World War*, 214–15; Stevenson, 127; Woodward, 87–92; and Antonius, 169–70. A cogent analysis of the relationship between the Arab nationalist societies, the Sharif of Mecca, and the British, is in Hourani, "*The Arab Awakening* Forty Years After," 31–32. The best discussion showing the erroneous nature of al-Faruqi's assertion that Germany and Turkey intended to grant the Arabs autonomy is in Friedman, *Question of Palestine*, 69–70.

5. Kedourie, *Chatham House Version*, 17–20; and Fromkin, 98, 100–1, 143–44, 169.

6. A statement that angered the Government of India; note Busch, *Britain, India, and the Arabs*, 68–69.

7. GOC Egypt to Secretary of State for War, 12 and 15 Oct. 1915, PRO/WO 33/747; and Fromkin, 177–78.

8. Kitchener to Asquith, 13 Nov. 1915; and Asquith to Kitchener, 12 Nov. 1915, PRO/WO 33/747.

9. Note below, 167, 182–83.

10. Woodward, 95–97.

11. See above, chapter 6.

12. McMahon to Grey, 24 Oct. 1915, PRO/FO 371/2354/163829, which enclosed a lengthy intelligence document titled "Note on Propaganda, etc. on the part of Germans giving the impression that they or their Sovereign and Government had em-

braced Islam or were in sympathy with Anti-Christian Manifestations on the part of Ignorant or Fanatical Moslems."

13. Ibid. At the end of the summer, major Allied newspapers had published a report purporting to quote from a letter of Wilhelm II to the Shaykh al-Sanussi claiming the kaiser had converted to Islam; see, for instance, "Allah's Envoy, Islam's Protector," *Daily Chronicle* (London), 30 Aug. 1915.

14. The paragraphs which follow, discussing the Abyssinian state and its ruler, are based on Marcus, 111–14; Boahen, 7:304; and Greenfield, 131–36.

15. See above, 105; and Syburg to AA, 27 June 1915, T-137/14/0091.

16. AA to Athens legation, 2 Sept. 1915; Syburg to Bethmann Hollweg, 22 Oct. 1915; and Neurath (Constantinople embassy) to AA, 5 Nov. 1915, NARA/T-136/30/0103, 0133, 0125 respectively.

17. Regarding the German negotiations for a treaty with Abyssinia, note Syburg to AA, 12 Dec. 1915, NARA/microcopy T-136 (Files of the German Foreign Ministry Archives, 1867–1920, filmed at St. Antony's College, Oxford)/reel 30/no frame [hereafter nf]; and mention of an "alliance" in Constantinople embassy to Sektion Politik Berlin, 1 Jan. 1916, NARA/T-137/14/0095.

18. Marcus, 114.

19. Thesiger to Grey, 31 Mar. and 1 May 1915, PRO/FO 371/2228/53518, 66020.

20. Thesiger to Grey, 16 June 1915, PRO/FO 371/2228/92293; and WO, "Sudan Intelligence Report, Nr. 252," July 1915, PRO/FO 371/2349/133114.

21. Thesiger to Grey, 6 Sept. 1915, PRO/FO 371/2228/141629; and E. G. Maechtig (Colonial Office) to Lord Eustace Percy, 18 Nov. 1915, PRO/FO 371/2227/174093.

22. The Porte delivered the message, mentioning the shipping of weapons and shells to the "Mad Mullah," to the Germans; see the Turkish document, "Notice confidentielle.," 11 Mar. 1916, containing Syburg to AA, 12 Dec. 1915, NARA/T-136/30/nf; WO, "Sudan Intelligence Report," Sept. 1915, FOS 371/2349/177154; Marcus, 114; and Greenfield, 136–37.

23. See above, 113.

24. Rodd to FO, 29 May 1915, PRO/FO 371/2489/68849.

25. Commander of the General Staff [hereafter "CGS"] Simla (summer capital of British India) to General Force "D," 12 June 1915, PRO/WO 157/776; and Sir H. Bax-Ironside (British minister in Sofia) to FO, 8 June 1915, PRO/FO371/2489/74465.

26. Wratislaw (Salonika) to FO, 1 July 1915, containing Sykes's message for the WO, PRO/FO 371/2489/897754. The standard work on Sykes's mission is Adelson, 185–96.

27. Sykes to Major-Gen. C. E. Callwell (DMO in the WO), No. 7, 29 July 1915, PRO/FO 371/2486/93937.

28. Ibid.

29. As examples, note "Intelligence Summary," 18 Sept. 1915, PRO/WO 157/779; and WO intelligence department, Cairo, "Intelligence Summary," 8 and 16 Sept. 1915, PRO/WO 157/695.

30. Clayton to Communications Mudros, 12 Nov. 1915, PRO/FO 882/12/KH/15/12; and Maxwell to Kitchener, 14 Oct. 1915, PRO/FO 33/747. On 13 Oct., Oppenheim reported to his superiors from Damascus that "my Sinai trip led me deep into occupied British territory." See Wangenheim to Bethmann Hollweg, 17 Oct. 1915, NARA/T-120/4952/L367820. Also note McKale, "German Policy toward the Sharif of Mecca," 310.

31. Sykes, "Memorandum," 28 Oct. 1915, in Sykes to Major Callwell, 15 Nov. 1915, PRO/FO 882/13/MIS/15/16.

32. "Note on Arab Movement," contained in WO to director, military operations, 21 Nov. 1915, PRO/FO 882/2/AP/15/18. Regarding the opposition of the IO, note Busch, *Britain, India, and the Arabs,* 64–100.

33. Wingate to Clayton, 15 Nov. 1915, PRO/FO 882/12/KH/15/16.

34. Clayton to Wingate, 22 Nov. 1915, PRO/FO 882/12/IND/15/2, which stated that the Aga Khan was "not well-disposed towards an Arab Khaliphate [*sic*], and that it would cause great trouble in India, if we got mixed up in such a movement." Also see Adelson, 193–94.

35. Dawn, *From Ottomanism to Arabism,* 31; Kedourie, *England and the Middle East,* 56–57; Fromkin, 185–89; Zeine, 116; Adelson, 193–94; and on the British promises to deliver weapons at the beginning of 1916 to the sharif, Antonius, 191–92.

36. Lacey, 124.

37. WO, "Intelligence Summary for Period from 7th December to 14th Inclusive," PRO/WO 157/698.

38. WO, "Intelligence Summary," 25 Dec. 1915, PRO/WO 157/698; and McMahon to FO, 7 and 21 Dec. 1915, PRO/FO 371/2357/195078, 196095.

39. See Lord Drogheda, "Memorandum on Turkish Peace Overtures," 20 Nov. 1917, PRO/FO 371/3057/222199; and above, 116.

40. Note the IO minute by Hirtzel, 3 Dec. 1915, IOLR/L/P&S/11/101.

41. Busch, *Britain, India, and the Arabs,* 81–89, 100–2; Adelson, 186–87, 193, 194; Kedourie, *Chatham House Version,* 20–21; and Fromkin, 170–72.

42. Adelson, 196–97.

43. Note above, chapter 6.

44. Guinn, *British Strategy,* 131–32, notes that in January 1916 almost two hundred thousand British troops were to be found in Egypt, Mesopotamia, and Salonika. Maxwell, according to Farnie, 539, fearing a Gallipoli in reverse in the Suez Canal zone, had asked for thirteen divisions to defend Egypt against a possible onslaught by 250,000 Turks.

45. Guinn, British Strategy, 132. Larcher, 617, estimates that the maximum number of British forces present at one time during the war on Gallipoli was 127,000, in Egypt-Syria 432,000, and Mesopotamia 447,000. Mühlmann, 90, claims that during 1915 Egypt and the Dardanelles between them tied down five hundred thousand British troops. Macmunn and Falls, *Military Operations Egypt & Palestine,* 371, observes, "During the Gallipoli campaign the high-water mark, including troops on the islands and in the Egyptian bases, was little above 200,000." According to Gilbert, *First World War,* 205, the British kept a hundred thousand troops in Egypt to protect against "a possible German-led Turkish attack on the Suez Canal." The number of Egyptian troops, most of them stationed in the Sudan, was roughly thirteen thousand; see Antonius, 136.

46. Good summaries are Herwig, *"Luxury" Fleet,* 154–55; and Keegan, 130–31.

47. Wallach, *Anatomie,* 187–88. Regarding the major conflicts between them, see Trumpener, *Germany and the Ottoman Empire,* chapters 3, 6–10.

48. The sources disagree on the date of Wangenheim's death. See Weber, 159, 163–67; Pomiankowski, 175–76; Friedman, *Germany, Turkey, and Zionism,* 260, 273; and Dadrian, 207, 425.

49. AA (Zimmermann) to Constantinople embassy, 26 Nov. 1915, NARA/T-137/25/ 0091; AA, memo, 5 Nov. 1915; and Oppenheim to Bethmann Hollweg, 10 Nov. 1915, NARA/T-120/4952/L367858-70, L367890-93.

50. Baghdad consulate to Constantinople embassy, 13 Aug. 1915, NARA/T-137/142/ 0513; and "Die Ereignisse im Irak," *Vossische Zeitung,* 3 Nov. 1915.

51. See above, 109–11.

52. Dr. Ranzi (Austro-Hungarian consul in Damascus) to Stephan Baron von Burián (foreign minister in Vienna), 10 Apr. 1915, PA/*Türkei* 165/Bd. 37.

53. Prüfer to Wolff-Metternich, 10 Dec. 1915, NARA/T-137/25/0150-57, enclosing the report he submitted to Jemal Pasha; Friedman, *Question of Palestine,* 70; and McKale, *Curt Prüfer,* 46.

54. See above, 159–60.

55. AA, memo, 5 Nov. 1915, NARA/T-120/4952/L367858.

56. Previously the war minister had opposed the Germans paying Muslim leaders in Persia and Libya; note Weber, 182.

57. Schoenberg, memo, contained in Neurath to Bethmann Hollweg, 16 Sept. 1915, PA/*Türkei* 165/Bd. 37. Prince Reuss, the German minister in Persia, held a similar view; see Reuss to Bethmann Hollweg, 13 July 1915, NARA/T-137/141/0271-72. Regarding German-Russian peace negotiations during 1915, see Egmont Zechlin, *Krieg und Kriegsrisiko. Zur deutschen Politik im Ersten Weltkrieg,* 279–89, 296-313; Fischer, *Germany's Aims,* 195–98; Trumpener, *Germany and the Ottoman Empire,* 147–48; Hans Herzfeld, *Der Erste Weltkrieg,* 145; and Stevenson, 93.

58. Weber, 183–84.

59. Wesendonk, memo, 17 Oct. 1915, NARA/T-137/25/0005.

60. Rathmann, *Stossrichtung Nahost,* 123; and Weber, 180–82.

61. AA (Zimmermann) to Constantinople embassy, 26 Nov. 1915, NARA/T-137/25/ 0091. Also, see above, 165.

62. Farwell, chapters 10–16; Boahen, 7:132–33; Herzfeld, 168–69; Gilbert, *First World War,* 279; and James, *Rise and Fall of the British Empire,* 365–66.

63. Note Solf, "Ganz geheim! Anweisung Nr. I für die I. Staffel des Arabisch-Ägyptischen Erkundungskommandos.," 23 Feb. 1915; Wangenheim to AA, 6 May 1915, NARA/T-137/138/0551, 0748; and Rathmann, *Stossrichtung Nahost,* 123–24.

64. For example, Prüfer, "Vertraulich," 6 Aug. 1915, NARA/T-137/24/0793, urged the conquest of Egypt and the Sudan as retribution for the British occupation of the German colonies. He also advocated using the Sudan as "a door for invading Uganda and British East Africa." Merely blocking the Suez Canal, he concluded, would be insufficient to destroy British routes to India and Australia.

65. The standard work is still Fischer, *Germany's Aims,* 102–9, 161, 170, 234-35. Also useful are Rathmann, *Stossrichtung Nahost,* 67–73, 101–3; Herzfeld, 151, 169–70; Stevenson, 91; and Stoecker, "The First World War: The War Aims," in *German Imperialism in Africa: From the Beginnings until the Second World War,* ed. Helmuth Stoecker, trans. Bernd Zöllner, 280–90.

66. As examples, see Hans Schmidt (an agent sent by the General Staff to Eritrea and Egypt), "Bericht," July 1915, NARA/T-137/139/0080-88; and Wesendonk, "G. A.," 12 May 1915, NARA/T-120/4951/L367085-93.

67. Constantinople embassy to AA, 21 Sept. 1915, NARA/T-137/139/0116. Regarding Mecklenburg, note Farwell, 23, 25.

68. Solf to Falkenhayn, 29 Dec. 1915, NARA/T-136/30/0143-48.
69. Ibid.
70. Falkenhayn, "Abschrift," n.d., NARA/T-136/30/0151-52.
71. Ibid.

8. BRITAIN AS WARTIME "REVOLUTIONARY": THE ARAB REVOLT, 1916

1. Basic sources include Moberly, 2:212–466; Guinn, 121–31; Gilbert, *First World War*, 213, 228–29; Steel and Hart, 383–412; Trumpener, "German Officers," 33–34; and Moorehead, 329–30; and James, *Rise and Fall of the British Empire*, 358–59.

2. Hirtzel, "The War with Turkey: Memorandum by Political Department, India Office," 25 May 1916, PRO/FO 371/2778/130553. Also see his "Memorandum by the Political Secretary, India Office, on German Press Opinion Regarding the Middle East," n.d. (but is spring 1916), IOLR/L/P&S/11/101. For the peaking during 1916 of German intentions, particularly of Oppenheim and numerous economic and military leaders, to dominate the Turkish economy, note Rathmann, *Stossrichtung Nahost*, 62–63, 92–94, 152–65, 189–91; Wallach, *Anatomie*, 203–5; and Gisbert von Romberg (minister at Bern), "Überblick über die Entstehungsgeschichte der Nachrichtensaal-Organisation in der Türkei.," 24 Mar. 1917, NARA/microcopy T-140 (German Foreign Ministry Archives, 1867–1920, filmed by the University of California)/reel 476/frame 0428.

3. See his memo, "The War with Turkey," 13 June 1916, PRO/FO 371/2778/130533.

4. Ibid.

5. Landau, 127.

6. "Secret. Report of the 3rd Visit of Messenger 'G' to the Sherif Hussein Ibn Ali at Mecca.," 25 Jan. 1916, PRO/FO 882/12/KH/16/1; and Dawn, *From Ottomanism to Arabism*, 31–32.

7. Regarding reports on the sharif, note "Intelligence Summary," 22 Jan. 1916; and "Intelligence Summary for Period from 26th January to 2nd February, 1916.," PRO/WO 157/700. For Ibn Saud's "loathing of the Turk, which is almost an obsession with him," see J. Keyes to Sir Mark Sykes, 10 Jan. 1916, PRO/FO 882/8/IS/16/1.

8. Director of Military Intelligence [hereafter "DMI"] Egypt to WO, 9, 13, 25, 26 Feb. 1916, PRO/WO 33/760. On the background of "Maurice," note Lawrence James, *The Golden Warrior: The Life and Legend of Lawrence of Arabia*, 81.

9. WO to GOC Egypt, 5 Jan. 1916; DMI Egypt to WO, 11 Jan. 1916; and General Headquarters, Force "D" to WO, 11 Jan. 1916, PRO/WO 33/760.

10. Sharif to McMahon, 18 Feb. 1916, IOLR/L/P&S/10/387; and Dawn, *From Ottomanism to Arabism*, 33. Also see Clayton to Governor General Khartoum, 28 Feb. 1916, PRO/FO 882/12/KH/16/4.

11. Recounted in "Arabia. Hejaz. Feisal's Table Talk," *Arab Bulletin*, 42 (15 Feb. 1917): 78, in PRO/FO 882/26. Also note Dawn, *From Ottomanism to Arabism*, 32; Zeine, 117; Fromkin, 219; Friedman, *Question of Palestine*, 75–76; and Antonius, 188.

12. The British seized later biographical material about him from Stotzingen himself; note "Appendix. Stotzingen-Neufeld Mission to Arabia.," *Arab Bulletin*, 13(1 Aug. 1916):133, PRO/FO 882/25.

13. See above, 167.

14. Prüfer to Metternich, 7 Dec. 1915, PA/*Türkei* 165/Bd. 38; and Humann,

"Vertraulich! Zur Lage am 16. Januar 1916.," YUL/Jäckh Papers/1/30. Also, see the interesting memo of the Hamburg Colonial Institute titled "Der nahe Orient (Die arabische Frage)," Jan. 1917, PA/*Türkei* 165/Bd. 41.

15. Humann, "Vertraulich! Zur Lage am 16. Januar 1916.," YUL/Jäckh Papers/1/30.

16. Ibid.

17. Wolff-Metternich to Bethmann Hollweg, 22 Jan. 1916, PA/*Türkei* 165/Bd. 38.

18. To be sure, on most other issues during 1916, including military matters, the Ottomans insisted on having their way with the Germans. For example, the Turks forced their allies to agree to a new discriminatory and protective tariff, to void a number of international treaties from the nineteenth century, and to agree not to conclude a separate peace without the Porte. The latter also pressed the Reich to approve the abolition of the capitulations, which it did in January 1917. Whether a connection existed between any of these issues and the Stotzingen mission is unclear. Note Trumpener, *Germany and the Ottoman Empire,* 90-98, 126-39; and Yapp, 271.

19. German legation Bern (Romberg) to Bethmann Hollweg, 8 Jan. 1916, NARA/T-136/30/no frame [hereafter "nf"].

20. Solf to AA, 17 Jan. 1916, NARA/T-136/30/nf; and Wesendonk's letter to Enver, n.d., NARA/T-120/4952/L368068-69. Regarding the appointment of Khalil Bey in October 1915, which strengthened the ties between the Turks and Central Powers, note Trumpener, *Germany and the Ottoman Empire,* 123-25. Lossow had apparently been on leave in Berlin; Trumpener, "German Officers," 35-36.

21. Wesendonk, "G. A.," 3 Feb. 1916, NARA/T-120/4952/L368080; and Wesendonk, memo, 6 Mar., 1916, NARA/T-120/4196/K202424.

22. Sektion Politik, "Instruktion für die im Süden der Provinz Yemen zu errichtende Nachrichtenstelle," Mar. 1916, NARA/T-137/25/0288-92.

23. Loytved to Wolff-Metternich, 26 Feb. 1916, NARA/T-137/25/0303-05; and Dawn, *From Ottomanism to Arabism,* 34.

24. Humann, "Zur Reise Enver Pascha.," 21 Feb. 1916, YUL/Jäckh Papers/1/31; and Dawn, *From Ottomanism to Arabism,* 34.

25. See, for example, Constantinople embassy to Sektion Politik, 15 May 1916 ("Anliegende Berichte des Majors Freiherrn von Stotzingen ergebenst übersandt."), particularly "I. Bericht," 15 Apr. 1916, NARA/T-137/139/0210-11; and "Emir Hussein and Jemal in 1916.," *Arab Bulletin,* 94(25 June 1918):215, PRO/FO 882/27.

26. "Abschrift. Telegramm des Militärattachés Pera Nr. 2333 vom 11.3.[1916]," to Sektion Politik, NARA/T-137/25/0277; Wesendonk, "G. A.," 12 Mar. 1916, NARA/T-120/4952/L368130-31; and Dawn, *From Ottomanism to Arabism,* 34.

27. See the Porte, "Notice confidentielle.," 11 Mar. 1916, which transmitted Syburg's message to the AA, dated 12 Dec. 1915, NARA/T-137/14/0098-99.

28. AA to Constantinople embassy, 30 Mar. 1916, T-137/14/0100. Rumors of such a trip by Ras Mikail worried the Germans throughout the summer.

29. Dawn, *From Ottomanism to Arabism,* 33.

30. Maxwell to Kitchener, 19 Jan., 29 Feb., and 15 Mar. 1916; GOC Egypt to CIGS, 23, 25 Jan., 25, 28 Feb., 1, 7, 17 Mar. 1916; and GOC Egypt to WO, 18, 22 Mar. 1916, PRO/WO 33/760; "British Rule in Egypt," *Morning Post* (London), 15 Mar. 1916; Evans-Pritchard, 128; and MacMunn and Falls, *Military Operations Egypt & Palestine,* 123-34. Also note above, 145-51.

31. McMahon to the sharif, 10 Mar. 1916, IOLR/L/P&S/10/387.

32. A point made particularly well by Anderson, "Development of Nationalist Sentiment," 234; and Boahen, 7:136. Contrary to popular belief, therefore, as first elaborated by Antonius, 206, the sharif's uprising against the Turks, which began in June 1916, had little impact on Britain's suppression of the Sanussis in Libya.

33. Lt. Gen. Jan Smuts to WO, 3 Apr. 1916, PRO/FO 371/2842/66283.

34. Storrs, memo, 10 June 1916, PRO/FO 371/2773/119324.

35. Dawn, *From Ottomanism to Arabism*, 34–37; and McKale, "German Policy Toward the Sharif of Mecca," 313.

36. Stotzingen, "4. Bericht," 5 May 1916, NARA/T-137/139/0215-16; "Emir Hussein and Jemal in 1916.," *Arab Bulletin*, 94(25 June 1918):215, PRO/FO 882/27; and Dawn, *From Ottomanism to Arabism*, 37.

37. Dawn, *From Ottomanism to Arabism*, 37–38; Zeine, 117–18; and on the backing of some Germans of Jemal's persecution of the Arabs, Hermann Müller (an NfdO official in Constantinople) to Wesendonk, 29 May 1916, PA/*Türkei* 165/Bd. 38.

38. Loytved Hardegg to Wolff–Metternich, 25 May 1916, NARA/T-137/139/0231.

39. "Abschrift. Telegramm aus Damaskus vom 3 Juni 1916.," PA/*Türkei* 165/Bd. 38.

40. The consul's message is in Wolff-Metternich to Bethmann Hollweg, 21 June 1916, NARA/T-137/139/0235.

41. "I. Telegramm. Damaskus (Konsulat), 5.6.16. Nr. 70," PA/*Türkei* 165/Bd. 38.

42. Ibid.

43. "Abschrift. Telegramm aus Damaskus vom 7. Juni 1916.," PA/*Türkei* 165/Bd. 38.

44. Their fate is discussed in the *Arab Bulletin*, 1(6 June 1916):7, PRO/FO 882/25; and "Militärbevollmächtigter Pera 2250 vom 7. Juni an Generalstab Sektion Politik Berlin.," NARA/T-137/139/0221. Also, note Eugen Mittwoch,"G. A.," 23 Mar. 1916, NARA/T-120/4952/L368189-191.

45. Constantinople embassy to AA, 28 June 1916; "Abschrift. Telegramm des Militärbevollmächtigten Pera vom 6. Juli 1916 an Generalstab Sektion Politik Berlin.," NARA/T-137/139/0240, 0244; Dawn, *From Ottomanism to Arabism*, 39; and Donald M. McKale, "Germany and the Arab Question in the First World War," *Middle Eastern Studies*, 29(1993):242.

46. Described in "Appendix. Stotzingen-Neufeld Mission to Arabia.," *Arab Bulletin*, 13(1 Aug. 1916):133–39, PRO/FO 882/25.

47. These themes predominate in this study, in both the present chapter and chapter 7.

48. "Abschrift. Telegramm. Damaskus (Konsulat), 9.6.1916. Nr. 77.," PA/*Türkei* 165/Bd. 38.

49. Wolff-Metternich to Bethmann Hollweg, 21 June 1916, NARA/T-137/139/0235. Regarding the immediate Turkish response to the revolt, note Antonius, 201–2.

50. "Telegramm. Damaskus (Konsulat), 25.6.16. an Therapia, 26.6.16.," PA/*Türkei* 165/Bd. 38.

51. See Wolff-Metternich's two notes to Bethmann Hollweg, 30 June 1916, PA/*Türkei* 165/Bd. 38.

52. Wolff-Metternich to Bethmann Hollweg, 30 June 1916, PA/*Türkei* 165/Bd. 38.

53. Wolff-Metternich to AA, 1 July 1916, PA/*Türkei* 165/Bd. 38.

54. Weber, "Aufzeichnung des ersten Botschaftsdragomans," 7 Aug. 1916 ("Die Araberverfolgungen in Syrien und den Aufstand in Arabien."), PA/*Türkei* 165/Bd. 39.

55. A sample of German newspapers is in "Report on German Press Opinion Eegarding the Middle East, June–August 1916.," IOLR/L/P&S/11/101. Also, note "Die Lage in Arabien," *Norddeutsche Allgemeine Zeitung,* 27 July 1916; "Englisches Geld im Hedschas," *Norddeutsche Allgemeine Zeitung,* 31 Aug. 1916; and Franz Stuhlmann, *Der Kampf um Arabien zwischen der Türkei und England.*

56. Prüfer, "Krieg," entries for 9 June and 8 July 1916, HIWRP/Prüfer Papers.

57. Liman, "Meine Auffassung über die türkische Kriegslage," 10 July 1916, PA/*Türkei* 165/Bd. 38.

58. Falkenhayn to treasury office, 5 Aug. 1916, PA/*Türkei* 165/Bd. 39; and Wallach, *Anatomie,* 218.

59. Humann to naval office, 12 July 1916 ("Zum Aufstand in Mekka."), YUL/Jäckh Papers/1/35.

60. For example, Werner Otto Freiherr von Grünau (Pless) to AA, 18 Aug. 1916, PA/*Türkei* 165/Bd. 39.

61. His views are in Wolff-Metternich to AA, 21 July 1916, PA/*Türkei* 165/Bd. 39.

62. Stotzingen, "7. Bericht," 14 Sept. 1916, NARA/T-137/139/0321. The German consul at Beirut, Gerhard Mutius, reported similar economic discontent among Syrian Arabs; Mutius to Bethmann 31 July 1916, PA/*Türkei* 165/Bd. 39. Some evidence exists that the Germans asked the Porte at the end of September to allow Stotzingen to attempt once again reaching Abyssinia via the Hijaz; reference to such a request is in the index to AA documents in NARA/T-137/14/0088.

63. Quoted in Wolff-Metternich to AA, 29 Aug. 1916, PA/*Türkei* 165/Bd. 39.

64. See Richard von Kühlmann (German ambassador in Constantinople) to AA, 17 Nov. 1916; and "Bericht des Kapitänleutnant Seyffardt über Tatigkeit und Erfahrungen am Euphrat.," n.d., PA/*Türkei* 165/Bd. 40.

65. Brode to Wolff-Metternich, 8 Sept. 1916; and Rössler (consul in Aleppo) to Constantinople embassy, 19 Oct. 1916, NARA/T-149/365/0332-44, 0350-51.

66. "Abschrift. Telegramm Damaskus vom 1. Oktober 16.," PA/*Türkei* 165/Bd. 40.

67. Madrid embassy to AA, 28 June 1916, NARA/T-120/4952/L368322.

68. MacMunn and Falls, *Military Operations Egypt & Palestine,* 154–70; Woodward, 116–18; Farnie, 541–43; and Liddell Hart, *Real War,* 207–8.

69. Standard accounts of the battle are Macmunn and Falls, *Military Operations Egypt & Palestine,* 184–98; Farnie, 544–45; Wavell, 38–50; Mühlmann, 99–102; and Kress, chapter 12.

70. Macmunn and Falls, *Military Operations Egypt & Palestine,* 225–28, 230–32; Antonius, 210–11, 214–15; and Suleiman Mousa, *T. E. Lawrence: An Arab View,* trans. Albert Burtos, 16–17.

71. Landau, 109–11; and Müller, 284.

72. Antonius, 211, 213; and Wallach, *Anatomie,* 218.

73. Loytved Hardegg to Wolff-Metternich, 6 Aug. 1916, PA/*Türkei* 165/Bd. 39.

74. Ibid. Regarding the previous idea of a consulate at Jidda, note above, 66, 108–9.

75. Wolff-Metternich to Bethmann Hollweg, 6 Sept. 1916, PA/*Türkei* 165/Bd. 39.

76. Constantinople embassy to Bethmann Hollweg, 24 Nov. 1916, NARA/T-149/365/0362.

77. Lossow to Sektion Politik, 20 Oct. 1916, enclosing a memo by a German official named Weitz, "Abschrift. Strengvertraulich!," 15 Oct. 1916, NARA/T-137/145/0193-94.

78. Otto Göppert (chargé d'affaires at the Constantinople embassy) to AA, 29 Dec. 1916, PA/*Türkei* 165/Bd. 40.

79. This is discussed in Edouard Brémond, *Le Hedjaz dans la Guerre Mondiale*, 103; and Kedourie, *England and the Middle East*, 99.

80. Macmunn and Falls, *Military Operations Egypt and Palestine*, 230. Also see Andersen, Seibert, and Wagner, 79.

81. Moberly, 2:439–66; Woodward, 107–10; and Desmond Stewart, *T. E. Lawrence*, 142–44.

82. Lacey, 124–27.

83. The entry for 1 July 1916, T. E. Lawrence, *The Home Letters of T. E. Lawrence and His Brothers*, 327. Some historians as well have attached too much significance to the revolt. For instance, according to Kinross, 608, the rebellion "was to spread to all Arab lands and to exercise a profound influence on the outcome of the war and its aftermath."

84. The full text is in "Great Britain and the Holy Places," *The Times* (London), 28 July 1916. Regarding the British army concern for the revolt, note Mousa, 17–18.

85. Eldar, 337–38; Larcher, 507; Nevakivi, 62–63; and Brémond.

86. For example, see the report by a British agent, Ibrahim Dmitri, "Secret. A Statement on My Visit to Jeddah and Yembo from 30th July to 17th August 1916.," PRO/FO 882/4/HRG/16/38; and Appendix F, "Cumulative Evidence of Enemy Political Activity in Arabia," in the pamphlet by the General Staff, WO, "Summary of the Hejaz Revolt," 31 Aug. 1918, IOLR/L/MIL/17/16/13.

87. Sykes, "The Problem of the Near East," 20 June 1916, PRO/FO 371/2774/137276; Adelson, 210–13; Busch, *Britain, India, and the Arabs*, 170–74; and Dawn, "Influence of T. E. Lawrence," 74–75. Regarding the War Committee (or War Council), see Kennedy, *Realities Behind Diplomacy*, 176.

88. McMahon to FO, 13 Sept. 1916, PRO/FO/2775/182577, 185308.

89. Macmunn and Falls, *Military Operations Egypt & Palestine*, 230–34; McMahon to FO, 11, 12 Oct. 1916, containing Wingate's views; and FO to McMahon, 13 Oct. 1916, PRO/FO/371/203616, 204128.

90. Although both Western powers agreed to recognize Husayn as king, until December the area of his sovereignty remained questionable to the Anglo-French who, as noted previously in this study, hoped themselves to control postwar Syria, Mesopotamia, and Palestine. See Eldar, 339–40; and Busch, *Britain, India and the Arabs*, 172–74.

91. For Lawrence's work and activity with the Arab forces, his *Seven Pillars of Wisdom* is still informative. Also see Dawn, "Influence of T. E. Lawrence," 76; Stewart, 148–65; Mousa, 16–28; and James, *Golden Warrior*, 141–74.

92. McMahon to FO, 7 July 1916, PRO/FO 371/2773/132208; Gershoni and Jankowski, *Egypt, Islam, and the Arabs*, 28–30; and Kedourie, *Chatham House Version*, 181.

93. Viceroy India to IO, 6 July 1916, PRO/FO 371/2773/132030.

94. Busch, *Britain, India, and the Arabs*, 164–71; Viceroy India to IO, 30 June, 7 July 1916, PRO/FO 371/2773/126523, 132237; and FO minute to McMahon to FO, 14 July 1916, PRO/FO 371/2774/137050, which noted that "our job is to make our Indian Moslems realize that we have no intention of interfering in the religious question, but that the Sherif, in so far as he is fighting our enemies, is fighting for us and therefore merits our support."

95. Burke and Quraishi, 148–57; and Burn, 582–84.

96. Remy to Hertling, 11 Nov. 1917, NARA/T-149/400/0151-52; and Dignan, 67–69. Jodh Singh had also turned informer for the British and Government of India in the 1915 Lahore conspiracy trials. Note above, 125, 126; Bernstorff to AA, 19 Jan. 1917; and Wesendonk, "G. A.," 21 Jan. 1917, NARA/T-149/399/0417, 0414, respectively.

97. Dignan, 70–71, 73; and Doerries, *Imperial Challenge*, 155.

98. GOC Egypt to CIGS, 2, 17, 22 Oct. 1916; 8, 21 Feb. 1917; and 4 Mar. 1917, PRO/WO 33/905; Maxwell to Kitchener, 15 Mar. 1916, PRO/FO 371/2669/50987; Anderson, "Development of Nationalist Sentiment in Libya," 234; Evans-Pritchard, 129–41; and MacMunn and Falls, *Military Operations Egypt & Palestine*, 135–45.

99. The troop numbers are in Evans-Pritchard, 130. Also note the summary of British military "Western Desert Intelligence" reports during May–December 1916 in PRO/FO 371/2669/91189-255870; and Nuri Pasha's surprisingly accurate estimate of the numbers of British troops used (thirty thousand), mentioned in "Abschrift. Telegramm des Militärbevollmächtigten Pera vom 12.8.16. an Politische Abteilung Deutsches Gr. Hauptquartier.," NARA/T-137/5/0782-83.

100. Nadolny to admiralty staff, 23, 24 Mar. and 3 May 1916; "Abschrift. Telegramm. Militärattaché Pera Nr. 2685 vom 25. III. an Generalstab Berlin Sektion Politik"; and Reinhard Koch (chief of the admiralty staff) to Sektion Politik, 15 Apr., 8 May 1916, NARA/T-137/5/0636-37, 0634,0684, 0639, 0672-73, 0685, respectively.

101. "Bericht des Oberleutnants Freiherrn v. Todenwarth über Transport und Landung der für Dr. Mannesmann bestimmten Munition und Gewehre.," 9 May 1916, NARA/T-137/5/0690-0710.

102. Todenwarth, "Bericht über meine Reisen in Nordafrika vom 5. Juli bis 5. November 1916. Auszug aus dem Kriegstagebuch.," NARA/T-137/5/0861-68.

103. See Ibid., the portion continued on reel 6/0001-0012; Anderson, "Development of Nationalist Sentiment in Libya," 234; and Evans-Pritchard, 130.

104. Todenwarth, "Beurteilung der Lage in Nord-Afrika.," 15 Nov. 1916, NARA/T-137/5/0852-55; and Müller, 329.

105. See Lossow to Constantinople embassy, 29 Nov. 1916, NARA/T-137/5/0396-97; and Humann, "Auf das dortige Schreiben B. 30249 III vom 21. November 1916 gerichtet an Mittelmeer-Division. Bericht des Kommandanten von 'U.39' zur Fernunternehmung vom 8.X.-1 XI. 1916.," NARA/T-137/6/0065-68.

106. Sektion Politik to AA, 9 Dec. 1916, NARA/T-137/6/0046-47.

107. Contained in McMahon to FO, 3 Oct. 1916, PRO/FO 371/2775/197067.

108. GOC Egypt to CIGS, 13 Feb. 1916; and DMI to Wingate, 18 Mar. 1916, PRO/WO 33/760. A good survey of the history of Darfur and Ali Dinar and their relationship to Sudan is MacMunn and Falls, *Military Operations Egypt & Palestine*, 147–48.

109. Todenwarth, "Bericht über meine Reisen in Nordafrika. . . ," NARA/T-137/6/0001-02; and Wesendonk, memo, 17 Apr. 1916, NARA/T-120/4196/K202591.

110. "Abschrift. Telegramm des Militärbevollmächtigten Pera vom 12.8.16. an Politische Abteilung Deutsches Gr. Hauptquartier.," NARA/T-137/5/0783.

111. MacMunn and Falls, *Military Operations Egypt & Palestine*, 150–52; Wingate to McMahon, 9 June 1916; Wingate to Grey, 2 July 1916; and Wingate to FO, 12 Nov. 1916, PRO/FO 371/2671/144046, 144115, 227491.

112. See above, 156–57.

113. AA to German embassy Madrid, 23 Mar. 1916, NARA/T-136/30/nf; von Syburg

to AA, 12 Dec. 1915, NARA/T-137/14/0098; and Thesiger to Grey, 12, 27 Jan. 1916, PRO/FO/371/2593/22487, 32101.

114. CIGS to GOC Egypt, 12 Feb. 1916; and GOC Egypt to CIGS, 13, 16 Feb. 1916, PRO/WO 33/760.

115. British Colonial Office to Government of Somaliland Protectorate, 23 May 1916; and Thesiger to FO, 17, 18 May 1916, PRO/FO 371/2593/99491, 94522, 113264, respectively.

116. Thesiger to Grey, 1 June 1916; and Thesiger to British commission in Berbera (British Somaliland), 17 May 1916, PRO/FO 371/2593/119940, 113263, respectively.

117. Thesiger to Grey, 22 June 1916, PRO/FO 371/2593/138936.

118. Archer to Andrew Bonar Law (secretary of state in the Colonial Office), 18, 20 July 1916, PRO/FO 371/2593/139236, 172763.

119. Grey to McMahon, 27 Sept. 1916, PRO/FO 371/2594/185543. Regarding the role of the Allied ministers in the conspiracy, see in this same collection of documents, Thesiger to Grey, 4 and 8 Sept. 1916, files 197713, 197715.

120. Thesiger to Grey, 28 Sept. 1916, PRO/FO 371/2594/228181. Also note Marcus, 114–16; and Greenfield, 138–40. Tafari became emperor in 1928, taking the imperial name of Haile Selassie I.

121. Mittwoch (head of the NfdO), "G. A.," 6 Oct. 1916; and Radowitz (chargé d'affaires at the embassy) to AA, 13 Oct. 1916, NARA/T-137/14/0117-18, 0119.

122. For example, "Arabien und das Kalifat," *Vossische Zeitung,* 17 Oct. 1916; "Mecca without the Turks," *The Times* (London), 4 Nov. 1916; "Königreich Arabien," *Hamburger Fremdenblatt,* 16 Nov. 1916; "En Arabie. Le nouveau manifeste du chérif," *Temps,* 12 Nov. 1916; "Arabia Accuses Turks of Brutality," *The Times* (London), 3 Dec. 1916; and "New Arabia Starts Well," *The Sun* (New York), 6 Dec. 1916.

123. Mainly to regain the favor of the French and Russians; Bern legation to AA, 21 and 27 July 1916, PA/*Türkei* 165/Bd. 38. On the background and ideas of Sabaheddin, see Ahmad, *Young Turks,* 177–78; Hourani, *Arabic Thought,* 181, 263, 265, 282; and Landau, 26–29. Also, note Romberg (minister in Bern) to Bethmann Hollweg, 27 July 1916, containing a report from the specialist on Oriental affairs at the consulate in Geneva, F. Marum, 15 July 1916, NARA/T-149/0298-0302; and Wesendonk, memo, 25 June 1916, NARA/T-137/144/0930.

124. Regarding Farid and the Egyptian nationalists and students, note Lt. Col. V. G. W. Kell (WO London) to R. H. Campbell (FO), 30 Mar. 1916, PRO/FO 371/2666/61638; and Romberg to Bethmann Hollweg, 4 Nov. 1916, NARA/T-137/137/0241. On the dislike of the Turkish exiles for the Egyptians, see Romberg to Bethmann Hollweg, 6 June 1916, NARA/T-120/4952/L368309.

125. Fischer, *Germany's Aims,* 224–28; and Romberg to Bethmann Hollweg, 6, 8 May 1916, NARA/T-149/402/0830-32, 0836. Other members of the Turkish opposition party in Switzerland included Gabriel Effendi Noradunghian, a former Turkish foreign minister; Hakki Halid Bey, a previous director of the treasury in Constantinople; Izzet Pasha, formerly Turkish minister in Washington, D.C.; Lutfi Bey, once Turkish consul general in Paris; Kemal Midhat Bey, an associate of Sabaheddin; Rashid Pasha, a previous Ottoman minister of the interior; Sharif Pasha, a former general; and Jean Teuni Bey, once an official at the Turkish embassy in London.

126. Lord Drogheda, "Memorandum on Turkish Peace Overtures," 20 Nov. 1917, PRO/FO 371/3057/222199; and Romberg to Bethmann Hollweg, 10 June and 4 July

1916, NARA/T-149/403/0066, 0212. The dragomen were Alphonse Ledoulx of France and Andreas N. Mandelstam of Russia, both of whom had once served at their embassies in Constantinople.

127. Romberg to Bethmann Hollweg, 24 Aug. and 6 Oct. 1916; Marum, "Aufzeichnung," 21 Aug. 1916; and Zimmermann to Bern legation, 24 Aug. 1916, NARA/T-149/403/0415, 0510, 0436-38, 0408-09, respectively.

128. Regarding Britain's suspicions of Sabaheddin, note *Arab Bulletin*, 6(23 June 1916):50, PRO/FO 882/25; and Drogheda, "Memorandum on Turkish Peace Overtures," 20 Nov. 1917, prepared for the War Cabinet, PRO/FO 371/3057/222199.

129. The latter included August de Candolle, a member of the local British consulate general; and H. Parodi, the representative of the Egyptian education ministry. Regarding the British network, see above, 119. On Parodi and Candolle, note Romberg to Bethmann Hollweg, 27 Oct. 1916, NARA/T-149/403/0562-63; and de Candolle to Duff, 4 May 1916, PRO/FO 371/2666/71394.

130. Romberg to AA, 1 Mar. 1916, NARA/T-149/402/0738; and Romberg to Bethmann Hollweg, 2 Nov. 1916, NARA/T-149/403/0581.

131. For example, note Romberg to Bethmann Hollweg, 4 May 1916, NARA/T-149/402/0823-24; and Bern legation to Bethmann Hollweg, 28 July 1916, NARA/T-149/403/0325.

132. On 18 July the FO decided to "let matters rest till the Khedive makes further overtures." See FO to McMahon, 28 June 1916; FO to McMahon, 18 July 1916; and FO, minutes, 3 July 1916, PRO/FO 371/2672/124192, 137277, 127635, respectively.

133. Zimmermann, memo, 20 Apr. 1916; Marum, "Aufzeichnung," 10 May 1916, NARA/T-137/137/0115-16, 0129; Romberg to Bethmann Hollweg, 19 Apr. 1916, containing a memo on the meeting of an official at the German legation in Bern with the ex-khedive, NARA/T-149/402/0776-77; Weber, 180; and Landau, 106.

134. See "Switzerland," *Arab Bulletin*, 14(7 Aug. 1916):143, PRO/FO 882/25.

135. Tschirschky to Jagow, 6 July 1916, PA/*Türkei* 165/Bd. 38.

136. AA to Falkenhayn, 12 Aug. 1916; Wolff Metternich to AA, 21 and 23 July 1916; and Wesendonk, "G. A.," 1 July 1916, PA/*Türkei* 165/Bd. 38.

137. Marum, "Aufzeichnung," 4 Nov. 1916; and Romberg to Bethmann Hollweg, 10 Nov. 1916, NARA/T-137/137/0249-50, 0256. Also, note military intelligence Bern, report no. 02555, 13 Nov. 1916, IOLR/L/P&S/10/467. Regarding the spy "Bernard," who worked for another British agent in Switzerland, Somerset Maugham, see Andrew, 152.

138. Moberly, 3:71–105; and Gilbert, *First World War*, 312.

139. Rumbold to FO, 14 July 1917, IOLR/L/P&S/10/467; Rumbold to FO, 20 Dec. 1916; FO to Rumbold, 28 Nov. 1916; Rumbold to FO, 12 Dec. 1916, PRO/FO 371/2672/258482, 251857, and 254982, respectively; and James, *Golden Warrior*, 81.

9. TOWARD AN ALLIED VICTORY, 1917

1. The basic histories include Guinn, 191–96, 217–23; Woodward, 110–11, 117–20; Macmunn and Falls, *Military Operations Egypt & Palestine*, 242–373; James, *Rise and Fall of the British Empire*, 363–64 Gilbert, *First World War*, 312–13; Cyril Falls, *Armageddon: 1918*, 9–14; Stevenson, 180–81; Yapp, 286; and Kinross, 608.

2. Wallach, *Anatomie*, 238–39; and Trumpener, "German Officers," 39.

3. Hagen, 29; and on the decline of Said Halim's power already during 1915 and 1916, Trumpener, *Germany and the Ottoman Empire,* 123–26.

4. Fischer, *Germany's Aims,* 583–86.

5. Kühlmann to AA, 19 Jan. 1917; Wesendonk to embassy, 14 Mar. 1917; Prüfer to Heinrich Röttger (an official in German industry's most powerful association, the General Federation of German Industrialists), 16 Feb. 1917; Prüfer to Wesendonk, 16 Feb. 1917; and Kühlmann to Bethmann Hollweg, 1 May 1917, NARA/T-140/476/0384-88, 0425, 0398, 0399-400, 0435, respectively. Also see Oppenheim, "Die Nachrichtenstelle der Kaiserlich Deutschen Botschaft in Konstantinopel und die deutsche wirtschaftliche Propaganda in der Türkei"; Rathmann, *Stossrichtung Nahost,* 191–93; and McKale, *Curt Prüfer,* 50–52.

6. Prüfer, "Vertraulich," 12 Apr. 1917, NARA/T-149/365/0400-1; and McKale, "Germany and the Arab Question," 244–45.

7. McKale, "Germany and the Arab Question," 245.

8. Mühlmann, 157–69; and Cyril Falls, *The History of the Great War,* pt. 1, *Military Operations Egypt & Palestine from June 1917 to the End of the War,* 2–6.

9. Kühlmann to AA, 23 Feb. 1917, PA/*Türkei* 165/Bd. 41; and Wallach, *Anatomie,* 208–212.

10. Trumpener, *Germany and the Ottoman Empire,* 156–57.

11. The other issues, for example, were the Porte's resistance to unrestricted Jewish immigration and colonization rights in Palestine, and also the Turkish demand, presented by Talaat during a visit to Berlin in March 1917, that Germany sign no treaty that would restore the capitulations, whose abolition the Germans had agreed to in January 1917. See Friedman, *Germany, Turkey, and Zionism,* 283–306; and Trumpener, *Germany and the Ottoman Empire,* 130, 157.

12. A useful summary of the sporadic and unsuccessful Turkish efforts during 1917 and 1918 at approaching Husayn is Bernstorff to Georg Count von Hertling (German chancellor), 19 July 1918, PA/*Türkei* 165/Bd. 42.

13. Loytved Hardegg to Bethmann Hollweg, 5 Jan. 1917, PA/*Türkei* 165/Bd. 41.

14. James, *Golden Warrior,* 176–77; Falls, *Military Operations Egypt & Palestine,* 1:236–37; Stewart, 163; Antonius, 211; and Dawn, "Influence of T. E. Lawrence," 76.

15. Kühlmann to Bethmann Hollweg, 31 Jan. 1917, PA/*Türkei* 165/Bd. 41.

16. Kühlmann to AA, 20, 23 Feb. 1917, PA/*Türkei* 165/Bd. 41.

17. The most extensive accusation is in Kühlmann to AA, 25 Apr. 1917, PA/*Türkei* 165/Bd. 42.

18. Wesendonk, "G. A.," 13 Mar. 1917, PA/*Türkei* 165/Bd. 41; and Macmunn and Falls, *Military Operations Egypt & Palestine,* 738.

19. Mutius to Bethmann Hollweg, 19 Mar. 1917, PA/*Türkei* 165/Bd. 41.

20. Rössler to Kühlmann, 2 May, 1917, PA/*Türkei* 165/Bd. 42.

21. Arab Bureau to DMI, 17 Jan. 1917, PRO/WO 33/905; and "Arabia. Hejaz. Summary of News," *Arab Bulletin,* 37(4 Jan. 1917):4, PRO/FO 882/26.

22. See, for example, Hirtzel, "British Intersts in Arabia. B. 247.," 20 Jan. 1917, PRO/FO 371/3055/132784; and Capt. N. N. E. Bray (Indian army officer at Jidda), "A Note on the Mohammedan Question. Its Bearing on Events in India and Arabia. The Future of the Great Islamic Revival Now That Turkey Ceases to Be the Power on Which the Hopes of the Moslem World Were Placed.," 25 Mar. 1917, given by the Arab Bureau to the FO, PRO/FO 371/3057/103481.

23. A figure that was not entirely incorrect; since the end of 1916, the Germans had sent £T200,000 per month to the Turks for subsidies for the sharif and other Arab leaders in Syria, Arabia, and Mesopotamia; see above, 181, 184. Also note Wilson to director, Arab Bureau, 29 Mar. 1917, PRO/FO 882/12/KH/17/9.

24. Wilson to director, Arab Bureau, 29 Mar. 1917, PRO/FO 882/12/KH/17/9. Further, note James, *Golden Warrior*, 160, who observes that the allowance was raised in May to £200,000 per month.

25. For example, Mesopotamian GHQ intelligence, "Daily Situation Summary, 24 Apr. 1917, PRO/WO 157/798; Hogarth, "Arabia. The Next Caliphate.," *Arab Bulletin*, 49(30 Apr. 1917):192; and "Hejaz. Intelligence," *Arab Bulletin*, 49(30 Apr. 1917):193, PRO/FO 882/26. The IO objected to any discussion of the caliphate, still fearing the sensitivity of the issue among Indian Muslims and among Shiites in Mesopotamia; note J. E. Schuckburgh (IO), memo, 11 May 1917, IOLR/L/P&S/11/119.

26. Wilson to Arab Bureau, 9 Apr. 1917, PRO/FO 882/12/KH/17/11; and "Mesopotamia. Baghdad and Moslem Feeling," *Arab Bulletin*, 47(11 Apr. 1917):157-58, PRO/FO 882/26.

27. Fuad al-Khatib to Wilson, 20 Apr. 1917, PRO/FO 882/KH/17/13.

28. Busch, *Britain, India, and the Arabs*, 182. Regarding the War Cabinet, see Kennedy, *Realities Behind Diplomacy*, 176-78.

29. Adelson, 229-33; Busch, *Britain, India, and the Arabs*, 183-84; Nevakivi, 60, 63-64; and Eldar, 342-43.

30. See, for example, Stewart, 167-80; and James, *Golden Warrior*, 169-200.

31. Note Adelson, 233-36, 238-43; Gilbert, *First World War*, 373; Eldar, 345-46; Stevenson, chapter 4; Dawn, "Influence of T. E. Lawrence," 78-79; and Yapp, 291-92.

32. Paul Johnson, *A History of the Jews*, 429-31.

33. According to Nevakivi, 59, Storrs, the Oriental secretary at the British Residency in Cairo, estimated that British aid to the sharif amounted during the entire revolt to £11 million. Also see Antonius, 218-26; Macmunn and Falls, *Military Operations Egypt & Palestine*, 239-41; James, *Golden Warrior*, 188-214; and Stewart, chapters 16-17.

34. Romberg to Bethmann Hollweg, 2 Jan. 1917; and Bern legation to Bethmann Hollweg, 29 Dec. 1916, NARA/T-149/403/0706 and 0689, respectively.

35. As examples, see Romberg to AA, 17 May 1917; and Wedel (official at the Vienna embassy) to Bethmann Hollweg, 24 Apr. 1917, NARA/T-137/138/0115 and 0113, respectively. Note, moreover, Baron von Richthofen (member of the German parliament) to Abbas Hilmi, 16 May 1917, NARA/T-137/137/0355.

36. The relevant files for February-November 1918 are in PRO/FO 371/3200/36431, 133692, 176350, and 188576. Also, see Rumbold to FO, 14 July 1917, IOLR/L/P&S/10/467.

37. Bern legation to Reich chancellor, 19 Sept. 1917 ("Inhalt: Prinz Abdoul Mouneim"), NARA/T-137/138/0200.

38. John Darwin, *Britain, Egypt and the Middle East: Imperial Policy in the Aftermath of War, 1918-1922*, 67. For British apprehensions about Turkey's use of the ex-khedive in the Arab question, note Rumbold to Balfour, 10 Oct. 1917, IOLR/L/P&S/10/467; and Wingate (high commissioner in Cairo) to FO, 17 Oct. 1917, PRO/FO 371/3057/199502. The ex-khedive arrived in Constantinople on 20 Oct. 1917; Pomiankowski, 301.

39. Johann Heinrich Count von Bernstorff (German ambassador) to the Reich chancellor, 11 Dec. 1917 ("Inhalt. Der Khedive."), NARA/T-137/138/0254; McKale, "Germany and the Arab Question," 243; and War Office (G/East/111), 22 Dec. 1917, enclosing a report from its Geneva bureau on pan-Turanism and pan-Germanism, PRO/WO 106 (Intelligence)/file no. 1420.

40. Rumbold to Balfour, 16 Nov. 1917, PRO/FO 371/3058/223845; McKale, "Germany and the Arab Question," 244. Regarding British concern that the Turks were using Abbas Hilmi with the sharif and his son, Faysal, note Wingate to FO, 24 Dec. 1917, IOLR/L/P&S/10/467.

41. Wingate to FO, 17 Oct. 1917, PRO/FO 371/3057/199502.

42. Romberg to Georg Michaelis (Reich chancellor), 25 July 1917; AA to Constantinople embassy, 8 Aug. 1917; Romberg to AA, 9 and 11 Aug. 1917; and Waldburg to AA, 13 Aug. 1917, NARA/T-149/404/0155, 0176, 0179, 0184, 0209. Further, note Waldburg to AA, 19 Aug. 1917, PA/*Türkei* 165/Bd. 42.

43. Bernstorff to Michaelis, 10 Sept. 1917; and Romberg to AA, 14 Sept. 1917, NARA/ T-149/404/0278, 0276, respectively.

44. Note the Sektion Politik memo, "Vernehmung des Seid Ahmed Nakib am 24.9.17.," NARA/T-149/404/0288-91; and British General Staff, WO, "Summary of the Hejaz Revolt," 31 Aug. 1918, particularly appendix E, "Maurice's Report," in IOLR/L/ MIL/17/16/13.

45. WO, "Summary of the Hejaz Revolt," 31 Aug. 1918, IOLR/L/MIL/17/16/13.

46. Examples are probably DMI to Arab Bureau, 12 Sept. 1917, PRO/WO 33/935; and Rumbold to FO, 25 Oct. 1917, IOLR/L/P&S/11/P4340. Also, note WO, "Summary of the Hejaz Revolt," 31 Aug. 1918, IOLR/L/MIL/17/16/13; and James, *Golden Warrior*, 230.

47. See Hesse (then in Berlin), memo, 10 Aug. 1917; and Wustrow (the dragoman at the consulate in Mosul) to AA, 1 Aug. 1917, PA/*Türkei* 165/Bd. 42.

48. "Enemy Intelligence on the Euphrates.," *Arab Bulletin*, 98(23 July 1918):257–59, PRO/FO 882/27.

49. Ibid.; Mesopotamia Expedition Force [hereafter "MEF"], "Daily Situation Summary," 10 and 26 Oct. 1917, PRO/WO 157/804; Moberly, 4:32–65; and McKale, "Germany and the Arab Question," 245.

50. MEF, "War Diary," 9 and 20 Oct. 1917, PRO/WO 157/804; Cox to Government of India, 24 Jan. 1917, IOLR/L/P&S/10/617; and Winstone, *Leachman*, 194–95.

51. See the MEF's "War Diary" for Dec. 1917, in PRO/WO 157/806.

52. Kedourie, *England and the Middle East*, 107; and Antonius, 227, 230.

53. Vogel, 26–30; and mention of Niedermayer in Syria in Bernstorff to AA, 23 Dec. 1917, NARA/T-137/142/0032. Niedermayer had gone to Syria after plans for him to lead a second expedition to Persia and Afghanistan had been given up; Army Group F to AA, 4 Nov. 1917, NARA/T-149/400/0118.

54. Prüfer, "Abschrift. Nachrichtenstelle der Kaiserlich Deutschen Botschaft Konstantinopel.," 11 Dec. 1917, NARA/T-120/4197/K203215-216.

55. Regarding the killing of a German officer working with the Sixth Army near Mosul, see Waldburg to AA, 23 Aug. 1917, PA/*Türkei* 165/Bd. 42. Also, note Wallach, *Anatomie*, 209–20, 228–29; and Mühlmann, 167–72. On Falkenhayn's takeover of much of the command in Palestine from Jemal Pasha, see above, 202.

56. Friedman, *Germany, Turkey, and Zionism*, 329–30; and Wallach, *Anatomie*, 213–14.

57. Contained in Bernstorff to AA, 16 Nov. 1917, PA/*Türkei* 165/Bd. 42.

58. Wingate to FO, 24 Dec. 1917, IOLR/L/P&S/10/467; and Antonius, 227–28.

59. Wingate to FO, 24 Dec. 1917, IOLR/L/P&S/10/467; Stewart, 178; Yapp, 285; and Fromkin, 221.

60. See the account of the speech in *Arab Bulletin*, 77(27 Jan. 1918):32, PRO/FO 882/27; and Kedourie, *England and the Middle East*, 107.

61. Evans-Pritchard, 141–42; and Col. M. G. Talbot, "Report on the Negotiations of the Anglo-Italian Mission with Mohammed Idris-el-Mahdi-el-Senussi (January, February, March, and April 1917).," PRO/FO 371/2670/198793.

62. Wesendonk, "G. A.," 8 Nov. 1917, NARA/T-120/4197/K203156-157; Sektion Politik to AA, 13 June and 10 Aug. 1917; and "Abschrift. Bericht des Leiters der Expedition Mirr, Rittmeister Frhr. von Todenwarth, in Misrata (Tripolis). Militärisches.," NARA/T-137/6/0153, 0165, 0188.

63. See, for example, "Libya.," *Arab Bulletin*, 64(27 Sept. 1917):394; and "Libya. Situation in Cyrenaica and Tripolitania.," *Arab Bulletin*, 71(27 Nov. 1917):478-79, in PRO/FO 882/26.

64. According to Farwell, 310, the British had about eighty thousand men, while the Germans had less than ten thousand; also note Boahen, 7:133. On the whereabouts of Lij Iyasu, see Marcus, 117. During the fall of 1917, the Italians caused Britain momentary concern when they reported that Iyasu was trying to reach the Arabian coast. Note Italian embassy, "Ethiopia," 5 Oct. 1917; FO to Thesiger, 16 Oct. 1917; and Thesiger to FO, 18 Oct. 1917, IOLR/L/P&S/11/128.

65. The plan was discussed in Adolf Müller (German minister in Switzerland) to AA, 12 June 1919 ("Inhalt. Abessinien."), which enclosed a memo by a previous resident of Abyssinia, Dr. Weinzinger, "Betrifft Abessinien.," 12 June 1919, NARA/T-137/14/0136-38.

66. Thesiger to Balfour, 22 Feb. 1917, PRO/FO 371/2855/68793; Bertie to FO, 3 June 1917; and Thesiger to FO, 5 June 1917, IOLR/L/P&S/11/122/P1988.

67. "Abyssinia," *Arab Bulletin*, 62(8 Sept. 1917):375-76 and 63(18 Sept. 1917):384, PRO/FO 882/26; and Bertie to FO, 10 July 1917, IOLR/L/P&S/11/122/P1988.

68. Campbell (Addis Abeba) to FO, 11 Dec. 1917, PRO/FO 371/2855/237723; and "Germans from Abyssinia.," *Arab Bulletin*, 72(5 Dec. 1917):493, PRO/FO 882/26. The Abyssinian regime was one of dual authority, in which power was shared between the empress and the regent, each with his or her own, often conflicting, policies. See Boahen, 7:305; and Marcus, 117-19.

69. Rathmann, *Stossrichtung Nahost*, 76-79; and Fischer, *Germany's Aims*, 359.

70. Kheiry to German foreign secretary, 1 May 1917; and Waldburg to Michaelis, 10 Aug. 1917, NARA/T-149/400/0039-43, 0013, respectively.

71. AA to German legation Stockholm, 12 Nov. 1917; Chattopadhyaya to Berlin Indian committee, 1 Nov. 1917, enclosing a document, "Projekt einer russisch-indischen Annäherung;" and committee to Wesendonk, 31 Dec. 1917, NARA/T-149/400/0122, 0123-26, 0271-72, 0277. Also see Indian committee to Wesendonk, 3 and 7 Feb. 1917, NARA/T-149/399/0435-38, 0447-48. Regarding the Stockholm conference, Stevenson, 156-62, is useful. For the German response to the conference, note Herzfeld, 224; and for Britain, Guinn, 235.

72. Quoted in Bernstorff to AA, 19 Jan. 1917, NARA/T-149/399/0417.

73. Dignan, 73-74. On Chakravarty's activities in the United States, note Berlin Indian committee to Wesendonk, 15 Mar. 1917, enclosing a letter from Chakravarty at

the end of 1916, NARA/T-149/399/0570-71. Regarding the arrest of Igel and capture of his papers, see above, 190.

74. Dignan, 57–58, 74.

75. Wesendonk, "Abschrift," 18 July 1917, NARA/T-149/399/0867.

76. Bern legation to Bethmann Hollweg, 16 Mar. 1917; Romberg to Bethmann Hollweg, 23 Mar. 1917, NARA/T-149/403/0821, 0864; and AA to Bern legation, 16 Apr. 1917, NARA/T-149/399/0634-35. For Gifford's background and recruitment by the Germans, note Romberg to Bethmann Hollweg, 22 Aug. 1915, NARA/T-149/402/0585-89.

77. Datta (general secretary of the committee) to Hertling, 30 Nov. 1917, NARA/T-149/400/0196-203.

78. The standard work on German war objectives, especially those of the army by 1917-1918 regarding Asia and the Middle East, is still Fischer, *Germany's Aims,* chapters 16–18, 20. Also, see Herwig, *First World War,* 374, 382–83.

79. See Guinn, chapters 9–10; and Stevenson, 139–95. Also the British finally announced in December 1917 that they had cleared the enemy out of his last African colony; Farwell, 317–18.

80. See Guinn, 283, which quotes from the prime minister's speech to Parliament on 20 December 1917, about the importance to the British Empire of the capture of Baghdad and Jerusalem. In addition, note James, *Rise and Fall of the British Empire,* 364.

81. Nevakivi, 48.

82. The feelers are summarized in Drogheda, "Memorandum on Turkish Peace Overtures," 20 Nov. 1917, prepared for the War Cabinet, PRO/FO 371/3057/222199.

83. See the standard work on the subject, Trumpener, *Germany and the Ottoman Empire,* 158 66; and Fromkin, 266–67. Also the British noted the wish by the Turks to place pressure on Germany; Rumbold to FO, PRO/FO 371/3388/10743.

84. This bizarre episode is documented in PRO/FO 371/3057/195257 and 198834.

85. Trumpener, *Germany and the Ottoman Empire,* 165.

86. Rumbold to FO, 27 July 1917, IOLR/L/P&S/11/125.

87. For this reason, in July Sykes had assisted the French and Zionists in halting the peace mission to Turkey of Henry Morgenthau, the former American ambassador to the Porte. Note Adelson, 234–35; Wingate to FO, 1 July 1917; FO to Spring Rice (British ambassador in Washington), 19 July 1917; and the extensive "Memorandum By Sir Mark Sykes," 29 July 1917, PRO/FO 371/3057/130633, 138184, 149776.

88. Sykes to Sir Maurice Hankey (secretary to the War Cabinet), 14 Nov. 1917, PRO/FO 371/3057/225559.

89. FO to Rumbold, 21 Dec. 1917, PRO/FO 371/3057/241322. Also see Guinn, 277.

90. "We are very anxious to secure peace with Turkey," the FO informed the minister on 1 January 1918, PRO/FO 371/3057/245518.

91. Rumbold to FO, 16 and 24 Jan. 1918, PRO/FO 371/3388/10743, 16415.

10. EPILOGUE: THE WAR'S END, 1918

1. Bernstorff to AA, 19 Jan. 1918, PA/*Türkei* 165/Bd. 42. Also see Dawn, "Influence of T. E. Lawrence," 79.

2. During March and April 1918, Ottoman forces invaded Transcaucasia, causing conflict with the Germans, who also viewed central Asia as a field for future expan-

sionism. See Trumpener, *Germany and the Ottoman Empire,* chapter 6; and Wallach, *Anatomie,* 241–44. Fromkin, 352, mentions that Enver's emphasis on pan-Turanism particularly increased with the collapse of tsarist Russia.

3. Niedermayer, "Zentralasien. Beurteilung der Lage und unseres Vorgehens," May 1918, NARA/T-137/142/0095; Vogel, 30; and Mühlmann, 217, 218.

4. The figures are in Antonius, 231–33. Also see the summaries of this much-discussed story in Macmunn and Falls, *Military Operations Egypt & Palestine,* 2:395–421; Woodward, 121–22; James, *Golden Warrior,* 238–46; Stewart, 198–99; Guinn, 307; and Dawn, "Influence of T. E. Lawrence," 79. For different estimates among the British on the value of the Arab revolt west of the Jordan River, note Fromkin, 328.

5. Wallach, *Anatomie,* 222–26; and Mühlmann, 213–19. According to the latter, General Hans von Seeckt, the German chief of staff of the Turkish army, denied to Berlin that the Turks were robbing the Palestine and Syrian fronts to favor Transcaucasia.

6. See Papen to Bernstorff, 24 May 1918, in Johann Heinrich Andreas Hermann Albrecht, Graf von Bernstorff, *Memoirs of Count Bernstorff,* trans. Eric Sutton, 213.

7. Ibid., 213–14.

8. Bernstorff to Papen, 14 June 1918, ibid., 215.

9. Papen to Bernstorff, 18 July 1918, ibid.

10. The British official history of the war, published in 1930, concluded that Husayn's views "did not affect the Northern Army" of Faysal; note Macmunn and Falls, *Military Operations Egypt & Palestine,* 2:411. See also, Busch, *Britain, India, and the Arabs,* 191–96; Adelson, 247; and Stewart, 192–93.

11. Arab Bureau to DMI, 4 Jan. 1918, PRO/WO 33/946.

12. A point mentioned by Fromkin, 328–29.

13. Eldar, 345–46. According to Nevakivi, 64: "Experience had shown in the course of 1918 that the French were quite unprepared to face the approaching peace settlement in Asiatic Turkey. In comparison with the gigantic British armies in Palestine and in Mesopotamia, they had fragmentary though well qualified units in Arabia, a small detachment in Palestine, and a half-trained Syro-Armenian voluntary force in Cyprus, from where it was sent only at the last moment of the war to the front in Palestine."

14. Quoted in Bernstorff to Hertling, 19 July 1918, PA/*Türkei* 165/Bd. 42.

15. See his memo, "Berlin, den 28. Juli 1918.," PA/*Türkei* 165/Bd. 42.

16. Bernstorff to AA, 22 Aug. 1918; and Berckheim (the AA's liaison at Germany's supreme military headquarters) to AA, 22 Aug. 1918, PA/*Türkei* 165/Bd. 43.

17. Quoted in Berckheim to AA, 22 Aug. 1918, PA/*Türkei* 165/Bd. 43.

18. Ibid.

19. Quoted in Berckheim to AA, 1 Sept. 1918, PA/*Türkei* 165/Bd. 43.

20. Constantinople embassy to AA, 4 Sept. 1918; and Berckheim to AA, 1 Sept. 1918, PA/*Türkei* 165/Bd. 43. On Seeckt, note Trumpener, "German Officers," 38.

21. Falls, *Military Operations Egypt & Palestine,* 2:468–625; Mühlmann, 226–34; and Gilbert, *First World War,* 463–65, 469, 484.

22. Moberly, *Campaign in Mesopotamia,* 4:258–332.

23. For the connection of the military to such civilian elements and the latter's massive membership figures, note Herwig, *Hammer or Anvil?* 216; Fischer, *Germany's Aims,* 431–34, 586–90; and Hillgruber, 44. Also see Rathmann, *Stossrichtung Nahost,*

72-73, 79, about the continuing ambitions of German leaders during 1917-18 in central Africa and the Indian Ocean.

24. Prüfer, "Krieg," entry for 30 June 1918, Prüfer Papers/HIWRP; and McKale, *Curt Prüfer*, 54.

25. Prüfer to AA, 1 Aug. 1918; Bernstorff to Hertling, 27 Apr. 1918, Romberg to AA, 2 Oct. 1918, NARA/T-137/138/0307, 0282, 0339, respectively; and McKale, *Curt Prüfer*, 54-55. Regarding German attempts to woo the ex-khedive's son, Abd al-Moneim, from Switzerland to Germany, note Prüfer, memo, 3 Sept. 1918, PA/*Nachlass* Curt Prüfer/*Politische Aufsätze;* and Prüfer, "Krieg," entry for 17 Aug. 1918, Prüfer Papers/HIWRP.

26. Bernstorff to AA, 27 Aug. 1918; Waldburg to Hertling, 16 Sept. 1918; and AA to Constantinople embassy, 29 Sept. 1918, NARA/T-137/6/0261, 0264, 0266.

27. Hagen (submarine commander), "Bericht über die Ausführung des Transport nach Misrata und über die Lage in Tripolis im Oktober/November 1918.," NARA/T-137/6/0273-274.

28. Chattopadhyaya's anti-British and pro-Indian propaganda had attracted the attention of the Bolsheviks and their negotiator at the Russo-German peace talks at Brest Litovsk, Leon Trotsky, who promised the Indian safe travel to Petrograd. See German legation Stockholm to AA, 14, 23 Jan. 1914; and Har Dayal to Datta, 18 Mar. 1918, NARA/T-149/400/0288, 303, 0434. Also, note Herwig, *First World War*, 382, on Trotsky's calling on Britain and France to apply the doctrine of self-determination to Ireland, Egypt, India, Madagascar, and Indochina.

29. Wesendonk, "G. A.," 6 Feb. 1918; and Freiherr Hilmar von dem Bussche-Haddenhausen (under secretary of state in the AA) to Stockholm legation, 19 Feb. 1918, NARA/T-149/400/0351-52, 0363-64.

30. AA to Stockholm legation, 27 Feb. 1918, NARA/T-149/400/0371-72; Rathmann, *Stossrichtung Nahost*, 70-71; and Fischer, *Germany's Aims*, 586-87.

31. Both the AA and German police, suspicious of the loyalty of the revolutionaries in Germany, kept them under surveillance. Note Glasenapp, "G. A.," 2 Mar. 1918; and Berlin Indian committee to Wesendonk, 26 Mar. 1918, NARA/T-149/400/0384, 0439.

32. While returning in 1917 through Russia to Germany, Pratap had met Trotsky and other Bolshevik leaders. See Grünau to AA, 8 Apr. 1918; "Oberkommando A.A. d. N.O. Nr. 5602 to AA," 22 Mar. 1918; AA to Grünau, Sektion Politik, Stockholm and Bern legations, and Vienna embassy, 27 Mar. 1918; Wesendonk, "G. A.," 27 Mar. 1918; Pratap, "For the gracious perusal of His Imperial Majesty the Emperor of the German Empire. An account of the trip from Berlin to Berlin through Turkey, Persia, Afghanistan, and Russia.," 2 Apr. 1918; and Hentig to AA, 3 Apr. 1918, NARA/T-149/400/0492, 0416, 0419-20, 0437-38, 0457-66, 0519-25, respectively.

33. Trumpener, *Germany and the Ottoman Empire*, 352-53; and Gilbert, *First World War*, 484-85.

34. Elie Kedourie, "Great Britain, the Other Powers, and the Middle East Before and After World War I," in *The Great Powers in the Middle East, 1919-1939*, ed. Uriel Dann, 3. Repeated mention of the hostility toward the Germans among the Turks and Arabs is in the issues of the *Arab Bulletin* from 1918, PRO/FO 882/vol. 27; and Wallach, *Anatomie*, 244-49. On the escape of the Young Turk leaders to Germany in Nov. 1918, notably with the aid of Seeckt (later the chief of the German high command, from 1920 to 1926), see Trumpener, *Germany and the Ottoman Empire*, 358-64.

35. Note, U.S. Government, *The Treaty of Versailles and After: Annotations of the Text of the Treaty*.

36. The principal published sources are Lukasz Hirszowicz, "The Course of German Foreign Policy in the Middle East between the World Wars," in *The Great Powers in the Middle East, 1919–1939*, ed. Uriel Dann (New York: Holmes and Meier, 1988),175–89; and Bernd Philipp Schröder, *Deutschland und der Mittlere Osten im Zweiten Weltkrieg*, 17–28. The objectives of German foreign policy in the Weimar years are outlined in Werner Weidenfeld, *Die Englandpolitik Gustav Stresemanns. Theoretische und praktische Aspekte der Aussenpolitik*, 36–61.

37. Prüfer, memo, 23 Nov. 1918; Jawish to Wesendonk, 25 Nov. 1918, NARA/T-120/ 4953/L368572-573, L368575-576; and Reich treasury office, "Im Anschluss an das Schreibens von 6.d.M.," 27 Nov. 1918, NARA/T-149/365/0002. Regarding postwar arrangements for Indian revolutionaries, see Glasenapp, "Bericht über meine amtliche Reise nach Stockholm.," 7 Dec. 1918; Indian Committee to Wesendonk, 13 Nov. 1918; and Glasenapp, "Bericht über meine Reise nach Stockholm und die dortigen Verhandlungen mit dem Indischen Nationalkomitee," n.d., NARA/T-149/400/0800- 05, 0848-53, 0651-63, respectively.

38. In March 1917 conflict between the sharif and al-Masri had led to the latter's dismissal from his command and return to Cairo. An Arab nationalist, al-Masri had held an ambiguous position toward the Arab revolt. At the war's beginning he told the British that he favored the creation of a united Arab state, independent of Turkey. But during May 1915 he had approached the Germans, urging the preservation of the Ottoman Empire, giving Turks and Arabs as well as other nationalities autonomous status. He advocated collaboration with Germany because he believed it would support such an Ottoman state and because he saw that a British victory would endanger Ottoman unity. In April 1918, after the British High Commissioner in Cairo, Wingate, had allowed al-Masri to go to Spain, he contacted the German embassy in Madrid. Although the Germans disagreed over al-Masri's political reliability, after the war they believed him useful—in the words of the AA—"for German policy in Arabia," and paid him accordingly. See AA, "G. A.," 6 Aug. 1919; Bassewitz (chargé d'affaires at the Madrid embassy) to AA, 23 Jan. 1919; Count Wedel (AA) to Sektion Politik, 13 Apr. 1918; AA to Sektion Politik, 23 June 1918; and AA (Wesendonk) to Sektion Politik, 19 Oct. 1918, NARA/T-120/4953/L368595, L368597, L368493-494, L368515-516, L368555-557, respectively. Also, see Prüfer to AA, 11 Aug. 1918, PA/*Türkei* 165/Bd. 43; Khadduri, 12–13; and Jankowski, "Egypt and Early Arab Nationalism," 257. For his contacting the Germans in 1915, note above, 116. Also during 1918, al-Masri visited Sir Arthur Hardinge, the British ambassador in Madrid; the FO called him a "dangerous pro-Turk" who would "play havoc with our plans" and cautioned the ambassador toward him. Nevertheless, the British paid and retained contact with al-Masri. See the FO minutes on Hardinge to Balfour, 14 Jan. 1918; Hardinge to FO, 4 May 1918; FO, memo, May 1918, with Wingate to FO, 5 May 1918, and FO minutes attached; and WO to FO, 23 Sept. 1918, PRO/FO 371/3396/14436, 79524, 79673, 161448.

39. Bern legation to AA, 8 Jan. 1919, NARA/T-149/365/0006; and AA, memo, 4 Sept. 1919, NARA/T-120/4953/L368630.

40. See above, 274 n.45. According to James, *Rise and Fall of the British Empire*, 367, at the war's end some "306,000 imperial troops including 92,000 Indians and 20,000

Australians were deployed in Egypt, Palestine, and Syria. There were 220,000 soldiers serving in Mesopotamia, of whom 120,000 were Indian and 102,000 British. There were over a third of a million native labourers working on the lines of communication throughout the Middle East."

41. Kedourie, "Great Britain, the Other Powers, and the Middle East," 3. Summaries of the peace settlements are in Nevakivi, 240–60; Aaron S. Klieman, *Foundations of British Policy in the Arab World: The Cairo Conference of 1921,* chapters 2–9; Macfie, 65–75; and Fromkin, 493–568.

42. The extensive literature on this subject is in the bibliography provided by Ovendale, 309–15. Also see Fromkin, 415–65; and Darwin, 67–79.

43. Weinberg, 12. Also, the expansion of Britain's War Cabinet in 1918 into an Imperial War Cabinet reflected the new influence of the Dominions and India; see Kennedy, *Realities Behind Diplomacy,* 177–78.

44. See Monroe; Hourani, "*The Arab Awakening* Forty Years After," 22; Reynolds, chapter 4; and Macfie, 79–81.

BIBLIOGRAPHY

A Comment on Archival Sources

Much of this study is based on large collections of unpublished records from before and during World War I, in German, British, and American archives. On the German side, the bulk of the documents used are from the German foreign ministry (*Auswärtiges Amt*, AA). A substantial portion of its records from 1867 to 1920 have been microfilmed, with most of the films located in the National Archives and Records Administration, Washington, D.C. (NARA). These sources were filmed by a joint Anglo-American and French team in the United Kingdom as well as by several universities and other institutions both in the United Kingdom and in the United States. Microfilms used in this study are cited according to their microcopy, reel, and frame numbers (e.g., T-137/143/0423).

The major collection of these records for the Middle East is microcopy T-137 (filmed by the University of Michigan). It contains materials on German pan-Islamic and anti-British activities before and during World War I in Turkey (including Syria, Arabia, and Mesopotamia), Egypt, Libya (the Sanussis), Persia, and Afghanistan. Also, interspersed throughout the collection is a modest, but useful, amount of correspondence during World War I between the AA and highest offices of the German army and navy. Few such army records (which come from the reserve section of the German General Staff, responsible for organizing the army's political operations in foreign countries), survived World War II.

A less substantial, but nevertheless crucial, collection for this study is microcopy T-149 (filmed by the American Historical Association); it contains war records on the AA's Information Service for the East (NfdO) and on German operations in Switzerland, Persia, and Afghanistan, and on those aimed at India. Microcopy T-136 (filmed by St. Antony's College, Oxford) has material on Abyssinia; T-120 (records received by the U.S. Department of State) on Libya (the Sanussis), Egypt, Syria, and Arabia; and T-140 (filmed by the University of California) on the NfdO.

The originals of these documents are deposited in the *Politisches Archiv des Auswärtigen Amts* in Bonn (PA). Most important for this book are the collections that possess the following references *(Aktenzeichen): Ägypten; Türkei 165 (Arabien); Weltkrieg Nr.11g (Unternehmungen und Aufwiegelungen gegen unsere Feinde in Ägypten, Syrien und Arabien); Weltkrieg Nr. 11g Geheim (Ägypten, Syrien und Arabien);* and *Nachlass* Curt Prüfer. These documents are cited by reference name and volume (e.g., *Ägypten* 1/Bd. 21).

In Britain the principal archive is the Public Record Office in London (PRO), which holds the enormous collections of Foreign Office political papers (FO 371) and War Office documents (WO). A vast secondary literature exists on British policy in the Middle East before and during World War I, and it is used significantly in this book; notwithstanding, much in the sections on Britain rests on FO 371 papers for Abyssinia, Egypt, Persia, Switzerland, Turkey, and the United States. The records used in this study are cited according to their collection, piece number, and file (e.g., FO 371/452/24070).

Also, the PRO has records of the Arab Bureau in Cairo (FO 882), an agency that received intelligence information from British offices and operatives throughout northern and eastern Africa, Arabia, and Syria. This group of documents includes the *Arab Bulletin,* the bureau's intelligence summaries. Available as well are the consular papers (FO 395). Several WO collections provide valuable military and intelligence material on the Arab revolt, security measures in Egypt, and the Gallipoli, Mesopotamian, and Palestine campaigns: WO 33 (Reports and Miscellaneous Papers), WO 106 (Directorate of Military Operations and Intelligence, 1837-1960), and WO 157 (Intelligence Summaries, 1914-1921).

Of further use for studying British policy toward Afghanistan, India, Mesopotamia, Persia, and the Persian Gulf, are papers of the India Office (IO) and Government of India, deposited at the India Office Library and Records in London (IOLR). The IOLR's extensive IO Political and Secret Department files (L/P and S) contain material on German propaganda and other political activities in India and neighboring lands.

In the United States, in addition to the microfilms located in the NARA, the other major archives used for this book are the Hoover Institution on War, Revolution, and Peace at Stanford University (HIWRP) and the Yale University Library, New Haven, Connecticut (YUL). The former holds the diaries and other papers of Curt Prüfer, a German consular and intelligence agent in the Middle East before and during World War I. Prüfer worked with or met most of the principal German and Turkish figures. For its part, the Yale University Library holds the papers of Ernst Jäckh, a German journalist, academic, and member during World War I of the diplomatic service. This collection for the war years includes the secret cables and reports from Constantinople of the German naval attaché, Hans Humann; Max von Oppenheim's memorandum on inciting the Islamic world to holy war against the Entente; information about Muslims used by German intelligence; and the Armenian massacres of 1915–1917, as reported to the German ambassador in Constantinople, Hans von Wangenheim, by observers in Asia Minor and by him to the AA. Another archive consulted for this study was the U.S. Military History Institute at the U.S. Army War College, Carlisle Barracks, Pennsylvania; it has papers of Edward Davis, an American officer who visited Egypt before World War I.

Guides, Archives Inventories, Bibliographies, and Other Reference Works

American Historical Association, Committee for the Study of War Documents. *A Catalogue of Files and Microfilms of the German Foreign Ministry Archives, 1867–1920.* New York: Oxford University Press, 1959.

Kent, George O. *A Catalog of the Files and Microfilms of the German Foreign Ministry Archives, 1920–1945.* 4 vols. Stanford, Calif.: Hoover Institution on War, Revolution and Peace, 1962–1973.

Newspapers, Journals, and Other Serials

Abendblatt der Frankfurter Zeitung
Berliner Lokal-Anzeiger
Berliner Tageblatt
The Civil and Military Gazette
Daily Chronicle (London)

Hamburger Fremdenblatt
Hamburger Montagsblatt
Le Journal du Caire (Cairo)
Kölnische Zeitung
The Morning Post (London)
National Zeitung (Berlin)
Neue Freie Presse (Vienna)
Neue Preussische Zeitung (Berlin)
The New York Times
Norddeutsche Allgemeine Zeitung (Hamburg)
The Standard (London)
The Sun (New York)
Der Tag (Berlin)
Temps (Paris)
The Times (London)
The Times of India (Bombay)
Vossische Zeitung (Berlin)

Memoirs, Diaries, Handbooks, Atlases, and Pamphlets

Adams, Michael, ed. *The Middle East: Handbooks to the Modern World.* New York and Oxford: Facts on File Publications, 1988.

Bernstorff, Johann Heinrich Andreas Hermann Albrecht, Graf von. *Memoirs of Count Bernstorff.* Trans. Eric Sutton. New York: Random House, 1936.

Brémond, Edouard. *Le Hedjaz dans la guerre mondiale.* Paris: Payot, 1931.

Bülow, Bernhard Prince von. *Memoirs of Prince von Bülow.* 2 vols. Boston: Little, Brown, 1931.

Djemal Pasha. *Memories of a Turkish Statesman, 1913–1919.* London: Hutchinson, n.d.

German Intrigues in Persia. The Diary of a German Agent. The Niedermayer Expedition through Persia to Afghanistan and India. Trans. from the German. London: Hodder and Stoughton, 1918.

Gilbert, Martin. *Atlas of World War I: The Complete History.* 2nd ed. New York: Oxford University Press, 1994.

Glasenapp, Helmut von. *Meine Lebensreise. Menschen, Länder und Dinge, die ich sah.* Wiesbaden: F. A. Brockhaus, 1964.

Hentig, Werner Otto von. *Mein Leben eine Dienstreise.* Göttingen: Vandenhoeck und Ruprecht, 1962.

Kress von Kressenstein, Friedrich Freiherr. *Mit den Türken zum Suezkanal.* Berlin: Vorhut-Verlag, 1938.

Lawrence, T. E. *Seven Pillars of Wisdom: A Triumph.* New York and London: Anchor Books, 1991; first pub. 1926.

Lührs, Hans. *Gegenspieler des Obersten Lawrence.* 9th ed. Berlin: Vorhut-Verlag, 1936.

Niedermayer, Oskar von. *Im Weltkrieg vor Indiens Toren: Der Wüstenzug der deutsche Expedition nach Persien und Afganistan.* 3rd ed. Hamburg: Hanseatische Verlagsanstalt, 1942.

———. *Unter der Glutsonne Irans. Kriegserlebnisse der deutschen Expedition nach Persien und Afghanistan.* Munich: Einhornverlag, 1925.

Oppenheim, Max von. "Die Nachrichtenstelle der Kaiserlich Deutschen Botschaft in Konstantinopel und die deutsche wirtschaftliche Propaganda in der Türkei." Berlin: Reichsdruckerei, 1916.

Pfanmüller, Gustav, ed. *Handbuch der Islam-Literatur.* Berlin and Leipzig: Walter de Gruyter, 1923.

Pomiankowski, Joseph. *Der Zusammenbruch des Ottomanischen Reiches. Erinnerungen an die Türkei aus der Zeit des Weltkrieges.* Zurich: Amalthea-Verlag, 1928.

Robinson, Francis. *Atlas of the Islamic World since 1500.* New York: Facts on File, 1989.

Storrs, Ronald. *Orientations.* London: Nicholson and Watson, 1943.

Stuhlmann, Franz. *Der Kampf um Arabien zwischen der Türkei und England.* Hamburg, Braunschweig, Berlin: Verlag Georg Westermann, n.d.

Documentary Collections

Great Britain. Foreign Office. *Correspondence Respecting Events Leading to the Rupture of Relations with Turkey, November 1914.* London: His Majesty's Stationery Office, 1914.

Die Grosse Politik der Europäischen Kabinette 1871–1914. Sammlung der Diplomatischen Akten des Auswärtigen Amtes. Ed. Johannes Lepsius, Albrecht Mendelssohn Bartholdy, and Friedrich Thimme. 40 vols. Berlin: Deutsche Verlagsgesellschaft für Politik und Geschichte, 1925–1926.

Lawrence, T. E. *The Home Letters of T. E. Lawrence and His Brothers.* New York: Macmillan, 1954.

———. *Secret Despatches from Arabia by T. E. Lawrence.* London: Golden Cockerel Press, n.d.

Levine, Isaac Don. *Letters From the Kaiser to the Czar: Copies from Government Archives in Petrograd Unpublished before 1920.* New York: Frederick A. Stokes, 1920.

United States. *Papers Relating to the Foreign Relations of the United States,* 1915, Supplement to the World War. Washington, D.C.: U.S. Government Printing Office, 1928.

United States. Department of State. *The Treaty of Versailles and After: Annotations of the Text of the Treaty.* Washington, D.C.: U.S. Government Printing Office, 1947.

Secondary Sources

Adamec, Ludwig. *Afghanistan's Foreign Affairs to the Mid-Twentieth Century: Relations with the USSR, Germany, and Britain.* Tucson: University of Arizona Press, 1974.

Adelson, Roger. *Mark Sykes: Portrait of an Amateur.* London: Jonathan Cape, 1975.

Ahmad, Feroz. "The Late Ottoman Empire." In Marian Kent, ed., *The Great Powers and the End of the Ottoman Empire.* London: George Allen and Unwin, 1984, 5–30.

———. *The Young Turks: The Committee of Union and Progress in Turkish Politics, 1908–1914.* Oxford: Oxford University Press, 1969.

Andersen, Roy R., Robert F. Seibert, and Jon G. Wagner. *Politics and Change in the Middle East: Sources of Conflict and Accommodation.* 3rd ed. Englewood Cliffs, N.J., 1990.

Anderson, Lisa. "The Development of Nationalist Sentiment in Libya, 1908–1922." In Rashid Khalidi, Lisa Anderson, Muhammad Muslih, and Reeva S. Simon, ed., *The Origins of Arab Nationalism.* New York: Columbia University Press, 1991, 225–42.

Anderson, M. S. *The Eastern Question, 1774–1923: A Study in International Relations.* New York: Macmillan, 1966.

Andrew, Christopher. *Her Majesty's Secret Service: The Making of the British Intelligence Community.* New York: Penguin, 1987.

Antonius, George. *The Arab Awakening: The Story of the Arab National Movement.* Philadelphia: Lippincott, 1939.

Armstrong, Karen. *Holy War: The Crusades and Their Impact on Today's World.* New York: Anchor, 1992.

Barboza, Steven, ed. *American Jihad: Islam after Malcolm X.* New York: Doubleday, 1993.

Bauer, Karl Johannes. *Alois Musil. Wahrheitssucher in der Wüste.* Vienna and Cologne: Böhlau Verlag, 1989.

Berghahn, Volker R. *Imperial Germany, 1871–1914: Economy, Society, Culture and Politics.* Providence, R.I., and Oxford: Berghahn Books, 1994.

Bidwell, Robin. *Travellers in Arabia.* London: Hamlyn, 1976.

Boahen, A. Adu. *General History of Africa.* Vol. 7, *Africa under Colonial Domination, 1880–1935.* London and New York: James Currey, University of California Press, UNESCO, 1990.

Bosworth, R. J. B. "Italy and the End of the Ottoman Empire." In Marian Kent, ed., *The Great Powers and the End of the Ottoman Empire.* London: George Allen and Unwin, 1984, 52–75.

Burke, Edmund. "Moroccan Resistance, Pan-Islam and German War Strategy, 1914–1918." *Francia. Forschungen zur Westeuropäischen Geschichte,* 3(1975):434–64.

Burke, S. M., and Salim Al-Din Quraishi. *The British Raj in India: An Historical Overview.* Oxford: Oxford University Press, 1995.

Burn, Richard. "Political Movements, 1909–1917." In H. H. Dodwell, ed., *The Cambridge History of India.* Vol. 6, *The Indian Empire, 1858–1918.* Delhi: S. Chand, 1972, 574–86.

Busch, Briton Cooper. *Britain and the Persian Gulf, 1894–1914.* Berkeley and Los Angeles: University of California Press, 1967.

———. *Britain, India, and the Arabs, 1914–1921.* Berkeley: University of California Press, 1971.

Cecil, Lamar. *Albert Ballin: Business and Politics in Imperial Germany, 1888–1918.* Princeton, N.J.: Princeton University Press, 1967.

———. *The German Diplomatic Service, 1871–1914.* Princeton, N.J.: Princeton University Press, 1976.

———. *Wilhelm II: Prince and Emperor, 1859–1900.* Chapel Hill: University of North Carolina Press, 1989.

Chickering, Roger. *We Men Who Feel Most German: A Cultural Study of the Pan German League, 1886–1914.* Boston: Allen and Unwin, 1984.

Cockfield, Jamie. "Germany and the Fashoda Crisis, 1898–99." *Central European History,* 16 (1983):256–75.

Cohen, Stuart A. *British Policy in Mesopotamia, 1903–1914.* London: Ithaca Press, 1976.

Corr, Edwin G., and Stephen Sloan, eds. *Low-Intensity Conflict: Old Threats in a New World.* Boulder, Colo.: Westview Press, 1992.

Craig, Gordon A. *Germany, 1866–1945.* New York: Oxford University Press, 1978.

Dadrian, Vahakn N. *The History of the Armenian Genocide: Ethnic Conflict from the Balkans to Anatolia to the Caucasus.* Providence, R.I., and Oxford: Berghahn Books, 1995.

Dann, Uriel. "Lawrence of Arabia—One More Appraisal." *Middle Eastern Studies,* 15(1979):154–62.

Darwin, John. *Britain, Egypt and the Middle East: Imperial Policy in the Aftermath of War, 1918–1922.* New York: St. Martin's Press, 1981.

Davies, C. C. "The North-West Frontier, 1843–1918." In H. H. Dodwell, ed., *The Cambridge History of India.* Vol. 6, *The Indian Empire 1858–1918.* Delhi: S. Chand, 1972, 448–76.

Dawn, C. Ernest. *From Ottomanism to Arabism: Essays on the Origins of Arab Nationalism.* Urbana: University of Illinois Press, 1973.

——. "The Influence of T. E. Lawrence on the Middle East." In Jeffrey Meyers, ed., *T. E. Lawrence: Soldier, Writer, Legend.* London: Macmillan, 1989, 58–86.

——. "The Origins of Arab Nationalism." In Rashid Khalidi, Lisa Anderson, Muhammad Muslih, and Reeva S. Simon, eds., *The Origins of Arab Nationalism.* New York: Columbia University Press, 1991, 3–30.

Dignan, Don K. "The Hindu Conspiracy in Anglo-American Relations During World War I." *Pacific Historical Review,* 40(1971):57–76.

Dinkel, Christoph. "German Officers and the Armenian Genocide." *Armenian Review,* 44(1991):77–133.

Doerries, Reinhard. "Die Mission Sir Roger Casements im Deutschen Reich 1914–1916." *Historische Zeitschrift,* 222(1976):578–625.

——. *Imperial Challenge: Ambassador Count Bernstorff and German-American Relations, 1908–1917.* Trans. Christa D. Shannon. Chapel Hill: University of North Carolina Press, 1989.

Earle, Edward Mead. *Turkey, the Great Powers, and the Bagdad Railway:*

A Study in Imperialism. New York: Macmillan, 1935.

Eldar, Dan. "French Policy towards Husayn, Sharif of Mecca." *Middle Eastern Studies,* 26(1990):329–50.

Eldridge, C. C. *England's Mission: The Imperial Idea in the Age of Gladstone and Disraeli, 1868–1880.* Chapel Hill: University of North Carolina Press, 1974.

Epstein, Klaus. *Matthias Erzberger and the Dilemma of German Democracy.* New York: Howard Fertig, 1971.

Esposito, John L. *The Islamic Threat: Myth or Reality?* New York and Oxford: Oxford University Press, 1992.

Evans-Pritchard, E. E. *The Sanusi of Cyrenaica.* Oxford: Clarendon Press, 1949.

Falls, Cyril. *Armageddon: 1918.* Philadelphia: J. B. Lippincott, 1964.

—— [Maps compiled by A. F. Becke]. *The History of the Great War: Military Operations Egypt and Palestine from June 1917 to the End of the War.* 2 pts. London: His Majesty's Stationery Office, 1930.

Farnie, D. A. *East and West of Suez: The Suez Canal in History, 1854–1956.* Oxford: Clarendon Press, 1969.

Farwell, Byron. *The Great War in Africa, 1914–1918.* New York and London: Norton, 1986.

Feigl, Erich. *Musil von Arabien: Vorkämpfer der islamischen Welt.* Vienna and Munich: Amalthea, 1985.

Fieldhouse, David K. *Die Kolonialreiche seit dem 18 Jahrhundert.* Frankfurt/Main: Fischer Taschenbuch, 1993; first pub. 1965.

Fischer, Fritz. *Bündnis der Eliten: Zur Kontinuität der Machts- trukturen in Deutschland 1871–1945.* Düsseldorf: Droste, 1979.

——. *Germany's Aims in the First World War.* New York, Norton, 1967.

——. *War of Illusions: German Policies from 1911 to 1914.* Trans. Marian Jackson. New York: Norton, 1975.

Fletcher, Arnold. *Afghanistan: Highway of Conquest.* Ithaca, N.Y.: Cornell University Press, 1965.

Fraser, Thomas G. "Germany and Indian Revolution, 1914–18." *Journal of Contemporary History,* 12(1977):255–72.

Friedman, Isaiah. *Germany, Turkey, and Zionism, 1897–1918.* Oxford: Clarendon Press, 1977.

——. *The Question of Palestine, 1914–1918: British-Jewish-Arab Relations.* New York: Schocken, 1973.

Fröhlich, Michael. *Imperialismus: Deutsche Kolonial–und Weltpolitik 1880–1914.* Munich: Deutscher Taschenbuch Verlag, 1994.

Fromkin, David. *A Peace to End All Peace: The Fall of the Ottoman Empire and the Creation of the Modern Middle East.* New York: Avon Books, 1989.

Fück, Johann. *Die Arabischen Studien in Europa bis in den Anfang des 20. Jahrhunderts.* Leipzig: Harrassowitz, 1955.

Gautschi, Willi. *Lenin als Emigrant in der Schweiz.* Zürich and Köln: Benziger, 1973.

Gehrke, Ulrich. "Germany and Persia up to 1919." In Jehuda L. Wallach, ed., *Germany and the Middle East, 1835–1939.* Tel Aviv: Israel Press, 1975, 104–16.

——. *Persien in der Deutschen Orientpolitik während des Ersten Weltkrieges.* 2 vols. Stuttgart: W. Kohlhammer, 1960.

Geiss, Imanuel. *Das Deutsche Reich und die Vorgeschichte des Ersten Weltkriegs.* 2nd ed. Munich: Carl Hanser Verlag, 1978.

Gellner, Ernest. *Anthropology and Politics: Revolutions in the Sacred Grove.* Oxford, U.K., and Cambridge, Mass.: Blackwell, 1995.

Gershoni, Israel, and James P. Jankowski. *Egypt, Islam and the Arabs: The Search for Egyptian Nationhood, 1900–1930.* New York: Oxford University Press, 1986.

Gilbert, Martin. *The First World War: A Complete History.* New York: Henry Holt, 1994.

Gooch, G. P. *Recent Revelations of European Diplomacy.* New York: Russell & Russell, 1967.

Goodheart, Eugene. "A Contest of Motives: T. E. Lawrence in *Seven Pillars of Wisdom.*" In Jeffrey Meyers, ed., *T. E. Lawrence: Soldier, Writer, Legend.* London: Macmillan, 1989, 110–27.

Gottlieb, W. W. *Studies in Secret Diplomacy.* London: Allen and Unwin, 1957.

Greenfield, Richard. *Ethiopia: A New Political History.* London: Pall Mall Press, 1969.

Grunwald, Kurt. "Pénétration Pacifique—The Financial Vehicles of Germany's 'Drang nach dem Osten.'" In Jehuda L. Wallach, ed., *Germany and the Middle East, 1835–1939.* Tel Aviv: Israel Press, 1975, 85–101.

Guillen, Pierre. "The Entente of 1904 as a Colonial Settlement." In Prosser Gifford and William Roger Louis, eds., *France and Britain in Africa:*

Imperial Rivalry and Colonial Rule. New Haven, Conn.: Yale University Press, 1971, 333–68.

Guinn, Paul. *British Strategy and Politics, 1914 to 1918.* Oxford: Clarendon Press, 1965.

Haddad, Mahmoud. "Iraq before World War I: A Case of Anti-European Arab Ottomanism." In Rashid Khalidi, Lisa Anderson, Mohammad Muslih, and Reeva S. Simon, eds., *The Origins of Arab Nationalism.* New York: Columbia University Press, 1991, 120–50.

Hagen, Gottfried. *Die Türkei im Ersten Weltkrieg. Flugblätter und Flugschriften in arabischer, persischer und osmanisch-türkischer Sprache aus einer Sammlung der Universitätsbibliothek Heidelberg eingeleitet, übersetzt und kommentiert.* Frankfurt/Main: Peter Lang, 1990.

Hahlweg, Werner. *Lenins Rückkehr nach Russland 1917. Die deutschen Akten.* 4th ed. Leiden: E. J. Brill, 1957.

Hanioglu, M. Sukru. "The Young Turks and the Arabs before the Revolution." In Rashid Khalidi, Lisa Anderson, Muhammad Muslih, and Reeva S. Simon, ed., *The Origins of Arab Nationalism.* New York: Columbia University Press, 1991, 31–49.

Hauner, Milan. *India in Axis Strategy: Germany, Japan, and Indian Nationalists in the Second World War.* Stuttgart: Klett-Cotta, 1981.

Heller, Joseph. *British Policy towards the Ottoman Empire, 1908–1914.* London: Frank Cass, 1983.

Henze, Dietmar. "Ewald Banse und seine Stellung in der Geographie auf Grund seiner Schriften, Tagebücher und Briefe." Unpublished Ph.D. dissertation. Universität Frankfurt, 1968.

Herwig, Holger H. *The First World War: Germany and Austria-Hungary, 1914–1918.* London and New York: Arnold, 1997.

———. *Hammer or Anvil? Modern Germany, 1648–Present.* Lexington, Mass.: D. C. Heath, 1994.

———. "Imperial Germany." In Ernest R. May, ed., *Knowing One's Enemies: Intelligence Assessment before the Two World Wars.* Princeton, N.J.: Princeton University Press, 1984, 62–97.

———. *"Luxury" Fleet: The Imperial German Navy, 1888–1918.* Winchester, Mass.: Allen and Unwin, 1980.

Herzfeld, Hans. *Der Erste Weltkrieg.* 6th ed. Munich: Deutsche Taschenbuch Verlag, 1982.

Hess, Robert L. *Ethiopia: The Modernization of Autocracy.* Ithaca: Cornell University Press, 1970.

Hillgruber, Andreas. *Germany and the Two World Wars.* Trans. William C. Kirby. Cambridge, Mass.: Harvard University Press, 1981.

Hirszowicz, Lukasz. "The Course of German Foreign Policy in the Middle East between the World Wars." In Jehuda L. Wallach, ed., *Germany and the Middle East, 1835–1939.* Tel Aviv: Israel Press, 1975.

———. "The Sultan and the Khedive, 1892–1908." *Middle Eastern Studies,* 8(1972):287–312.

Hopkirk, Peter. *The Great Game: The Struggle for Empire in Central Asia.* 2nd ed. New York: Kodansha International, 1994.

Hopwood, Derek. *Tales of Empire: The British in the Middle East, 1880–1952.* London: I. B. Tauris, 1989.

Hourani, Albert. "*The Arab Awakening* Forty Years After." In Derek Hopwood, ed., *Studies in Arab History: The Antonius Lectures, 1978–87.* London: Macmillan, 1990, 21–40.

———. *Arabic Thought in the Liberal Age, 1798–1939.* Cambridge: Cambridge University Press, 1984; first pub. 1962.

———. *A History of the Arab Peoples.* Cambridge, Mass.: Harvard University Press, 1991.

Hoyt, Edwin P. *The Last Cruise of the Emden.* London: Mayflower, 1969.

Imperial War Museum. *Operations in Persia, 1914–1919.* London: Her Majesty's Stationery Office, 1987.

"The Invasion of Chaldea." *The Times History of the War,* 3(9 Mar. 1915):81–120.

James, Lawrence. *The Golden Warrior: The Life and Legend of Lawrence of Arabia.* London: Weidenfeld and Nicolson, 1990.

———. *The Rise and Fall of the British Empire.* New York: St. Martin's, 1994.

Jankowski, James. "Egypt and Early Arab Nationalism, 1908–1922." In Rashid Khalidi, Lisa Anderson, Muhammad Muslih, and Reeva S. Simon, eds., *The Origins of Arab Nationalism.* New York: Columbia University Press, 1991, 243–70.

Jarausch, Konrad. *The Enigmatic Chancellor: Bethmann Hollweg and the Hubris of Imperial Germany.* New Haven, Conn.: Yale University Press, 1973.

Johnson, Paul. *A History of the Jews.* New York: Harper, 1987.

Joll, James. *The Origins of the First World War.* 2nd ed. London and New York: Longman, 1992.

Katkov, George. "German Political Intervention in Russia during World War I." In Richard Pipes, ed., *Revolutionary Russia: A Symposium.* Garden City, N.Y.: Doubleday, 1969, 80–112.

Kedourie, Elie. *Arabic Political Memoirs and Other Studies.* London: Frank Cass, 1974.

———. *The Chatham House Version and Other Middle-Eastern Studies.* London: Weidenfeld and Nicolson, 1970.

———. "The End of the Ottoman Empire." *Journal of Contemporary History,* 3 (1968):19–28.

———. *England and the Middle East: The Destruction of the Ottoman Empire, 1914–1921.* London: Bowes and Bowes, 1956.

———. "Great Britain, the Other Powers, and the Middle East before and after World War I." In Uriel Dann, ed., *The Great Powers in the Middle East, 1919–1939.* New York: Holmes and Meier, 1988, 3–11.

Keegan, John. *The Price of Admiralty: The Evolution of Naval Warfare.* London and New York: Penguin, 1988.

Kennedy, Paul M. "Great Britain before 1914." In Ernest R. May, ed., *Knowing One's Enemies: Intelligence Assessment before the Two World Wars.* Princeton, N.J.: Princeton University Press, 1984, 172–204.

———. *Preparing for the Twenty-First Century.* New York: Random House, 1993.

———. *The Realities behind Diplomacy: Background Influences on British External Policy, 1865–1980.* London: Fontana, 1985.

———. *The Rise and Fall of the Great Powers: Economic Change and Military Conflict from 1500 to 2000.* New York: Vintage, 1987.

———. *The Rise of the Anglo-German Antagonism, 1860–1914.* London: George Allen and Unwin, 1980.

———. *The Samoan Triangle: A Study in Anglo-German-American Relations.* New York: Barnes and Noble, 1974.

Kent, George O. *Bismarck and His Times.* Carbondale and Edwardsville: Southern Illinois University Press, 1978.

Kent, Marian. "Asiatic Turkey, 1914–1916." In F. H. Hinsley, ed., *British Foreign Policy under Sir Edward Grey.* Cambridge: Cambridge University Press, 1977, 436–51.

———. "Constantinople and Asiatic Turkey, 1905–1914." In F. H. Hinsley, ed., *British Foreign Policy under Sir Edward Grey.* Cambridge: Cambridge University Press, 1977, 148–64.

——. *Oil and Empire: British Policy and Mesopotamian Oil, 1900–1920.* New York: Barnes and Noble, 1976.

Khadduri, Majid. *Arab Contemporaries: The Role of Personalities in Politics.* Baltimore and London: Johns Hopkins University Press, 1973.

Khalidi, Rashid Ismail. *British Policy towards Syria and Palestine, 1906–1914: A Study of the Antecedents of the Hussein-McMahon Correspondence, the Sykes-Picot Agreement, and the Balfour Declaration.* London: Ithaca Press, 1980.

——. "Ottomanism and Arabism in Syria before 1914." In Rashid Khalidi, Lisa Anderson, Muhammad Muslih, and Reeva S. Simon, ed., *The Origins of Arab Nationalism.* New York: Columbia University Press, 1991, 50–72.

Khoury, Philip S. *Urban Notables and Arab Nationalism: The Politics of Damascus, 1860–1920.* Cambridge: Cambridge University Press, 1983.

Kinross, Lord. *The Ottoman Centuries: The Rise and Fall of the Turkish Empire.* New York: Morrow Quill Paperbacks, 1977.

Klieman, Aaron S. *Foundations of British Policy in the Arab World: The Cairo Conference of 1921.* Baltimore: Johns Hopkins University Press, 1970.

Kramer, Thomas. *Deutsch-ägyptische Beziehungen in Vergangenheit und Gegenwart.* Tübingen and Basel: Horst Erdmann, 1974.

Kröger, Martin. "Revolution als Programm. Ziele und Realität deutscher Orientpolitik im Ersten Weltkrieg." In Wolfgang Michalka, ed., *Der Erste Weltkrieg. Wirkung, Wahrnehmung, Analyse.* Munich: Piper, 1994, 366–91.

Krüger, Horst. "Har Dayal in Deutschland." *Mitteilungen des Instituts für Orientforschung*, 10 (1964):141–69.

Lacey, Robert. *The Kingdom: Arabia and the House of Sa'ud.* New York: Avon Books, 1981.

Landau, Jacob. *The Politics of Pan-Islam: Ideology and Organization.* Oxford: Clarendon Press, 1990.

Landes, David S. *Bankers and Pashas: International Finance and Economic Imperialism in Egypt.* Cambridge, Mass.: Harvard University Press, 1958.

Langer, William L., ed. *An Encyclopedia of World History.* 5th ed. Boston: Houghton Mifflin, 1980.

Larcher, M. *La guerre turque dans la guerre mondiale.* Paris: Berger-Levrault, 1926.

Lasswell, H. D. *Propaganda Technique in the World War.* New York: Peter Smith, 1938.

Leshnik, Lawrence S. "Vor den Augen des Waffenbruders. Das Massaker an den Armeniern im Ersten Weltkrieg und die deutsche Mitverantwortung." *Die Zeit,* 17(20 Apr. 1990):41–42.

Lewis, Geoffrey. "The Ottoman Proclamation of Jihad in 1914." *The Islamic Quarterly,* 19(1975):157–63.

Liddell Hart, B. H. *The Real War, 1914–1918.* Boston: Little, Brown, 1930.

Lovett, H. Verney. "The Rise of an Extremist Party." In H. H. Dodwell, ed., *The Cambridge History of India.* Vol. 6, *The Indian Empire, 1858–1918.* Delhi: S. Chand, 1972, 548–60.

Lowe, C. J., and M. L. Dockrill. *The Mirage of Power.* Vol. 1, *British Foreign Policy, 1902–14.* London and Boston: Routledge and Kegan Paul, 1972. Vol. 2, *British Foreign Policy, 1914–22.* London and Boston: Routledge and Kegan Paul, 1972.

Macfie, A. L. *The Eastern Question, 1774–1923.* London and New York: Longman, 1989.

McKale, Donald M. *Curt Prüfer: German Diplomat from the Kaiser to Hitler.* Kent, Ohio: Kent State University Press, 1987.

——. "German Policy Toward the Sharif of Mecca, 1914–1916." *The Historian,* 55(1993):303–14.

——. "Germany and the Arab Question before World War I." *The Historian,* 59(1997):311–26.

——. "Germany and the Arab Question in the First World War." *Middle Eastern Studies,* 29(1993):236–53.

——. "'The Kaiser's Spy': Max von Oppenheim and the Anglo-German Rivalry before and during the First World War," *European History Quarterly,* 27(1997):199–220.

——. "*Weltpolitik* versus *Imperium Britannica*: Anglo-German Rivalry in Egypt, 1904–14." *Canadian Journal of History,* 22(1987):195–207.

Macmunn, George, and Cyril Falls. *The History of the Great War: Military Operations Egypt and Palestine from the Outbreak of War with Germany to June 1917.* London: His Majesty's Stationery Office, 1928.

Mai, Gunther. *Das Ende des Kaiserreichs. Politik und Kriegführung im*

Ersten Weltkrieg. 2nd ed. Munich: Deutsche Taschenbuch Verlag, 1983.

Mansfield, Peter. *The Ottoman Empire and Its Successors*. London: Macmillan, 1973.

Marcus, Harold G. *A History of Ethiopia*. Berkeley and Los Angeles: University of California Press, 1994.

Matthew, H. C. G. "The Liberal Age (1851–1914)." In Kenneth O. Morgan, ed., *The Oxford History of Britain*. Oxford and New York: Oxford University Press, 1988, 518–81.

Melka, R. L. "Max Freiherr von Oppenheim: Sixty Years of Scholarship and Political Intrigue in the Middle East." *Middle Eastern Studies*, 9(1973):81–93.

Mikusch, Dagobert. *Wassmuss der deutsche Lawrence*. Leipzig: Paul List Verlag, 1937.

Moberly, F. J. *The History of the Great War Based on Documents: The Campaign in Mesopotamia, 1914–1918*. 4 vols. London: His Majesty's Stationery Office, 1927–28.

Mommsen, Wolfgang J. *Der autoritäre Nationalstaat. Verfassung, Gesellschaft und Kultur des deutschen Kaiserreiches*. Munich: Fischer Taschenbuch Verlag, 1990.

Monroe, Elizabeth. *Britain's Moment in the Middle East, 1914–1971*. Baltimore: Johns Hopkins University Press, 1981.

Moorehead, Alan. *Gallipoli*. New York: Ballantine Books, 1958.

Morgan, Kenneth O. "The Twentieth Century (1914–1987)." In Kenneth O. Morgan, ed., *The Oxford History of Britain*. Oxford and New York: Oxford University Press, 1988, 582–660.

Morsey, Konrad. *T. E. Lawrence und der arabische Aufstand 1916/18*. Osnabrück: Biblio Verlag, 1976.

Mousa, Suleiman. *T. E. Lawrence: An Arab View*. Trans. Albert Butros. London and New York: Oxford University Press, 1966.

Mühlmann, Carl. *Das Deutsch-Türkische Waffenbündnis im Weltkriege*. Leipzig: Verlag Koehler und Amelang, 1940.

Müller, Herbert Landolin. *Islam, gihad ("Heiliger Krieg") und Deutsches Reich. Ein Nachspiel zur wilhelminischen Weltpolitik im Maghreb 1914–1918*. Frankfurt/Main: Peter Lang, 1991.

Munson, Jr. Henry. *Islam and Revolution in the Middle East*. New Haven, Conn.: Yale University Press, 1988.

Nevakivi, Jukka. *Britain, France and the Arab Middle East, 1914-1920.* London: Athlone Press, 1969.

Nouschi, Andre. *La Naissance du nationalisme algérien.* Paris: Les Editions de Minuit, 1962.

Ochsenwald, William. *The Hijaz Railroad.* Charlottesville: University Press of Virginia, 1980.

——. "Ironic Origins: Arab Nationalism in the Hijaz, 1882-1914." In Rashid Khalidi, Lisa Anderson, Muhammad Muslih, and Reeva S. Simon, eds., *The Origins of Arab Nationalism.* New York: Columbia University Press, 1991, 189-203.

Ovendale, Ritchie. *The Longman Companion to the Middle East since 1914.* London and New York: Longman, 1992.

Owen, Roger. *State, Power and Politics in the Making of the Modern Middle East.* London and New York: Routledge, 1993.

Paret, Rudi. *The Study of Arabic and Islam at German Universities: German Orientalists since Theodor Nöldeke.* Wiesbaden: Franz Steiner Verlag, 1968.

Pick, Pinhas Walter. "German Railway Constructions in the Middle East." In Jehuda L. Wallach, ed., *Germany and the Middle East, 1835-1939.* Tel Aviv: Israel Press, 1975, 72-84.

Prätor, Sabine. *Der arabische Faktor in der jungtürkischen Politik. Eine Studie zum osmanischen Parlament der II. Konstitution (1908-1918).* Berlin: Klaus Schwarz Verlag, 1993.

Ramsaur, Ernest Edmonson, Jr. *The Young Turks: Prelude to the Revolution of 1908.* New York: Russell and Russell, 1970; first pub. 1957.

Rathmann, Lothar. *Berlin-Bagdad. Die imperialistische Nahostpolitik des kaiserlichen Deutschlands.* [East] Berlin: Dietz Verlag, 1962.

——. *Stossrichtung Nahost, 1914-1918. Zur Expansions politik des deutschen Imperialismus im ersten Weltkrieg.* [Eqst] Berlin: Rütten und Leoning, 1963.

Reynolds, David. *Britannia Overruled: British Policy and World Power in the Twentieth Century.* London and New York: Longman, 1991.

Robbins, K. G. "Public Opinion, the Press and Pressure Groups." In F. H. Hinsley, ed., *British Foreign Policy under Sir Edward Grey.* Cambridge: Cambridge University Press, 1977, 70-88.

Robinson, Ronald, and John Gallagher. *Africa and the Victorians: The Official Mind of Imperialism.* London: Macmillan, 1974; first pub. 1961.

Rodinson, Maxime. *Europe and the Mystique of Islam.* Trans. Roger Veinus. London: I. B. Tauris, 1987.

Rushbrook Williams, L. F. "India and the War." In H. H. Dodwell, ed., *The Cambridge History of India.* Vol. 6, *The Indian Empire, 1858–1918.* Delhi: S. Chand, 1972, 476–88.

Safran, Nadav. *Egypt in Search of Political Community: An Analysis of the Intellectual and Political Evolution of Egypt, 1804–1952.* Cambridge, Mass.: Harvard University Press, 1961.

Said, Edward W. *Culture and Imperialism.* New York: Knopf, 1978.

———. *Orientalism.* New York: Pantheon Books, 1978.

Sauer, George. "Alois Musil's Reisen nach Arabien im Ersten Weltkrieg." *Archiv Orientální,* 37(1969):243–63.

Schöllgen, Gregor. *Imperialismus und Gleichgewicht. Deutschland, England und die orientalische Frage 1871–1914.* Munich: R. Oldenbourg Verlag, 1984.

Schröder, Bernd Philipp. *Deutschland und der Mittlere Osten im Zweiten Weltkrieg.* Göttingen: Musterschmidt, 1975.

Silberman, Neil Asher. *Digging for God and Country: Exploration, Archeology, and the Secret Struggle for the Holy Land, 1799–1917.* New York: Knopf, 1982.

Silberstein, Gerard E. *The Troubled Alliance: German-Austrian Relations, 1914 to 1917.* Lexington: University Press of Kentucky, 1970.

Simon, Reeva S. "The Education of an Iraqi Ottoman Army Officer." In Rashid Khalidi, Lisa Anderson, Muhammad Muslih, and Reeva S.Simon, ed., *The Origins of Arab Nationalism.* New York: Columbia University Press, 1991, 151–67.

Smith, C. G. "The Emergence of the Middle East." *Journal of Contemporary History,* 3(1968):3–18.

Smith, Vincent A. *The Oxford History of India.* Oxford: Clarendon Press, 1958.

Smith, Woodruff D. *The Ideological Origins of Nazi Imperialism.* New York: Oxford University Press, 1986.

Sontag, Raymond James. *Germany and England: Background of Conflict, 1848–1894.* New York: Norton, 1969.

Staley, Eugene. "Business and Politics in the Persian Gulf: The Story of the Wönckhaus Firm." *Political Science Quarterly,* 48(1933):367–85.

Steel, Nigel, and Peter Hart. *Defeat at Gallipoli.* London: Papermac, 1994.

Steiner, Zara S. *Britain and the Origins of the First World War.* New York: St. Martin's Press, 1977.

———. *The Foreign Office and Foreign Policy, 1898-1914.* Cambridge: Cambridge University Press, 1969.

———. "The Foreign Office under Sir Edward Grey, 1905-1914." In F. H. Hinsley, ed., *British Foreign Policy under Sir Edward Grey.* Cambridge: Cambridge University Press, 1977, 22-69.

Stevenson, David. *The First World War and International Politics.* Oxford: Clarendon Press, 1988.

Stewart, Desmond. *T. E. Lawrence.* London: Paladin, 1986.

Stoecker, Helmuth. "The First World War: The War Aims." In Helmuth Stoecker, ed., *German Imperialism in Africa: From the Beginnings until the Second World War.* Trans. Bernd Zöllner. Atlantic Highlands, N.J.: Humanities Press International, 1986, 280-96.

———. "The First World War: The War in Africa." In Helmuth Stoecker, ed., *German Imperialism in Africa: From the Beginnings until the Second World War.* Trans. Bernd Zöllner. Atlantic Highlands, N.J.: Humanities Press International, 1986, 270-80.

———. "German East Africa 1885-1906." In Helmuth Stoecker, ed., *German Imperialism in Africa: From the Beginnings until the Second World War.* Trans. Bernd Zöllner. Atlantic Highlands, N.J.: Humanities Press International, 1986, 93-113.

———. "The Quest for 'German Central Africa.'" In Helmuth Stoecker, ed., *German Imperialism in Africa: From the Beginnings until the Second World War.* Trans. Bernd Zöllner. Atlantic Highlands, N.J.: Humanities Press International, 1986, 249-62.

Stoecker, Helmuth, and Helmut Nimschowski. "Morocco, 1898-1914." In Helmuth Stoecker, ed., *German Imperialism in Africa: From the Beginnings until the Second World War.* Trans. Bernd Zöllner. Atlantic Highlands, N.J.: Humanities Press International, 1986, 230-49.

Sykes, Christopher. *Wassmuss: "The German Lawrence."* London: Longmans, Green and Co., 1936.

Tignor, Robert L. *Modernization and British Colonial Rule in Egypt, 1882-1914.* Princeton, N.J.: Princeton University Press, 1966.

Treue, Wilhelm. "Max Freiherr von Oppenheim—Der Archäologe und die Politik," *Historische Zeitschrift.* 209(1969):37-74.

Trumpener, Ulrich. "Germany and the End of the Ottoman Empire." In

Marian Kent, ed., *The Great Powers and the End of the Ottoman Empire*. London: George Allen and Unwin, 1984, 111–40.

——. *Germany and the Ottoman Empire, 1914–1918*. Princeton, N.J.: Princeton University Press, 1968.

——. "German Officers in the Ottoman Empire, 1880–1918: Some Comments on Their Backgrounds, Functions, and Accomplishments." In Jehuda L. Wallach, ed., *Germany and the Middle East, 1835–1939*. Tel Aviv: Israel Press, 1975, 30–43.

Tuchmann, Barbara W. *The Zimmermann Telegram*. New York: Ballantine Books, 1991; first pub. 1958.

Vatikiotis, P. J. *The History of Modern Egypt: From Muhammad Ali to Mubarak*. 4th ed. Baltimore: Johns Hopkins University Press, 1991.

Vogel, Renate. *Die Persien- und Afghanistanexpedition Oskar Ritter v. Niedermayers 1915/16*. Osnabrück: Biblio Verlag, 1976.

Wallach, Jehuda L. *Anatomie einer Militärhilfe. Die preussisch-deutschen Militärmissionen in der Türkei 1835–1919*. Düsseldorf: Droste, 1976.

——. "The Weimar Republic and the Middle East: Salient Points." In Uriel Dann, ed., *The Great Powers in the Middle East, 1919–1939*. New York: Holmes and Meier, 1988, 271–73.

Watt, William Montgomery. *Muslim-Christian Encounters: Perceptions and Misperceptions*. London: Routledge, 1991.

Wavell, A. P. *The Palestine Campaigns*. 2nd ed. London: Constable, 1929.

Weber, Frank G. *Eagles on the Crescent: Germany, Austria, and the Diplomacy of the Turkish Alliance, 1914–1918*. Ithaca, N.Y.: Cornell University Press, 1970.

Wehler, Hans-Ulrich. *Das Deutsche Kaiserreich 1871–1918*. 5th ed. Göttingen: Vandenhoeck and Ruprecht, 1983.

Weidenfeld, Werner. *Die Englandpolitik Gustav Stresemanns. Theoretische und praktische Aspekte der Aussenpolitik*. Mainz: v. Hase and Koehler Verlag, 1972.

Weinberg, Gerhard L. *A World at Arms: A Global History of World War II*. Cambridge: Cambridge University Press, 1994.

Wilson, Mary C. "The Hashemites, the Arab Revolt, and Arab Nationalism." In Rashid Khalidi, Lisa Anderson, Muhammad Muslih, and Reeva S. Simon, eds., *The Origins of Arab Nationalism*. New York: Columbia University Press, 1991, 204–24.

Winstone, H. V. F. *The Illicit Adventure: The Story of Political and Military Intelligence in the Middle East from 1898 to 1926. London: Jonathan Cape, 1982.

——. Leachman: 'OC Desert': The Life of Lieutenant-Colonel Gerard Leachman D.S.O. London: Quartet Books, 1982.

Wolpert, Stanley. A New History of India. 4th ed. New York and Oxford: Oxford University Press, 1993.

Woodward, Llewellyn. Great Britain and the War of 1914–1918. London: Methuen, 1967.

Wrigley, W. David. "Germany and the Turco-Italian War, 1911–1912." International Journal of Middle East Studies, 11(1980):313–38.

Yapp, M. E. The Making of the Modern Near East, 1792–1923. London and New York: Longman, 1987.

Yisraeli, David. "Germany and Zionism." In Jehuda L. Wallach, ed., Germany and the Middle East, 1835–1939. Tel Aviv: Israel Press, 1975, 142–64.

Zechlin, Egmont. "Cabinet versus Economic Warfare in Germany: Policy and Strategy during the Early Months of the First World War." In H. W. Koch, ed., The Origins of the First World War: Great Power Rivalry and German War Aims. 2nd ed. New York: Macmillan, 1984.

——. Die Deutsche Politik und die Juden im Ersten Weltkrieg. Göttingen: Vandenhoeck und Ruprecht, 1969.

——. "Friedensbestrebungen und Revolutionierungsversuche," Aus Politik und Zeitgeschichte. Beilage zur Wochenzeitung 'DasParlament,' B20(17 May 1961):269–88; B24(14 June 1961):325–37; B25(21 June 1961):341–67.

——. Krieg und Kriegsrisiko. Zur deutschen Politik im Ersten Weltkrieg. Düsseldorf: Droste Verlag, 1979.

Zeine, Zeine N. The Emergence of Arab Nationalism: With a Background Study of Arab-Turkish Relations in the Near East. 3rd ed. Delmar, N.Y.: Caravan Books, 1976.

Zeman, Z. A. B. Germany and the Revolution in Russia, 1915–1918: Documents from the Archives of the German Foreign Ministry. London: Oxford University Press, 1958.

Zetterberg, Seppo. Die Liga der Fremdvölker Russlands 1916–1918. Ein Beitrag zu Deutschlands antirussischem Propagandakrieg unter den Fremdvölkern Russlands im ersten Weltkrieg. Helsinki: Akateeminen kirjakauppa, 1978.

INDEX

The main entries "Germany" and "Great Britain" identify subjects before World War I or that had little connection in the war to each country's policy in the Middle East of inciting revolution among the native peoples of its enemy's empire or ally. The main entries "War by revolution (Germany)" and "War by revolution (Great Britain)" list subjects related to both countries' revolutionary policies during the World War.

Abadan, 37, 40, 82–85, 132

Abbas Hilmi II, 24; and son, 103, 199, 208; and Abdullah, 43; and Arab revolt, 198, 209; attempt on life of, 53; and Austria-Hungary, 53, 90, 116–17; and Britain, 21–22, 32, 53, 71, 89–90, 103, 117–19, 198–99, 208–9; and caliphate, 23, 27, 29, 31, 41; and Cromer, 21–22; deposed, 90, 92; and Egypt, 12, 53, 71; and Egyptian nationalists, 22–23, 89, 117; and Enver Pasha, 53, 117, 198; and espionage, 199; and Foreign Office, 199; and France, 208; and Germany, 21–22, 53, 71, 90, 116–17, 198–99, 208–9, 225; and Jemal Pasha, 198; and Kitchener, 32; and Oppenheim, 12, 22–23; pilgrimage of, 243n. 53; and Prüfer, 223; and Rashid Rida, 31, 41; and Said Halim, 53; and Sanussis, 23; and Sharif of Mecca, 209, 223; and Switzerland, 117, 197–98; and Turks, 53, 56, 89–90, 116, 117, 198–99, 208–9, 225,

247n. 106; and Wangenheim, 53; and Wilhelm II, 117, 225

Abduh, Muhammad, 13, 238n. 47

Abd ul-Hamid, 2, 8–10, 19, 23, 25, 26

Abdullah, 31, 41, 43, 75, 98, 103, 153, 160

Abdullah, Sayyid Muhammad ("Mad Mullah"), 157, 158, 168, 193–95

Abu Musa, 37

Abyssinia, 63, 64–65, 104–6, 156–58, 174–75, 193–96, 214

Adelson, Roger, ix

Aden, 95

Admiralty (Britain), 82, 95

Afghanistan, 7, 37, 47, 51, 79–82, 128, 136–37, 143–45

Aga Khan, 76, 92, 161, 245n. 79

al-Ahd ("Covenant"), 153, 247n. 106

Ahmad, 134, 141

Ahmad Fuad, 209

Ajaimi, 44, 135, 210–12, 247n. 107

Albanians, 24

Algeria, 51

Ali, 178
Ali, Muhammad, 92
Allenby, Edmund, 200, 207, 208, 214, 220, 221, 224
All India Muslim League, 245n. 79
Altengrabow, 68
Amir (Muslim ruler), 7
Amirate (office of commander, governor, or minor ruler of a province), 34
Anatolian railroad, 4, 8, 14
Anaza, 38, 65
Andaman islands, 126
Anglo-Persian Oil Company, 37, 82
Annie Larsen, 125
Antonius, George, ix
Aqaba incident, 17, 19–20
Arab Bureau, 161, 171, 188, 205, 206, 222
Arabism, 27
Arab question, 26, 28, 42, 75
Arabs: and Britain, 41, 116, 153–54, 219; and caliphate, 3, 27, 41, 42; congress in Paris, 42; and France, 41, 219; frustration of, xi; and Germany, 4, 39, 41–44, 61–62, 94, 116, 164–66; nationalism among, 27, 110–11, 116, 153, 165–66; and peace settlement, 229–30; persecution of, 114, 115–16, 164, 177; and reawakening of Islam, 3; reform committees of, 42; response to *jihad*, 114; revolt of, 177–78, 181–83, 189, 203–4, 207, 213, 220–25; secret societies of, 31, 110–11; and Turks, 3, 24, 26–33, 41, 43, 56, 58; and wartime actions, xiii. *See also* Germany; Great Britain; Shiites; Sunnis; war by revolution (Germany); war by revolution (Great Britain)
Archer, G. F., 195
Armenians, 3, 7, 9, 24, 35, 113–14, 164, 262n. 67
Arms Act (India), 77
Army Group F (German), 200–202, 211, 212, 221–22, 224

Arslan, Shekib, 227
Asia Korps. *See* Pasha II
Askari, Jaafir Bey, al-, 146
Askeri, Sulayman, 50, 129, 132
Asquith, Herbert Henry, 154–55, 162
Aulad Ali, 146
Austria-Hungary, 40, 88, 116–17, 226
Austro-Prussian War, 6
al-Azhar University, 12–13, 171

Bachmann, Walter, 81
Baghdad railroad, 8–9, 14–15, 24, 35–36, 38, 40–41, 44, 201, 211
Bakhtiaris, 85, 132, 138
Balfour, A. J., 208, 219
Balfour Declaration, 208
Balkan wars, 26, 33, 34, 77
Ballin, Albert, 83
Bani Lam, 132
al-Barani, Sulayman, 88, 93, 146, 191, 214
Barenfels, 52
Barkatullah, Maulvi, 78, 120, 122–23, 128, 145
Bas Hamba, Ali, 50, 248n. 12
Basra Reform Committee, 42
Bentheim, Baron von, 88, 102
"Bernard," 199
Bernstorff, Johann Heinrich Count von: and Arab revolt, 220, 222–24; and capitulations in Egypt, 21; and CUP, 222; imperialism of, 225; and Jemal Pasha, 220; and "Maurice," 210; and Oppenheim, 24; and revolution in India, 123–26; and Sharif of Mecca, 223; and Talaat Pasha, 223; and United States, 78–79, 125
Bethmann Hollweg, Theobald von, and Britain, 39, 46, 54; and Egypt, 52–53, 54, 56–58; and Habibullah, 128; and India, 51, 54, 128; and Jews, 112; and Oppenheim, 51, 80; and peace proposal, 86; and Persia, 80, 139; and Turkey, 39, 58; war aims of, 55, 106

Bieberstein, Adolf Freiherr Marschall von, 8, 13, 20
Bismarck, Otto Prince von, 4, 6
Boehm, George Paul, 124
Boer War, 15
Bolo Pasha, 117
Bosnian crisis, 25, 241n. 31
Boyle, Harry, 19
Brémond, Edouard, 206
Breslau, 49, 69, 85
Brest Litovsk, 219
British Empire, 31; extent of, 2; German war against, 46; Muslims in, 2, 91; provides troops, 57, 72, 87, 92, 150, 167, 190, 291n. 40; threat to, 17, 84; weakening of, xiii, 122, 230, 292n. 43
British General Staff, 20, 31, 155. *See also* Imperial General Staff (Great Britain)
British Indian Army, 72, 84, 90, 122, 170, 185–86, 199, 200, 211–12
Brode, Heinrich, 182
Bülow, Bernhard von, 6, 8, 21
Bulgaria, 80, 139, 154, 226
Busch, Brinton Cooper, ix

Cairo museum, 33
Canada, 78
Caucasus, 86
Cecil, Robert, 207–8
Central Office for the Indian Revolution, 123, 124
Central Office for the Islamic Movement, 50
Central Powers, 46; and Abbas Hilmi, 90; Bulgaria joins, 139, 154; defeat of, 230; and eastern front, 97; and Egyptians, 54; Enver and, 47, 49; and Italy, 56; and Muslims, 68; and peace overtures, 218; and Persia, 133; Turks join, 76, 80
Chakravarty, C. K., 190, 216
Chandra, Harish, 127
Chandra, Ram, 122–23, 125

Chattopadhyaya, Virendranath, 78, 120, 122, 127, 128, 216, 290n. 28
Cheetham, Sir Milne, 70–72, 74–75, 94–95
Clayton, Gilbert, 72–73, 153–54, 160, 187
Colli, Count, 194–95
Colonial Office (Great Britain), 157
Committee of Imperial Defence (Great Britain), 20
Committee of Union and Progress (CUP), 24–25, 33–34, 108, 202–3, 222
Constantinople Agreement, 152
Cox, Sir Percy, 37, 99, 211
Crow, Eyre, 74
Crew, Lord, 36
Cromer, Evelyn Baring Lord, 12, 19–23, 32
Ctesiphon, 162
Cumberbatch, H. A., 30–31
Curzon, George, 15

Danakils, 215
Dardanelles. *See* Gallipoli Peninsula
Darfur, 105, 190, 192–93, 260n. 38
Das, Taraknath, 78
Datta, Bhupendranath, 78, 217
Dawn, C. Ernest, ix
De Bunsen, Maurice, 102
Defence of India Act, 77
Dekker, Douwes, 123, 125
Democrats, 134, 136, 138, 141
Dering, Herbert, 125
Deutsche Bank, 14, 44, 92
Deutsche Orientbank, 14, 21
Deutsche-Palästina Bank, 14
Dhows (small boats), 94
Dinar, Ali, 105, 149, 192–93
Dinshawai incident, 20
Djember, 126
"Dr. Mann." *See* Mannesmann, Otto
Duff, Grant, 118

"Easterners," 95, 97, 163, 187
Egypt: and Arab revolt, 189; and Britain,

Egypt *(cont.)*
xi–xii, 2, 15–16, 20, 69–72, 92, 155, 163, 182–83, 185; capitulations in, 21; and *entente cordiale,* 15–16; and Germans, 17–24, 32–33, 47; nationalists of, 12–13, 20–21, 23, 32–33, 89, 196, 227; opinion in, 69–70, 92, 102–3, 189, 252n. 2; and pan-Islamism, 20, 31; protectorate proclaimed in, 92; sultan of, 92, 103, 209; troop numbers in, 33, 57, 72, 87, 97, 101–2, 163, 190, 274n. 45; Turkish–German attack on, 52–59, 69–72, 97–98, 100–101, 155, 182–83. *See also* Abbas Hilmi II

Egyptian Expeditionary Force (EEF; Great Britain), and Anatolia, 224; formation of, 182; and Palestine, 199, 200, 202, 207–8, 212, 214, 224; and Sinai Peninsula, 182, 185; and Transjordan, 220, 221

Egyptian national library, 33, 38

Ekbatana, 83

Emden, 77, 106

Enver Pasha: and Abadan, 83; and Abbas Hilmi, 53, 117; and Afghanistan, 79; and Ali Dinar, 192, 193; and Arab revolt, 181, 184, 222; background of, 33; and Central Office for the Islamic Movement, 50; and coup of 1913, 33; draws Turks into war, 85; and Egypt, 56, 167; Falkenhayn and, 151, 212; flees, 227; and Germans, 47, 66, 107, 108–9, 114–15, 128–30, 140, 148, 151, 174–75, 176, 191, 212; and Ibn Saud, 107; and Ibn Rashid, 107; and India, 51; and Italy, 88; and al-Jawish, 44; and Jemal Pasha, 115, 174–75, 179–80; and *jihad,* 107; and "Maurice," 210; member of ruling faction, 87, 201–2; and Mesopotamia, 212; and Obeidullah's mission, 79; pan-Turanism of, 79, 86, 128, 201–2, 221; and Palestine, 212; and peace overtures, 218; and Persia, 128–

30; preparations for war, 49, 58; and Rauf Bey, 133, 135; replacement of, 226; and Sanussis, 88–89, 146–47,151, 191; and Sharif of Mecca, 111, 115, 166, 173–76, 179, 184; and *Taskilat-i Mahsusa,* 50; and Wahib Bey, 179; and Wangenheim, 53–54, 108, 133, 135, 164; and Wolff-Metternich, 164, 166; Zimmermann and, 107, 108, 133, 151

Erzberger, Matthias, 117

Euphrates and Tigris Steam Navigation Company, 35

Ex-khedive. *See* Abbas Hilmi II

Falkenhayn, Erich von, 57, 169, 181, 168–69, 200–201, 212, 221

Farid, Muhammad, 23, 32–33, 53–54, 71, 89, 196, 227

Farman Farma, 141, 142

al-Faruqi, Muhammad Sharif, 153–54

Fatherland party, 225

Fauzi Bey, Omar, 56

Faysal: and Arab revolt, 177–78, 187, 203, 207, 213, 221–22; demands of, 224; and Germans, 64, 108, 109–11, 117, 158, 172, 212, 224; and Jemal Pasha, 177, 213; and Lawrence, 111, 203, 207, 224; and nationalist societies, 110–11; and peace settlement, 229–30; and Sharif of Mecca, 110, 222–23; and Turks, 109–10, 174–75, 177–78, 213, 222–24

Fifth Army (Turkish), 180–81

Le Figaro, 117

Fischer, Fritz, 48

Fitzmaurice, Gerald, 75, 241n. 32

Flotow, Johannes von, 57, 88

Foreign Office (Great Britain), and Abbas Hilmi, 89–90, 199; and Abyssinia, 157, 194; and Arab revolt, 188, 205; and Egypt, 20, 32, 70; and Hijaz railroad, 19, 20; and al-Idrisi, 75, 95; and India, 76; and Italy, 93, 147, 150; and Jemal Pasha, 162; and

Libya, 147; and al-Masri, 72; and Oppenheim, 19; and pan-Islamism, 25–26; and peace overtures, 218–19; and Sharif of Mecca, 160, 161; and Turkey, 37, 40, 41, 69, 71; and Yahya, 75

Fourth Army (Turkish), 50, 58–59, 61, 70–71, 86, 97–98, 100–101, 164, 212, 222

France: and Ali Dinar, 192; and Arab alliance, 75; and Arab revolt, 75, 186–88; and Baghdad railroad, 8; and Britain, 15, 75, 161, 186–88, 206–8, 223; and Constantinople Agreement, 152; and Germany, 7; imperialist aims of, 280n. 90; and Oppenheim, 22; and peace settlement, 289n. 13; and Sharif of Mecca, 75, 206; and Switzerland, 197; and Sykes-Picot Agreement, 162, 206–7; and Syria, 75, 155, 162, 206–7, 223, 280n. 90; and Triple Entente, 15

Franz Joseph, 117

Freemasons, 241n. 32

French Foreign Legion, 22, 257n. 82

French Somaliland, 214–15

Frobenius, Leo, 63, 64–65, 105–6, 156–57

Fromkin, David, ix, 229

Fuad Selim, 173–74, 197–98, 210

Fundamentalism (Islam), xiii

Gali, Ali, 173

Gallipoli Peninsula, 76, 95–96, 101–2, 155, 162, 170

German-Armenian Society, 114

German army, 13, 225

German colonial ministry, 167–68, 225

German East Africa, 104, 167–68, 176, 214, 260n. 33, 287n. 64. See also Stotzingen, Othmar von

German foreign ministry: and Abadan, 83; and Abbas Hilmi, 198; and Abyssinia, 156; and Afghanistan, 52, 79–82; and Ali Dinar, 192; and Amir Said, 51; anti-Semitism in, 11–12, 237–38n. 40; and Arab revolt, 179, 181, 198, 202–3, 220, 224; and Arabs, 42–43, 151, 223; and Armenians, 114; and Baghdad railroad, 44–45; and colonial ministry, 168; and Egypt, 21–22, 51, 54–55, 57–58, 87; and Enver Pasha, 79, 151; and expeditions to Middle East, 59–66, 128; and Ibn Saud, 164; imperialism of, 168; and India, 51, 54, 120, 122–23, 128, 217, 226; and Information Service for the East, 67, 108; Islamic section of, 50; and Italy, 88; and Jemal Pasha, 115, 164–65, 167; and Libya, 89, 151, 190; and the navy, 53, 190; and Oppenheim, 11, 108–12, 201; and Orientals, 227–28; and pan-Islamism, 13–14, 167; and Persia, 80, 129–30, 136, 139, 141; and Persian Gulf, 82–84; political department of, 50, 51, 108; and propaganda, 51, 59, 201; and Rauf Bey, 135; and reserve General Staff (stellvertretende Generalstab), 50, 51, 129–30; and Sanussis, 191; and Sharif of Mecca, 164, 166; and Sudan, 168–69; and Turkey, 9–10, 58, 108–9, 151, 202–3

German General Staff: and Abadan, 83; and Abyssinia, 156; and Afghanistan, 52, 79; and Arab revolt, 181; and British forces, 49; and East Africa, 167–69; and Egypt, 49, 52, 167; and Enver Pasha, 79, 140; and expeditions to Middle East, 59–66, 174; and foreign ministry, 50, 51, 129–30; and Jemal Pasha, 165, 167; and Libya, 89, 190; and the navy, 190; and pan-Islamism, 167; and Persia, 128–30; and Persian Gulf, 82, 84; reserve section (stellvertretende Generalstab) of, 50, 106; and Sanussis, 191; Sektion IIIb Politik of, 50, 257n. 82; and Sudan, 168–69; and von der Goltz, 140; and war by revolution, 49; and Young Turks, 58

German navy, 6, 46–47, 52–55, 83, 125, 168, 190, 225
German Oriental Institute, 227
Germany: and Abadan, 82–85, 132; and Abbas Hilmi, 21–22; and Afghanistan, 7, 47, 52; and Anatolian railroad, 4, 8; and Anglo-Turkish convention, 39; and Arabs, xii, 4, 27–30, 38–39, 41–44, 81; and Armenians, 7, 9; and Baghdad railroad, 14–15, 24, 38, 40, 44–45; and Britain, x, xi, 15–16, 28, 30, 35–40, 44, 46–47, 61, 67; and central African empire, 55, 105, 168, 260n. 36; defeat of, 226; and Egypt, 17–24, 32–33, 47; encirclement of, 39; and *entente cordiale*, 15–16; and France, 53, 55, 220; and German East Africa, 104, 167–68, 260n. 33; and Hijaz railroad, 19; imperialism of, 3–4, 39, 55, 235n. 19, 260n. 36; and Jemal Pasha, 114–15, 164–65, 177–78, 204, 212–14; and Jews, 112–13; and July crisis, 44–45; and Klein expedition, 83–85, 129–30; loss of colonies of, 260n. 33; and Mesopotamia, 19, 24, 28–29, 35, 38, 40, 42, 43–44; military strategy of, 46–47; and Morocco, 17, 39, 51; Muslim subjects of, 4; and nazism, 230; and oil, 40, 82–85; and Orientalists, 11; and pan-Islamism, x, xii, 17, 22, 30; paranoia of, 15; and peace feelers, 197; and Persia, 37–38, 47; and Persian Gulf, 14, 37, 82–84; and Russia, 166; and Syria, 12, 19, 24, 28, 38; and Transjordan, 221; and Turkey, 4–10, 14–15, 28, 34, 39–40, 47–48, 55–56, 69, 86, 95–96, 235n. 13, 237n. 28; and Versailles treaty, 227; view of Orient and Orientals, 8, 58; war aims of, x, xii, 46, 48, 55, 106, 168; war's impact on, 227–28, 230; and Weimar Republic, 227–28; and *Weltpolitik*, xii, 6, 13. *See also* Army Group F (German); German foreign ministry; German General Staff; Turkey; war by revolution (Germany)

Ghadr (Mutiny) party, 77–78, 122, 123
Gifford, Gerald, 217
Giorgis, Habte, 158, 193, 195
Glasenapp, Helmuth von, 76
Goeben, 49, 69, 85
Goltz, Colmar Freiherr von der, 13, 140, 142–43, 170, 185–86, 211
Gondos, Franz, 63, 64, 251n. 61
Gorst, Sir Eldon, 23, 31
Grahame, T.G., 138
Grand vizier (prime minister), 34
Great Britain: and Abadan, 37, 40, 82, 84, 132; and Abbas Hilmi, 21–22, 32, 53, 71, 89–90, 103, 117–19, 198–99; and Aden, 2, 95; and Aqaba incident, 19–20; and Arabs xi, 30–33, 40–41; and Armenians, 7, 35, 114; and Baghdad railroad, 8, 35–36, 40; and Burma, 125; and Constantinople Agreement, 152; and "Easterners," 95, 163, 187; Egypt, xi–xii, 2, 15–16, 17–24, 52, 69–72, 90, 92, 100–102, 163, 182–83, 185; and India, x, xii, 3, 7, 15, 76–77, 122–25, 189; and Farid, 71; and France, 15; and French Somaliland, 215; and Gallipoli, xi, 101–2, 163, 170; and Germany, x–xi, 6–7, 15–16, 17–24, 28, 31, 34, 35–40, 47, 104; and India, Government of, 2, 7, 123; and Hijaz railroad, 19; and Ibn Saud, 36–37; impact of war on, 228–30; and Italy, 93–94, 102, 147, 150; and Jews, xi, 113; and Kuwait, 2, 15, 36, 39; and Libya, 93–94, 145–51, 175–76, 190; and al-Masri, 72, 116; and Mesopotamia, xi, 35, 36, 39–40, 84, 102, 132–33, 135, 142, 162, 163, 165, 170, 185–86, 199, 200, 211–12, 224–25; and military strategy, 95; and Muhammarah, 2, 37; and Oppenheim, 22; and Palestine, 32, 43, 200, 202, 205, 207–8, 213, 224, 229; and pan-Islamism, x–xi, xii, 3, 7, 17, 25;

and peace feelers, 197, 217–19; and Persia, 37, 80, 81–82, 133–34, 137–38, 140–45; and Persian Gulf, 2, 14–15, 35–36, 74, 81–82, 84; and Red Sea, 104; and Russia, 2, 7, 15, 40; and Siam, 125; and Sudan, 7; and Syria, 20, 30–31, 41, 214, 220, 229; and Transjordan, 220, 221; and Turkey, xi, 1–3, 6–7, 17, 25–26, 31–32, 34, 35–39, 44, 47, 76; and United States, 126, 189–90; and Versailles treaty, 227; view of Muslims, 3, 234n. 8; and Weimar Republic, 227; and "Westerners," 163, 188; and Young Turks, 25–26, 35. *See also* British Empire; Egypt; Foreign Office (Great Britain); India Office (Great Britain); Turkey; war by revolution (Great Britain); War Office (Great Britain)

Grey, Sir Edward: and Abbas Hilmi, 118–19; and Abyssinia, 195; and Arabia, 31; and Egypt, 20–21, 70; and Gallipoli, 102; imperialism of, 102; and Islam, 21, 25; and McMahon, 155–56, 195; and Muslim feeling, 103; and Sharif of Mecca, 118, 187, 195; and Stotzingen mission, 195; and Turkey, 34–35, 38, 40–41, 73, 152, 155; Griesinger, Walter, 130, 138, 143

Gumppenberg, Otto von, 102, 148

Gupta, Heramba Lal, 122, 124, 190

Habibullah, 52, 79, 128, 143–45, 270n. 89

Haidar, Ali, 180

Halid, Hakki, 282n. 125

Halim, Said, and Abbas Hilmi, 34, 47, 53, 87, 89–90, 184, 201, 208

Hall, Salomon, 156

Hamburg-Amerika Line, 37, 79, 83

Hamilton, Sir Ian, 101, 154

Har Dayal, Lala, 78, 120, 122, 127

Hardinge, Charles, 36, 76

Harerge, 195

Hassan, Aziz, 92, 182

Hassan, Muhammad Anim Bey ibn, 173

Hatzfeldt, Hermann Count von, 32

Hatzfeldt, Paul Graf von, 11

Helfferich, Emil, 124

Helfferich, Theodor, 124

Henry S., 124

Hentig, Werner Otto von, 128, 136–37, 138–39, 143–45, 225

Hesse, W. G., 28, 29–30, 40, 43–44

Hijaz railroad, 30; and Arab revolt, 177–78, 183, 187, 203, 207, 221; Bedouins plunder, 28, 182; and Britain, 19; construction of, 9; and Sharif of Mecca, 34

Hilgendorf, 63, 64

Hirtzel, Sir Arthur, 36, 74, 170–71

Hogarth, David G., 41

Hohenlohe-Langenburg, Ernst Fürst zu, 113

Holderness, T. W., 171

Holtzendorff, Arndt von, 79–80, 83

Holy War. *See* Jihad; Turkey; war by revolution (Germany)

Holz, Arnold, 214–15

Hourani, Albert, ix

Humann, Hans, 55, 88, 107, 108, 135, 148, 173, 181

Husayn ibn Ali (Sharif of Mecca), Abbas Hilmi on, 223; and Arab nationalists, 27, 109, 116; Austria-Hungary and, 165; and Balfour Declaration, 222; and Britain, 109, 153, 155, 161, 170–72, 175, 187–88, 205–7, 213; and caliphate, 103; Enver Pasha and, 111, 176–77; and Faysal, 109–10, 174–75, 177, 222–23; and France, 187, 188, 206; and Germans, 61–64, 108–9, 165–66, 172–74, 180; and Ibn Rashid, 73; and Ibn Saud, 73, 171, 186, 222; and al-Idrisi, 73; and Jemal Pasha, 174, 177, 213; and Kitchener, 75, 153; Lawrence and, 189; and McMahon, 103, 116, 153, 175; and non-Muslims, 64; and Oppenheim, 22, 109, 165–66, 184–85, 205; and Picot,

Husayn ibn Ali *(cont.)*
206–7; revolt of, 177–82, 203–4; and
Stotzingen mission, 171–72, 206; and
Sykes, 206–7; and Sykes-Picot Agreement, 162, 206, 222; and Turks, 29, 34,
43, 73, 94, 99, 109, 165, 174–77, 202–3;
and Wahib Bey, 62, 64, 91, 106, 109;
and Yahya, 73; and Yemen, 29
Husayn Kamil, 92, 103, 209

Ibn Rashid: and Enver Pasha, 107; and
Germany, 42, 106; and Ibn Saud, 29,
36, 62, 73, 99–100, 104, 106; Musil mission and, 65, 91, 107; and Nuri ibn
Shaalan, 66, 91; and Sharif of Mecca,
73, 204; and Turks, 54, 65, 99, 203–4
Ibn Saud: and Britain, 29, 36–37, 161,
164, 186; and Germans, 164, 166; and
India, government of, 36, 84, 98–99;
and Ibn Rashid, 29, 36, 62, 73, 91, 99–
100, 104, 106; Musil mission and, 65,
107; and Nuri ibn Shaalan, 66; and
peace settlement, 229; and Shakespear, 36–37, 74, 84, 98–100; and
Sharif of Mecca, 73, 106, 186; and
Turks, 36–37, 54, 65, 99, 107, 171, 203
Ibn Shaalan, 38, 65–66, 91
Ibrahim Bey, 203
Idris, Muhammad, 190–91, 214
al-Idrisi, Sayyid, 54, 73, 95, 99
Igel, Wolf Walter Franz von, 190, 216
Imam (spiritual leader), 30
Imperial General Staff (Great Britain),
163. *See also* British General Staff
India: and Arab revolt, 189; Bengal in,
77–78; Germany and, 76–79, 120–27;
and Great Rebellion, 3; and Lahore
trial, 216; Muslims of, 3, 7, 36, 189,
234n. 9, 245n. 79; and nationalists, 36,
245n. 79; North-West Frontier Province in, 7, 37, 144, 236n. 23; and pan-
Islamism, 36, 77; Punjab in, 76–78,
122, 265n. 8; revolutionaries of, in Far

East, 122–26; revolutionaries of, in
United States, 77–79, 120, 123–25; and
Singapore revolt, 122; and troops for
war, 57, 72, 87, 92, 122. *See also* India,
Government of; India Office (Great
Britain); United States
India, Government of: and Arab alliance, 73–74, 103; and Arab revolt, 188;
and Cairo, 103; and defending India,
76–77, 91, 123, 189; and Habibullah,
144; and Ibn Saud, 36, 84, 98–99, 103;
and al-Idrisi, 103–4; influence of, 2;
and *jihad,* 98; and Muslim subjects,
41; and pan-Islamism, 7, 36; and Persia, 145; and Persian Gulf, 2, 103; and
Red Sea, 103–4; and Sharif of Mecca,
160; and shaykh of Kuwait, 15, 245n.
81; troops of, 137; and Turkey, 41; and
Wassmuss, 131. *See also* India; India
Office (Great Britain)
Indian Expeditionary Force D (IEF D),
84, 132–33
Indian Independence Committee (Berlin), Stockholm branch of, 216–17,
226; formation of, 77–78, 120; and
German policy, 217, 226; and Indian
revolutionaries, 78, 216–17; and Jagow,
127; members of, 78; and missions to
Middle East, 126–27; problems of, 122,
127, 215–16, 225–26; revolutionary
schemes of, 120; and Russian revolutionaries, 216, 217, 226; and Turkey,
162
India Office (Great Britain), 25, 35–36,
73–74, 103, 170, 171, 205
Information Service for the East
(*Nachrichtenstelle für den Orient;*
Germany), 67–68, 76, 108, 112, 118, 120,
184, 227. *See also* German foreign
ministry; German Oriental Institute
Inger, Solomon, 102
International socialist conference
(Stockholm), 216

Ishaak, 195

Italy: and Abyssinia, 156–57, 193–95; and Britain, 93–94, 147, 150, 214; enters war, 93, 106, 135, 147; and Frobenius, 105, 156; and Germans, 56–58, 88–89, 105, 145–47; and Sami Bey, 62; and Sanussis, 56–57, 105–6, 145–51, 190, 214

Iyasu, Lij, 105, 156–58, 174–75, 193–96

Izzet Pasha, 282n. 125

Jabbar Kheiry, Abd, al-, 78

Jacoby, Heinrich, 118–19, 198, 217

Jacob, H. F., 95

Jäckh, Ernst, 39, 50, 79, 113

Jagow, Gottlieb von, 39, 46, 48–49, 58, 59, 83, 86, 127, 198

Javid Bey, 87, 197, 202, 218

al-Jawish, Abd al-Aziz, 23, 32–33, 44, 56–57, 71, 227

Jemal Pasha, and Allies, 116, 162, 263n. 81; and Arabs, 114–16, 16w4–65, 177, 204, 223; and Arab revolt, 181, 202, 213, 222; and coup of 1913, 33; and Egypt, 100; and Enver Pasha, 115, 174, 212; and Faysal, 177, 180; flees, 227; and Fourth Army, 86, 164; and Germans, 29, 115–16, 164–65, 177–78, 204, 212–14; and Ibn Rashid, 115; and Ibn Saud, 115; and Jews, 112, 213; and Kressenstein, 100, 115, 202, 212; and loss of command, 202, 212; and "Maurice," 210; and Oppenheim, 165, 177; pan-Islamism of, 86; replacement of, 226; and ruling faction, 87; rumors about, 203; and Sharif of Mecca, 174, 177, 179–80, 214, 222; and Sykes-Picot agreement, 213; and Stotzingen mission, 174–75, 177; and Zionism, 213

Jessrasinghi, Thakur Shri, 216–17

Jews, 112–13, 208, 241n. 32

Jihad (holy war). See Turkey; war by revolution (Germany)

Kaiser Friedrich Museum, 38

Kalisch, 90

Kamerun, 104

Kamil, Mustafa, 12, 20, 23

Kanitz, Georg von, 135, 140–42

Karbala, 28, 35, 85, 131, 135

Kardorff, Radolf von, 80, 82, 129, 133, 134

Kayser, Paul, 11

Kedourie, Elie, ix

Khabur valley, 38

Khairy Bey, 184

Khalil Bey, 174

al-Khatib, Fuad, 185, 206

Khazal, 37

Khedive. See Abbas Hilmi II

Kiderlen-Wächter, Alfred von, 13, 39

Kitchener, Horatio Herbert Lord: and Abbas Hilmi, 32, 118–19; and Abdullah, 41, 74–75; and Alexandretta, 155; and Arabs, 32, 41, 72–76, 152; and caliphate, 30, 75; and defending Egypt, 32, 42, 72, 101, 155; as "Easterner," 95; and Egyptian nationalists, 32–33; and Gallipoli, 101–2, 155; and Germans, 32–33; imperialism of, 102; and Italy, 147; and al-Masri, 32; and Mors, 71; and pan-Islamism, 74, 95; replaced, 163; shapes policy, 32; and Sharif of Mecca, 73, 75, 118–19, 153; and Turkey, 31–32, 41, 152; as war minister, 70

Klein, Fritz, 33, 83–85, 129, 131–32, 135, 141

Kraft, Vincent, 126

Kressenstein, Friedrich Freiherr Kress von: and Arab revolt, 202; and Egypt, 63, 100–101, 167, 182–83; and Enver Pasha, 212; and Falkenhayn, 212; and Fourth Army, 58; and intelligence information, 98; and Jemal Pasha, 100, 115, 167, 212; and Moritz expedition, 62–64; reward for, 71

Krupp, 7, 21, 79, 235–36n. 20

Kühlmann, Richard von, 202–4, 210

Kut al-Amara, 170, 185

Kuwait, 2, 14–15, 36, 99, 245n. 81

Lahore trial, 216
Langwerth von Simmern, Ernst Freiherr, 51, 81, 83, 108
Lascelles, Sir Frank, 19–21
Lawrence, T. E., ix, xii, 32, 41, 111; and Arab revolt, ix, 186, 188, 203, 207, 221, 224
Leachman, Gerard, 36–37, 211
Ledoulx, Alphonse, 282n. 126
Lenders, Theodor, 131
Lepsius, Johannes, 114
Lettow-Vorbeck, Paul von, 167
Libya, 26, 33; and Britain, 93–94, 145–51, 175–76, 190; Germans and, 214, 225; and Italy, 56–57, 105–6, 145–51, 190, 214; Mannesmann mission to, 57, 88–89, 93, 146–51, 191; Sanussis in, 56, 88, 93–94, 145–51, 163, 176, 190–91, 214
Lichnowsky, Karl von, 40
Listemann, Helmuth, 82, 131
Lloyd George, David, 188, 200, 206–8, 217–19
Logothetti, Count, 133
Lorimer, J. G., 30
Lossow, Otto von, 140, 141, 174, 184
Lowther, Gerard, 25–26, 35, 41
Loytved Hardegg, Julius, 107, 173, 177–78, 179, 181–82, 184, 203
Ludendorff, Erich, 224
Lührs, Hans, 81, 132
Lutfi Bey, 282n. 125
Lutfullah, Habib, 118–19

Macedonians, 24
McMahon, Sir Henry, and Abbas Hilmi, 103, 118–19; and Arab revolt, 187–88; and Grey, 155–56, 195; and Husayn Kamil, 103; and Ibn Rashid, 104; and Italy, 102, 147; and Muslim feeling, 103, 147; and policy coordination, 103; and Sanussis, 102, 176; and Sharif of Mecca, 103, 116, 153, 155, 161, 175

"Mad Mullah." See Abdullah, Sayyid Muhammad
Maharajah of Nepal, 128
Mallet, Sir Louis, 35, 41, 49, 64, 69, 70–71, 73–75
Malta, 71, 92
Mandelstam, Andreas N., 282n. 126
Mannesmann, Otto, 51, 57, 88–89, 93, 146–47, 148–51, 191, 257n. 82
Mannesmann, Reinhard, 51, 80–81, 235–36n. 20
Marathay, Narajenawai, 123
Maresch, Paul, 81
al-Masri, Aziz Bey, 32, 43, 72, 106, 116, 227, 247n. 106, 291n. 38
Maude, F. S., 186
Maugham, William Somerset, 119, 198
"Maurice." See Mustafa Bey
Maverick, 125
Maxwell, Sir John, 70–71, 92, 101, 147, 154–55, 163
Mazhar Bey, 157
Mecklenburg, Duke Adolf Friedrich zu, 104, 168
Mediterranean Expeditionary Force (MEF; Great Britain), xviii–xix, 101–2. See also Mesopotamia Expeditionary Force
Megiddo, 224
Mehmed V, 25, 85
Mehmed VI, 224
Meissner, Heinrich August, 239n. 5
Menilek, 156, 196
Mersa Matruh, 150–51
Mesopotamia: and Anglo-German agreement, 40; and Arab revolt, 181–82; and Arabs of, 29, 43–44, 135, 211; Britain and, 35–36; and German-Turkish conflicts, 129; pan-Islamism in, 85; and peace settlement, 229; Shiism in, 25–26, 28, 30, 35, 85, 135; war in, 132–33, 140, 162, 170, 182, 185–86, 199, 200–201, 210–12, 224–25

Mesopotamia Expeditionary Force
(MEF; Great Britain), xviii–xix, 205.
See also Mediterranean Expedition-
ary Force
Middle East: defined, 231n. 1; peace
settlement in, xi, 231n. 1, 231n. 3
Midhat, Kemal, 282n. 125
Mikail, Ras, 156, 175, 196
Miquel, Hans von, 42–43
Missmont. *See* Muntafiq Mission;
Preusser, Conrad
Mittwoch, Eugen, 67
Moltke, Helmuth von, 13, 47–49
al-Moneim, Abd, 103, 199, 208–9
Monroe, Elizabeth, 230
Moritz, Bernhard, 38, 61–64
Moroccan Crisis, 17
Morocco, 51, 235–36n. 20
Morocco Mine Syndicate, 51
Mors, Robert, 53, 55–57, 71
Moshi document, 176
Moukhtar Pasha, 19
Mousa, Suleiman, ix
al-Muayyad, 12
Mudros, 226
Müller, Adolf, 228
Mufti (one learned in Islamic law and
who issues decisions on the law), 61
Muhammad, 10, 17, 97
Muhammarah, 2, 37, 99, 132
Mukherjee, Jatin, 126
Mukhtar Pasha, 219
Muntafiq, 29, 38, 44, 211
Muntafiq Mission (Missmont), 211
Murray, Archibald, 182, 185–86
Musil, Alois, 30, 38, 65–66, 91, 107
Mustafa Bey ("Maurice"), 171, 199, 209–10
Mustaufi ul-Mamalik, 140–41
al-Mutasim, 38
Mutius, Gerhard von, 204, 279n. 62

Nachrichtenstelle für den Orient. See
Information Service for the East

Nadolny, Rudolf, 50–51, 106–7, 129–30,
132, 135, 140, 146, 151, 257n. 82
Najaf, 28, 30, 35, 85, 131, 135
Napoleon III, 235n. 17
Naqib, Sayyid Talib, al- 28, 42, 253n. 24
Nasrullah, 144
Nawwaf, 66, 91
Nazim Pasha, 30
Neufeld, Karl, 64, 174–75
Neurath, Konstantin von, 166
Nicholas II: and Wilhelm II, 9–10
Nicolson, Arthur, 25, 35–36
Niedermayer, Oskar von, 134; and
Abadan, 83; and Faysal, 212, 221; and
Habibullah, 143–45; and mission to
Afghanistan, 80–81, 85, 128, 130, 136–37,
138–39, 143–45; and pan-Turanism,
221; and Persia, 130, 136, 138
Noradunghian, Gabriel Effendi, 282n. 125
Nureddin Bey, 218
Nuri ibn Shaalan. *See* Ibn Shaalan
Nuri Pasha, 89, 146–48, 191–92

Obeidullah Effendi, 79
O'Connor, W. F. T., 142
Ogaden Somalis, 193–94
Oppenheim, Max Freiherr von, 32; and
Abadan, 83, 85; and Abbas Hilmi, 22–
23, 98; and Afghanistan, 51–52, 79–80;
and Arabs, 171; and Armenians, 113–14,
158; background of, 10–12; and Baghdad railroad, 24, 38; and Bernstorff,
24; and Bethmann Hollweg, 51, 80;
and British, 12, 19–20, 29; Cairo's fear
of, 159–60; called "Kaiser's spy," 22,
24; and Constantinople embassy, 87–
88; disputed influence of, 13, 238n. 49;
and Egypt, 12–13, 19, 22–24, 66–67, 86–
87; and Enver Pasha, 51, 108; and
Faysal, 109–11, 117; and foreign ministry, 11, 50; and Frobenius expedition,
64; and Ibn Saud, 65, 67; and Ibn
Rashid, 65; and India, 51–52, 66, 77–

Oppenheim, Max Freiherr von, *(cont.)* 78, 80, 122, 127; and India, government of, 158; imperialism of, 276n. 2; and Information Service for the East, 67–68, 108, 112; and Jemal Pasha, 115, 165, 167, 223; and Jews, 112–13; and *jihad,* 51, 66–67, 90, 98; meets Husayn ibn Ali, 22; memorandum of, 66–67; in Mesopotamia, 38; mission of, 107–12, 158–60, 171; and Moritz expedition, 62; and Moukhtar Pasha, 19; and Musil mission, 65; nationalism of, 68; and pan-Islamism, 13, 22, 24, 77, 111–12, 158; and Persia, 79–80; and propaganda, 51, 66–68, 108, 110, 111, 201; and Prüfer, 57, 111; and Sharif of Mecca, 61, 62, 65, 109, 160, 184–85, 205, 223; Sykes's fear of, 159–60; and Tell Halaf, 12, 24, 38; and Young Turks, 24
Orientalists, 11
Ottoman Empire. *See* Turkey

Padel, Wilhelm, 28, 106
Palestine: and peace settlement, 229; war in, 200–201, 202, 205, 207–8, 213, 214, 220, 222, 224
Palestine Exploration Fund, 32
Pan Arab movement, 75
Pan-German League, 39, 55, 168, 215, 225, 235n. 19
Pan-Islamism: doctrine of, x, 2–3. *See also* Egypt; Germany; Great Britain; India; Mesopotamia; Oppenheim, Max Freiherr von; Turkey; war by revolution (Germany); war by revolution (Great Britain)
Pannwitz, von, 52
Pan-Turanism. *See* Enver Pasha; Talaat Pasha; Turkey; Young Turks
Papen, Franz von, 79, 123, 125–26, 222–24
Parodi, H., 218
Paschen, Peter, 130
Pasha I, 167

Pasha II (Asia Korps), 212
La Patrie Egyptienne (The Egyptian Fatherland), 54
Persia: and British, 37, 80, 129, 140–43; declares neutrality, 82; and Germans, 37–38, 47, 79–82, 128–43; and Russians, 37, 129, 140–43; and Turks, 131, 133–45; and Shiism, 131, 134. *See also* Germany; Great Britain; Russia; war by revolution (Germany)
Persian Carpet Company, 80
Persian Committee, 133
Persian Gulf, 2, 14–15, 27–28, 35–36, 74, 81–82, 84
Picot, François Georges, 206–7
Pillai, Chempakaraman, recruited by Germans, 78
Pilling, J. R., 219
Prabhakar, Marthe, 78
Pratap Singh, Mahendra, 127–28, 136–37, 145, 226
Press Act (India), 77
Preusser, Conrad, 81, 211, 225
Pröbster, Edgar, 108–9, 150–51
Prüfer, Curt: and Abbas Hilmi, 223; and Abdullah, 98; and Arabs, 56, 58, 59, 61, 165–66; and Arab revolt, 180, 212; and Egypt, 22, 32–33, 55–56, 63, 101; and Enver Pasha, 56; and Fourth Army, 58; imperialism of, 225, 275n. 64; and Information Service for the East, 223; and al-Jawish, 57, 71; and Jemal Pasha, 165–66; and Jews, 112–13; and *jihad,* 90–91, 98, 101; and Kitchener, 33; and "Maurice," 210; and Mors, 55–57, 71; and propaganda, 201; reward for, 71; and Sanussis, 212; and Sharif of Mecca, 62, 91, 173, 212; and Wangenheim, 57

al-Qadir, Abd, 51
Qashgais, 85, 138
Qawam-ul-Mulk, 142

Quadt, Alfred Graf von, 61

Rais Ali, 139
Rashid Pasha, 42, 218, 282n. 125
Rauf Bey, 81, 129, 133, 135, 139
Red Sea, 104
Remy, Erwin, 124
Reserve General Staff (*stellvertretende
    Generalstab*). See German General
    Staff
Reuss, Prince Heinrich XXXI of, 133–36,
    137–39, 140, 142
Reventlow, Ernst von, 215
Rida, Muhammad Rashid, 31, 41–42
Rifat, Mansur, 54
Robertson, William, 163, 188
Rodd, Sir Rennell, 93, 158
Rössler, Walter, 204
Rohlfs, Gerhard, 11
Rohrbach, Paul, 39, 113
Roloff, Max, 62
Romani, Battle of, 182–83
Romberg, Baron Gisbert von, 54, 119,
    174, 209–10, 228
Rosen, Friedrich von, 14, 238–39n. 51
Rothschild, Moritz, 113
Royle, L. V., 93–94, 147
Rualla, 38, 65
Romania, 80, 82, 84
Rumbold, Horace, 199, 218–19
Russia: and Bolsheviks, 213, 217; collapse
    in war, 201; and Germany, 6, 7, 34,
    166; and Persia, 37, 129, 131, 134, 137,
    139, 140–45; and Sykes-Picot agree-
    ment, 213; and Switzerland, 197; and
    Turkey, 6, 34, 102
Russo-Turkish War (1877–78), 3
Ryan, Sir Andrew, 73

as-Sabah, Mubarak, 15, 29
Sabaheddin, Prince, 196–97
Saddik, Yussuf Bey, 24
Sadhun Pasha, 29, 247n. 107

Said, Amir, 51
Salandra, Antonio, 88
Salar ud-Daula, 82
Salih, Shaykh. See al-Sharif al-Tunisi,
    Salih
Salisbury, Lord, 7
Samarra, 28, 38
Sami Bey, 62
Sanders, Liman von, 34, 49, 55–56, 63,
    95–96, 180–81, 221–22
Sanjak (flag of the prophet), 97
Sanussis, 70; and Abbas Hilmi, 23; and
    Ali Dinar, 192; and British, 93–94, 147,
    150, 190, 214; defeat of, 176; and Egypt,
    100, 150–51, 167, 225; and Italians, 56,
    105–6, 145–47, 214; and Mannesmann,
    57, 88, 146–47, 148–51; order of, 145–
    46; shaykh of, replaced, 190; and
    Turks, 146, 148, 191. See also Libya;
    war by revolution (Germany); war by
    revolution (Great Britain)
Sarre, Friedrich, 38, 130, 133, 141, 267n. 33
al-Sattar Kheiry, Abd, 78
Saud ibn Subhan, 107
Sayyid Ahmad. See al-Sharif, Sayyid
    Ahmad (Shaykh al-Sanussi)
al-Sayyid, Ahmad Lutfi, 23, 244n. 69
Schellendorff, Fritz Bronsart von, 104
Schlieffen, Alfred Count von, 172
Schlieffen, Countess von, 172
Schnee, Heinrich, 176
Schöllgen, Gregor, x
Schoenberg, Fritz, 166
Schowingen, Karl Emil Schabinger
    Freiherr von, 67
Schuenemann, Max Otto, 80–81, 130–31,
    133, 137
Schulze, Max, 124
Schwabe, 63, 64
Seeckt, Hans von, 224
Seiler, Eduard, 81, 130–31, 138, 142–43
Sektion IIIb Politik. See German Gen-
    eral Staff

Seminar for Oriental Languages, 4
Senne, 68
Seventh Army (Turkish), 201–2, 212
Shakespear, William, 36–37, 74, 84, 98–100
Shammar, 38, 204
Sharif of Mecca. See Husayn ibn Ali
Sharif Pasha, 282n. 125
al-Sharif, Sayyid Ahmad, (Shaykh al-Sanussi), 57, 145; and Ali Dinar, 192; and British, 93–94, 147, 150–51; defeat of, 176, 190; and Germans, 93, 146–47, 225; and jihad, 149; and khedivat, 89; and Mannesmann, 57, 88–89, 146, 148–51; replaced by cousin, 190, 191; and Sharif of Mecca, 146
al-Sharif al-Tunisi, Salih, 109, 180
Shaykh al-Sanussi. See al-Sharif, Sayyid Ahmad; Idris, Sayyid Muhammad
Sheffik, Ahmad, 110, 117
Shiites: beliefs of, 25–26, 28, 30, 35, 85, 131, 134–35, 182, 242n. 36
Siam, 123–25
Sinai Peninsula: and Aqaba incident, 19–20, 33, 38, 63–64, 72, 100–101, 155, 182
Singh, Bhagvan, 123
Singh, Jodh, 124–25, 189, 216
Sixth Army (Turkish), 140, 142, 170, 185, 201
Snow, C. L., 147, 150
Society for the Progress of Islam (Société Progrés de l'Islam), 53
Solf, Wilhelm, 105, 167–69, 226
South-West Africa, 104
Spitta, Wilhelm, 11
Steinwachs, Hans, 51
Stellvertretende Generalstab (reserve section of German General Staff), 50–51
Storrs, Ronald, 70, 72, 176
Stotzingen, Othmar von, 172–75, 177–78, 181, 279n. 62

Strempel, Major von, 29
Sublime Porte, 4. See also Turkey
Sudan, British defense measures in, 7, 62–65, 93, 104–6, 168, 173–74
Suez Canal, 22; and Britain, 19, 20, 69–72, 92, 154–55; Turkish-German attack on, 49–50, 52–61, 69–72, 98, 100, 165, 167, 182–83. See also Egypt
Sunnis, 26, 85, 134, 242n. 36
Sun Yat-sen, 123
Suwayhli, Ramadan, al-, 191, 214
Switzerland, 54, 118, 119, 196–99, 218–19
Syburg, von, 65, 175, 156–58, 193, 214–15
Sykes, Mark: and Anglo-Arab alliance, 1, 162; and France, 162, 206; and Grey, 187; and Oppenheim, 159–60; and peace feelers, 219; and Sharif of Mecca, 161, 187, 206; and Sykes-Picot agreement, 162, 206–7; and War Cabinet, 206, 219; and War Committee, 162, 187–88; and Turkey, 1
Sykes-Picot agreement, 162, 206–7, 213–14
Syria: Arabs of, 27; and Britain, 20, 30–31, 41; and caliphate, 31; and France, 40, 44, 75, 155, 162, 206–7, 223, 280n. 90; and Germany, 12, 19, 24, 28, 38; and Hijaz railroad, 19; and peace settlement, 229; war in, 214, 220

Tafari Makonnen, Ras, 195–96, 215
Talaat Pasha, and Arab revolt, 220, 224; and coup of 1913, 33–34; flees, 227; and Germany, 47; and "Maurice," 210; and Musil, 107; and pan-Turanism, 128, 201, 221; and peace feelers, 197, 218; as prime minister, 201, 208; replacement of, 226; and ruling faction, 87, 201–2, 208; and Stotzingen mission, 174
Tangistanis, 134, 138–39, 143
Taskilat-i Mahsusa (secret service), 50
Tauscher, Hans, 79
Tell Halaf, 12, 24, 38

Teuni, Jean, 282n. 125
Thesiger, Wilfried G., 157–58, 194–96, 215
Tilger, Alfred, 51, 89
The Times (London), 217
Tirpitz, Alfred von, 47, 53
Todenwarth, Freiherr Wolff von, 191–92, 214, 225
Togoland, 104
Transcaucasia, 221–22, 288n. 2
Transjordan, 221–22
Triple Alliance, 56
Triple Entente, 15, 58
Trotsky, Leon, 290n. 28
Trumpener, Ulrich, x
Tschirschky, Heinrich von, 20, 65, 117, 198
Tunis, 51
Turkey, and Abbas Hilmi, 56, 89, 90, 116–18, 198–99, 208–9, 225, 247n. 106; and Abyssinia, 157–58, 193–96; and Afghanistan, 79, 80; and Ali Dinar, 192; and Anatolian railroad, 4, 6, 8–9, 14; and Arabs, 26–33, 34–35, 56, 58, 66, 135, 173–75, 223; and Arab revolt, 177–85, 202–3, 220–25; and Armenians, 3, 7, 9, 35, 113–14, 262n. 67; and Army Group F (German), 200–202, 211–12, 224; and Baghdad railroad, 8–9, 14–15, 38; and Britain, xi, 19–20, 28, 35, 38–39, 49; and Caucasus, 86; and Central Office for the Islamic Movement, 50; and Central Powers, 76, 80, 87; defeat and dismantling of, 226, 229; and Egypt, 49–50, 52–59, 86, 92, 97–98, 100–101, 182–83; and Egyptian nationalists, 89, 117, 196; enters war, 76, 80, 84, 85; exiles of, 196–97, 209, 282n. 125; and factionalism, 87, 201–2; and Faysal, 109–10, 174–75, 177–78, 213, 222–24; Fifth Army of, 180–81; Fourth Army of, 50, 58, 212, 222; and France, 44; and Gallipoli, 95–96, 163–64, 170; and Germans, xi, 4, 6, 47–48, 55–56, 63–64, 66, 108–9, 114, 128–43,

164–66, 227; and Ibn Rashid, 56, 99, 203–4; and Ibn Saud, 36, 99, 203; and al-Idrisi, 99; and al-Jawish, 56; and Jews, 112, 284n. 11; and *jihad,* xi–xii, 85–86, 94, 131, 226; and Libya, 88–89, 145–51, 225; and loss of lands, 2, 26; and al-Masri, 116; and "Maurice," 210; and Mesopotamia, 132–33, 142, 162–63, 170, 185–86, 200, 224–25; as Muslim power, 2; neutrality of, 49; non-Turks in, 24; and Palestine, 200–202, 205, 207–8, 213, 220, 222, 224; and pan-Islamism, 9, 19, 25, 26, 33, 50, 85, 117; pan-Turanism of, ix, 34, 79, 86, 113, 128, 201, 221; and peace feelers, 197, 218–19; and Persia, 79, 128–45; and preparations for war, 49–50, 58, 69–72; and replacement of CUP, 226; and Sanussis, 146, 148, 191; Seventh Army of, 201–2, 212; and Sharif of Mecca, 34, 43, 94, 99, 109, 165–66, 173–79, 184, 202, 223; and Shiite-Sunni schism, 133, 135; Sixth Army of, 140, 142, 170,185, 200; and Stotzingen mission, 172–75, 279n. 62; and Syria, 44, 201, 220, 222; and *Taskilat-i Mahsusa,* 50; and Transcaucasia, 221–22, 288n. 2; and Transjordan, 221–22; and Wilhelm II, x, 8–10, 13–14, 209; and Yemen, 26, 28–29; war casualties of, 200; xenophobia of, 113; and Yahya, 94, 99, 173; and Young Turk revolution, 24–25, 33, 241n. 30. *See also* Arabs; Enver Pasha; Germany; Jemal Pasha; war by revolution (Germany); Young Turks
Turkish-Greek War (1897), 7
Turkish-Italian war (1911–12), 26, 33, 77

Ulamas (persons learned in Islamic theology and law), 85, 171
United States, 78–79, 120, 123–27, 189–90, 216

Vali (Turkish governor), 29
Vatican, 217
Versailles treaty, 227
Voigt, Günther, 81
Voretzsch, Dr., 124

Wagner, Wilhelm, 81
Wahhabis, 36
Wahib Bey, 62, 64, 91, 106, 109, 179, 257n. 89
Wangenheim, Baron Hans von: and Abadan, 83; and Abbas Hilmi, 53; and Arabs, 42–43; and Armenians, 113, 262n. 68; death of, 164; and Egypt, 55; and Enver Pasha, 53–54, 108–9, 133, 164; and foreign ministry, 108; and Ibn Rashid, 42; and Italy, 56, 58, 88; and Jemal Pasha, 115; and Jews, 112; and *jihad,* 86; and al-Masri,43, 116; and Oppenheim, 108–9; and pan-Islamism, 14, 44; and Persia, 129, 133, 135; personal rivalries of, 55–57; and Sanussis, 89; and Sharif of Mecca, 111; and Turks, 39, 42–43, 47–49, 108
War by revolution (Germany), and Abbas Hilmi, 53, 89–90, 116–17, 198–99, 208–9, 225; and Abyssinia, 104, 156–58, 193–94, 214; and Afghanistan, 51–52, 79–81, 128, 139, 143–45; aims of, xi–xii, 46–50, 51, 151; and Ali Dinar, 192; and Arabia, 168–69; and Arabs, 61–63, 67, 98, 106–7, 114, 135, 165–66, 171, 210–12; archaeologists in, 81; and Armenians, 113–14; arrogance of, 68, 213; and British, xi–xii, 46–48, 53, 61, 67, 140–63, 167, 170–76, 220; and caliphate, 61, 67; diplomatic blunders of, 88–89; as diversion, x, xii, 46, 49–50, 101, 140, 168, 248n. 16; earliest expeditions of, 59–66; and Egypt, 49–61, 69–72, 86, 97–98, 100–101, 165, 167, 182–83; and Enver Pasha, 51, 54, 56, 108, 114–15, 173; and Faysal, 109–11, 175,

212; financing of, 67, 87, 181, 184, 205, 284n. 23; Frobenius mission of, 63–65, 105–6, 156–57; Hall mission of, 156; historiography on, 232–33nn. 12; and Holz, 214–15; and Ibn Saud, 62, 107, 164, 166, 203; and Ibn Rashid, 62, 106–7, 203; imperialist aims of, 80, 104–5, 167–68, 201, 215, 217, 225–26, 276n. 2, 288n. 2; and India, 51–52, 76–79, 120–27, 215–17, 225–26; and Italy, 56–58, 88–89; and Jidda consulate, 66, 168; and *jihad,* xi–xii, 46, 48, 50–51, 66–67, 90–91, 97–99, 106–7, 117, 131, 134; Klein expedition of, 131, 135; in Libya, 56–57, 88–89, 145–51, 190–91, 214, 225; Mannesmann mission of, 88–89, 146–51, 191; and al-Masri, 116; "Maurice" and, 209–10; Mesopotamia and, 90, 129, 135, 181–82, 200–201, 210–12, 224–25; misperceptions of, 68; Muntafiq mission of, 211; Musil mission of, 65–66, 91, 107; Niedermayer and, 80–82, 128, 130–31, 136–39, 143–45, 212; Oppenheim and, 66–67, 107–12, 114, 166, 184–85; opposes Arab revolt, 179–85, 187, 201, 203–4, 212–13, 220–25; origins of, 1, 6, 17, 46–48, 233n. 13, 235n. 17; in Palestine, 212–13, 222, 224; pan-Islamism of, 48–51, 68, 69, 78, 86, 114, 117; and Persia, 52, 79–85, 128–43; plans for, 48–50; and postwar contacts, 227–28; Pratap-Hentig expedition of, 128, 136–39, 143–45; and prisoners of war, 68; problems of, 46–47, 52, 66, 67, 81–82, 86–88, 98, 104, 122–27, 134–39, 140–41, 164, 178–79, 184, 203–4; propaganda of, 51, 66–68, 108, 110, 112, 114, 133, 157, 184, 211; and Sanussis, 56–57, 88–89, 145–51, 190–91, 225; Sharif of Mecca and, 61–63, 66, 106, 108–10, 165–66, 169, 172–75, 178–81, 223; significance of, 228–30; Stotzingen mission of, 172–78, 279n.

62; and Sudan, 104, 156–57, 173–74, 192–93; and Switzerland, 54, 118–19, 197–99, 216–17; in Syria, 90, 212, 222, 224; and Turks, 52–59, 97–98, 100–101, 108, 128–43, 164–66, 180–83, 202–4, 212–13, 220–25, 277n. 18; and Wilhelm II, 48; and Yemen, 172, 174–75, 177–78. *See also* Egypt; Germany; German General Staff; India; Persia; Turkey; war by revolution (Great Britain)

War by revolution (Great Britain), and Abbas Hilmi, 208, 209; and Abdullah, 75, 153, 160; and Abyssinia, 157–58, 193–94; and Ajaimi, 211–12; and Ali Dinar, 192–93; Arab alliance of, xi, 1, 30–33, 72–76, 103–4, 152–56, 160, 170–72, 175; Arab Bureau and, 171, 188, 205–6; Arab revolt of, 175–79, 185–88, 203, 207, 228; Asquith and, 154–55, 162–63; and Balfour Declaration, 208; Cairo's influence on, 75, 103, 153–56, 158–61, 207; and caliphate, 72–75, 99, 103, 154; Clayton and, 72–73, 153–54, 160, 187; and dismantling Turkey, 152–53, 160–62, 170, 200, 208, 229; and al-Faruqi, 153–54; financing of, 187, 205, 208, 285n. 33; Fitzmaurice and, 75; Foreign Office and, 154, 161–62, 205; France and, 75, 161, 186–88, 206–8, 223; and German-Turkish threat, 152–56, 158–60, 170, 205–9; and Gallipoli, 154–55; Grey and, 73, 152, 155, 187; Hamilton and, 154; Hirtzel and, 74, 170; historiography on, ix–x, 231n. 3; and holy places, 186, 188; and Holz, 215; and Ibn Rashid, 73; and Ibn Saud, 73, 84, 98–100, 103, 161, 171, 186; and al-Idrisi, 73; imperialist aims of, 152, 154, 186, 188, 200, 207–8, 217, 218, 280n. 90; India, government of, and, 73–74, 103, 158, 188; India Office and, 73–74, 170–71, 205; intelligence information for, 73; and Jews, 208, 229; and

jihad, xi, 91, 92, 95, 98–99, 153–56, 159–60, 162–63, 192–93; Kitchener and, 72–75, 152–55; Lawrence and, 186, 189, 203; Lloyd George and, 207–8, 217; Mc-Mahon and, 153–56, 161, 175–76, 188; al-Masri and, 72; "Maurice" and, 171, 199, 209–10; Maxwell and, 154–55; and Mors, 71; and Moshi document, 176; Oppenheim and, 114, 158–60 162, 171, 205; and pan-Islamism, 73–75, 93, 95–96, 114, 170, 205, 228; and peace settlement, 206–7, 229–30; policy differences regarding, 103–4, 160, 171, 187–88; propaganda of, 65, 208; Rodd and, 158; Ryan and, 73; and Sanussis, 175–76, 190–91, 214; Shakespear and, 99–100; and Sharif of Mecca, 72–76, 94, 109, 118–19, 161, 171–72, 175–76, 187–88, 205–7, 213; significance of, 228–30; Stotzingen mission and, 171–72, 178, 185; Sudan and, 93, 192–93; and Switzerland, 118–19, 196, 198–99, 217; Sykes and, 159–63, 187–88, 206; Thesiger and, 157–58, 194–96, 215; and troops in Middle East, 33, 57, 72, 87, 92, 97, 101–2, 163, 190, 228, 274nn. 44, 45, 29n. 40; War Cabinet and, 206, 219, 221, 223; War Committee and, 162, 187–88; War Office and, 153–54, 159–62; and Wilhelm II, 156; Wingate and, 160–61; and Yahya, 73. *See also* Arabs; Egypt; Great Britain; India; Persia; Turkey; war by revolution (Germany)

War Office (Great Britain), 70, 72, 153–54, 159–60, 218

Wassmuss, Wilhelm, 37, 80–81, 131, 138–39, 142–43

Weber, Theodor, 87–88, 180

Wehde, Albert H., 124

Weimar Republic, 227–28

Weizmann, Chaim, 113

Weizmann, Minna, 113

Welo, 196, 214

Wesendonk, Otto Günther von, 50–51, 107, 122, 146, 198, 204, 210, 226

"Westerner," 163, 188

Wilhelm II: and Abbas Hilmi, 117, 225; and Abd ul-Hamid, 8, 10; and Afghanistan, 81, 128; and Armenians, 113; and Britain, 6, 15, 30, 46, 48, 61; and Egypt, 57; and France, 48; and Islam, 9, 17, 48, 70, 156; and Nicholas II, 9–10; and Oppenheim, 22; and Orient, 8; and pan-Islamism, x, 6, 10, 22, 48; and Persia, 139; as "revolutionary," 48; and Russia, 48; and Turkey, x, 7–10, 13, 14, 39, 44, 47–48, 209; wartime decisions of, xii; *Weltpolitik* of, 6, 13

Wilson, C. E., 188, 205–6

Wingate, Sir Francis Reginald, 93, 160, 188, 192, 213, 219

Woenckhaus, Robert, 14, 37, 82, 83

Wolff-Metternich zur Gracht, Paul Graf, 14, 113–14, 164, 166, 173, 179–80, 184

Woolley, Leonard, 32

World War I, historiography of, ix–x. *See also* Germany; Great Britain; war by revolution (Germany); war by revolution (Great Britain)

Wustrow, Kurt, 138, 139, 142

Yahya, Imam, 54, 73, 94, 99, 173

Yeghen, Muhammad, 199

Yemen, 26, 28, 29, 172, 174–75, 177–78

Yilderim. See Army Group F (German)

Young Egypt, 196

Young Turks, 42; and Abbas Hilmi, 53, 56, 89–90, 118, 198–99, 209; and Anglo-Turkish settlement, 38; and Arabs, 27, 37, 99, 135, 202; and Armenians, 113; Britain and, 25–26, 35; and Egypt, 52; and Egyptian nationalists, 196; factionalism among, 87, 201; and France, 44; and Germany, xiii, 39, 47–49, 64–66, 82, 118, 148; and Ibn Rashid, 42; and Libya, 89, 148; and al-Masri, 32; and Oppenheim, 24; and pan-Islamism, xi, 24, 25–26, 33, 34, 85; and pan-Turanism, xi, 34, 79, 128, 201, 221; revolution of, 24–25, 33; and Sharif of Mecca, 34, 94, 223; and Turkish exiles, 197. *See also* Turkey

Yusuf, Ali, 12

Zawditu, 196, 215

Zia Bey, 198

Zimmermann, Arthur, and Abbas Hilmi, 198; and Afghanistan, 81; and Armenians, 114; arrogance of, 108; and Baghdad railroad, 45; and Britain, 86, 106–7; and Enver Pasha, 107, 108, 133; and Egypt, 55; and Information Service for the East, 67; and Italy, 58; and Jemal Pasha, 165; and Musil, 107; and Oppenheim, 66, 165; and pan-Islamism, 48, 86; and peace proposal, 86; and Persia, 81, 133; and Sharif of Mecca, 108–9; as "strong man," 86; and Turks, 48, 58; and Wangenheim, 108; and war by revolution, 48; and Wilhelm II, 48, 81

Zimmermann telegram, 131, 267n. 36

Zionism, 112, 213

Zionist World Congress, 113

Zossen, 68

Zugmayer, Erich, 80–81, 130–31, 138, 143

WAR BY REVOLUTION

was composed in 10.5/14 Legacy Book on a Power Macintosh using PageMaker 6.5

at The Kent State University Press;

printed by sheet-fed offset on 50-pound Lions Falls Turin Book Natural stock

(an acid-free, totally chlorine-free paper),

Smyth sewn and bound over binder's boards in ICG Arrestox B cloth,

and wrapped with dust jackets printed in 2 colors on

100-pound enamel stock by Thomson-Shore, Inc.;

designed by Diana Dickson;

and published by

THE KENT STATE UNIVERSITY PRESS

Kent, Ohio 44242